Glenna Snow's Cook Book

BUCHTEL BOOKS

Miss Harriet Angel, editor, *Recipes by Ladies of St. Paul's Church: A New Edition with a Photo Insert and an Introduction by Jon Miller*

Glenna Snow, editor, *Glenna Snow's Cook Books: A New Edition with a Photo Insert and an Introduction by Kevin Kern*

Glenna Snow's Cook Book

A NEW EDITION WITH A PHOTO INSERT
AND AN INTRODUCTION BY KEVIN KERN

BUCHTEL BOOKS • AKRON, OHIO

Originally published 1944 by The Akron Beacon Journal Company

14 13 12 11 10 5 4 3 2

ISBN 978-1-931968-86-7

The paper used in this publication meets the minimum requirements of American National Standard for Information Sciences—Permanence of Paper for Printed Library Materials, ansi z39.48–1984. ∞

Cover design: Amanda Gilliland

Glenna Snow's Cook Book

1385 Home Tested Recipes by Beacon Journal Readers

PREFACE
Lisa Abraham

Generations of Akron cooks may never have heard of Glenna Snow, even though they pay her tribute each time they pull out their yellowed, tattered recipes and prepare an old-fashioned favorite. Without Glenna Snow, frying pans might not produce the delightful smells of Potato Doughnuts as they sizzle in hot oil, awaiting their dusting of powdered sugar. This popular recipe, which appeared in the original 1938 edition of *Glenna Snow's Cook Book*, remains a community favorite to this day.

Mrs. Snow didn't create all of the recipes in her book—most were submitted by readers of the *Akron Beacon Journal*, where she was Home Economics Editor from 1932 to 1946. But she was the community's conduit for thousands of homemade favorites. Readers would send her their favorite recipes and she tested each one. If she deemed the recipe good enough, it would be printed in the newspaper—a sought-after prize for homemakers of the era.

She wrote her daily column from her home on North Firestone Boulevard, where she would take calls from readers about cooking and meal planning. She often retold a story of a young woman who called and said, "I've opened the can. Now what do I do?"

Mrs. Snow guided readers through some of the most challenging times in our country's history. She taught readers how to prepare economical meals and stretch their food budgets during the Great Depression, when cooking was more about feeding the mouths around the table than an expression of culinary creativity. In 1932, Mrs. Snow fed her family for a week using only the food included in a weekly order from the Family Service Society, just to show that feeding a family on charity could be accomplished. During World War II, when food was in short supply and Akron residents raised victory gardens, she advised readers how to make the most of their rations and how to can their fruits and vegetables to enjoy all winter long.

In her fourteen years on the job, more than fifteen thousand recipes found their way onto the pages of the *Akron Beacon Journal*, including the one for Potato Doughnuts, originally submitted by Mrs. Richard A. Huth. Mrs. Snow decided to compile the recipes into a cook book to provide those who were learning to cook with a tome of tested favorites. The first edition appeared in 1938, with other editions following in 1942 and 1947, the year after she retired. More than six thousand of her cook books were given as prizes to local homemakers who were lucky enough to have their recipes printed in the paper.

A few years after her retirement, Mrs. Snow and her husband, Mason Snow, former president of Akron's Permanent Federal Savings & Loan Co., moved to Bradenton, Fla., where she resided until her death in November 1976 at age 86.

During her retirement, Mrs. Snow traveled around the world and visited all fifty states. She liked to boast that her travel was paid for by the royalties that her husband had invested from her three cookbooks.

Copies of her original cookbooks are scarce. They are found most often on the shelves of used book dealers, on tables at garage sales, and in grandmothers' basements and attics—their pages yellowed from age and tattered from frequent use. But the recipes are woven into the culinary fabric of Akron, Ohio, where they are still used by cooks today.

INTRODUCTION

Kevin Kern

To many, the thought of a historian writing the introduction to a cookbook might seem as absurd as a chef writing the introduction to an encyclopedia (and even more absurd to those who are aware of the culinary limits of this particular historian). Yet apart from their obvious utility as repositories of recipes, cookbooks are—like any written work—historical documents that are a product of their time and place of origin. Looking beyond the ingredients, measurements, and oven settings that are standard to any cookbook, a careful reader of *Glenna Snow's Cook Book* can find evidence of the everyday life and culture that shaped its construction.

While some of these clues are simple dated semantic usages (ground beef is "hamburg" instead of "hamburger," a porcelain-enameled pot is a "granite kettle"), most of the historically distinctive features of this volume reflect larger trends in American national and domestic life. Compiled from recipes submitted by readers to the *Akron Beacon Journal* from 1932 to 1944, this text is not only an extremely practical kitchen companion, but also represents a unique opportunity to better understand these trends and gain a glimpse into everyday life in Akron, Ohio during the 1930s and 1940s.

Portions of this book subtly reflect the dynamic place in which it was written. In the years leading up to the 1930s and 1940s, Akron was the scene of remarkable demographic changes. It became the fastest-growing city in the country during the decade between 1910 and 1920—a product of the more than 900 percent growth of the rubber industry—tripling in size from 69,067 to 208,435 and jumping from the 81st to the 32nd largest city in the U.S. It added yet another small city's worth of population by 1930, when that year's census listed its population at 255,040. The Great Depression dramatically reversed this trend, causing the city to lose more than 10,000 people by 1940; but the economic boom caused by World War II created yet another boomlet, placing the city's population at nearly 275,000 by 1950.

Some of Akron's phenomenal growth during the early part of this period came from Europe, particularly immigrants from Germany, Austria, and Hungary. Together, these places accounted for more than 15,000 of Akron's foreign-born population, and built on the already substantial first- and second-generation German presence that had characterized the city in earlier decades. Although the "New Immigration" from Eastern and Southern Europe touched Akron as well, the two largest contributors (Italy and Russia) accounted for far fewer new Akronites (3,614 and 3,065 respectively) before the immigration restriction laws of the early 1920s effectively shut the door on these countries.

However, most of Akron's population increase—more than fifty thousand—came from internal migration from other states, particularly the Appalachian regions of Pennsylvania, West Virginia, Kentucky, and Tennessee. The influx from these regions was so great that some would joke that the correct answer to the question "What is the capital of West Virginia?" was "Akron, Ohio." Although this time period was also marked by the "Great Migration" of African-Americans to northern cities, and although Akron's African-American population did indeed increase substantially from 1910 to 1940, most of Akron's new southern-born population was white. African-Americans comprised less than 5 percent of the city's total population when this book was originally published.

Glenna Snow's Cook Book makes few overt references to its geographic origin (one notable exception being a discussion of the best cooking apples to be found in Northeast Ohio [p. 125]). However, some hints of Akron's demographic history lie in the types of recipes it includes—or, in some cases, omits. The ethnic recipes favored seem to be from those regions that donated the largest percentages of Akron's foreign-born population, particularly Hungary (Hungarian Butter Pastry [p. 269], and Goulash, Noodles, and Pigs in Blankets [p. 263]) and Germany/Austria (including Hassenpfeffer [*sic*], several "Bavarian" and "Austrian"-named deserts and "kuchens," and numerous slaw and sauerkraut recipes).

In contrast, the book lists relatively few Italian dishes as such (Ravioli [p. 202], Spaghetti [p. 203], and Stew [p. 409]). Macaroni makes a brief appearance [p. 201], but the two recipes—Macaroni, Eggs, and Mushrooms and Macaroni Mousse (the closest the book comes to macaroni and cheese)—are hardly in forms standard to Italian cuisine. There is no Chicken Parmesan, no Lasagna, no Fettuccini Alfredo, nor any other currently popular Italian food (there is a Chicken Tetrazzini recipe [p. 232], but that dish was essentially an American invention). The book does make mention of going to an "Italian importing store," but only as a way to purchase dried mushrooms for a completely different ethnic dish: Egg Foo Yong [p. 174]. Perhaps this is not surprising, as Italian immigrants were barely 3 percent of Akron's population at the time. However, it does serve to illustrate the point that Akron's demographic profile cast a shadow on the construction of this book. If these "home-tested" recipes were selected, as Snow states in her introduction, because they "would be the most universally used" [vii], then these inclusions and deletions say much about the ethnic background of most of her readers.

Some recipes that seem to represent foreign immigration actually represent either long-established ethnic patterns, or the far more substantial internal migration that swelled the city during its phenomenal growth. Several "Dutch" recipes (Apple Pie [p. 272], Peach Cake [p. 161]), plus such dishes as Schnitz un Knepp [p. 225], Scrapple [p. 225], and Pon Hoss [p. 253]) are staples of Pennsylvania Dutch cooking, indicating the strong presence of Pennsylvanian immigrants of German descent in parts of Northeast Ohio. Although the roots of this immigration trace back to the mid-1800s, evidence of the early twentieth-century Pennsylvanian Appalachian invasion can also be found in such recipes as Pittsburgh Potatoes [p. 442] and the deceptively-named City Chicken [p. 227], a dish originally thought to be from Western Pennsylvania. City Chicken is still a regional favorite in both Ohio and Pennsylvania.Similarly, there are numerous reflections of Akron's southern influx in these recipes, in both names and ingredients. Southern Canapés [p. 6], Jambalaya [p. 377], and Louisiana Rice Pudding [p. 164] are among the most obvious examples of southern influence, but more subtle linguistic evidence appears, too, such as the term "mush" for boiled cornmeal cereals [pp. 87–88] and "craklin" for pork rinds (Cracklin Bread [p. 33]). Of course, most of the numerous cornmeal-, hominy-, and okra-based recipes themselves betoken a southern and African-American flavor to the cookbook that many southern immigrants of the time must have appreciated. This does not mean the appreciation was always reciprocated—Glenna Snow states rather matter-of-factly, "Okra is a vegetable used extensively in the south. It has a slimy appearance which the northerner does not care for." Yet despite this pronouncement, five okra-based recipes immediately follow. In this way, life imitated food—although many long-time Akron residents perhaps did not care for the Appalachian/southern invasion, they eventually learned to live with it.

While a careful reading of the cookbook reveals hints of the place where it was written, reflections of its place in time are ubiquitous and often plain to see. The years during which it was compiled were ones of great change, affecting everything from the world stage to the kitchen cupboard. A global depression, followed immediately by a world war (still raging when this second edition found its way into Akron homes), left marks on these pages, as did an even longer-term revolution of the American kitchen. Major transitions in American foodways and culinary practices that began in the late 1800s made 1940s American kitchens very different than those of previous generations, and they would be even more different still less than a generation later. Paging through almost any section of this book, the reverberations these international and domestic events had on the book's original audience are almost palpable.

The Great Depression and World War II may have been vastly different events, but in some ways had very similar effects on American household economies. Both caused privation and the need for frugality in the kitchen, either from lack of money or from wartime rationing. American families squeezed the most out of the resources at hand, from stretching dollars to stretching food. Although few examples of this could be clearer than the recipes for War Cake [p. 63], Economical Cakes [p. 69], Economical Gingerbread [p. 31], or Economy Oatmeal Cookies [p. 107], this volume is replete with other unambiguous references to the types of constraints under which Akron's homemakers had to operate.

Some of the clearest evidence of these restrictions lies in the ingredients lists that accompany the recipes. The most economical ingredient, of course, is one that costs nothing at all, and there are several recipes devoted to such items. Dandelions, a free ingredient literally (and lamentably) at Akronites' doorsteps, show up several times throughout the book, as canned greens [p. 326], cooked greens (two ways) [p. 427], Mock Mushrooms [p. 428], and Dandelion Wine [p. 451]. For those willing to go a little further to forage, the book also provides two recipes for Crab Apple Jelly [pp. 350, 369], with the implicit assumption that these could be easily gathered from the ordinarily commercially useless crab apple trees that were found with some frequency around the area. Similarly, one of the many helpful hints that Snow throws in states, "Since elderberries grow by the roadside they are almost always free for the picking. The blossoms are especially good for wine." The book elsewhere gives recipes for cobbler [p. 155], jam [p. 363], jelly [p. 370], and preserves [p. 375] made from this windfall ingredient, as well as Elderberry Blossom Fritters [p. 123]. For the even more committed foragers, there are several pages of recipes for game animals, including several preparations of rabbit, and one for the most plentiful game animal in Akron: squirrel [pp. 213–215].

Other recipes reflect the need to make ingredients that are cheap, but perhaps less-than-appealing, seem more appetizing. Organ meat, for example, was often relatively less expensive, allowing a frugal homemaker to put meat on the table if she could get her family to eat it. Although the cookbook introduces the poultry section with brief recommendations for giblets, it spends several pages on these "variety meats" in beef and calves [pp. 237–243], including multiple preparations for livers, kidneys, pancreases, tongues, brains, and tripe. Other lesser-used parts of animals find some use, too, including a recipe for Oxtail Soup [p. 406] and one for Pickled Pig's feet [p. 223]. Perhaps the most unusual of these (to twenty-first century eyes, at least) is the recipe for Souse, traditionally a kind of headcheese made from the parts of the animal that were otherwise cast off. This book's recipe calls for pig's knuckles, but also helpfully suggests that heart and tongue can be used. Souse also apparently had the advantage of being easy to slice, and would keep for up to two weeks in a cool place, if the family did not choose to finish it at the first or second try. Along similar lines, the book frequently addresses the issue of making the most of food the family did not finish, not only incidentally ("Croquettes are a good method of using up leftover materials"), but also with a four-page section devoted entirely to repurposing leftover food [pp. 197–200]. Helpfully alphabetized by food, a second life for almost any food described in the book is here, including bean sandwiches and brain patties.

A number of recipes imply the need to pinch pennies, either by giving instructions on how to make even the most commonly-purchased things at home, or by making the most of every item that passes through the kitchen. In the first group are recipes for various candies, gumdrops, after-dinner mints, and lollypops [pp. 80–82]; snack foods like crackers [p. 113] and potato chips [p. 122]; and condiments like catsups [p. 341]; all of which could be made more economically at home, given the time and the will to do so. For those with even more will, the book also gives instructions on how to render lard and make soap [p. 253]. The latter recipe calls for ten pounds of "waste fat," a reference to the second group of "waste not, want not" ideas that pervade the text. In the canning section, Snow commands that if the tops of the canning beets are young and tender, "do not throw them away, but can them the same as spinach for a winter green." Similarly in introducing a discussion about cooking vegetables, Snow adds that "All liquor drained from cooked vegetables should be saved for soup or added to tomato juice for a beverage." Even chicken feet find a use, with Snow recommending they be used for making chicken broth. For the frugal homemaker, Snow's book provides numerous ways to stretch the family food dollar nearly as far as it can go.

Although making do was something common to both the Great Depression and World War II, many instances in these pages seem to refer more to wartime rationing. A number of recipes actually advertise the limited amount of rationed ingredients in their names, including Sugarless Brownies [p. 412], One-Egg Cakes [pp. 50, 62, 73], and Butterless, Eggless, Milkless Cake [p. 57]. Furthermore, Snow devotes an entire section to substitutes and extenders [pp. 410–414], which includes instructions on how to stretch or replace butter (using margarine, fat, lard, milk, cream, or gelatin), sugar (using molasses, maple syrup, corn syrup, or honey), coffee (using roasted whole grain wheat), and in an instance of a substitute for a substitute, synthetic maple syrup (using boiled corn cobs and brown sugar). The section also has handy charts for making the transition between ingredients, giving equivalents in standard measures, and warning about the different properties between, for example, cake flour and bread flour. Elsewhere [pp. 250–251] is a list of meat substitutes, using carrots, cheese, rice, nuts, and soybeans. Sprinkled throughout the rest of the text are a number of "mock" recipes, including Mock Chicken A La King (tuna) [p. 189], Mock Sausage (lima beans) [p. 432], and Mock Whipped Cream (egg whites and apple sauce) [p. 148]. Snow states in her introduction that these had been added "because of the war," but she also supposed that they would "be used universally from now on. There are often in peace times occasions which require that we use another ingredient rather than the one called for in the recipe." Given the decades-long experience of rationing and privation between two world wars and a great depression, Snow certainly could be forgiven for assuming such trends might continue. Furthermore, shortages did not apply only to foods and ingredients, but also to other important kitchen supplies. Pressure cookers had only become widely available to most American homes in the late 1930s, but the conversion to a wartime industrial footing ended most consumer production of these coveted items. While Snow strongly recommends the use of pressure cookers in her canning section, she also acknowledges their scarcity on more than one occasion [pp. 301, 316, and 324] and provides alternative methods of canning.

Snow's discussion of canning points to another long-term trend that this cookbook illustrates—the evolution of American domestic foodways. During the 1930s and 1940s, American kitchens were in the midst of a transition from older, traditional practices toward the modern kitchen life that became common the 1950s. There is no better example of the past, "present" (1944), and future of this transition than in Snow's section on food preservation. At nearly ninety pages [pp. 289–376] (almost 20 percent of the book), it is by far the longest section, highlighting the great changes that took place in American kitchens and pantries during the previous decades. Although the book concentrates on contemporary techniques, there are plenty of references to older methods and equipment throughout. Salting, drying, pickling, sulphuring, and preserving with sugar were preservation methods with ancient histories, and all draw some attention in this section. Furthermore, Snow feels obligated to point out that in order to can effectively, an oven with automatic heat control is mandatory, ruling out the use of older coal-, gasoline-, oil-, or wood-heated ovens that some homes still used. Other references to pre-automatic ovens pop up elsewhere, especially the use of the terms "slow oven" [p. 48] or "moderate oven" [p. 49], which describe the more general way homemakers used to judge cooking heat.

Other sets of recipes illustrate an older mindset toward food and its relative value. One telling insight into the traditional closeness that American homemakers had to their food comes in the section on canning meats; Snow's very first instruction is to make sure that the "animal heat" has left the body [p.

316]—an indication of just how fresh meat could be (for veal, for example, she recommends a full 24 hours for this to happen [p. 319]). As if to reinforce the point, her instructions for chicken include the provision "If the chickens are in your possession, they should be confined 12 to 24 hours before killing. Give water but no feed. Kill six to twelve hours before canning. Avoid bruising, bleed thoroughly." Other references to chicken reveal a startling (to twenty-first century eyes) assumption about the relative popularity and value of different meats. Until large-scale poultry-raising operations had begun in the 1940s, chicken was a relatively expensive kind of meat, often reserved for Sunday meals or special occasions. Thus, Snow provides several "mock chicken" recipes such as California Chicken [p. 226], City Chicken [p. 227], Mock Chicken Stew [p. 409], or Poor Man's Chicken [p. 236] using the then-cheaper substitute ingredient of veal. "Although it is a young meat, it is a tough meat," Snow explains in her introduction of veal recipes [p. 235], reflecting the contemporary perception of veal as a generally inferior product. Dairy farms often cast off male calves as relatively useless, so it is perhaps easy to see how this perception arose. Nevertheless, recipes like this, as well as statements like "Salmon is the most used of the canned fish. Although it may be purchased fresh, there are few who buy it that way," show some very distinct differences in traditional foodways that still persisted into the 1940s.

Despite the lingering signs of earlier times and traditions, Snow's book also illustrates the departures from them by the 1930s and 1940s. Again, the section on food preservation is most revealing in this respect. By the 1930s and 1940s, canning had made tremendous advances, and American homemakers were canning more than ever before. Part of this was due to wartime exigencies: the government encouraged American households to grow victory gardens and can the surplus, to allow more of the nation's food production (as well as the tin and steel that would ordinarily go into cans) to be directed to the war effort. However, the scale and scope of canning had been steadily increasing for decades, especially with the introduction of pressure canners, the mechanization of the glass jar-making process (which made canning jars much less expensive), and scientific experimentation that set standards for the amount of time for each method that was "safe" for each kind of food. This is clearly evident throughout this section, with detailed descriptions of the science behind the canning process and explicit references to minimum times for each food using each method.

The "Canning Budget" [pp. 302–303] reveals just how thoroughly canning had become an ingrained part of the American household. Snow explains here that households should can from 80 to 120 quarts of food for each family member—divided up in lots of green and yellow vegetables (30–45 quarts), tomatoes (20–30 quarts), fruit (30–45 quarts), and meat (10 quarts)—and includes a helpful accompanying chart that converts raw measures to canned quantities. For a family of four (the average-size U.S. family in 1940), this budget could mean canning close to 500 quarts of food every year. The weeks that this would entail, working over batches of boiling water for hours on end in the heat of the late summer—and all in the days before home air conditioning—should give every reader renewed respect for the efforts of American homemakers of that generation.

Snow's knowledgeable comments in the canning section and elsewhere touch on another indication of a transition from earlier times. The book's very construction and its author's official title—Home Economics Editor—mark a major shift in American culinary practices. Home economics as an academic discipline was a rather new development, first becoming widespread in the 1910s and 1920s. The cookbook reads like a home economics text, with nutritional and descriptive information provided for most major ingredients. Read Snow's explanation of the causes of spoilage [p. 300] or her description of vitamins [p. 415], and see how this was much more than just a traditional collection of recipes. Indeed, even though her detailed description of how to kill and butcher a chicken [p. 316–317] serves as an example of more traditional cooking duties, it is also an example of transition in the American kitchen. Previously, homemakers did not need a book to tell them how to do this—it was knowledge that was passed down, usually from mother to daughter, as part of the gendered education common in American culture. This book, then, serves as a departure from that time, assuming little knowledge on the part of the reader, and explaining everything fully in a systematic way.

Another departure from the past appears in Snow's nod to the fact that Akron homemakers were getting cooking information from another relatively new medium: processed food packaging. These references crop up here and there, but most pointedly in the discussion of cereals, where she states that although some cereals need to be cooked, "Since there are directions on the boxes we are not using our space to repeat them here." Such a line would be unimaginable in a cookbook of a previous generation (when consumers often purchased food in bulk using their own containers), and acknowledged the inroads that pre-packaged and processed foods were beginning to make in American life. This trend would of course continue in the years to come.

This book provides other glimpses into the future of American kitchens, with the section on food preservation again providing some of the best examples. Snow devotes three pages [pp. 338–340] to methods of freezing various foods. Although virtually no private homes had freezers in 1944, families were able to rent space in freezer lockers found in butcher's shops, grocery stores, farmers' co-ops, and other businesses that could afford to purchase and maintain these large, room-like freezers. Snow gives explicit instructions on how to prepare food for freezing, including the directive to label each package with the kind of meat, its weight, the date, and the locker number. Electric home freezers may have been several years in the future, but in other ways the future had already arrived in Akron kitchens, particularly in the electrification of other appliances. Instructions in many recipes give different times for hand mixing as opposed to using an electric mixer [pp. 65, 396]. Similarly, while the book has many "ice-box" recipes (Ice Box Cake, Ice Box Pie, Ice Box Cookies), it also has such items as Apricot Refrigerator Cake [p. 126], Refrigerator Frosting [p. 195], Refrigerator Rolls [p. 26], and Refrigerator Sour Cream Cookies [p. 112]. Within a few years after the publication of this book, the post-war economic boom completed the electrification of the American kitchen, with most homes eventually gaining refrigerators, freezers, and other laborsaving appliances.

Although this introduction could provide many other examples of the ways *Glenna Snow's Cook Book* reflects its time and place, there is no substitute for actually reading and enjoying the recipes themselves. The book is thoroughly indexed, but to really get a sense of it, page through it and select recipes at random. Read them not only for ideas for dishes to serve, but also for insight into the lives of the hundreds of people who submitted them. In doing so, you will not only be getting a taste of some authentic home cooking from an earlier era, but also a taste of the era itself.

Glenna Snow's Cook Book

Introduction

(TO THE SECOND EDITION)

We take pleasure in presenting to our readers the second edition of the Glenna Snow cook book. The recipes in the first edition were chosen from the columns of the Akron Beacon Journal, published from 1932 to 1938 — this book contains almost all of those same recipes, as we found very few could be omitted, they being the best of their kind. We have added a great many more recipes which we have taken from the column since 1938.

We know that we have not published all your favorite recipes, but we have tried to select those which would be the most universally used, and have put in blank pages so that you could add your individually preferred ones.

We have made a complete index which will be found in the back of the book. It is cross indexed so that you should not have any trouble finding the recipe you want.

The recipes in this book are plain recipes, each one being written in a form easy to follow; as one reads, the ingredients stand out in bold face type and the directions go right along as the ingredients are added. Explanations are often given in the recipe so that the reason for so doing will be more readily understood.

We have written all recipes in a readable form so that each ingredient, with its amount falls into the proper place at the proper time, to give the best results.

We advise the reading of each recipe completely before starting to make the product. It not only tells what is needed but it also gives a definite idea as to what you are going to do. Some things need to stand, while others must be put immediately into an oven which should be ready for them. A few minutes spent in reading a recipe will save many mistakes.

The cover of this book is washable. Just wipe it off with a damp cloth, if some egg or fat happens to drop on it, but do it immediately as it will be much harder to remove if it has dried on the cover.

We hope our readers will feel that this is their book. We had to omit the names of those contributing to make space for more recipes.

We have added a chapter on substitutes which have had to be

used because of the war, but which will be used universally from now on. There are often in peace times occasions which require that we use another ingredient rather than the one called for in the recipe.

We have enlarged the chapter on food preservation to meet your needs in what ever manner you plan to store food for winter.

We wish to thank the management of the Akron Beacon Journal for this opportunity of giving to you these recipes in book form. We especially want to acknowledge the help throughout the years of our Woman's Editor, Mrs. Ethel Myers and Mrs. J. B. Romer, a housewife, who devoted much of her time in arranging the recipes in this book.

GLENNA H. SNOW.

Home Economics Editor
Akron Beacon Journal

Appetizers

Appetizers are dainty bits of food served before the meal to give zest to the appetite. They usually have a sharp tang as cheese or cured fish would have.

A Canape is a small open faced sandwich used as an appetizer. Relishes, chopped meats and fish usually are the basis of these appetizers.

Small rounds of baked pie crust may be used for the base of canapes.

APPETIZERS

Spread small squares of fresh bread with butter, then with a very fine soft cheese. Roll like a jelly roll, fasten a strip of bacon around the center holding it in place with a tooth pick. Toast these on all sides. It is well to leave the last side to be toasted after the guests have arrived, so they will be very hot when served.

Small frankfurters may be heated and served on hors d'oeuvre sticks.

Small pickled onions may have a bit of melted cheese poured over the top and served on sticks.

Ground dried beef mixed with garlic and cottage cheese may be made either into balls and served on sticks, or rolled in another piece of dried beef.

Sardines may be crushed and mixed with butter and served on crackers. Anchovies and caviar are two other small fish products, which when mixed with mayonnaise and served on crackers make excellent appetizers.

Hard cooked eggs, parsley, chives, paprika and pimentos make excellent garnishes for any of these.

Assorted plate of these appetizers served with a cocktail (either alcoholic or not) makes very pleasing first course for an evening dinner.

CURRY COCOANUT BALLS

Mix **1 tablespoonful butter, 1 tablespoonful Indian Chutney, 1 teaspoonful curry powder** and **1 cup cream cheese** together well. Roll in balls, cover with freshly grated **cocoanut.**

PINEAPPLE WEDGES

This is an attractive appetizer. Wash the **whole pineapple** thoroughly, cut off the top. Do not peel. With a sharp knife follow the outline of the eye of the pineapple, cutting in cone shape towards the core. Each eye makes a wedge—serve on a salad plate with the apex of the cones towards the center of plate. A **mound of confectioner's sugar** may be in the center.

ROQUEFORT ROLLS

Blend 2-3 oz. packages of cream cheese with **1/7 lb. Roquefort cheese,** add **2 tablespoonfuls** finely chopped **celery, 1 tablespoonful** finely chopped **onion, a dash** of **cayenne** and enough **salad dressing** to moisten. Form into rolls. Roll in **ground nuts.** Chill. Serve with tomato juice and crackers.

SARDINE CANAPES

Cut slices of bread with a diamond cutter and spread with **sardine butter.** This is made by mashing sardines and adding just enough creamed butter to make a paste. Season the mixture highly with **cayenne** and **lemon juice.** After spreading with butter, put a border of very finely **chopped egg whites** around the edge and over the border place at intervals the tiniest shreds of **fresh green pepper.** Vary the canapes by decorating every other one with a border of **sifted egg yolk** over which is placed the same size shreds of **red pepper.** If the green pepper is first parboiled in water containing a bit of soda it will have a brighter color.

SOUTHERN CANAPES

Chop a **few spoonfuls of cold chicken,** the same amount of **cooked ham,** moisten to a paste with **creamed butter.** Spread this on fancy cuts of **sauted bread.** Cover with **grated cheese** and run under the gas flame to heat and melt cheese. Garnish with **olive** sections.

Cocktails

Cantaloupe is a very excellent melon used mostly in the fresh stage. It is excellent for appetizers, for breakfast fruit and makes a lovely dessert for supper.

CANTALOUPE BALL

Cut melon in half and remove seeds. Scoop out the balls, using a French cutter or the half teaspoonful in your measuring set, for this purpose. Cover with grape juice to which a few drops of lemon or lime juice has been added. Place in refrigerator and chill. At serving time arrange in cocktail glasses and garnish with mint.

CRANBERRY

Boil **2 cups sugar** and **2 cups water** together for 5 minutes. Add **1 pound cranberries** and cover, cooking slowly until popping stops. Strain through a fine wire sieve (reserve cranberries for sauce). Now add the juice of **1 large grapefruit, 1 lemon** and **3 large oranges** to cranberry juice and stir well. Pour into a glass covered jar and chill. A little water or sugar may be added if it seems too strong or not quite sweet enough.

EGGNOG

Beat **16 egg yolks** thoroughly. Add **1 pound powdered sugar,** rolled fine and stir again until mixture is smooth. Then add **1 quart good whisky** very slowly, a few tablespoonfuls at a time. Next add **1 pint of white Jamaica rum** slowly. Next add **1 pint whipped cream** and **1 quart milk** to which **vanilla** or **nutmeg** have been added to suit the taste. Add **whites of the 16 eggs** beaten stiff. Do not stop stirring or beating and always stir in the same direction; clockwise or counterclockwise. This mixture should be made at least a day before use and kept cold. After eggnog has set it develops a crust. This should be cut through to quarter the crust and the nog stirred in the same direction as when made.

Buttered pop-corn makes a good appetizer. Freshly popped corn salted, makes a good substitute for cereal, with sugar and cream.

FROZEN TOMATO JUICE

Soak **1 teaspoonful gelatin in ¼ cup' cold tomato juice**, then melt over hot water. Add **2 tablespoonfuls sugar, 1 teaspoonful salt, ⅛ teaspoonful pepper, ⅛ teaspoonful celery salt, ¼ teaspoonful onion juice, dash tabasco sauce, ½ teaspoonful Worcestershire** sauce and garlic to the rest of the tomato juice. Add a little of the cold seasoned tomato to the melted gelatin. Finally mix all together. Freeze with fast unit. After it is frozen 1 inch from the edge of freezing tray stir vigorously. If a very smooth texture is desired, stir twice while freezing.

MELON BALLS

Just a simple arrangement of different kinds of **melon balls** makes an attractive entree. **Watermelon, honeydew** and **golden canteloupe** balls with **few blackberries** and **sprigs of mint** makes about the most attractive dish. A **paper doily** may be used as a garnish, pasting it to the outside of glass thus giving the appearance of a bouquet. The canteloupe may be cut in rings with seeds and rind removed. Place other balls in the center. This does well where there are no cocktail glasses.

OYSTER

Raw oysters are used for cocktail. For each service allow **six oysters.** Arrange oysters in cocktail glasses and pour over them the following sauce. Mix **1 teaspoonful salt, ¼ teaspoonful parsley, 1 teaspoonful chopped chives or onions, 1 teaspoonful melted butter, two tablespoonfuls vinegar, ¼ teaspoonful tabasco sauce, 1 teaspoonful Worcestershire sauce, 1 teaspoonful horseradish, ½ cup catsup,** and **¼ cup finely cut celery.** Mix well together and chill thoroughly before pouring over the oysters.

SAUCE

Take **½ cup catsup** or **chili sauce, 3 tablespoonfuls lemon juice, few drops tabasco, ¼ teaspoonful salt, ½ cup finely chopped celely, 2 teaspoonfuls Worcestershire sauce** and **horseradish** to taste. Mix all ingredients together and keep in a screw top jar in a cool place. This is good over all kinds of shell fish.

TOMATO JUICE

Bring 1 **quart can of tomato soup** to a boil. Rub through colander and chill. Season with **salt** and **sugar** for children. For grownups, use a little **Worcestershire sauce. Horseradish** may be added. Serve very cold in cocktail glasses, if you have them. If not, then use stemmed sherbet cups or just plain sherbet cups.

WATERMELON

Scoop out **melon** in little balls, using a French cutter or the ½ teaspoon of your measuring set. Pour over them a **syrup made of lemon and orange or any other fruit juice.** Chill thoroughly. These look inviting served in pale green glasses. Garnished with either plain or powdered mint. **Powdered mint** is simply mint leaves dusted with powdered sugar. These balls also look nice set in circles of **yellow canteloupe** which has the outer green rind left on or in crescents of **honey dew melons** which have little holes dug out so the watermelon ball will set firm.

A cocktail may be a beverage, a fish served with a sauce, or a fruit as an appetizer to a meal.

Beverages

Since a beverage is a drink of any description we have placed all recipes for drinks under this title, that are not classed separately.

Chocolate and cocoa are related in the fact that cocoa is chocolate with the cocoa butter removed.

METHOD OF MAKING COCOA

Mix **2 tablespoonfuls cocoa, dash salt, 4 tablespoonfuls sugar,** and **½ cup cold water** in sauce pan and place over direct flame. Stir until smooth. Boil 2 minutes. Add **1½ cups milk** and heat over slow fire. Do not boil. Serves two.

CREAMY HOT CHOCOLATE

Cook **2½ squares bitter chocolate** and **½ cup cold water** over direct heat 4 minutes, stirring constantly. Beat until smooth. Add **¾ cup sugar** and **dash salt.** Return to fire and cook 4 minutes longer. Cool. Fold into **½ cup of whipped cream.** Place **1 rounding tablespoonful** of the mixture in cup. Pour hot milk over it. Stir well to blend.

METHODS OF MAKING COFFEE

1. Percolated coffee; **1 tablespoonful coffee to 1 cup cold water.** Percolate 10 to 15 minutes. 2. Drip coffee; **1 tablespoonful coffee to 1 cup boiling water.** Pour boiling water over coffee, let stand until all drips through. 3. Steeped coffee; **1 tablespoonful coffee to 1 cup boiling water.** Pour boiling water over coffee, set aside in warm place 3-4 minutes. 4. Coffee with egg; **1 tablespoonful of coffee plus ¼ beaten egg** to **1 cup cold water.** Combine coffee and egg in pot, pour in water, bring to a boil, set in warm place 3 to 5 minutes.

RULES FOR COFFEE MAKING

One may use regular coffee or coffee which has had the caffein removed. Use the latter if one has headaches or sleeplessness because of the use of regular coffee. 1—Always use fresh water. 2—Measure both coffee and water each time. 3——Never allow coffee to boil. 4—Use a clean pot and scald before making. 5—Remove grounds from coffee as soon as it is made. 6—Serve coffee immediately, if possible. 7—Serve freshly made coffee. Reheated coffee loses its flavor. 8—Always serve piping hot.

A pinch of salt in coffee really does improve the flavor.

Heat lemons if you want the most juice from them.

Keep a supply of sugar syrup in ice box during the summer season to add to fruit juices used for beverages.

4 cups sugar to 1 quart water.

FRUIT PUNCH

Extract juice from **2 lemons, 3 oranges** and **2 limes.** Add **1½ cups sugar** and stir until dissolved. Then add **6 glasses water** and serve immediately, pouring into glasses over crushed ice.

SYRUP FOR LEMONADE

Grate rind from **6 lemons.** Squeeze juice from **12 lemons** and pour over lemon rind. Let this stand for 1 hour. Put **4 lbs. sugar** and **2 cups water** in kettle and bring to boil. Let boil for 10 minutes, then strain lemon juice into syrup. Stir well, set aside to cool. When cold pour into quart jar and keep in ice box if all is not needed at once. Allow **1 tablespoonful syrup** and **1 cube ice** to each glass water—This should serve 50.

Use pipe cleaners for glass lemonade spoons.

Chill a thermos bottle in refrigerator before adding cold liquid, it enables it to remain cold longer.

ORIENTAL PUNCH

Dissolve **1 cup sugar** in **1 cup boiling water.** Add to **2 cups cold tea, 1 cup lemon juice, 1 cup grape juice** and **½ cup pineapple juice.** Dilute with **2 cups cold water.** Chill thoroughly before serving.

TEA

The following classification is made according to the size of the leaf of tea. The bud and smallest leaves are considered the best quality and are highest in price. Green tea is unfermented. Black tea is fermented. Oolong is a combination of both. Leaves—Black and green. Bud—Flowery pekoe. Flower—Jasmine. First Leaf—Black, broken orange pekoe. Green, first gunpowder. Second leaf—Black, orange pekoe. Green, second gunpowder. Third leaf—Black, pekoe. Green, young hyson. Fourth leaf—Black, English breakfast. Green Imperial.

The brew made from the leaves of the tea plant is almost as universally used as that of the coffee berry.

ICED TEA

Some form of Black tea makes the best iced tea, as it will dilute better, still retaining a good color. Use **4 teaspoonfuls tea** to **1 cup boiling water.** Dilute to desired consistency with ice and cold water. Boiling tea poured over chipped ice makes a very good iced tea, but if tea is cooled first not nearly so much ice is required.

Very strong ice tea will become cloudy.

HOT TEA

1 teaspoonful of tea to 1 cup of water is the rule given by most tea companies, however you may make as high as **six** cups of tea from **1 teaspoonful** tea if you do not care for it so strong. Always use fresh cold water, bringing it to a quick boil. Pour over tea, remove leaves after 1 minute of infusion.

Be sure the water for tea is freshly boiled.

Tea should always be made in a china or earthenware pot.

Tea is a good foundation for all kinds of cooling drinks during the summer.

WASSAIL

Make a mixture of **1 gallon sweet cider, ½ teaspoonful ground nutmeg, 3 teaspoonfuls allspice, 1 teaspoon ground cloves, 4 sticks cinnamon, juice of 8 oranges, juice of 4 lemons** and **2 cups sugar.** Bring this mixture to boiling point and serve hot.

Yeast Bread--Plain

Bread is the staff of life. We have classed all those breads which we have recipes for under this heading. The leavening and flour may vary but the results are always a bread of some kind.

It is best to scald all liquids used in yeast breads so as to insure the destruction of any organisms which might develop in the dough.

To get yeast bread to rise quicker set bowl containing dough over a pan of hot water.

LIGHT BREAD

Take an 8 or 10 quart pan or kettle. Measure **3 quarts of any kind of flour.** Sift before measuring. Put into kettle and add **2 tablespoonfuls sugar.** Heat to lukewarm **3 pints of water or milk,** break up **2 cakes of yeast** into a cup and cover with the **lukewarm water.** Let stand until yeast is dissolved. Pour yeast water and balance of water into flour and sugar. Stir well. Add **3 more quarts of sifted flour, 2 tablespoonfuls salt** and **2 heaping tablespoonfuls of soft lard.** Knead until well mixed, about 10 minutes. Let rise 1 hour (keeping well covered with cloth). Work down, let rise 15 minutes. Work into loaves. Put into well greased baking pans, let rise 2½ hours, bake for 1 hour in hot oven (450°F.). If it browns too much then reduce heat to 375° F., but keep in oven 1 hour. This recipe makes 6 loaves.

YEAST STARTER FOR BREAD

Boil **2 or 3 medium sized potatoes** in **2 quarts water.** When done, mash fine. Add **1 cup flour,** alternating with hot potato water. Add enough liquid to make **2 quarts.** Then add **2 cakes yeast** (either kind) and **2 tablespoonfuls sugar** which has been dissolved in **½ cup warm water.** Let rise over night in warm place. This makes enough for 3 large loaves, after taking out 1 pint for the next "Starter." For next baking follow above procedure, using starter in place of yeast cakes. This will last indefinitely if kept in a cool place.

Breads made with yeasts must have their temperature kept at lukewarm. If liquids are scalded, they must be cooled to this temperature before yeast is added, otherwise yeast plants will be killed and there will be no leavening agent present. The result is a heavy bread.

BREAD USING STARTER

After taking from starter **1 pint of the liquid** (to be placed in a cold place to keep for the next baking) add enough flour to make a stiff batter. Let stand about 1 hour or until light. Measure **8 cups flour,** place in a bowl hollowing out the center. Add **starter, 3 tablespoonfuls soft lard** and **1 tablespoonful salt** (lard keeps bread moist until used). Mix well, being careful not to get batter too stiff. More flour can be added, so do not start with too much. When well mixed, grease bottom and sides of pan and top of bread. (This is important as it keeps bread from forming a hard crust or cracking.)

Let rise until twice its size. Work down once and let rise. This makes finer texture but may be omitted. When light, work out into loaves, remembering to grease well. Let rise for about 1 hour. Put into hot oven, 450° F., reducing heat after first 15 minutes to 350° F. Bake about 1 hour or until it sounds hollow when tapped on bottom. The above recipe makes 3 large or 4 small loaves. It may be baked in regular bread pans or in pie pans.

SHORT PROCESS BREAD (1 Loaf)

Scald **1 cup water** (to kill all other bacteria). Add **1 tablespoonful lard, 1 tablespoonful sugar** and **¼ teaspoonful salt.** Cool to lukewarm. (Too cold water will not start plants growing. Too hot water will kill yeasts and spoil bread). When bottom of pan is so it can rest comfortably on palm of hand, add **1 cake compressed yeast,** softened in **¼ cup lukewarm water.** Stir in **1½ cups flour,** beat well, set aside in a warm place for a half hour or until the mixture doubles in bulk, stir down, add another **1½ cups flour,** gradually beating vigorously until the dough leaves a clean bowl. Place on slightly floured board and knead until smooth and elastic to touch. This assures thorough mixing and adds to texture. Place in greased bowl, cover, let rise until double in bulk, "work down," but do not add any flour, shape in a loaf, place in greased pan, let rise again until double in bulk. Bake in hot oven until it starts to brown. (This kills all yeast plants and prevents more rising.) Reduce heat to moderate oven and finish baking—about 30 minutes.

CRACKED WHEAT BREAD

Starter. Pare and slice 4 **medium potatoes.** Cook in **1 pint water** until soft. Mash or put through ricer. Add more water if needed to make **1 pint.** Add ½ **teaspoonful salt, 2 tablespoonfuls sugar.** When lukewarm add **1 cake yeast** which has been soaked in ½ **cup warm water,** then mix with **1 cup flour.** Beat well. Set in warm place over night. Next morning add **1 pint of water** that has been scalded and cooled. Stir well, then take out **1 pint of starter** and set aside in a cold place for the next baking.

Bread. Pour boiling water **(2 cups)** over **1½ cups cracked wheat, 2 tablespoonfuls sugar, 2 tablespoonfuls lard** and **1 tablespoonful fat.** Allow to cool until lukewarm. Add starter, then **white flour,** enough to make a soft dough that can just be handled, not too stiff. If dough is too stiff it makes dry bread. Place in greased bowl. Allow to rise until double in bulk, knead down, allow to rise again until double in bulk. Knead again, shape into loaves or rolls. Allow to rise again until double in bulk. Bake in a 450°F. oven for 20 minutes, then lower temperature to 350° F. and continue baking for 40 minutes more. (1 hour in all.)

ROLLED OATS BREAD

Crumble **1 cake yeast** in ¼ **cup warm water (with speck of sugar).** Pour **2 cups boiling water** over **1½ cups rolled oats, ½ cup sugar, 2 teaspoonfuls salt** and **2 tablespoonfuls lard.** Allow to cool until lukewarm. Add **yeast** and **5 or 6 cups flour.** Knead until well mixed. Let rise until double in bulk. Knead down, shape into loaves (or rolls if preferred). Allow to double in bulk. Bake in hot oven.

RYE BREAD

Take **2 quarts of rye flour** and add sufficient warm water to make a batter. Add **1 cake quick yeast** and mix well. Allow to stand over night. In the morning add 1 **tablespoonful salt** and **1 cup molasses.** Add **wheat flour** enough to make a stiff dough, let rise. Then knead it, and let rise again. Make into loaves. Let stand until it has reached edge of pan. Bake in moderate oven for 1 hour and 15 minutes.

RYE BREAD (No Wheat Flour)

Cook **1 cup cornmeal** in **1 pint water,** then cool. Mix **1 cake yeast** in little warm water. Add **½ cup corn syrup, 2 teaspoonfuls salt** to **1 cup rye flour** and when cornmeal is lukewarm mix all together. Makes a very thick dough. Set aside to rise. Work down, mold and place in pan to rise again. Bake like ordinary bread only somewhat slower. Bake 35 to 45 minutes.

SALT RISING BREAD

Pare and slice **2 large sized potatoes** in a crock at night. Add **1 teaspoonful salt** and **1 cup cornmeal,** pour over **1 quart boiling water,** cover and keep warm. Next morning remove potatoes and stir in flour to make a stiff batter. Set in a warm place until light. Make into loaves and set to rise. When it has risen twice the size, bake in moderate oven (350°F.) 1 hour.

Bread kept in a cool refrigerator will resist mold and stay fresh longer.

SOY BEAN YEAST BREAD

Scald **1 cup milk,** add **2 tablespoonfuls sugar, 2 teaspoonfuls salt, 2 tablespoonfuls shortening** and **1 cup water.** Cool to lukewarm. Add **1 cake quick yeast** which has been soltened in **¼ cup lukewarm water.** Sift **soy flour** then measure **6 tablespoonfuls; sift all purpose flour** and measure **5½ cups,** then sift together. Add gradually to lukewarm milk mixture until a stiff dough is formed. Turn out on lightly floured board and knead until smooth and satiny. Shape into a smooth ball. Place in a greased bowl and grease top of dough lightly. Cover and let rise until double in bulk. Punch down. Let rise again. When again double in bulk separate into two portions. Round each portion into a smooth ball. Cover and let rise 15 minutes, then shape into loaves. Place in greased standard bread loaf pans and let rise until double in bulk. Bake in a moderately hot oven (375° F.) for 20 minutes, then reduce to 350° F. and bake 25 minutes more. Brush with melted fat, remove from pans and cool on cake rake.

BREAD STICKS

Cut bread in slices 2 inches thick, remove crusts, cut in strips 1 inch wide. This makes rectangles about 1x1x4 inches. Brush or spread with butter on all four sides. Toast in broiler until all sides are brown, turning as often as possible. Serve piping hot.

Stale bread may be freshened by dipping loaf in cold water quickly, then placing it in a hot oven until thoroughly heated.

Soy flour is really ground soy beans. It is too concentrated to act as a flour by itself. It is always better when used with other flours.

CRUMBS

Dry or stale bread may be made into crumbs by completely drying it in a slow oven until crisp, then run through the food grinder until it is fine. Bread crumbs are best kept in a glass jar that is sealed tightly.

TOAST

Plain toast is made either in the broiler of the stove or a toaster made for that purpose. It is usually soft bread browned quickly on both sides, allowing the interior to still remain soft. It should be buttered while hot.

MELBA TOAST

Slice white bread very thin. (Remove crusts if desired but they are good for the teeth and excellent for children as the more they chew the more space there is for their second teeth.) Toast very slowly in oven until golden brown and crisp.

Yeast Bread -- Fancy

CHEESE BREAD

Grind ¼ **lb. strong American cheese** and **2 canned pimentos.** Scald **1 cup milk.** Make a paste of **3 tablespoonfuls flour** and **¼ cup milk.** Add to scalded milk with **1 tablespoonful sugar** and **2 teaspoonfuls salt.** Cook until thick. Add **2 tablespoonfuls butter** and **½ cup cheese mixture.** Cool. Add **1 cake yeast** dissolved in **3 tablespoonfuls lukewarm water** and **3 cups flour.** Knead into a dough. Let rise for 1½ hours. Work down and rise about double. Work down and place in greased pan. Let rise for about 40 minutes. Do not allow it to become as light as other bread. Bake 1 hour in moderate oven (350° F.).

CINNAMON KUCHEN

Scald **1¼ cups milk.** Add **3 tablespoonfuls butter, ½ teaspoonful salt** and **¼ cup sugar.** When lukewarm add **½ cake yeast** crumbled. Stir until dissolved. Add **1 egg** beaten and **2 or 3 cups flour,** enough to make a stiff batter. Cover and let rise until double in bulk. Grease an oblong pan. Pour dough in pan ½ inch thick. Melt **2 tablespoonfuls butter.** Spread over cake, then sprinkle with **3 tablespoonfuls sugar** that has had **1 teaspoonful cinnamon** mixed with it. Bake in hot oven (400° F.) for 1 hour.

CINNAMON ROLL BREAD

Combine **1 cup scalded milk** with **4 tablespoonfuls sugar, 1 teaspoonful salt** and **4 tablespoonfuls shortening.** Cool until lukewarm. Meanwhile soften **1 cake compressed yeast** in **2 tablespoonfuls lukewarm water,** then stir into first mixture. Next add **1 egg,** well beaten, and as much of **4 cups sifted flour** as can be stirred into the dough without kneading. Turn onto lightly floured board. Knead until easily handled. Roll ½ inch thick and spread with **1 tablespoonful melted butter.** Sprinkle with **¼ cup sugar** and **1 tablespoonful cinnamon** mixed. Roll up like jelly roll, place seam side down in greased loaf pan. Cover with clean cloth and let rise until nearly double in bulk. Bake in moderate oven at 375° F. for 45 minutes. Brush with **melted butter** and remove to cake rack to cool. This makes 1 large loaf or 2 small ones.

GRAHAM BREAD

Put **2 tablespoonfuls fat, ¼ cup brown sugar, 2 teaspoonfuls** salt in mixing bowl. Add **1 cake compressed yeast** that has been dissolved in a little lukewarm water. Mix, add remainder of **2 cups of sterilized liquid.** Stir in **2 cups white flour,** beat with spoon until smooth and set in a warm place to rise. Afterward add **3 cups Graham flour,** knead dough until smooth and elastic. Let rise until double in bulk then knead again. Form into loaves, placing in greased pans, then let rise again until double in bulk. Bake in hot oven, 450° F. at first, but reduce heat to 350° F. after crust has taken on a soft brown color.

RAISIN BREAD

Dissolve **1 cake compressed yeast** in **¼ cup luke warm water.** Scald **1 cup milk** and cool to lukewarm, then add dissolved yeast and **1½ cups flour.** Beat until smooth. Put in warm place for 1 hour. Sponge is light and ready when full of bubbles. Add **½ cup melted butter, ¼ cup sugar, 1 egg,** well beaten, **½ teaspoonful salt, ¼ cup raisins,** and **3 level cups flour.** Turn on board, knead until smooth and elastic, and does not stick to hand or board. Place in well greased bowl. Brush over top with melted shortening. Allow to rise 2 hours. Shape. Place in greased pans and bake. If a richer dough is desired, double the quantity of shortening and eggs, using only ¼ cup milk.

Yeast Rolls

Buns and rolls are yeast bread dough baked in individual servings.

HOT CROSS BUNS

Dissolve **1 cake yeast** and **1 tablespoonful sugar** in **1 cup lukewarm milk.** Add **1½ cups of flour** to make a sponge. Beat until smooth. Cover and let rise until light in a warm place free from draft. This takes about 1 hour. Then add **¼ cup butter, 1/3 cup sugar, 1 egg well beaten, ¼ cup raisins or currants** that have been **floured, ¼ teaspoonful salt** and **2 more cups flour.** Turn on board, knead lightly. Place in greased bowl. Cover and set in warm place until double the bulk, which should be about 2 hours. Then knead dough down. Shape into medium sized round buns. Place on well greased pans about 2 inches apart. Cover and let rise again, this time about 1 hour. Glaze with **egg diluted with water.** With a sharp knife cut a cross on top of each bun. Bake 20 minutes. Just before removing from oven brush with **sugar, moistened with water.** While hot fill cross with plain frosting. These are good eaten hot, but if allowed to get stale, are good cut in two, toasted and then spread with butter.

FRUITED HOT CROSS BUNS

Scald **1 cup milk** with **½ teaspoonful salt** and **¼ cup sugar.** Cool to lukewarm. Dissolve **1 cake yeast** in **¼ cup warm water** and add to milk. Whip in **2 cups sifted flour,** beat well. Set aside in warm place to rise for 2 hours or until light and fluffy. Fold in **3 tablespoonfuls melted shortening, 2 well beaten eggs, ¼ teaspoonful cinnamon, ¼ teaspoonful nutmeg, ¼ cup small seedless raisins, 2 tablespoonfuls candied citron,** shaved fine, and flour to make dough stiff enough to handle. Add flour gradually, keeping dough soft. Knead well and let rise again. When double in bulk, form into round buns about 2 inches in diameter. Place on buttered baking pans, allow to rise once more. When light, press or cut the form of a cross on each bun. Bake in hot oven 15 minutes. When finished, brush over top with mixture of **1 tablespoonful of cream** and **1 tablespoonful sugar.** When cool fill cross with plain white confectioner's icing, **powdered sugar and milk or water.**

BUTTER BUNS

Crumble **1 cake yeast** with **one tablespoonful sugar.** Add **1 cup lukewarm milk** and **½ pound** of **melted butter.** Then add **½ cup sugar, 1 teaspoonful salt, 3 eggs,** beaten, and **4 to 5 cups of flour.** Dough should be stiff enough to handle. Stir well. Let stand over night. Cut in 6 parts and roll each round like pie dough. Cut in 6 pieces like a pie. Place orange filling on wide end, then roll to small end, making a long roll. Let rise 4 hours. Bake in hot oven, 400° F., 10 to 15 minutes.

ORANGE FILLING FOR BUNS

Use **juice of 2 oranges** and **rinds cut fine.** The white pulp is removed after the juice is extracted before the rind is cut. Add **1 cup sugar** and cook until thick. Using about **1 teaspoonful** to a bun, there is just enough for the 36 that are made.

BUTTERSCOTCH ROLLS

Sift **1¾ cups flour, 2 teaspoonfuls baking powder** and **½ teaspoonful salt.** Cut in **4 tablespoonfuls shortening,** add **2/3 cup milk** and **½ teaspoonful vanilla.** Mix lightly, turn out on a floured board. Knead for a few seconds, then roll ¼ inch thick. Brush with **melted butter,** sprinkle with **brown sugar and cinnamon.** Roll firmly like a jelly roll. Cream together **¼ cup butter** and **2/3 cup brown sugar,** cover bottom of baking pan generously. Cut the biscuit dough, roll in ½ inch slices and place cut side up in this mixture. Bake about 20 minutes in a moderate oven 350° F., turn out of pan at once. Serve upside down. This recipe makes 1 dozen rolls.

CINNAMON PUFFS

Scald **1 cup milk,** add **2 tablespoonfuls sugar, 1/3 cup melted fat, 1 teaspoonful salt** and cool to lukewarm. Dissolve **1 yeast cake** in **¼ cup lukewarm water.** Sift **flour,** measure **2 cups** and sift into milk mixture, adding it gradually and stirring it in as added. Add yeast, **2 beaten eggs** and blend in thoroughly. Add 1¼ cups more flour, beating it in gradually. Beat until smooth. Cover and let rise till light. Stir down and drop by spoonfuls into greased muffin pans. Sprinkle with a mixture of **¼ cup sugar** and **¼ teaspoonful cinnamon.** Let rise until light (about 30 minutes). Bake 20 to 25 minutes at 375° F.

CINNAMON ROLLS

Mix ¼ **cup sugar, 1 cup mashed potatoes, 1 cup warm water** and **1 cake compressed yeast** and allow to stand 2 hours. Add **2 beaten eggs, ½ tablespoonful salt, 1 quart flour, ½ cup shortening.** Let rise. Roll out dough a piece at a time and spread with the following mixture: ½ **cup melted butter, 1½ cups light brown sugar, 1½ tablespoonfuls cinnamon.** Roll up like jelly roll. Cut in 1 inch slices and let rise again. Bake in moderate oven.

PECAN CARAMEL ROLLS

Mix **1 cup** of boiling **potato water** (water in which potatoes were cooked), ½ **cup butter,** ½ **cup sugar** and ½ **teaspoonful salt** together. Cool to lukewarm. Soften **1 cake yeast** in **2 tablespoonfuls** of **warm water** with ½ **teaspoonful sugar.** Add to first mixture. Add **2 well beaten eggs,** gradually stir in **2 cups** of **flour** and beat thoroughly. Add **2 more cups** of **flour,** stir but do not knead. Place in refrigerator with cover over top until wanted. This will keep for a week. When wanted, roll dough out on floured board to **½ inch thick.** Spread with **butter,** then sprinkle with **sugar, cinnamon** and **chopped pecans.** Roll and cut into slices ½ inch thick. Place these, cut side down, in baking pan in which **2 tablespoonfuls butter,** ½ **cup sugar** and **2 tablespoonfuls water** have been **blended,** slightly cooked and chopped pecans added. Set in warm place to rise until double in size. Bake in **400° F.** oven for **15** or **20 minutes.**

To put a glaze on rolls, brush over with slightly beaten egg yolk just before removing from oven.

To freshen rolls sprinkle with water, place in a paper bag and put in a hot oven for a few minutes.

REFRIGERATOR ROLLS

Crumble **1 cake compressed yeast** into a large bowl. Add **½ cup sugar, 1 teaspoonful salt** and **2 cups lukewarm water.** Add **1 egg,** well beaten. Sift **7 cups flour** once before measuring. Add half flour, then beat well. Add **3 tablespoonfuls melted shortening** and mix in remainder of flour. Let rise until double its bulk. Punch down, cover tightly and place in refrigerator. About 2 hours before baking, remove desired amount of dough. Shape into rolls and place on greased pan (use muffin pans for cloverleaf rolls, making three small rolls in each pan). Let rise slowly to double their bulk, then bake in hot oven, 425° F., for 20 to 25 minutes. This dough can be kept in refrigerator and used from as desired. Shapes may be prepared in the morning and placed back in the refrigerator to be ready for quick baking. Allow just enough time for the dough to rise and the rolls to bake, so they will come from the oven piping hot.

Biscuits

Biscuits are a hot quick bread. All are made on the same principle. If different flavors are desired they are added to the basic recipe. A very hot oven for baking is the secret of good biscuits.

Baking powder biscuits may be mixed, cut, placed on oiled pans and kept for hours in refrigerator before baking.

Biscuit mix may be made at home by mixing the dry ingredients with fat following a regular recipe. Set in refrigerator until needed then add either water or milk to make dough.

BISCUITS (Baking Powder)

Mix **2 cups flour** with **2 tablespoonfuls lard, ½ teaspoonful salt** and **4 teaspoonfuls baking powder** thoroughly. Add **¾ cup milk or water** and mix quickly. Pat out on board, cut with cutter. Bake in very hot oven 10 to 15 minutes.

BISCUITS (or Soda Biscuits)

Sift **2 cups flour** once before measuring. Then to 2 cups flour add **1 teaspoonful salt, 2 teaspoonfuls baking powder** and **¼ teaspoonful soda.** Mix in **4 tablespoonfuls shortening,** add **¾ cup sour milk** to make a soft dough. Roll out, cut with biscuit cutter and bake 8 minutes in a very hot oven (475° F.).

CHEESE BISCUITS

Mix **4 cups flour, 1 teaspoonful salt,** and **8 teaspoonfuls baking powder** and sift together. Work in **4 tablespoonfuls shortening.** Add **1½ cups milk,** mix with finger tips. Toss onto floured board. Roll out thin. Brush over with **melted butter.** Sprinkle well with **½ cup of finely grated cheese.** Fold one half over other half and press down to hold cheese in place and cut with biscuit cutter. Set oven at 450° F. Preheat oven 10 minutes. Bake 12 minutes.

To warm over biscuits, muffins or rolls, sprinkle lightly with water, place pan containing them in a pan of hot water and put in a moderate oven for a few minutes.

CREAM BISCUITS

Sift **2 cups flour.** Add **½ teaspoonful salt** and **4 teaspoonfuls baking powder.** Sift it all together three times. Add **1 cup whipping cream** and blend well with first mixture, using a fork. Put on floured board, pat out, cut and bake in oven 450° F. for 10 to 12 minutes. To make a Lenten dish which is very tasty, cover the biscuits with creamed peas and salmon before putting in oven and then bake at least 12 minutes.

HOT CROSS BISCUITS (With Baking Powder)

Sift **2 cups flour** with **dash of cinnamon** and **nutmeg, 4 teaspoonfuls baking powder** and **½ teaspoonful salt.** Cut in **4 tablespoonfuls shortening.** Add **½ cup chopped raisins.** Combine **¾ cup milk** with **1 well beaten egg yolk** and add gradually to flour mixture to form a soft dough. Roll out on slightly floured board to ½ inch thickness. Cut with biscuit cutter. Bake in hot oven, 450° F., for 10 to 15 minutes. Garnish each biscuit with a cross of confectioner's frosting.

Rolls, biscuits, muffins, etc., should be baked at high temperature. Slow baking dries them out.

MINCEMEAT BISCUITS

Make a rich baking powder biscuit by mixing **2 cups flour, 4 tablespoonfuls lard, 4 teaspoonfuls baking powder,** and **½ teaspoonful salt** together quickly and lightly, add **2/3 cup water** and work until it is absorbed. A fork mixes the water in without overworking. (Different flours require different amounts of moisture, so the amount of water may vary. A moist dough is a good dough.) Turn out dough on floured board. Roll until ½ inch thick. Spread with **soft butter,** then with a mixture of **½ cup mincemeat** and **½ cup chopped apples.** Roll as a jelly roll. Slice in 1 inch slices. Place in a greased shallow pan, cut side flat and bake in a hot oven until brown. Serve with the following sauce: Cook **1 cup brown sugar** and **½ cup water** together until they form a syrup, then add **2 tablespoonfuls butter.** Keep hot. When ready to serve roll, pour a small amount of syrup over each portion.

POPOVERS

Sift **1 cup flour** and **¼ teaspoonful salt.** Add **1 cup milk,** stirring until smooth. Drop in **1 egg unbeaten.** Beat until smooth. Pour into very hot, well greased muffin tins. Bake until puffed and firm in a hot oven for 25 minutes, then reduce to lower temperature for 20 minutes more. (Serves six.)

Popovers are a baked batter which depends entirely upon the incorporation of steam for its leavening agent.

SWEET BISCUITS

Mix **3 cups flour** with **2 teaspoonfuls baking powder, 2/3 cup sugar** and **½ teaspoonful salt.** Rub in **3 tablespoonfuls butter.** Beat **1 egg** and add to **1 cup milk.** Add this to the dry ingredients and mix to a soft dough. Roll to ¼ inch thickness. Cut and bake in a hot oven. These are nice for luncheons and may be cut as small as the hole of the doughnut.

Quick Breads

GINGERBREAD

Beat well 3 **eggs** and add **1 cup lard, 1 cup sugar** and **1 cup molasses.** Beat well together. Sift **3 cups flour** with **2 teaspoonfuls soda, ½ teaspoonful salt, 1 teaspoonful cinnamon** and **2 teaspoonfuls ginger.** Add to first mixture. Lastly, add **1 cup hot water.** The batter is very thin, but don't add more flour. Bake in a greased shallow pan in a moderate oven 350° F. until done. Cut from pan in squares and serve with whipped cream.

ECONOMICAL GINGERBREAD

Cream **2 tablespoonfuls butter** and **1 cup sugar.** Add **½ cup dark molasses.** Beat **2 cups flour, ½ teaspoonful cinnamon, ½ teaspoonful cloves, ½ teaspoonful ginger** and **1 teaspoonful soda** into first part, using a cup of cold coffee or tea to moisten. Have pan greased and floured. Bake slowly so it will rise evenly and avoid molasses burning. This makes rich, moist, dark gingerbread and never fails.

Gingerbread is a cross between a bread and a cake and may take the place of either at a meal.

GLORIFIED GINGERBREAD

Mix as for pie dough the following: **2 cups flour, 1 cup sugar, ¼ teaspoonful salt, ½ teaspoonful cinnamon, ½ teaspoonful ginger** and **½ cup shortening.** When well mixed remove **½ cup** for the **crumbs** on top. To the rest add **1 egg, 2 tablespoonfuls baking molasses, 1 cup thick sour milk, 1 teaspoonful soda,** and **1 teaspoonful baking powder.** Beat well and pour in greased pan. Sprinkle the ½ cup crumbs on top. Bake at 350° F. for 45 minutes.

Loaves

APPLE KUCHEN

Measure 2 cups of sifted flour (pastry flour is best). Add **2 teaspoonfuls baking powder, ¼ teaspoonful salt** and **2 tablespoonfuls sugar** and sift three times. Chop in **¼ cup butter** or **margarine** with two knives. Beat **1 egg** and add **2/3 cup sweet milk.** Mix all together until smooth. Spread in a shallow greased tin and cover with **melted butter.** Core, quarter and slice in eighths about **5 or 6 tart apples,** pared. Lay in rows, lapping each other on top of dough. Cover with more melted butter, **3 tablespoonfuls sugar** and **1 teaspoonful cinnamon.** Bake in moderate oven (350° F.) 40 minutes or until apples are done.

BANANA BREAD

Cream **½ cup sugar** and **2 tablespoonfuls shortening,** then add **1 teaspoonful salt, 1 egg,** beaten separately, **3 bananas crushed, 2 cups flour, 1 teaspoonful soda** and **¼ cup nut meats.** Place in greased bread tin and bake in a slow oven 40 minutes.

BOSTON BROWN BREAD

Mix and sift **1 cup granulated corn meal, 1 cup bread flour, ¾ teaspoonful soda** and **1 teaspoonful salt.** Add **1 cup graham flour, ¾ cup New Orleans molasses, 2 cups sour or buttermilk** and **½ cup seedless raisins.** Steam in 1 pound coffee cans three hours, or in 1 pound baking powder cans two hours. Place cans on a trivet in a kettle of boiling water. Let water come up half-way around molds. Cover closely and steam, adding boiling water as it may be needed. Stale bread, cake, cookies and doughnuts soaked in a little water and beaten free of lumps may be added to the brown bread batter.

Cracklins are the bits of substance left after rendering lard.

CRACKLIN BREAD

Sift **1 cup white cornmeal** with **1 tablespoonful flour, ½ teaspoonful soda, ½ teaspoonful baking powder** and **½ teaspoonful salt.** Add **¾ cup buttermilk** and **¼ cup cracklins.** Beat in **1 egg.** Pour into a greased skillet or pan and bake in a very hot oven (450° F.) until done. Serve hot.

CORNBREAD

Sift ¾ **cup cornmeal** with **1½ cups flour, 2 teaspoonfuls baking powder, 2 tablespoonfuls sugar, ½ teaspoonful salt.** Combine **1 egg,** well beaten, **1 cup milk, 4 tablespoonfuls shortening** and pour into dry ingredients all at once. Stir quickly until all ingredients are just mixed and have lumpy appearance. Turn into greased shallow pan about 8 inches square and bake 30 minutes at 375° F.

DATE NUT BREAD

Mix **1¾ cups sugar, 1 tablespoonful melted butter** and **1 egg.** Beat well. Pour **1½ cups boiling water over 1½ cups cut-up dates,** and add this to sugar, butter and egg mixture. Add **2¾ cups sifted flour** with **2 level teaspoonfuls soda** and **1 teaspoonful salt.** Add **1 cup walnut meats** and **1 teaspoonful vanilla.** Bake in 2 greased loaf pans in moderate oven for 1 hour. This bread is delicious when made into sandwiches with a filling of cream cheese and stuffed olives.

HEALTH BREAD

Mix **1 quart bran, 1 pint white flour, ½ cup baking molasses** (or sorghum), **1 teaspoonful soda** dissolved in a little of the molasses, **1 teaspoonful salt, 1 pint buttermilk** and **½ cup raisins.** Bake in a square or oblong pan for 1 hour, at (350° F.) moderate temperature.

JOHNNY CAKE

Cream **½ cup sugar** with **½ cup lard.** Stir in **one egg, 1 cup sour milk, 1 cup flour, 2 cups cornmeal, 1 teaspoonful baking powder, 2 teaspoonfuls soda** dissolved in a little **water** and pinch of **salt.** When well mixed, put into greased pan and bake in moderate oven about 20 minutes.

NUT BREAD

Mix **4 cups graham flour unsifted, 2 cups white flour, 1 cup brown sugar, 3 cups sour milk, 2 teaspoonfuls salt, 2 teaspoonfuls soda, 1 cup raisins** and **1 cup nut meats,** together and bake 1 hour in moderate oven (350° F.)

OLD-FASHIONED NUT BREAD

Sift **cake flour** and measure **2 cups.** Sift again with **2 teaspoonfuls baking powder** and **½ teaspoonful salt.** Cream **2/3 cup butter** (½ lard may be used). Add **1 cup sugar** gradually. Cream together until light and fluffy. Add 3 **eggs,** one at a time, beating thoroughly after each addition. Add 1 **cup finely chopped walnut meats** and blend. Add flour alternately with **6 tablespoonfuls milk.** Beat until smooth. Add **1 teaspoonful vanilla.** Pour into greased loaf pan 8x4x3 and let stand 20 minutes before baking. Bake in moderate oven 350° F. for 1¼ hours or until done.

ORANGE NUT BREAD

Mix **⅝ cup sugar** and **1 tablespoonful shortening** with **2 eggs, 1 cup candied orange peel, 2 teaspoonfuls salt, 1⅛ cups milk** and **3 cups flour** which has had **6 teaspoonfuls baking powder** sifted in it. Let rise 20 minutes in a greased loaf pan. Bake slowly about 50 minutes. Makes 2 medium loaves. Excellent for sandwiches. Method for making peel: Cut peel from **2 or 3 oranges** into small pieces. Cover with cold water and bring to boil. Pour off water and repeat the process 3 times. Make syrup of **1 cup sugar** and **1 cup water** and cook peel in this until tender. Drain off syrup which is not used. It may be used in a sauce or pudding.

PRUNE WHOLE WHEAT BREAD

Beat **1 egg,** add **¾ cup brown sugar** and mix well. Add **1 cup sour milk.** Soak **1 cup prunes** in small amount of water over night. Drain well, stone and cut into small pieces. Add prunes and **½ cup nut meats** to **¾ cup pastry flour** sifted with **1 teaspoonful baking powder, ½ teaspoonful salt** and **½ teaspoonful soda.** Then add **1½ cups whole wheat flour.** Then add alternately to first mixture. Let rise 25 minutes. Bake in oven 45 minutes at 325° F.

SPOON BREAD

Scald **1½ cups of cornmeal** and allow it to cool. Separate **three eggs** and add **yolks** to cornmeal, then add **1½ tablespoonfuls bacon fat, 2½ teaspoonfuls baking powder, ½ teaspoonful salt** and enough **milk** to make a thin batter. (**One pint** is usually the amount needed.) Fold in stiffly beaten **egg whites.** Bake in moderate oven (350) until well set. Serve at once.

RAISIN BREAD

Cream ¾ **cup shortening,** which should be half butter, with **1 cup sugar,** slightly beat **3 small or 2 large eggs** and add to sugar. Sift 3 **cups flour** with 8 **teaspoonfuls baking powder** and a **pinch of salt** (use more salt if all unsalted fat is used). Add this to sugar mixture alternately with **1½ cups of milk** and **water** mixed. The batter should be rather stiff, not runny. Add liquid slowly, it may not require it all. Lastly, flour, ½ **package of seeded raisins** and add to batter. (The seeded raisins have a better flavor than the seedless ones.) Pour into greased loaf pans. This makes one large loaf or two small ones. Bake at 350° F. for 40 minutes, then raise heat to 375° F. and continue to bake until brown. (Should be about 10 more minutes.)

Raisins are a dried grape raised for that purpose. They may be either seeded or seedless, according to the variety. The seeded are very sticky but are really better than the seedless in some recipes, so use the ones called for when reading a recipe.

Muffins

Muffins are a quick bread which are very easy to make. They should be mixed very little, as too much mixing causes large tunnels through the center. The pattern given at first may be used for all muffins if the substitutes used are kept in right amounts.

MUFFIN RECIPE PATTERN

Mix **2 cups flour** with **4 tablespoonfuls fat, 4 tablespoonfuls sugar, 4 teaspoonfuls baking powder** and **½ teaspoonful salt.** Beat **1 egg,** add **1 cup milk.** Mix well. Pour on to the dry ingredients and stir until mixed but do not over work. Pour into greased muffin tins and bake in a very hot oven (450° F.) 15 minutes or until nicely brown.

APPLE MUFFINS

Sift **2 cups flour, 4 tablespoonfuls baking powder, 1 teaspoonful salt, 1 tablespoonful sugar.** Add **1 cup milk** and **1 beaten egg.** Mix well. Add **4 teaspoonfuls melted shortening.** Drop spoonfuls of mixture separately in greased muffin tins. Add **1 tablespoonful apple sauce** to each muffin. Then cover the sauce with more muffin mixture. Bake from 25 to 30 minutes in a hot oven. This recipe makes 12 muffins.

BLUEBERRY MUFFINS

Cream **1 cup sugar** with **¼ cup butter.** Add **2 beaten egg yolks, 1 cup milk** and **2½ cups flour** sifted with **4 teaspoonfuls baking powder,** a little **nutmeg,** pinch **salt.** Add **2 cups blueberries** washed and drained. Lastly fold in **2 beaten egg whites.** Bake in muffin tins in moderate oven for about 20 minutes.

Blueberries are a small dark blue berry, whose family consists of the huckleberry and cranberry.

BRAN MUFFINS

Mix **1 cup flour** with **1 cup bran, 1 teaspoonful salt, 3 teaspoonfuls baking powder** and **¼ teaspoonful soda.** Cut in **4 tablespoonfuls fat.** Beat **1 egg,** add **2 tablespoonfuls New Orleans molasses** and stir until thoroughly mixed. Add **¾ cup sour milk** and combine the two mixtures. Pour into greased muffin tins. Bake in hot oven or 450° F. for 15 minutes.

BRAN GINGERBREAD MUFFINS

Sift **2 cups flour, 3½ teaspoonfuls baking powder, 1½ teaspoonfuls salt** and **½ cup brown sugar** together. Add **2 cups bran.** Beat **2 eggs,** add **2¾ cups milk** and **1/3 cup shortening,** melted and cooled. Add liquid to dry ingredients. When moist add **½ cup molasses, 1 teaspoonful ginger** and **1 teaspoonful cinnamon.** Stir until well mixed but not too long. Bake in greased muffin pans in moderate oven 20 to 25 minutes.

When muffins are wanted for breakfast, measure the dry ingredients and mix the night before. Mix the liquid with eggs and in the morning combine the two.

BREAD CRUMB MUFFINS

Pour **2½ cups milk** over **3 cups bread crumbs.** Let stand until soft, then beat with egg beater. Add **3 egg yolks** and **1 cup flour,** sifted, with **2 teaspoonfuls baking powder** and **½ teaspoonful salt.** Beat well, add **2 tablespoonfuls melted butter** and fold in **3 egg whites,** stiffly beaten. Bake in buttered muffin tins, 20 to 25 minutes at 375° F. or moderately hot oven.

Bran is the outside covering of the wheat kernel. It has no food value, as it is not absorbed by the digestive tract, but it does have value in that the intestines need bulk in order to do their work well. Bran acts as this agent.

CORN MUFFINS OR STICKS

Sift together **1 cup flour, 1 cup cornmeal, 3 teaspoonfuls baking powder, ¼ teaspoonful soda, 4 tablespoonfuls sugar,** and **1 teaspoonful salt.** Work in **4 tablespoonfuls fat** (either lard, butter or substitute for both). Beat **1 egg** slightly and add **1 cup thick sour milk** (less if thin milk is used). Combine the two mixtures and pour immediately into well greased pan, whether stick or muffins. Bake at a high temperature until done (450° F. to 500° F.).

CRACKED WHEAT MUFFINS

Measure **1 cup cracked wheat flour** and **1 cup soft wheat flour.** Add 4 **teaspoonfuls baking powder** and ½ **teaspoonful salt** to the soft wheat flour. Break **1 egg** in a mixing bowl and beat it well. Add **1 cup milk** and **4 tablespoonfuls sugar.** Measure **4 tablespoonfuls butter** and melt it, then add it to egg mixture. Mix well. Pour dry ingredients, except cracked wheat, into sifter and sift into egg mixture. Beat until all materials are blended. Add cracked wheat flour, then pour into greased muffin pans. Bake in hot oven 400° F. for 25 minutes. Makes 12 muffins. **Raisins** may be added if desired.

CRANBERRY MUFFINS

Sift **3 cups flour** with 3 **teaspoonfuls baking powder, 3 tablespoonfuls sugar** and ½ **teaspoonful salt.** Add **¾ cup raw cranberries** chopped. Combine **¾ cups milk, 1 beaten egg** and **3 tablespoonfuls melted shortening** and add all at once to first mixture. Stir only until flour is dampened. Fill greased muffin tins about ¾ full. Bake 25 minutes in a 425° F. oven. These muffins can be mixed an hour or two before baking if desired.

FEATHER MOLASSES MUFFINS

Cream ½ **cup shortening** with ½ **cup sugar.** Add **2 eggs** which have been beaten slightly. Stir in ½ **cup molasses, 1¼ cups flour** sifted with ½ **teaspoonful cinnamon,** ½ **teaspoonful soda** and ¼ **teaspoonful ginger.** Lastly, add ½ **cup fresh** or **sour milk.** Bake in oiled muffin pans in slow oven (325° F.) This recipe makes 12 muffins.

GINGER MUFFINS

Break **1 egg** in bowl. Add ½ **cup sugar** and ½ **cup molasses** and **1½ tablespoonfuls melted butter.** Dissolve ½ **teaspoonful soda** in ½ **cup boiling water** and add to above mixture. Sift ½ **teaspoonful ginger,** ½ **teaspoonful cinnamon** and ¼ **teaspoonful salt** with **1¾ cups flour,** then mix with the first mixture. Bake in muffin pans 10 to 15 minutes (400° F.). Makes 12 muffins. *Note*—This recipe may be baked in a low, flat pan but the time for baking will be longer.

SOY FLOUR MUFFINS

Place **1 unbeaten egg, ½ cup soy flour** and **1¼ cups milk** in a bowl. Thoroughly mix, add **2 tablespoonfuls melted shortening** and beat again. Sift **1 2/3 cups flour** with **¼ cup sugar, 1¼ teaspoonful salt** and **3 teaspoonfuls baking powder** into large bowl. Add soy mixture and beat just enough to mix. Bake in greased muffin pans in moderately hot oven about 25 minutes.

WHOLE WHEAT MUFFINS

Beat **1 egg** and add **1 cup milk.** Mix and sift together **2 cups whole wheat flour, 5 teaspoonfuls baking powder, 2 tablespoonfuls sugar, ½ teaspoonful salt** and add to first mixture. Beat just enough to blend thoroughly and add **4 tablespoonfuls shortening.** Turn into greased muffin pans and bake in hot oven (400° F.) for 25 minutes. **Dried fruits** or **nuts** may be added for variety. This recpe makes 12 muffins. *Note* — Where no flour is used but whole wheat, the product is rather heavy. Unless it is necessary, part white flour gives better results.

Pancakes

Pancakes are a quick bread baked on a griddle or fried in a skillet with a small amount of fat.

BUCKWHEAT CAKES

Use **1 cup of wheat flour** to **3 cups of buckwheat flour.** Add **2 tablespoonfuls sugar** and enough **water** to make a batter that will pour but will not break from spoon or run like a mere liquid. Mix until smooth, then beat over and over with a slotted spoon until large bubbles form and break. This will take about 5 minutes. Then stir in **1/3 cake of compressed yeast** dissolved in **½ cup warm water.** Cover and set to rise over night in a warm place. (A pitcher is nice to use so one can pour the batter out.) In the morning beat batter well and add **1 teaspoonful salt, ½ teaspoonful soda** and enough **warm milk** or **water** to make batter of right consistency. Water makes cakes more crisp while milk makes them brown better. Bake on griddle hot enough for fat to sizzle when rubbed over it.

Editor's Note: When all cakes are baked for one morning add buckwheat flour and wheat flour in the proportion of half and half until the batter is very stiff. Set aside in a cool place until the next morning, when ½ or a teaspoonful of soda is added, according to the amount of batter and enough boiling water to make batter the right consistency for baking. This is repeated every day that the batter is used until all is gone.

CORN-MEAL PANCAKES OR FLAPJACKS

Pour **1 cup boiling water** over **¾ cup yellow cornmeal** and stir until it thickens, then add **1 tablespoonful molasses, 1 cup sour milk** and **2 whole eggs.** Beat thoroughly. Let cool. Sift together **1½ cups flour, 3 teaspoonfuls baking powder, 1½ teaspoonfuls salt, ¼ teaspoonful soda** and **3 tablespoonfuls melted shortening.** Combine mixtures. Beat thoroughly. Bake on hot griddle.

PLAIN PANCAKES

Beat **2 eggs** well, add **12 tablespoonfuls milk** (sweet or sour), sift **1 cup flour** once, then measure, add **2 teaspoonfuls baking powder** if **sweet milk** is used, if **sour milk** is used then add **1 teaspoonful baking powder** and **¼ teaspoonful soda.** Beat into egg and milk mixture. Add **½ teaspoonful salt.** Bake at once. Should make 12 pancakes. A good measure for pancakes is 1 tablespoonful liquid to each pancake. (If pancakes are too thick, add more milk, if too thin, add more flour.)

POTATO PANCAKES

Mix **½ cup of canned milk** with **½ cup fine bread crumbs.** The crumbs should soak up all the milk. Stir in **1 egg, 1 teaspoonful minced onion, 2 cups grated raw potato** and **1½ teaspoonfuls salt.** Put bacon drippings on griddle or in frying pan. When hot, drop pancakes from tablespoon and press rather thin. Cook slowly until nicely browned. Turn and brown the other side.

RICE PANCAKES

Mix **1 cup cooked rice** with **1 tablespoonful melted butter, 1 teaspoonful salt, 1 egg,** well beaten and **1 cup sweet milk.** Sift **1 cup flour** with **2 teaspoonfuls baking powder** and add to liquid ingredients. Bake on hot greased griddle. Good use for left over rice.

Left over pancake batter may be thickened and used as muffins.

Buckwheat is a three cornered grain which is used in this country mostly for flour in pancakes. In buying buckwheat flour, small, frequent purchases are best. It should be kept cool and well covered, as it is much sought by insects.

Waffles

Waffles are a particular form of bread baked on a specially made griddle.

GINGERBREAD WAFFLES

Cream ½ **cup shortening** with 2/3 **cup brown sugar.** Add **2 eggs** well beaten, ½ **cup molasses** and ¾ **cup sour milk,** then **1½ cups flour** sifted with **1 teaspoonful baking powder, 1 scant teaspoonful soda, 1 teaspoonful ginger,** ½ **teaspoonful cinnamon** and ⅛ **teaspoonful cloves.** Beat until just smooth. Bake as ordinary waffles, putting cakes together with whipped cream at the moment of serving or with the accompaniment of a rather tart apple sauce.

SUGAR WAFFLES OR ROSETTES

Beat **2 eggs** slightly with **1 teaspoonful sugar** and ¼ **teaspoonful salt.** Add **1 cup milk** and **1 cup flour.** These are made with rosette irons. Screw handle into iron, then dip in **hot lard** or **oil** before dipping into batter, not allowing batter to come over top of iron. Return iron to hot lard for at least 20 seconds or until brown. Remove with piece of clean cheese cloth or clean cloth. Sprinkle with **powdered sugar.** These hints are to be observed in making rosettes. When waffles do not come off freely from iron, it indicates they are not sufficiently fried to be dry in center. Should rosettes blister, thus absorbing fat, it indicates eggs are beaten too much. Beat very little. Should waffles drop off in hot oil, it indicates the iron is not deep enough in the oil. Should batter slip from iron into bowl, it indicates iron is too hot.

Waffles may be kept crisp before serving if baked and placed on a rack in a slow oven.

WAFFLES (Sour Milk)

Mix **2 cups flour** with **1 teaspoonful baking powder** and **1 teaspoonful salt.** Add **2 eggs** well beaten and **2 cups** of **sour milk,** or **buttermilk,** which has had **1 teaspoonful soda** dissolved in it. Lastly, add **6 tablespoonfuls melted butter** or **lard.** Bake on hot iron. Makes 8 to 9 waffles, according to size of the iron.

WAFFLES (Sweet Milk)

Sift together **2 cups flour, 4 teaspoonfuls baking powder, ¼ teaspoonful salt, 2 tablespoonfuls sugar.** Beat **2 egg whites** stiff and **2 yolks** slightly. Add yolks to **1¼ cups milk,** then to dry ingredients. Add **6 tablespoonfuls melted butter,** then fold in beaten egg whites. Bake on hot waffle iron.

Cakes

Cake is a baked batter, which is sweet, and may have many different flavors. It usually uses for its leavening agent, either baking powder or soda but may have yeast, and in sponge cakes, air. Usually, cake failures are due to over anxiety to produce a good product, thus, continued beating, after the addition of the leavening agent, reduces its function, as the gas incorporated is again driven out. Do all the heavy beating or creaming of a cake in the early stages.

Better results are obtained in baking cakes if they are first given a lower temperature than called for in the recipe and then raised to that temperature after 15 minutes of baking time. For example: if a cake is to be baked at 350° F., put it in a 325° F. oven and do not raise the temperature to 350° F. for about 15 minutes, or one fourth of the baking time. This is especially true of loaf or tube cakes.

REASONS FOR CAKE FAILURES

1. Cakes that are not even may be due to an uneven oven or heat.

2. Cakes that are coarse may have too much leavening agent, too much sugar, baked at too low a temperature or poor blending of ingredients.

3. Cakes that are wet on bottom may come from insufficient blending of ingredients, especially sponge cakes, but it is more apt to be that the oven does not heat well on bottom.

4. Cakes with large holes usually means that you beat the cake too much after adding flour. It may be a poor recipe, using too little shortening for the flour.

5. Cakes that fall have too much sugar as a rule, but may have too much baking powder. If cake is removed from oven before being done it will fall, as the framework has not been set.

6. **Cakes that are dry are usually baked too long at too low a temperature. They could have too much flour also.**

7. **Cakes that hump and crack in center are usually baked too fast or have too much flour.**

When measuring flour for cakes, sift flour, then lift by spoonfuls into measuring cup. Do not shake down by any method. Recipes are based on gently lifting flour into the cup and then leveling with a spatula for accuracy.

Angel Food

Angel food cake obtains its lightness from the air incorporated while it is being made. After the egg whites have been beaten, the rest of the ingredients should be carefully folded in, so as not to force out the air already there.

ANGEL FOOD CAKE

Beat **1 cup egg whites** with flat whip until frothy. Beat in **1 teaspoonful cream of tartar** and **pinch of salt.** Continue beating until egg whites are glossy, fine grained and will stand up in peaks. Add **1 cup sugar** gradually, gently beating and folding after each addition. Fold in **1 teaspoonful flavoring** (usually half almond and half vanilla is used) Sift **¾ cup cake fllour** with **¼ cup sugar** and gradually add this to egg mixture, folding it in gently. Pour into dry, ungreased tube pan and bake at 300° F. for 15 minutes, then 325° F. until done. Remove from oven, invert pan and allow to cool before removing from pan.

ANGEL STRAWBERRY SHORTCAKE

Use **1 whole Angel food cake.** When cake is cold, slice in two, as for layers. Place a layer of **brick ice cream** between layers, laying the 2 baked crusts next to the ice cream. Cover top with **whipped cream** sweetened with **confectioner's sugar.** Garnish thickly with halves of fresh **strawberries.** Cut as one would layer cake when serving.

CHOCOLATE ANGEL FOOD CAKE

To **1¼ cups egg whites** add **¼ teaspoonful salt** and beat until foamy, then add **1 teaspoonful cream of tartar** and continue beating until they stand in peaks, but not dry: Sift **¾ cup flour, ¼ cup cocoa** and **1¼ cups sugar** six times. Fold into egg whites with **1 teaspoonful vanilla.** Pour into an ungreased angel food pan, bake 1 hour, the first 30 minutes at 275° F., increase to 350° F. for the last 30 minutes. Cool by inverting pan. Do not remove until cake is cold.

FILLED ANGEL FOOD CAKE

When **cake** is cold remove from pan with a sharp knife. Cut out part of the center. Fill the cavity with **ice cream, whipped cream,** into which has been folded **fresh fruit** or **whipped, flavored, and colored gelatin.** Garnish with whipped cream or fruit.

Egg whites beat better if they are at room temperature, rather than just removed from the ice box. Freshly laid eggs do not whip as well as those that are about 3 days old.

STRAWBERRY MERINGUE CAKE

Have **6 egg whites** very cold. Add **¼ teaspoonful salt** and beat with wire whip. Sift **1 pound powdered sugar** and combine with egg whites, beating with a rotary beater. Add **¾ teaspoonful vanilla.** Pour into 3 buttered layer cake pans and bake in a slow oven (275° F.) 35 minutes, until delicately browned. Let cool. Cover with **strawberries,** place layers one on top of the other and serve with **whipped cream**

Chocolate Cocoa Cakes

CHOCOLATE PEPPERMINT CAKE

Cream ¼ **cup butter** with **1 cup sugar.** Add **2 egg yolks** and beat briskly. Add **2 squares of melted unsweetened chocolate.** Sift **1½ cups pastry flour, ½ teaspoonful salt** and **1 teaspoonful soda.** Add to butter mixture alternately with **1 cup sour milk.** Mix thoroughly, add **1 teaspoonful vanilla.** Pour in square cake pan or oblong cake pan that has been greased and floured. Bake in moderate oven (350° F.) 50 to 60 minutes. Ice with a white icing flavored with peppermint. After cake is iced with white icing, melt 2 squares of bitter chocolate and pour over the top, allowing it to run down sides in uneven formation.

CHOCOLATE CAKE WITH MASHED POTATOES

Beat **1 cup hot mashed potatoes** until very light, then add **1 cup butter** substitute and beat again. Add **2 cups sugar** and beat well. Add 3 **squares** of **melted chocolate, 1 grated lemon rind** and **grated rind of 1 orange.** Sift together **1¾ cups cake flour, 2 teaspoonfuls baking powder, 1 teaspoonful cloves, 1 teaspoonful nutmeg, ½ teaspoonful salt** and add to mixture alternately with **½ cup milk.** Add 4 **eggs well beaten** and **1 cup nut meats.** Bake 45 minutes in moderate oven. Ice with any preferred icing, but caramel is always good.

CRAZY CHOCOLATE CAKE

Put the following ingredients in a mixing bowl in the order given: (Do not stir until boiling coffee is added and then beat 3 minutes with electric beater, or 5 minutes if mixed by hand.) **2 cups sugar, 2 eggs, 1 cup sour milk** or **buttermilk, 1 cup cocoa, 1 cup butter,** or any desired shortening, **2 teaspoonfuls soda, 2 teaspoonfuls vanilla, ⅛ teaspoonful salt, 3 cups sifted flour** and **1 cup boiling hot coffee.** Makes three 9-inch layer, four 8-inch layer, or one large pan 10-15. Bake at 325° F. from 25 to 45 minutes, depending upon which pan is used.

ECONOMICAL CHOCOLATE CAKE

Grate or melt **2 squares chocolate** over hot water. Cream **¼ cup butter** or **margarine** and **1 cup white sugar.** Add **2 unbeaten eggs,** one at a time, and beat well. Add **½ cup milk,** alternately with **1¼ cups flour,** which has had sifted with it **½ teaspoonful salt** and **1 teaspoonful baking powder.** Lastly, add **1 teaspoonful vanilla** and melted **chocolate.** Bake in 2 layers in a 325° F. to 350° F. oven for 20 to 25 minutes.

EGGLESS CHOCOLATE CAKE

Cream **1 cup brown sugar, 2 tablespoonfuls cocoa** and **4 level tablespoonfuls shortening** (half lard and butter or all vegetable compound). Add **1 teaspoonful soda** and **1 teaspoonful vanilla** to **1 cup thick sour milk or buttermilk.** Starting with **1½ cups flour** to which **¼ teaspoonful salt** has been added, add to creamed butter and sugar, alternating with milk and soda. (Add more flour if needed.) Bake in a moderate oven about 30 minutes.

ONE-EGG CHOCOLATE CAKE

Put **1 square of bitter chocolate** and **1 cup water** in a sauce pan and let come to a boil. Cool. Cream **¼ cup shortening.** Add **1 cup sugar** gradually, then **1 egg yolk** beaten. Add chocolate mixture. Add **¾ cup flour** and **2 teaspoonfuls baking powder,** while slowly beating batter. Add **½ teaspoonful vanilla** and fold in **1 egg white** beaten stiff. Bake in a shallow pan. Frost with a brown sugar icing.

RAISED DEVIL'S FOOD CAKE

Cream **1 cup butter** or other shortening, add **2 cups white sugar** while creaming. Add **3 squares melted chocolate** and mix well. Add **3 egg yolks** and beat mixture thoroughly. Sift **2¾ cups cake flour** with **½ teaspoonful salt** and add alternately with **1 cup sweet milk.** Stir in **1 teaspoonful vanilla.** Add **½ yeast cake** dissolved in **¼ cup lukewarm water.** Fold in **3 stiffly beaten egg whites** and place in refrigerator for 12 hours or overnight. Then add **1 teaspoonful soda** dissolved in **4 teaspoonfuls lukewarm water** and bake in moderate oven.

RED DEVIL CAKE

Place 3 **squares of bitter chocolate** to melt in double boiler. Cream ½ **cup shortening.** Add 2 **cups sugar** gradually. Cream until fluffy. Add 2 **egg yolks** well beaten. Mix well. Sift together 3 times, 2½ **cups cake flour** with 2 **teaspoonfuls baking powder** and ½ **teaspoonful salt.** Add alternately with 1 **cup buttermilk.** When all is smoothly combined, add 1¼ **cups boiling water** to melted chocolate, stir until smooth, add 1½ **teaspoonfuls soda** and stir again. Use a very deep boiler as mixture will foam. Cool slightly. Add slowly with **1 teaspoonful vanilla** to batter. Lastly, fold in **2 beaten egg whites.** Bake at 375° F. May be large loaf or 2 or 3 layers.

SOUR CREAM CHOCOLATE CAKE

Cream 2 **cups brown sugar** with ½ **cup butter,** add 3 **beaten eggs.** Sift all purpose **flour,** measure **2 cups,** add **1 teaspoonful soda** to **1 cup sour cream.** Add flour and sour cream alternately to first mixture. Add **2 squares baking chocolate,** melted, and **1 teaspoonful vanilla.** Pour into two 9-inch greased pans and bake in moderate oven (350° F.), 30 to 35 minutes.

Devil's food is a chocolate cake made with sour or buttermilk.

WELLESLEY FUDGE CAKE

Cream ½ **cup butter** with 2 **cups sugar,** add 3 **egg yolks** and beat until creamy. Sift 3 **cups flour** with 3 **teaspoonfuls baking powder** and ½ **teaspoonful salt.** Melt 4 **squares bitter chocolate.** Add melted chocolate to sugar and butter mixture. When well mixed add flour and ¾ **cup milk** and ¾ **cup coffee** alternately, until all is used. Lastly, add 1 **cup English Walnut meats.** Bake in 1 large sheet in 350° F. oven. Cut in squares. May or may not be iced.

Coffee Cakes

COFFEE CAKE (Baking Powder)

Sift 1½ **cups flour**, 4 **tablespoonfuls light brown sugar**, 3 **teaspoonfuls baking powder** and ¼ **teaspoonful salt** into a bowl. Work in 4 **tablespoonfuls solid butter.** Add 1 **well beaten egg** with ¼ **cup milk** and 1 **teaspoonful vanilla.** Mix until it forms a dough. Divide dough into two pieces and work in lengths about 24 inches long. Take 1 **tablespoonful butter** and work until soft. Spread each length with butter and sprinkle with ½ **cup nuts** and ¾ **cup raisins.** Lift one length upon the other and twist. Bake in round cake pan. Use moderate oven (350° F.) for 30 minutes. Remove from oven and frost with 1 **tablespoonful water** and enough **powdered sugar** to make like thick cream. Return to oven for a short time to dry.

COFFEE CAKE (Soda)

Cream 1 **cup sugar** with 2 **tablespoonfuls shortening.** Add 1 **egg** well beaten. Mix well and add 1 **cup sour milk,** 1 **teaspoonful soda,** ¼ **teaspoonful salt,** 2¼ **cups flour** and ¼ **cup raisins.** Beat until smooth. Spread in a baking pan so that it will be about ½ inch thick. Top with following: 1 **cup brown sugar,** 4 **teaspoonfuls flour** and 1 **teaspoonful cinnamon** mixed well together. Spread well over the top and dot with **butter.** Bake 20 minutes in moderate oven (350° F.)

COFFEE CRUMB CAKE

Cream ½ **cup sugar** with ¼ **cup butter,** add 1 **teaspoonful vanilla** to ¾ **cup milk** and 2 **teaspoonfuls baking powder** to 2 **cups flour.** Add alternately to first mixture and beat until smooth. Bake in hot oven in shallow pan. Make this mixture for the top: 3 **tablespoonfuls butter,** 3 **tablespoonfuls sugar,** 1 **teaspoonful cinnamon,** 1 **teaspoonful cocoanut** and 3 **tablespoonfuls flour** rubbed together. Put on top of baked cake and return to oven to brown.

Cup Cakes

Cup Cakes—Reduce the amount of flour by 2 tablespoonfuls per cup, if using a cake recipe for cup cakes.

CHOCOLATE CUP CAKES

Put into a bowl the following ingredients: **1 egg, ½ cup cocoa, ½ cup shortening, 1½ cups flour, ½ cup sour milk, 1 teaspoonful vanilla, 1 teaspoonful soda, 1 cup sugar** and **½ cup hot water. Do** not mix until the last item has been added. Beat well and bake **in** a moderate oven **(350° F.), about 20 to 25 minutes.**

DEVIL'S FOOD CUP CAKES

Cream **½ cup butter** or **lard** with **1½ cups sugar,** add **2 whole eggs** and beat. Cut **2 squares chocolate** into small pieces and melt over hot water. Stir in **1 cup sour milk** and **1 teaspoonful vanilla.** Sift **flour** and measure **2 cups,** add **½ teaspoonful salt,** add to mixture. Dissolve **1 teaspoonful soda** in **1 tablespoonful vinegar,** add the very last thing. Bake in hot oven in well greased muffin pans for 30 minutes.

Chocolate Icing:

Mix **½ cup sugar, ½ cup water** and **2 tablespoonfuls butter,** bring to a boil, stirring constantly. Remove from fire. Add **2½ cups powdered sugar.** Add **1 oz. melted chocolate** and stir until smooth. Lastly, add **¾ teaspoonful vanilla.** Spread on sides and tops of cakes. If tops only are to be iced, then use only ½ the recipe.

LEMON CUP CAKES

Cream **½ cup shortening** and **½ cup sugar.** Add **1 egg** and beat well. Add **grated rind of 1 lemon** and mix again. Add **½ cup milk** and **½ cup molasses** (New Orleans) to the creamed mixture. Sift together **2 cups flour, 1½ teaspoonfuls baking powder, 1½ teaspoonfuls cinnamon, ¼ teaspoonful salt.** Add to mixture with **1 teaspoonful lemon juice.** Mix well. Pour into muffin pans. Bake in moderate oven (350° F.) about 25 minutes.

ORANGE CUP CAKES

Cream **1/3 cups shortening** with **1 cup sugar.** Add **2 egg yolks** and beat well. Sift together **1¾ cups sifted flour, ¼ teaspoonful salt** and **2 teaspoonfuls baking powder.** Add alternately to creamed mixture with **2/3 cup milk.** Stir in **1 teaspoonful orange juice** and **grated rind of 1 orange.** Fold in 2 stiffly beaten **egg whites.** Bake in a moderate oven about 25 minutes. Use the remainder of the orange juice for powdered sugar icing.

SPICE CUP CAKES

Cream **½ cup butter** or **shortening, 1 cup sugar** and **1 egg** together. Add **1 cup sour milk,** then **2 cups flour** that has had **1 teaspoonful soda, 1 teaspoonful cinnamon, 1 teaspoonful cloves, 1 teaspoonful allspice** and **½ teaspoonful salt** sifted with it. Bake in greased muffin tins about 20 minutes. This recipe will fill 2 eight-pan muffln tins.

WHITE CUP CAKES

Separate **2 eggs.** Cream **½ cup butter** with **1 cup sugar.** Add beaten **egg yolks.** Sift **2 cups flour** with **2 teaspoonfuls baking powder** and add alternately with **½ cup milk** to the creamed mixture. Whip **2 egg whites** until very stiff and add to batter, folding them in lightly. Add **1 teaspoonful vanilla** for flavor. Bake in a moderate oven (350° F.) about 25 minutes.

Fruit Cakes

BUTTERLESS, EGGLESS, MILKLESS CAKE

Put into a pan the following ingredients: **1 cup brown sugar, 1 cup water, 2 cups seedless raisins, ½ cup lard, 1 teaspoonful cloves, 1 teaspoonful cinnamon, ½ teaspoonful salt** and **1 teaspoonful nutmeg.** Boil together for 3 minutes after it comes to a boil. Cool. When cold add **1 teaspoonful soda** dissolved in a little hot water and **2 cups flour,** to which **½ teaspoonful baking powder** has been added. Bake in moderate oven about 40 minutes.

EASY FRUIT CAKE

Cream **1 cup butter or lard** with **1 cup brown sugar.** Add **1 egg,** then **1 cup molasses** with **2 level teaspoonfuls soda** stirred in, and **1 cup sour milk.** Put **2 teaspoonfuls of spices** with **3 cups flour, sift.** Add **1 cup raisins** with a **little flour.** Bake in a greased **loaf** pan in a moderate oven until done.

FRUIT CAKE

Cream **½ cup butter,** add **1 cup sugar** and **2 egg yolks** and stir well. Mix **1 teaspoonful soda** in **1 cup sour milk** and alternate with **2½ cups flour.** Put **2 teaspoonfuls baking powder** in the well-beaten **whites of 2 eggs** and add to mixture. Next add **1 box white raisins, 1 cup nuts, 2 slices candied pineapple, ¼ lb. candied cherries, ¼ lb. citron, ¼ lb. candied orange peel** and **¼ lb. candied lemon peel.** Mix well and bake in slow oven for 1 hour.

If you have trouble with fruit falling to bottom in cake try adding half the batter, then the floured fruit, then the other half of batter.

OLD ENGLISH FRUIT CAKE

Cream **1 cup dark brown sugar, 2 cups white sugar** with **¾ pound butter** thoroughly, add **6 well beaten eggs,** mix well, add **½ cup grape juice** and **1 wine glass of brandy.** Add 3½ **cups flour** and 3 **teaspoonfuls baking powder** sifted together, then **1 teaspoonful nutmeg** and **1 teaspoonful cinnamon** and **2 teaspoonfuls lemon extract,** mixing thoroughly after each addition. Mix **2 cups seeded raisins** with ½ **cup flour** and **1 cup chopped dates, ½ cup chopped figs, 2 cups candied cherries, 1 cup blanched almonds, 1 cup English walnuts, 1 cup finely cut citron, ½ cup candied pineapple, ½ cup candied orange peel, ½ cup candied lemon peel** or **grated rind of 1 lemon and 1 orange.** Mix into batter mixture. Bake three hours in a slow oven (250° F.) Cool in pan. When cold wrap in oiled paper and store in a tin or other container to ripen for several weeks before using.

PORK FRUIT CAKE

Pour **1½ cups of boiling water** over **½ lb. ground fat pork** and set aside. Put the following fruit and nuts through a food chopper: **2 boxes raisins, 1 box cocoanut, 1 lb. figs, 1 lb. dates, ½ lb. English walnuts** and **½ lb. cream nuts.** Add all this fruit and nuts to **5 cups of flour** and mix well. Add 3½ **cups light brown sugar, 1 teaspoonful nutmeg, 1 teaspoonful cinnamon** and **1 teaspoonful cloves.** Pour in meat and water. Dissolve **1½ teaspoonfuls soda** in small amount of cold water and add to the batter. Mix well and **bake in slow oven 300° F. about 2 or 2½ hours.**

WHITE FRUIT CAKE

Cream **1 cup of vegetable shortening** with **2 cups sugar.** Add **3 cups flour,** which has been sifted with **2 teaspoonfuls baking powder** alternately with **1 cup milk.** Stir in **1 pound of white raisins** (Sultanas), **1 cup candied cherries** cut in pieces, then **1 cup candied pineapple** cut fine and **¼ lb. mixed citron, lemon** and **orange peel.** Sprinkle the candied fruits over the batter a little at a time to avoid them sticking together. Fold in **7 stiffly beaten egg whites.** Bake in paper-lined tube pans. Bake at 250° F. for 3½ hours, then **increase to 300° F. for 15 minutes. Makes 2 large tube pans.**

Spice Cakes

ORIGIN OF SPICES

ALLSPICE—From a West Indian tree, about the size of a small pea, dried and ground or left whole.

ANISE—The minute seed of an annual plant cultivated chiefly in Spain.

BAY LEAVES—The aromatic leaves of the sweet bay or laurel tree.

CAPERS—The flower buds of the caper bush.

CARAWAY—The aromatic seeds of a plant which grows wild in the meadows of Holland.

CARDAMON—The fruit of a reed-like plant, native to the Malabar coast of India.

CASSIA BUDS—The dried flower buds of the tree that yields cassia cinnamon.

CAYENNE PEPPER—From very small narrow red pepper pods.

CELERY SEED— The seed of the celery plant.

CINNAMON—The inner bark of young wood of a cinnamon tree.

CLOVES—Dried flower buds of the clove tree.

CORIANDER—A smooth, round, yellowish, seedlike fruit, borne by a small plant to the South of Europe.

CUMIN—An herb of the caraway type producing seeds of aromatic odor.

DILL—A hardy, easily grown herb used for pickles.

GINGER—The root stock of a reed-like plant, dried and ground.

HORSERADISH—The ground root of the horseradish plant.

MACE—The outside covering of the nutmeg.

MARJORAM—An aromatic, sweet herb whose tops and leaves are both used.

MINT—A plant whose leaves give an aromatic flavor.

PARSLEY—An herb grown for seasoning and garnishing.

PAPRIKA—Ground sweet red Spanish pepper.

NUTMEG—The kernel of the fruit of a tropical tree.

MUSTARD—The seeds of a widely grown plant.

PEPPER—The dried berry of the pepper plant.

SAFFRON—Dried orange-red stigmas and styles of a purple crocus.

TARRAGON—An aromatic herb used for flavoring vinegar.

THYME—An herb cultivated for leaves and tops.

TUMERIC—The aromatic root stock of a plant grown in Southern Asia.

APPLE BUTTER CAKE

Cream **½ cup shortening** with **1 cup brown sugar,** then add **1 cup apple butter** and **2 eggs.** Beat until smooth. Sift flour, measure **2½ cups** and sift with **½ teaspoonful baking powder, ½ teaspoonful allspice, ½ teaspoonful nutmeg** and **1 teaspoonful soda.** Add alternately with **½ cup milk** to first **mixture.** Wash **¾ cup raisins,** then dry and add the last thing to batter. Bake in loaf pan in slow oven (350° F.) for 30 to 35 minutes.

APPLE SAUCE CAKE

Cream **2 cups sugar** and **1 cup shortening,** stir in **2 cups hot apple sauce.** Add **1 cup English walnuts, 1 cup raisins, 3 teaspoonfuls cinnamon, 1 teaspoonful cloves, 2 teaspoonfuls vanilla, 2 teaspoonfuls soda, ½ teaspoonful salt** and **3½ cups flour, 2 well beaten eggs.** Bake slowly for 1 hour in 300° F. oven.

ARABY SPICE CAKE

Cream **¾ cup shortening,** add **1 cup sugar** gradually and cream thoroughly. Add 3 **eggs,** one at a time, beating after each egg is added. Add 2 **cups flour** which has had sifted with it the following: **½ teaspoonful baking powder, ½ teaspoonful soda, ½ teaspoonful salt, ¾ teaspoonful nutmeg, 1 teaspoonful cinnamon** and **2 tablespoonfuls cocoa,** alternately with **¾ cup buttermilk or sour milk.** Blend in **1 teaspoonful vanilla** and **1 teaspoonful lemon.** Add **½ cup** coarsely cut **nuts,** toasted. Bake in 2 cake pans 30 minutes in moderate oven (350° F.)

Blackberry is a native berry of North America. It grows mostly in the wild state and may be had for the gathering.

BLACKBERRY JAM CAKE

Cream ½ **cup shortening.** Add **1 cup brown sugar** gradually and beat until light and fluffy. Add **3 beaten egg yolks.** Sift **1¾ cups flour** with **1 teaspoonful soda, 1 teaspoonful cinnamon,** and **½ teaspoonful ground cloves.** Add this mixture alternately to creamed mixture with **1 cup blackberry jam** and **3 tablespoonfuls sour milk** which have been stirred together. Add **½ cup chopped raisins** which have been floured. Fold in **3 egg whites,** beaten. Bake in two layers in a moderately hot oven (375° F.) until done.

CRUMB CAKE

Cut **¾ cup shortening** (½ butter and ½ lard) into **2 cups cake flour** and **1 cup brown sugar** until mixture is about the consistency of crumbs. Reserve **¾ cup** of these **crumbs.** To remaining crumbs, add **1 teaspoonful soda, ½ teaspoonful cloves, 1 teaspoonful cinnamon, 1 teaspoonful baking powder** and **¼ teaspoonful salt.** Mix thoroughly. Stir in **1 cup light cream** and **1 well beaten egg.** Add **1 cup chopped nut meats** and pour in well greased baking pan 8 inches square. Sprinkle with reserved crumbs and bake in a moderate oven (350° F.) This cake is delicious served warm with whipped cream.

HEAVENLY SPICE CAKE

Cream **1 cup butter** with **2½ cups sugar.** Add **2 well beaten eggs,** then **2 cups buttermilk** which has had **2 teaspoonfuls soda** dissolved in it, alternately with **3¼ cups flour** that has had **¼ teaspoonful cloves, 1 teaspoonful ground cinnamon, 1 teaspoonful ground allspice** and **4 teaspoonfuls cocoa** sifted with it. Add **1 teaspoonful vanilla.** Bake either in layers or a large loaf pan about 8x10x2. Bake in moderate oven for 45 minutes or longer, if needed. Test with toothpick. When it comes out clean, cake is done.

LIGHTNING CAKE

Put ingredients in mixing bowl in order given and beat together for 3 minutes, **1/3 cup brown sugar, 1/3 cup shortening, 2 eggs, ½ cup milk, 1 1/3 cups pastry flour, ½ teaspoonful cinnamon, ½ teaspoonful nutmeg,** and **3 teaspoonfuls baking powder.** Bake 40 minutes in a square pan at 375° F.

MARBLE CAKE

White Part: Cream **½ cup butter** with **1 cup sugar** until **fluffy.** Add alternately **½ cup sweet milk** and **2½ cups of flour** that has been sifted before measuring, then again with **2 teaspoonfuls baking powder** and a **pinch salt.** Lastly fold in **4 egg whites** whipped until stiff and **1 teaspoonful vanilla.** *Dark Part*: Cream well **½ cup butter** with **1 cup brown sugar.** Add **4 egg yolks** well beaten and cream again. Add **½ cup baking molasses.** To **1½ cups of sifted flour** add **1 teaspoonful cinnamon, 1 teaspoonful cloves, 1 teaspoonful mace, 1 teaspoonful nutmeg** and **1 teaspoonful soda** and sift again. Add to batter alternately with **½ cup sour milk.** Drop by tablespoonfuls into greased tube pan alternating with white and dark batter. Draw spoon through batter in pan once or twice to give it the marble effect. Bake in moderate oven, raising the temperature at the last to make a nice crust. It takes about 1 hour for this cake to bake. When cold, frost it with a boiled white icing.

ONE EGG SPICE CAKE

Cream 3 **heaping tablespoonfuls butter** (this is probably ½ cup level) and **1 cup sugar.** Mix well and add **1 beaten egg.** Sift together **1½ cups cake flour, 1 teaspoonful cinnamon, 1 teaspoonful nutmeg, ¼ teaspoonful cloves** and **¼ teaspoonful allspice.** Into **1 cup sour milk** put **1 teaspoonful vanilla** and **1 teaspoonful soda** and add alternately with dry ingredients to first mixture. Bake in loaf pan 45 minutes in 350° F. oven. Cover with a rich chocolate icing or any other desired frosting.

TOASTED SPICE CAKE

Cream **2 cups sifted brown sugar, ¾ cup butter, 2 egg yolks** (well beaten.) Dissolve **1 teaspoonful soda** in **1¼ cups sour milk;** add alternately with sifted dry ingredients which includes **2 1/3 cups flour, 1 teaspoonful baking powder, 1 teaspoonful cloves, 1 teaspoonful cinnamon,** and **¾ teaspoonful salt.** Add **1 teaspoonful vanilla** and pour in shallow pan. Beat **2 egg whites** until stiff. Add **1 cup sifted brown sugar** slowly. Stir until smooth, then spread this mixture over raw cake batter. Sprinkle with broken **nut meats.** Bake 40 to 50 minutes in moderate oven

WAR CAKE

Boil together for 5 minutes **2 cups brown sugar, 2 cups hot water, 2 tablespoonfuls fat, 1 teaspoonful** salt, **1 package raisins, 1 teaspoonful cloves, 1 teaspoonful cinnamon.** When cold, add **3 cups flour** which have been sifted once before measuring, **add 1 teaspoonful soda** dissolved in **1 teaspoonful hot water.** This makes 2 loaves of cake. Bake 45 minutes in 325° F. oven. This cake is of good texture and will keep moist for weeks.

Sponge Cakes

Sponge cakes will have a browner crust if a little fine white sugar is sprinkled over the top before baking.

SPONGE CAKE

Beat **yolks of 2 eggs** until thick and lemon colored. Add **½ cup sugar** gradually and continue beating. Add another **½ cup sugar, ¼ teaspoonful lemon extract, whites of 2 eggs** beaten stiff and **1 cup flour** mixed and sifted with **1½ teaspoonfuls baking powder and ¼ teaspoonful salt.** (For upside down apple cake.)

SPONGE CAKE WITH ELECTRIC BEATER

Sift **cake flour** once, then measure **1 cup.** Add **¼ teaspoonful salt** and sift 4 times more. Beat **6 egg whites,** using high speed, then **6 egg yolks,** using high speed till thick and lemon colored. Add **1 cup sugar** gradually, still using high speed. Add **1 tablespoonful vinegar** and **½ teaspoonful flavoring.** Beat 30 seconds longer. Fold in flour slowly by hand. Fold in egg whites slowly by hand. Bake in ungreased tube pan **1 hour, moderate oven.**

Icing: Put **2 egg whites, 1½ cups sugar, 1 tablespoonful light corn syrup, 5 tablespoonfuls water** and **½ teaspoonful vanilla** in top of double boiler. Bring water in bottom to a boil. Stir the mixture enough to dissolve sugar. Cook 2 minutes longer without stirring. Remove from fire and stir or beat 7 minutes at high speed. Add **flavoring** and spread on cake.

EGG YOLK SPONGE CAKE

Sift **flour** then measure **2¼ cups. Add 3 teaspoonfuls baking powder** and sift again. Beat **9 egg yolks** with rotary beater until thick and ivory colored. Add **1½ cups sugar** gradually; continue beating. Add **¾ cup boiling water** and **1 teaspoonful lemon extract** and beat well. Sift flour and baking powder into egg mixture. Bake in tube pan which has been sprinkled with flour on the bottom. Bake 45 to 60 minutes in moderate oven (325° F.). Invert and cool 1 hour before removing from pan.

HOT WATER SPONGE CAKE

Sift 1¼ **cups cake flour** that has already been sifted with **1¼ teaspoonfuls baking powder** and **½ teaspoonful salt,** then sift together three times. Beat **4 egg yolks** until thick and light. Add **½ cup sugar** gradually, beating constantly. Beat **4 egg whites** with flat wire whisk until light and foamy throughout; add **¾ cups sugar** very gradually and continue beating until stiff enough to hold up in definite satiny peaks. Add **vanilla** and **lemon rind.** Add **2/3 cup boiling water** to egg yolks, stirring well; then add flour all at once and beat with spoon until smooth. Fold quickly into egg whites. Turn into ungreased tube pan and bake in moderate oven (350° F.) 1 hour and 5 minutes, or until done. Invert pan 1 hour, or until cold.

YELLOW OR SUNSHINE CAKE

Beat **7 egg whites** until half thick. Add **pinch salt.** Beat, then add **½ teaspoonful cream of tartar** and beat again. Add **2 tablespoonfuls sugar,** then beat some more. Beat **yolks of 7 eggs.** Add remainder of **1 cup sugar** with **¾ teaspoonful vanilla** and **¼ teaspoonful almond extract.** Beat thoroughly, then fold into the whites of eggs. Lastly, fold in **1 cup cake flour** sifted 6 times. Bake slowly for 50 minutes in 300° F. oven.

JELLY ROLL

Beat **3 whole eggs** and **1 cup sugar** together, then add **3 tablespoonfuls water** and **1 teaspoonful vanilla.** Carefully fold in **1 cup flour** that has had **1 teaspoonful baking powder** added. Turn into large paper lined pan and bake. It should be rather thin. When done, invert pan on paper sprinkled with powdered sugar. Tear off paper and sprinkle with more powdered sugar. Spread with **jelly** and trim edges. Wrap in towel or napkin, rolling at the same time. Marshmallow filling or strawberry preserves are delicious if used in place of jelly.

Upside Down Cakes

Upside down cakes are so named because they have their best part on the bottom and must be turned upside down before serving.

APPLE UPSIDE DOWN CAKE

Spread **brown sugar** on bottom of a baking dish to depth of ½ inch. Dot with small pieces of **butter.** Pare and slice thin enough **apples** to fill baking dish 1 inch more. Sprinkle **cinnamon** on top of apples. Make a **simple sponge cake** and pour over top of apples. Bake for 1 hour in moderate oven. After cake browns cover with brown paper. Let cake stay in oven for full hour, so apples will cook thoroughly. This may be served from the dish without turning the cake out, if desired. Delicious with **whipped cream.** (See Sponge Cake.)

PINEAPPLE UPSIDE DOWN CAKE

Melt **2 tablespoonfuls butter** with **1 cup brown sugar** and put in a skillet. Place **one pineapple ring** in center and **small pieces** around. Add **2 tablespoonfuls pineapple juice.** Set aside until batter is ready. Beat well **2 egg yolks** with **1 cup white sugar.** Scald **½ cup sweet milk** and pour over eggs and sugar. Put in **1 cup pastry flour** that has had 1 teaspoonful baking powder added. Lastly, fold in **2 well beaten egg whites.** Pour over first mixture that is in skillet. Bake in oven until done. Turn out of skillet as soon as done to allow the candied pineapple to come out easily. If allowed to cool in pan it will harden and is impossible to remove. Serve with **whipped cream.**

White Cakes

Flavoring in a cake is not nearly so apt to be forgotten if measured into the liquid to be used.

BLACK WALNUT BUTTER CAKE WITH COCOANUT ICING

Sift and measure **2 cups cake flour.** Add **3 teaspoonfuls baking powder.** Cream **½ cup butter** and **1 cup sugar** to consistency of whipped cream. Add **2/3 cup milk** and flour mixture alternately to the creamed ingredients. Add **½ cup black walnuts** ground and **1 teaspoonful vanilla.** Fold in **3 beaten egg whites** last of all. Bake in two layers, in moderately hot oven at 375° F. to 400° F. for 12 to 15 minutes. Frost with cocoanut icing.

ECONOMICAL WHITE CAKE

Sift **flour,** measure **2½ cups** and add **2½ teaspoonfuls baking powder.** Sift again three times. Cream thoroughly **½ cup shortening** and **½ teaspoonful salt,** then add gradually **1½ cups sugar.** Cream together until light and fluffy. Add flour to creamed mixture, alternating with **1 cup sweet milk.** Beat after each addition until smooth. Add **1 teaspoonful vanilla.** Bake in layers in a moderate oven until done.

PINEAPPLE CAKE

Cream **½ cup butter** and **1½ cups sugar** together. Add **1 teaspoonful vanilla** and **1 cup crushed pineapple** as it comes from the can. Then a part of **2½ cups cake flour** that has had **⅛ teaspoonful salt, 3 teaspoonfuls baking powder** sifted with it. Add **¼ cup water** alternately with remaining flour, stirring until smooth. Fold in3 stiffly beaten **egg whites.** Bake in 2 eight-inch round greased and floured layer cake pans. Bake in moderate oven (350° F.) for 25 to 30 minutes. When cool cover with any white icing.

WHIPPED CREAM CAKE

Whip **1 cup of heavy cream** until slightly thickened, but not stiff enough to hold a peak. Fold in **1 cup sugar, 2 beaten eggs** and **1 teaspoonful vanilla.** Add **1½ cups cake flour** which has been sifted with **2 teaspoonfuls baking powder** and **¼ teaspoonful salt.** Mix only till smooth. Place in two small layer cake pans or in one shallow loaf pan and bake in moderate oven 350° F. to 375° F. Cool and ice with boiled or fudge icing. This makes a delicious cocoanut cake if boiled icing is used and a generous amount of cocoanut is sprinkled over the surface.

WHITE CAKE

Cream well **2 cups sugar** and **½ cup butter.** Add **2 tablespoonfuls boiling water** to creamed mixture and cream again until light. Sift **cake flour,** then measure **3½ cups** and sift 4 times more. Add a small amount of flour to creamed mixture. Alternate, adding the remainder of flour with **1½ cups cold water,** a **pinch salt** and **2 teaspoonfuls vanilla.** Lastly, fold in **4 egg whites** well beaten. Then sprinkle **4 teaspoonfuls baking powder** over batter. Fold in baking powder. Bake in three layers or a loaf pan.

Always sift flour before measuring.

Whole Egg Cakes

There are 2 cups of butter in a one-pound brick. Just divide in half for 1 cup and in fourths for ½ cup.

When creaming butter allow it to reach room temperature, then rub with the back of a spoon until soft and uniform.

Cut butter with a knife covered with the wrapping from the butter, it will cut smooth and evenly without sticking.

BANANA CAKE

Cream **1 cup butter** with **2 cups sugar.** Add 2 eggs **slightly** beaten, and **2 or 3 large bananas,** crushed to a cream mixture. **Add 1 cup sour milk** alternately with **3 cups flour** to which **1 teaspoonful soda** and **1 teaspoonful baking powder** have been added. Lastly add **½ teaspoonful vanilla** and a **pinch salt.** Bake in layers or a shallow loaf pan in moderate oven until done.

To prevent a bowl from slipping during the process of cake making wring a cloth out of cold water. Double it several times and place on table, then set bowl on cloth.

CORNSTARCH CAKE

Cream 2/3 **cup butter.** Add **2 cups sugar** gradually and cream thoroughly. Mix **1 cup cornstarch** with **2 cups flour, 2 teaspoonfuls cream of tartar** and **1 teaspoonful soda** and sift several times. Add alternately with **1 cup sweet milk** to creamed butter and sugar. Whip **whites** of **4 eggs,** but not too stiff. Add to other mixture by folding in gently. At the same time fold in **1 teaspoonful lemon extract.** Bake in loaf pan for ¾ hour at 350° F. It is best to start this cake at 325° F., then, after the first 10 minutes, raise temperature to 350° F.

EASY SOUR CREAM CAKE

Put 2 **eggs** in a cup and fill with **sour cream.** Place in mixing bowl. Add **1½ cups sifted pastry flour, 1 teaspoonful cream of tartar, 1 teaspoonful soda, 1 teaspoonful lemon flavoring** (other may be used) and **1 cup sugar.** Beat with dover or electric beater for 3 minutes. Pour into buttered nine inch pans and bake in a moderately hot oven 375° F. for 20 minutes.

GOLD CAKE

Sift flour once, then measure **2½ cups (pastry flour)**, add **2½ teaspoonfuls baking powder** and sift together three times. Cream **¾ cup butter** well. Add **1¼ cups sugar** gradually and cream together until light and fluffy. Add 8 **egg yolks,** beaten until thick, then beat again. Add flour alternately with **¾ cup milk,** a small amount at a time. Beat well after each addition. Add **1 teaspoonful lemon extract.** Bake in greased layer pans in moderate oven (350° F.) for 25 minutes. Put together with any desired icing. A lemon filling and a lemon frosting makes this an excellent cake.

GRAHAM CAKE

Cream 4 **tablespoonfuls butter.** Slowly add **1½ cups sugar.** Drop in 3 **egg yolks** and beat thoroughly. Roll with rolling pin **40 graham crackers** until they are like flour. Add these to first mixture alternately with **1½ cups milk.** Add **1 teaspoonful vanilla.** Mix 4 **tablespoonfuls white flour** with **¼ teaspoonful salt,** and **4 teaspoonfuls baking powder** and add to batter. Fold in beaten **whites of 3 eggs.** Pour batter into three-layer tins. Have oven at 350° F. before cake is set in oven. Bake ½ hour. Ice with an icing made of **¼ lb. butter,** creamed with **1 lb. powdered sugar, 4 tablespoonfuls cream** and **½ teaspoonful vanilla.**

Flour a cake pan after it has been greased and it will not stick.

JIFFY CAKE

Sift together 1 2/3 **cups flour, 1 cup sugar, ¼ teaspoonful salt, 2½ teaspoonfuls baking powder** in a mixing bowl. Add **1/3 cup shortening, 2/3 cup milk, 1 egg** and **1 teaspoonful vanilla.** Beat all ingredients together well for 2 minutes. Pour into a greased and floured pan about 8 inches square or round. Bake 35 minutes at 350° F.

Icing For Jiffy Cake

Mix together **3 tablespoonfuls melted butter, 5 tablespoonfuls brown sugar, 2 tablespoonfuls cream** and **½ cup shredded cocoanut.** Spread this on cake while cake is warm. Place very low under broiler. Broil until it bubbles all over and becomes brown.

ONE-EGG CAKE

Mix **1 2/3 cups flour** with **1 cup sugar, ¼ teaspoonful salt** and **2½ teaspoonfuls baking powder.** Melt **1/3 cup shortening** (butter is best) in **2/3 cup lukewarm milk.** When melted add **1 teaspoonful flavoring** and **1 beaten egg.** Add to dry ingredients slowly with egg beater. Beat until smooth. Pour into greased 8x8x2 pan and bake 25 to 30 minutes in 350° F. oven.

Do not place a hot cake in an open window or cold place to cool quickly. The steam will condense and make it heavy.

ORANGE CAKE

Mix well the following ingredients: **1 cup sugar, ½ cup butter, 2 beaten eggs, 1 cup sour milk, 2 cups all purpose flour, 1 teaspoonful soda, 1 teaspoonful vanilla, 1 cup raisins** and **rind of 1 orange,** ground fine. Bake in loaf pan about 40 minutes at 350° F. Icing: Use **juice** of **orange,** and add **¾ cup sugar.** Heat enough to dissolve sugar. As soon as cake is taken out of the oven, spread this icing on and it will form a crust of sugar for the icing.

POUND CAKE

Cream **1 pound butter,** add **1 pound sugar** gradually and continue beating. Add **10 egg yolks** beaten until thick and lemon colored, **10 egg whites** beaten until stiff, **1 pound flour, ½ teaspoonful mace,** and **2 tablespoonfuls** of **rum** or **sherry** flavoring. Beat vigorously for 5 minutes. Bake in deep pan 1¼ hours in slow oven (300° F.)

QUICK CAKE

This cake recipe is sufficient as "just cake", with or without icing. It is excellent for a shortcake foundation with any kind of fruit. The batter is very thin, so be sure to follow recipe. Beat **2 eggs** thoroughly (with dover or electric beater), then add **1 cup sugar** and continue beating until very fluffy. Bring **½ cup milk** to scalding temperature, **melting 1 tablespoonful butter** in it. Pour hot milk mixture over eggs and sugar, beat again. Add **1 cup flour** which has been sifted with **1 teaspoonful baking powder.** Add **1 teaspoonful flavoring** (vanilla or lemon), beat until smooth. Pour into a greased pan and bake 30 minutes in a 350° F. oven.

VEGETABLE OIL CAKE

Sift together in a bowl **1 cup cake flour, ¾ cup sugar, 2 teaspoonfuls baking powder** and **½ teaspoonful salt,** add **¼ cup cooking oil** and **1/3 cup cold water.** Beat **2 egg yolks until** lemon colored, add to above mixture and beat again. Beat **2 egg whites** stiff, but not dry, with **¼ teaspoonful cream tartar.** Fold into batter with **½ teaspoonful flavoring.** Bake in an 8x8x2 square pan at 325° F. for 30 minutes. Test center by touching lightly with forefinger. If it springs back it is done.

Candy

Different candies are made by varying the methods of cooking the sugar and liquid. The higher the temperature goes, the different is the candy. Learn that candies start at soft ball and end at the caramel stage. As sugar and water are cooked together the water evaporates and the result is a solution of pure sugar treated with heat. Sugar crystals are reduced in size by cooking, then cooling before being beaten. The presence of an invert sugar will help, that is the reason for the addition of either corn syrup or cream tartar to candy, the latter changes the sugar into a simpler form which is non-crystaline.

ALMOND MINTS

Dip an **almond** in **fondant, mint flavored** and colored green, leaving uncovered the part of the almond held by the fingers. Dip again in **melted chocolate,** just half way up the mint fondant. It makes a lovely candy for luncheons or decorative pieces in a holiday box.

BUTTERSCOTCH

Mix **1 1/3 cups brown sugar, 2 tablespoonfuls vinegar, 2/3 cup butter** and **2/3 cup water** in a pan. Boil without stirring to 290° F. Add **½ tablespoonful vanilla** and pour into buttered pan. Cool slightly and mark in squares.

CARAMELS

Put **1 pound brown sugar, ½ cup water** and **½ cup white corn syrup** in deep sauce pan. Stir and boil until sugar is thoroughly dissolved, then slowly add **2½ cups thin cream.** Stir constantly, do not allow mixture to stop boiling while cream is being added. This takes about 20 minutes. Add **¼ cup** (⅛ pound) **butter.** Cook, stirring frequently until a firm, but not hard ball is formed in cold water (240° F. to 242° F.) Remove from fire, add **1 teaspoonful vanilla (2/3 cup broken walnut meats,** optional), and a sprinkle of **salt.** Pour into buttered tin. When cold cut into cubes with scissors and wrap in wax paper. Yield, 100 pieces.

CANDIED CHERRIES

Select round **ripe sour cherries,** pit and drop into cold water. For every pound of cherries allow **2 cups sugar** and **½ cup water.** Make a syrup of sugar and water, boil to thread stage. Drain cherries, put into crock, pour boiling syrup over them and press down with plate. Let stand overnight. Next morning and for two mornings following, drain off syrup, heat to boiling, pour over cherries. On fourth morning, drain well, put on large platters, covered with waxed paper. Sift **powdered sugar** over cherries and dry in a warming closet or slow oven. When dry, pack in tin boxes with waxed paper in between.

CANDIED GRAPEFRUIT PEEL

Remove the heavy inside membrane that remains after pulp has been removed from the grapefruit. This comes out easily if a dull knife is placed under one edge prying out a small part, then with the fingers pull the rest away from the shell. Cut in strips any size or shape. If wanted for a valentine party, one could cut out small hearts as the peel is very soft. Take **2 ½ cups grapefruit peel.** Cover with cold water and bring to a boil. Boil 20 minutes. Drain and cover again with cold water and bring to a boil. Again boil for 20 minutes. Drain and cover again with cold water. Bring to a boil and boil again for 20 minutes. Drain, then add **2 cups sugar, ¼ cup grapefruit juice, ¼ cup water** that has been boiled together until the sugar is dissolved. Now cook grapefruit peel (it is in this syrup that the color is added if wanted) until nearly all the sugar is absorbed. We find, if cooked until all is absorbed, most people let it go too long and make it hard. Remove the grapefruit several pieces at a time and roll in **granulated sugar.** Place on cake racks and dry in oven. Use a slow oven with the door open.

CHOCOLATE PEANUT CLUSTERS

Melt ½ **lb.** of **dipping chocolate** over warm water or in a double boiler. Add **1½ cups** of **roasted red skinned Spanish peanuts,** stirring until well coated. Drop from teaspoon on waxed paper and keep in a cool place until firm. This makes about 2½ dozen clusters.

CHOCOLATE COATING OR DIPPING

A successful dipper uses a large amount of chocolate to work with. We suggest **2 lbs. of sweet chocolate** and **1 lb. of bitter chocolate.** Shave or cut into small pieces and place in top of double boiler. Melt slowly over warm water (never boiling) until it is completely melted, stirring all the time to keep the cocoa butter evenly distributed. Remove from heat and beat until it sets. Now this will take a long time and often the beginner will stop beating or hurry by cooling more quickly than is good for the chocolate. This all works best if the room temperature is between 60° F. to 65° F. When chocolate has set, after first heating, then return the top part of boiler to its place over the bottom part and reheat slowly until the chocolate is just the consistency of whipped cream. Some find that the heat from the floor register is sufficient for this heating. Dip one center at a time. If when placed on the waxed paper the chocolate runs, it is too warm for dipping and should be stirred until it is cooler. Too much heat, too much cold, affects the coating so that there are white spots or gray streaks on the chocolate. The chocolate solidifies very quickly and must be reheated and cooled quite often while dipping.

CREAM DROPS

Peppermint, white or green; Wintergreen, pink; Lemon, yellow; Orange, orange. Melt **½ cup fondant** (see fondant) over hot water. Work in coloring (on tip of toothpick or medicine dropper) carefully. Add **flavoring.** If fondant is quite thick add a **few drops of boiling water.** Drop from tip of teaspoon or pastry tube, held vertically, on paraffin paper. Bits of fruit or nuts may be dipped in melted fondant.

EASTER EGGS

Free **1 lb. powdered sugar** from lumps and knead the following ingredients together: **1/3 cup hot mashed potatoes, ¾ lb. butter, 1/3 cup cocoanut, 1/3 cup chopped nuts** and **1/3 teaspoonful vanilla.** Shape into eggs. Set aside a few days to ripen. Melt **dipping chocolate** over warm water and dip eggs in until completely covered. Place on waxed paper or a cold marble slab to dry.

FONDANT

Put 3 **cups sugar, 2 tablespoonfuls light corn sirup, ½ teaspoonful cream of tartar** and **1½ cups boiling water** in a sauce pan. Stir well until sugar is dissolved. Do not stir in but wipe down crystals from sides of pan with wet cloth. Boil until soft ball stage is reached, then pour on buttered platter, let cook until lukewarm. Beat with wooden spatula, then knead with hands until soft and creamy. Divide in parts, flavor with desired flavor and mold in shapes for candy desired. Roll in **cool melted sweet chocolate,** if one is making chocolate drops. Lay away in dry place.

HAND ROLLED BUTTER CREAMS

To **2½ pounds sugar** add **¼ teaspoonful cream of tartar.** Add enough **water** to dissolve, which should be about **2 cups.** Cook to 234° F. Add **⅛ teaspoonful salt** and **¼ pound butter.** After butter has been melted in batch, wash down kettle well and cook to 240° F. Pour on slab. When cooled, begin to work up. When batch begins to look cloudy add **¾ pound marshmallow whip** and finish working. Let stand 1 hour then roll and dip. This center has exceptional keeping qualities. For a chocolate center add **3 ounces melted chocolate.**

ORIENTALS

Put **2½ lbs. sugar** and **1 pint of cold water** in kettle. When sugar is dissolved add **½ teaspoonful glycerin.** When it starts to boil add **6 drops** of **acetic acid.** Cook until 236° F. by the thermometer (soft ball stage). Pour on a platter and let stand until perfectly cold, then beat in the **whites** of **2 eggs** with **½ teaspoonful vanilla.** Work until it gets hard enough to mold. Dip in **chocolate.**

PEPPERMINT PATTIES

To make cream centers, boil and mash enough **white potatoes to fill 1 cup.** Mash through a sieve and remove every lump. Stir and work in **2 lbs. powdered sugar.** At first the mass will be wet, then moist, but by constant working it becomes a fine creamy fondant. Work in **essence of peppermint** to suit taste. Make into patties. Lay on tin sheet and set in ice box for an hour, then with a broad bladed knife turn on the other side and let dry. Dip one by one in **melted coating chocolate** and dry on wax paper.

CHOCOLATE FUDGE

Mix 2 **cups sugar, 2 tablespoonfuls white corn syrup,** 2 **squares** of finely cut **chocolate** and ¾ **cup milk.** Cook without stirring until a very soft ball is formed in cold water. Remove from fire, add 2 **tablespoonfuls butter** and ½ **teaspoonful vanilla.** Set aside to cool. Do not stir until mixture is entirely cold. When cold, heat until creamy. If mixture becomes crumbly, add a few drops of cream or hot water and knead as for fondant. When of proper consistency, pour into a well buttered pan and mark in squares or form into balls with the fingers. The secret of good fudge lies in the method of handling. The smallest sugar crystals are desired. These can only be obtained by not stirring until cold as heat allows large crystals to precipitate. Do not hurry fudge.

CREAMY WHITE NUT FUDGE

Measure 3 **cups white sugar,** 1 **cup white corn syrup** and ½ **cup hot water** into sauce pan. Stir well, bring to boil. While syrup boils beat 2 **egg whites** until stiff enough to hold a peak. Chop 1 **cup nuts** and 1 **small jar** of **maraschino cherries** well drained. Rub small amount of **butter** on surface of platter with waxed paper, remove all extra butter from dish. Cook sugar mixture to brittle test in cold water. Remove from heat. Let cool partly, then begin adding egg whites by spoonful. Beat until all egg whites have been added. Add nuts, cherries and 1 **teaspoonful vanilla.** When candy holds a swirl, pour into platter to cool. To cut into squares put blade of knife in boiling water, wipe dry on towel and cut candy into squares while blade is hot. The cherries and nuts may be omitted for economy sake, but they do improve both flavor and appearance.

SHORT CUT FUDGE

Melt 3 **squares** of **unsweetened chocolate** in double boiler. Add 1 1/3 **cups condensed milk** and cook for 5 minutes, stirring occasionally until mixture thickens. Remove from fire. Add 1½ **tablespoonfuls butter** and 1 **tablespoonful vanilla** and work in 2 **cups powdered sugar.** Fold in ½ **cup chopped nuts** and ½ **cup chopped dates** (if desired). Pour into a shallow buttered pan. Chill, cut in squares for serving.

DIVINITY

Place 2½ **cups sugar, 2/3 cup light corn syrup, ½ cup water** and ¼ **teaspoonful salt** in a sauce pan and bring to a boil, stirring until sugar is dissolved. Continue cooking without stirring until a hard ball is formed in cold water, (240° on thermometer). Remove from stove and pour gradually over **2 beaten egg whites,** beating all the time. Continue beating until candy will hold its shape when dropped from spoon. Add ½ **teaspoonful vanilla** and **1 cup broken nut meats.** Mix thoroughly. Drop by spoonfuls on waxed paper. This makes 1¼ lbs. of candy.

HARD CANDY

Boil together **2 cups sugar, 1 cup hot water,** ¼ **teaspoonful cream tartar** to very hard crack stage or 310° F. without stirring. Remove from fire, add desired coloring and flavoring as listed below. Pour on lightly greased surface as marble slab, cooky sheet or top of porcelain table. In a few minutes lift edge of candy. Cut in thin strips with large scissors. Do not lift entire batch from slab as it will harden instantly. Break strips in very small pieces.

Use oil flavoring for this candy:

Peppermint — ¼ **teaspoonful** — Color white
Lemon — ¼ **teaspoonful** — Color yellow
Orange — ¼ **teaspoonful** — Color orange
Wintergreen — **1 teaspoonful** — Color pink
Cinnamon — ¼ **teaspoonful** — Color green
Clove — ¼ **teaspoonful** — Color red.

LEMON GUM DROPS

Soak 2 level tablespoonfuls of plain gelatin in ½ cup water about 5 minutes. Place 2 cups sugar and ¾ cup boiling water on fire and when sugar is dissolved add the soaked gelatin and boil slowly 10 minutes. Remove from fire add 3 tablespoonfuls lemon juice and 2 teaspoonfuls lemon extract. Add any coloring desired. Pour into pans (which have been dipped in cold water), to the deptp of ¾ inch. Let stand overnight. Turn out, cut in squares and roll in powdered or granulated sugar. Other flavoring and coloring may be used, but always add lemon juice for tartness.

MAPLE SUGAR CREAMS

Boil any amount of **maple syrup** until it forms a soft ball when dropped in cold water. A little butter rubbed on the edge of the kettle will prevent it from boiling over. After the syrup reaches the soft ball stage pour into cereal dishes, filling them ¾ full. Add a piece of **butter** the size of a walnut to each dish of syrup. Let it stand until thoroughly cold, then stir until it thickens. Drop with a teaspoon onto waxed paper. It is important that the syrup is cold before starting to stir to be sure to have creamy maple creams.

MARSHMALLOW CANDY

Take 3 **cups granulated sugar** and **16 tablespoonfuls water.** Boil until it threads in cold water. Soak **4 tablespoonfuls of gelatin in 12 tablespoonfuls cold water** 10 minutes. Add to syrup and cook 1 minute. Take from stove and beat 30 minutes. Flavor with **vanilla.** Put in cake pan and sprinkle with **powdered sugar.** Cut into squares when cool. Roll in powdered sugar.

AFTER DINNER MINTS

Mix **4 cups powdered sugar** with **1 cup water** and bring to boil. Wipe down sides of pan just before it starts to boil. Add **¼ teaspoonful of cream of tartar** or **4 drops of acetic acid,** put tight lid on kettle and let steam for a few minutes. Boil to 260° F. Pour on greased slab and let cool. When edges are cool add **9 drops of oil of peppermint** and **2 drops of oil of lemon.** Fold edges over so that the flavor is folded in. When cool enough to handle, pull until white and cut in small cushions with scissors, letting the pieces fall into a pan of powdered sugar so that they do not touch each other. Put in cardboard box and set aside until candy changes from a chewy to a creamy substance. Then pour into sieve and shake free from sugar. Make a day or two before desired use.

PULLED MINTS

Mix **2 cups sugar, 1 tablespoonful corn syrup, 1 cup water** and **4 tablespoonfuls butter** together and cook until it cracks in cold water. When cool enough pull as you do taffy. When ready to cut pull into very slender rolls and cut off in small pieces. If cut properly they look very much like after dinner mints, only they have delicious rich buttery taste. When cool, store in airtight containers for four or five days. They will be soft and tender, but never sticky. They may be flavored and colored as desired.

MOLASSES LOLLIPOPS

Cook 1½ **cups sugar,** ½ **cup water,** 1½ **tablespoonfuls vinegar** and ½ **cup New Orleans molasses** and stir well. When boiling add ¼ **teaspoonful cream of tartar.** Boil to 250° F. or until brittle when tested in cold water. When nearly done, add ⅛ **teaspoonful soda** and 2 **tablespoonfuls soft butter** and stir. Pour mixture into buttered muffin tins to cool or pour by tablespoonfuls on a flat buttered surface. When nearly cool, insert wooden skewers.

These may be decorated for Halloween with faces made with frosting.

PEANUT BRITTLE

Cook 2 **cups sugar,** 1 **cup light corn syrup** and ½ **cup water** until it spins a thread or 250° F. Then add 1 **teaspoonful butter** and 2 **cups raw Spanish peanuts** (with red skins), stirring constantly. Cook until peanuts get brown. When skins pop open they are done. Remove from fire. Add ½ **teaspoonful vanilla,** ¼ **teaspoonful salt** and 2 **teaspoonfuls soda.** Stir thoroughly and pour quickly on buttered cold cookie sheet or slab. Spread and pull thin.

PEANUT BUTTER CANDY

Mix ½ **pint peanut butter** with ½ **box powdered sugar** and enough **cream** to make easy handling. Knead well. Add 1 **teaspoonful vanilla.** Roll in **cinnamon.** Put in cold place for 1 hour. Then cut in slices ⅛ inch thick. This makes a good center for chocolate creams.

PRALINES

Combine 3 **cups brown sugar** with 1 **small can of evaporated milk,** the **juice** and **grated rind** of 1 **large orange** and mix thoroughly. Put over fire and stir until it starts boiling. Cook until a few drops in cold water form a soft ball. Remove from stove. Add 3 **tablespoonfuls butter.** Let cool a few minutes, then beat until it thickens. Add 1 **cup pecan meats** and drop by spoonfuls on oiled paper. This recipe will make a large amount of candy with very little effort.

TOFFEE

Butter a platter or pan and sprinkle with ½ **cup of blanched and chopped almonds.** Put ½ **lb. butter** in skillet, add **1 cup brown sugar** and mix thoroughly. Bring to boil and boil about 12 minutes, stirring constantly. Do not have fire too high. Pour over almonds in buttered platter in a thin sheet. Arrange 2 **chocolate milk bars** over mixture and spread as they melt. Sprinkle another ½ **cup of blanched chopped almonds** over candy. Mark in squares and cool.

Popcorn

Popcorn, a peculiar type of small grained corn which when heated, expands and pops.

CARAMEL CRISP POP-CORN

Cook **2 lbs. light brown sugar, 1 lb. light corn syrup, ¾ cup butter, ½ cup water, 1 teaspoonful salt** to 260° F., or having no thermometer, to the soft ball stage, then add **1 teaspoonful salt** and bring to 280° F., or almost the hard ball. At this point, turn out the fire and pour syrup over **3 gallons of popped corn.** Pour syrup slowly and stir until well covered. Spread out on trays to dry. One delicious combination used with this same syrup is to pour some over 2 **cups** of **puffed cereal** and **half a cup of nut meats,** using butternut or black walnut if possible.

EASY POP-CORN BALLS

Boil **1 cup dark or light corn syrup, ½ cup sugar** and **1 teaspoonful cream of tartar** to the hard ball stage. Add **¼ teaspoonful soda** and **1 tablespoonful butter.** Beat well. Pour over **4 quarts** of **freshly popped corn.** This amount makes 16 balls.

SEA FOAM

Mix **2 cups brown sugar, 1 cup water, 1 tablespoonful butter,** and **1 tablespoonful vinegar** together and cook (248° F.) until it forms a hard ball when dropped in cold water. Remove from fire, and add slowly to 2 stiffly beaten **egg whites,** beating continuously with rotary egg beater. Add **2 teaspoonfuls baking powder, 1 cup chopped nuts** and **1 teaspoonful vanilla** while beating. Beat until creamy and stiff. Turn into buttered pan or drop by spoonfuls on oiled paper.

SPANISH PENOCHE

Mix **4 cups light brown sugar, 1 cup sweet cream, 2 tablespoonfuls butter** and boil, stirring constantly until it forms a soft ball in cold water. Remove from fire. Add **1 cup chopped walnuts** (black ones are best) and **flavoring.** Allow to cool. Stir until it becomes creamy or doughy. Pour into pans.

Chopped raisins, dates, prunes, figs, orange peel, etc., make a variety.

TAFFY APPLES

Heat **1 cup corn sirup** and **1 cup sugar** slowly, stirring constantly until dissolved. Boil until a little tried in cold water becomes brittle. Place pan at once over boiling water, add **1 tablespoonful butter.** Dip in apples, washed, dried and with skewers inserted. When coated put on buttered tins to cool. By placing over boiling water the syrup does not become too brittle for coating.

PLAIN TAFFY

Put **2 cups white sugar, ½ cup vinegar** and **½ cup water** in pan and stir for a few minutes. Place over fire and cook until ½ teaspoonful dropped in a cup of cold water will form a hard ball. Add **1 teaspoonful butter.** Pour on well greased platter. **Add 1 teaspoonful vanilla** and when cool, pull, using the finger tips as much as possible.

PULLING TAFFY

Take **1 lb. brown sugar, 1 cup molasses, ½ cup water,** and **3 tablespoonfuls butter.** Boil over a hot fire until it hardens when dropped in cold water. Pour on a greased platter. When ready to handle, gather in buttered hands and pull until light.

Cereals

Cereal grains used for breakfast foods are barley, corn, oats, rice and wheat. These may be purchased in many forms prepared for breakfast foods. Some are ready to serve while others must be cooked. Since there are directions on the boxes we are not using our space to repeat them here.

Hominy, a corn preparation, where the outside cover of the kernel has been removed by lye.

HOME-MADE HOMINY

Put **2 tablespoonfuls lye** into kettle and add **1 pint cold water.** When dissolved add **1 gallon boiling water** and mix thoroughly. Stir in **2 quarts shelled corn** and bring to boiling point. Boil 20 minutes, stirring constantly. Remove from stove and fill kettle with cold water and stir. Drain off water, repeating 4 or 5 times. Cover corn with cold water and bring to boil. Drain off and repeat 3 or 4 times. After last boiling, cover corn with water and boil 3 or 4 hours. Do not use anything but iron kettle and stir with paddle. Do not put hands into first 4 wash waters.

MUSH IN DOUBLE BOILER

Place **1 cup corn meal,** either color, in double boiler. Add **4 cups cold water, 1 teaspoonful salt** and **1 teaspoonful sugar.** Put hot water in lower part and place on fire. Heat slowly. In 10 minutes stir thoroughly and your work as far as cooking mush is over. The cooking should continue slowly for 2 hours. Serve in bowls with milk or pour in molds for frying.

To prepare Wheatena, Cream of Wheat, cornmeal mush or any fine cereal, mix with 1 cup water before adding to boiling water. 1 cup cereal to 4 cups boiling water is the rule for all cereals to be cooked.

MUSH

Mix **1 cup cornmeal** with **1 cup water.** Add **1 teaspoonful** salt. Bring 3 **cups of water** to boiling, add moistened cornmeal and cook stirring constantly for 20 minutes. May be served with sugar and cream or packed into a mold to solidify after which it may be sliced and fried.

Water ground whole grain cornmeal requires only **3 cups of** water to **one cup of cornmeal.**

ROLLED OATS (Fried)

Take **equal amounts of leftover rolled oats** and **leftover mashed potatoes.** Season with **salt** and **pepper** if needed. Mix thoroughly and pack in bowl or oblong pan. Slice, fry in fat, make into patties, or dip in egg and cracker crumbs, then fry in fat.

Cheese

Cheese is the product produced by hardening the curd of milk. The different methods and milks employed give different cheeses. The flavors differ by methods and seasonings together with the different bacteria used in the making.

BAVARIAN CHEESE PIE

Beat **4 egg whites** very stiff. Beat **2/3 cup cream** until stiff. Add to cream **1¼ cups of cottage or cream cheese, 1 teaspoonful vanilla** and **4 tablespoonfuls flour** mixed with **2/3 cup sugar.** Combine with beaten egg whites. Line a pie pan with rich pastry. Pour in filling. Bake in slow oven until filling is firm. This takes about 1 hour. The oven should be between 300° F. and 325° F.

BREAD AND CHEESE SQUARES

Cut **bread** into **2 inch slices** then in **2 inch cubes.** With a sharp knife hollow out a small hole in the center of top. Dip in melted butter. Place a smal piece of soft American cheese in each cavity. Set in toaster until tops are well browned and cheese is melted. Serve immediately.

CHEESE FONDUE

Mix **1 cup scalded milk** with **1 cup soft stale bread crumbs, 1 cup mild cheese** (cut in small pieces), **1 tablespoonful butter** and **½ teaspoonful salt;** add **yolks of three eggs,** beaten until lemon colored, cut and fold in whites of **3 eggs beaten** until stiff. Pour into buttered baking dish. Bake 20 minutes in moderate oven. Serve hot. Excellent served with **mushroom sauce.**

Zweibach, a bread product with a German name. It usually has more milk, butter and eggs than ordinary bread. It is toasted after slicing and sold in that manner. Soaked in milk it is an excellent food for the baby.

CHEESE CAKE

Roll **1 package zwiebach** into crumbs and add to **2 tablespoonfuls butter** and **2 tablespoonfuls sugar** that have been creamed together. Rub this mixture until well blended. Put in bottom of baking dish and press down evenly all around. Cream **1 cup of sugar** with **1 pound white cream cheese** until well blended. Add **2 tablespoonfuls flour, pinch of salt, 1 teaspoonful vanilla,** and **4 beaten egg yolks.** Mix well and add **1 cup milk.** Fold in **4 beaten egg whites.** Pour into baking pan on top of crumbs. Bake in a slow oven, 325° F. 1 hour or more, until no depression is left when touched in the center with finger.

CHEESE AND MUSHROOM SOUFFLE

Pan fry **½ cup mushrooms,** cut fine, in **2 tablespoonfuls butter** for a few minutes. Blend in **3 tablespoonfuls flour** and **½ cup milk** slowly, stirring constantly until thick and smooth. Remove from fire and add to well beaten **yolks of 3 eggs.** Cool. Season with **¼ teaspoonful paprika, ½ teaspoonful salt, ¼ teaspoonful black pepper.** Grate **½ cup American cheese** and mix with **2 tablespoonfuls chopped parsley.** Mix with first mixture. Lastly, fold in **whites of three eggs.** Turn into buttered baking dish. Set dish in pan of water and bake at 325° F. for 45 minutes. Serve with horseradish sauce.

Put soft American cheese through a food chopper when too soft for grating.

CHEESE POP-CORN

Pop **½ cup of dry pop-corn.** Melt **¼ cup butter** with **½ cup grated American type, very dry cheese.** Mix thoroughly. Pour over freshly popped corn and stir until every kernel has been coated. Sprinkle with salt to taste and dust with more cheese if you think it is needed.

Dry cheese rinds in open air, grate off cheese and save for dishes requiring grated cheese.

CHEESE STRAWS

Make these as if one were making pie dough. To **1 cup flour** add ½ **teaspoonful salt, 4 tablespoonfuls fat, 1 cup grated cheese** and dash of **cayenne pepper.** Mix well with pie dough mixer or finger tips. Add **3 tablespoonfuls water** and mix just until blended. Roll out and cut in small strips. Bake in moderate oven until brown. Too hot an oven will spoil the cheese.

COTTAGE CHEESE FROM PASTEURIZED MILK

To **1 quart skimmed milk** add **2 tablespoonfuls buttermilk.** Let stand overnight at room temperature. Put in double boiler or other pan over low heat and heat to 98° F. or 110° F., not any higher. Pour through cloth into colander and drain off whey, letting it stand until thoroughly drained. Then wash it by running cold water through it several times, draining well each time. Add salt, sweet or sour cream as preferred. A dash of pepper perks up flavor.

GRAHAM CRACKER CHEESE CAKE

Break **1 pound** of **dry cottage cheese** into very small bits (a pastry blender is excellent for this purpose). Mix cheese with **2 tablespoonfuls flour, 2 egg yolks,** ¾ **cup sugar,** ¼ **teaspoonful salt,** ½ **lemon (juice and grated rind)** and ½ **teaspoonful vanilla.** Then slowly add **1 cup milk** a little at a time. Beat **egg whites** stiff, fold in lightly.

Melt ¼ **pound butter,** add ½ **pound rolled graham crackers.** Line cake pan and fill with cheese mixture. Sprinkle more graham cracker crumbs on top. Bake 50 minutes at 350° F

ROQUEFORT CHEESE RING WITH FRUIT SALAD

Soak **1 tablespoonful plain gelatin** in ¼ **cup cold milk** for 5 minutes. In the meantime mash **4 ounces of Roquefort** (blue) **cheese** with a fork and blend thoroughly with **2 cups creamed cottage cheese** taking care to remove all lumps. Add ¼ **cup salad dressing,** ¼ **teaspoonful** salt, **1 teaspoonful Worcestershire sauce,** and **3 drops tobasco sauce.** Dissolve gelatin by holding milk over hot water (use double boiler), then stir gelatin into cheese mixture. Allow mixture to cool, then fold in ½ **cup whipped cream.** Rinse 6 small ring molds in cold water, fill them with cheese mixture and place in refrigerator until firm. At serving time arrange lettuce on salad plate, unmold cheese ring, fill center with **fruit salad** and serve with **French Dressing.**

The fruit salad may be any fruit in season.

Rarebits

Originally in England dishes made with cheese to take the place of meat were called Cheese rabbits. But in the course of years the name has been changed to rarebit by Americans. Either name is now correct.

ALMOND RAREBIT

Melt 4 **tablespoonfuls butter** in a sauce pan. Add **1 cup flour.** When well blended add **1 quart milk** and cook until thick. Add ¼ **lb. grated American cheese. Salt** and **pepper** to taste. Serve on **Melba toast** sprinkling grated cheese on top. Garnish liberally with hot **buttered toasted almonds.**

Serve orange and grapefruit salad with this rarebit.

QUICK RAREBIT

Melt **1 package of fine American cheese** in a double boiler. Add **1 can tomato soup** and stir until thoroughly dissolved. Add **1 egg yolk,** slightly beaten. Remove from fire, add stiffly **beaten egg white.** Serve on **toast triangles or crackers.**

WELSH RAREBIT

Prepare a white sauce of **2 tablespoonfuls butter, 2 tablespoonfuls flour** and **1 cup milk.** When done add **1 cup grated cheese** and **stir** until melted. Add **1 egg yolk** slightly beaten, remove from **stove,** stir until yolk is evenly distributed. Beat **egg white** and fold into mixture. Serve on **crackers** with a dash of **paprika** on top.

To keep cheese from molding wrap in a cloth soaked in vinegar. Pour paraffin over cut surface of cheese.

Cookies

Cookies are small bits of sweetened dough baked in all sizes and shapes. They vary according to flavor and texture. No home is complete without a cookie jar and that one well filled at all times.

Almonds may be used either with or without blanching. To blanch, pour boiling water over shelled nuts, allow to stand for a few minutes, then remove outside covering with thumb and forefinger. Spread out to dry before using.

ALMOND HILLS

Pour boiling water over **15 dates.** (This is to clean and soften them.) The amount does not matter as it is poured off. Remove stones and chop fine. Add **1 cup unblanched chopped almonds.** Beat **2 egg whites** until stiff. Add **1 cup powdered sugar** and **½ teaspoonful vanilla.** Beat until stiff. Add **nuts** and **dates,** folding them in carefully. Drop by teaspoonfuls on waxed paper and bake in a moderate oven until light brown. Undercooking would cause them to fall, but they are still very good to eat even if that does happen. Overcooking would cause them to get too hard. Watch for the light brown color.

APRICOT FILLED COOKIES

Cream **1 cup lard** and **2 cups sugar.** Add **2 unbeaten eggs,** one at a time. Beat well. Sift **6 cups flour, 2 teaspoonfuls soda, 4 teaspoonfuls baking powder** and **1 teaspoonful salt.** Add dry ingredients alternately with **1 cup milk.** Add **2 teaspoonfuls vanilla** last.

Filling

Soak **1 pound dried apricots** until soft. Mash, add **1 cup sugar.** Roll out cookie dough and cut in desired shapes. Put **½ teaspoonful** filling on one cookie then cover with another and press edges together. Bake in moderate oven 350° F. until a light brown. This recipe makes 100 cookies.

ALMOND MACAROONS

Beat 3 **egg whites.** Add **1 cup sugar** very slowly, beating constantly. Add ½ **lb. finely chopped almonds, 10 drops almond flavoring** and **1 tablespoonful melted shortening.** Mix well. Drop by teaspoonfuls on wet paper which has been placed on a cookie sheet. Bake in slow oven 30 to 40 minutes. Makes about 45 macaroons.

AUSTRIAN NUT BARS

Grind 2 **cups** either **black walnuts** or **English walnuts,** mix with **1 cup soft bread crumbs,** ½ **cup sugar** and **1 egg** (add another egg if needed). When well mixed roll out on a sugared board about ½ inch thick. Spread frosting on all dough. Then cut into bars 2 inches long and 1 inch wide. Place in greased pan with a long knife, then into a previously heated oven to dry, turning all heat off. Frosting: **2 egg whites, 12 tablespoonfuls granulated sugar** and **1 tablespoonful lemon juice.** Stir with an electric mixer until stiff.

BLACK WALNUT ICE BOX COOKIES

Cream **1 cup butter** with **2 cups brown sugar.** Add **2 eggs, ¼ teaspoonful salt, 1 teaspoonful soda, 1 teaspoonful baking powder, 3½ cups flour, 1 teaspoonful** vanilla and **1 cup black walnuts.** Knead well on board and keep over night in refrigerator. Next morning cut very thin, bake 12 minutes in hot oven. Thickness of cookie determines temperature and time of baking. Watch first pan for exact time. They must be a golden brown to be crisp when cold.

BRANDY SNAPS

Beat ½ **cup butter** with **2/3 cup powdered sugar.** Add ½ **cup molasses** and blend well. Add **1 teaspoonful lemon juice** and **grated rind.** Finally, add **1 cup flour.** Drop from tip of a small spoon onto well greased flat tins, three inches apart (these spread and flatten). Bake in moderate oven and watch carefully as molasses burns easily. While snaps are still warm roll over the handle of a wooden spoon into curls. This is a crisp, tasty snap that may be used in place of candy.

BROWN SUGAR COOKIES

Mix **1 cup brown sugar** with **½ cup butter** and **2 eggs**. Sift **3 cups flour** with **1 teaspoonful soda, 2 teaspoonfuls cream of tartar** and **¼ teaspoonful salt.** Add to first mixture with **1 teaspoonful vanilla.** Roll, cut and bake in a moderately hot oven. The older they get the better, as they obtain moisture and are soft.

Brown sugar will remain soft if kept in a closed glass container.

BUTTERETTES

Cream **1 cup butter** and **1 cup brown sugar.** Add **2 well beaten eggs** and beat well. Sift **flour,** then measure **2½ cups.** Sift again with **4 teaspoonfuls baking powder** and **¼ teaspoonful salt.** Blend with egg mixture and **2 teaspoonfuls vanilla.** Roll into small marble-sized balls and press top with fork. Place half a **maraschino cherry** on each. Bake on greased cookie sheet in moderate oven until brown. This makes 4 dozen cookies.

BUTTERSCOTCH ICE BOX COOKIES

Cream **1 cup shortening** and **2 cups dark brown sugar.** Add **2 eggs,** beat well. Combine **1 teaspoonful vanilla, 1 teaspoonful baking powder, ½ teaspoonful salt, 1 cup nut meats, 3 cups flour, 1 teaspoonful soda, 2 tablespoonfuls sour milk** and shape into 2 rolls, 1½ inches in diameter. Chill over night. Next morning slice very thin. Bake on cooky sheet 10 minutes in hot oven.

BRAZIL NUT STICKS

Beat **2 eggs** until light. Add **2 cups brown sugar** and beat again. Hull and grind **1 pound Brazil nuts** in coarse grinder and add to **1¾ cups flour.** Stir flour mixture into egg mixture and beat until thoroughly mixed. Let stand 1 to 2 hours in cold place. Cut off chunks, roll between the palms of the hands into sticks three inches long. Bake in moderate oven. When cold roll in **powdered sugar.** Place in container and cover with waxed paper. Bake a week or two before using.

BREAD CRUMB COOKIES

Cream ½ **cup shortening** with **1 cup sugar,** either brown or white. Add **2 eggs** well beaten, then ½ cup cold coffee, **½ cup molasses, 2½ cups bread crumbs, 2½ cups flour** sifted with **1 teaspoonful soda, 1 teaspoonful salt, 1 teaspoonful nutmeg** and ¼ **teaspoonful cinnamon.** Mix thoroughly. Drop from teaspoon on greased sheet and bake 20 minutes at 375° F.

BROWNIES

Beat **2 eggs,** add **1 cup sugar** gradually. Melt 3 **tablespoonfuls cocoa** and **6 tablespoonfuls butter** together over a flame. Pour into egg mixture slowly, add **1 cup nuts, 1 teaspoonful vanilla** and ½ **cup sifted flour.** Bake in slow oven in shallow cake pan. Cut into squares when cool.

CHOCOLATE CHIP COOKIES

Cream **1 cup butter** and gradually add **¾ cup white sugar** and **¾ cup brown sugar.** Blend well. Add 2 **eggs** well beaten, then **2 tablespoonfuls hot water.** Add 3 **cups flour** which have been sifted with 1 **teaspoonful soda.** Add 1 **teaspoonful vanilla** and **1 cup chopped nut meats.** Chip or purchase **½ lb. of semi-sweet chocolate bits** and fold into batter. Drop on greased cooky pan and bake at 350° F. for 15 to 20 minutes. This makes 6 dozen cookies.

If less soda is preferred use **2 teaspoonfuls baking powder** and **½ teaspoonful soda** in recipe. Add ½ **teaspoonful salt** if shortening is used in place of butter.

CHOCOLATE DROP COOKIES

Sift flour once then measure **2 cups cake flour,** add **½ teaspoonful soda** and a **dash salt.** Sift again. Cream ½ **cup butter** thoroughly, add 2/3 **cup brown sugar** gradually and cream together until light and fluffy. Add 1 **egg,** well beaten, then 3 **squares unsweetened chocolate,** melted. Add flour alternately with ½ **cup milk,** a small amount at a time. Beat smooth after each addition. Add **1 teaspoonful vanilla** and ½ **cup broken walnuts.** Drop from teaspoon on greased baking sheet and bake in moderate oven 350° F. about 7 minutes. Makes 50 cookies.

CHOCOLATE MACAROONS

Beat the **whites of 2 eggs** until stiff, fold in **1 cup sugar, 1½ squares** of **melted chocolate, ¼ teaspoonful salt, 1½ cups cocoanut** and **1 teaspoonful vanilla.** Place in greased pan by teaspoonfuls not making them larger than a quarter. Bake in slow oven 300° F. about 30 minutes. When they crust over on top and crackle they are done. Do not bake until hard.

The baking is very important with these cookies.

CHOCOLATE PINWHEELS

Cream **1 cup butter, 1 scant teaspoonful salt** and **2 cups brown sugar** together, add **4 egg yolks** and mix well. Sift **flour** and measure **4 cups** into sifter, add **1 teaspoonful soda** and **1 teaspoonful cream tartar** and sift three times. Knead into mixture, adding **2 teaspoonfuls vanilla.** Divide dough into halves. To one half add **2 squares melted chocolate** and knead thoroughly. They may be rolled separately but to make pinwheels they should be rolled flat, placed one upon the other and then rolled as a jelly roll giving the pinwheel effect when sliced.

CHOCOLATE WHEAT GERM COOKIES

Mix and cream **1 cup brown sugar, ½ cup butter or margarine,** add **1 egg, ¾ cup milk, 2 ozs. melted chocolate** (2 squares), **½ cup wheat germ** and **¼ teaspoonful salt.** Sift **1½ cups flour** with **1 teaspoonful baking powder** and **½ teaspoonful soda.** Add to first mixture. Add **1 teaspoonful vanilla.** Beat thoroughly. Add **½ cup seedless raisins.** Drop on buttered cookie sheets. Bake at 350° F. for 15 minutes. Cool and spread with **chocolate icing** and **chopped nut meats** if desired.

CHRISTMAS COOKIES (Pie Dough)

Part I: Take **4½ cups cake flour, 1 cup shortening** (½ butter, ½ lard). Cut flour and shortening together as for pie crust. Part II: Add to mixture No. I, **1 cup sugar** beaten into **2 beaten eggs.** Part III: Take **5 tablespoonfuls sweet milk, 1 teaspoonful vanilla, 1 teaspoonful soda** and **nutmeg** if desired. Add this mixture to mixture No. 1. No more flour is necessary for rolling. Cut with fancy cutters. Bake in hot oven about 10 minutes.

CHRISTMAS COOKIES

Cream **1 cup butter** with **2 cups sugar.** Add **2 eggs** well beaten, also **¼ teaspoonful salt, ½ teaspoonful soda** mixed with **4 cups flour.** Mix all together, add **1 teaspoonful vanilla** with the last mixing. Cut these in fancy shapes. Bake in hot oven. When cool cover with a frosting made of **powdered sugar** and **cream.** Sprinkle with **colored sugars.** Make a holly wreath by adding green and red sugar around the edge of a round cookie. Add the many colored sugars to Christmas tree cookies, making them look as though they had ornaments.

CHRISTMAS FILLED COOKIES

Cream **½ cup shortening** with **1 cup sugar.** Add **1 egg** and **3¼ cups flour** (sifted before measuring), **1 teaspoonful salt, 3 teaspoonfuls baking powder, ½ cup milk** and **1 teaspoonful vanilla.** Add the milk and flour alternately for the best results. Chill dough. Roll out as thin as possible on cloth covered board. Rub flour into cloth to prevent sticking. Cut and put in filling. Cut opening in top cover so filling may be seen. Wet edges and put together. Bake in moderate oven for about 12 minutes. Fruit filling: Take **½ cup crushed pineapple, 1 cup grapes** (seeded), **1 cup orange marmalade** and **½ cup shredded cocoanut.** Mix and place between cookies.

CHUNKS OF GOODNESS

Mix **2½ cups flour** with **1 cup brown sugar, 2½ cups rolled oats,** then add **1 cup butter** and **½ teaspoonful salt.** Mix as for piecrust. Then add **1 teaspoonful soda** dissolved in **½ cup hot water.** Form into 2 rolls. Roll out in two pieces of the same size. Spread the following filling on one piece: Pit **1 pound dates** and cut fine, add **½ cup hot water** and **1 cup sugar** and cook for a few minutes, then cool. Add **1 cup pecans,** broken. Spread this filling on the dough and cover with the second piece, patting it down so it covers the lower piece. Cut in pieces 1 inch square with a floured knife. Bake at 350° F. for 10 to 12 minutes. When cool, store in tin box.

CINNAMON STARS (No. 1)

Beat 3 **egg whites** stiff but not dry. Add 2 **cups powdered sugar** gradually, then **grated rind ½ lemon,** and continue **beating.** Reserve ¼ of mixture to put on center of cookies. To the remaining mixture add ½ **teaspoonful cinnamon** and ½ **lb. blanched almonds,** grated. Roll out on board, using powdered sugar to prevent sticking. Cut into star shapes. Place a small portion of reserve mixture on each cooky. Bake 15 minutes at 350° F. (moderate oven). Makes 3 dozen cookies. No flour is used. Add more powdered sugar if necessary.

CINNAMON STARS (No. 2)

Beat **whites of 4 eggs** until stiff and dry, gradually beat in ¾ **lbs. (1½ cups sugar)** ½ **lb. ground blanched almonds,** ½ **tablespoonful cinnamon,** and 12 **tablespoonfuls flour.** Mix lightly and roll to ¼ inch thickness. Shape with a very small star cutter. After they are baked in a slow oven, glaze with **confectioner's sugar** mixed with **lemon juice** to a thin consistency. Bake only until they are a light brown.

COCOANUT MACAROONS

Cream ¼ **cup shortening.** Add ½ **cup sugar, 1 egg** and ¼ **teaspoonful lemon juice.** Beat well. Sift 1½ **cups flour,** ⅛ **teaspoonful salt, 3 teaspoonfuls baking powder** together and add to first mixture, alternately with ½ **cup milk.** Lastly, add 2 **cups grated cocoanut.** The batter should be quite stiff. Drop by small spoonfuls on greased pan allowing space to spread. Bake in moderate oven at 385° F. for 15 to 20 minutes.

Brown sugar which has become very hard may be softened by placing it in bread box for several days.

Butter for cooky press cookies should be very soft before mixing it with other ingredients.

COOKY PRESS COOKIES

Mix 1½ **cups of butter** (butter substitute or lard or lard substitute, adding salt if the unsalted fat is used) with **1 cup sugar.** Add **2 eggs** and beat well. Add ½ **teaspoonful vanilla** then gradually **3¼ cups all purpose flour.** Press out and bake on cooky sheet in moderately hot oven.

COCOANUT SQUARES

Mix ½ **cup butter,** ½ **cup brown sugar,** and **1 cup flour** together until fine. Put in an 8x13 pan, spreading evenly over the bottom. Bake for 10 minutes at 375° F. Now mix **1 cup brown sugar, 1 cup walnuts** chopped, **3 tablespoonfuls flour,** ½ **teaspoonful salt** and **1½ cups cocoanut** together until well blended. Then add **2 eggs** slightly beaten and **1 teaspoonful vanilla.** Place over other mixture that has baked 10 minutes. It can not be spread but dropped on and patted in place. Replace in oven and bake for 20 minutes at the same temperature.

Brown sugar may be softened by heating in oven at low temperature. Use immediately as it hardens quickly.

DATE BARS

Cream **1 cup sugar** with **3 beaten egg yolks.** Mix **1 cup chopped dates** and **1 cup chopped walnuts** with **1 cup flour,** ⅛ **teaspoonful salt** and **1 teaspoonful baking powder** sifted together. Combine with sugar and egg mixture. Fold in **3 beaten egg whites.** Spread ½ inch thick in shallow pan. Bake in moderate oven 15 to 20 minutes. When cool, cut into bars. Roll in powdered sugar just before serving.

DATE AND APRICOT BARS

Filling: Blend **1 cup pitted dates** cut in small pieces with **1¾ cups drained, cooked, unsweetened apricots,** ½ **cup sugar** and **2 tablespoonfuls liquid** from cooked apricots. Boil until mixture thickens (which is about 3 minutes.) Cool slightly. Spread between layers of cooky dough for filled cookies.

Dough—Blend ¾ **cup shortening** (½ **butter for flavor)** with **1 cup brown sugar.** Sift **flour** once then measure **2 cups.** Sift again with **1 teaspoonful soda** and blend with **2 cups** of **quick-cooking rolled oats.** Blend this dry mixture into the sugar and butter mixture, using the hand. Press half of this dough on the bottom of a well greased baking pan. Spread date and apricot mixture over the entire surface. Top with remaining mixture, pressing gently down into filling with hand or back of spoon. Bake at 350° F. 30 minutes. Cool, cut in bars.

DATE NUT COOKIES

Sift **2 cups flour, ½ teaspoonful salt, 2 teaspoonfuls baking powder.** Cream **½ cup shortening** with **2/3 cup sugar.** Add **1 egg,** beaten, and **1 cup dates,** cut fine. Add **4 tablespoonfuls milk, 1 teaspoonful vanilla** and mix well. Stir in dry ingredients and **¾ cup chopped nuts.** Batter should be stiff. Drop by teaspoonful on greased cooky sheet or shallow pan. Bake at 350° F. or 375° F. 20 minutes.

DROP SOUR CREAM COOKIES

Mix **2 cups brown sugar** and **2 well beaten eggs,** add **1 teaspoonful soda** to **1 cup sour cream** and put in above mixture. Sift flour, measure **3 cups,** sift again with **1 teaspoonful baking powder** and a **pinch salt,** then add to mixture, add **1 teaspoonful vanilla.** Drop from spoon on a well greased baking sheet. Sprinkle with nuts if desired. Bake in a moderate oven about 15 to 20 minutes.

DROP SPRINGERLES

Beat **1 dozen eggs for ½ hour.** Add **1 pound sugar** and continue beating. Then gradually add **1 pound flour** with **anise extract** to taste. When well mixed, drop from a spoon onto a greased cooky sheet and bake until a light brown color in a moderate oven.

DUTCH COOKIES

Cream **2 cups sugar** with **1 cup shortening (lard).** Add **2 eggs, beaten, 1 cup dark molasses** and **1 cup sour milk,** plus **1 tablespoonful soda.** Mix **¾ teaspoonful ginger, ¾ teaspoonful cloves, 1 teaspoonful salt, 2 teaspoonfuls cinnamon** in **4 cups flour.** Mix lightly, handling as little as possible. Add **1 more cup of flour** if not stiff enough to roll out. Roll, cut in any desired shape and bake in 425° F. oven until done. Candied fruit or nuts may be added.

ENGLISH TEA CAKES

Cream **4 tablespoonfuls butter** and **2 tablespoonfuls lard** and **1 cup sugar.** Add **1 egg, 1 scant quart of flour, 2 teaspoonfuls baking powder, 1 teaspoonful salt** and **1 teaspoonful nutmeg** that have been sifted together. Add **1 cup floured currants** or **raisins** and **½ cup milk or water.** Roll out on floured board and cut with biscuit cutter. Bake a golden brown. Time about 30 minutes. Serve warm with butter. They are good several days old.

The fig is a subtropical fruit which depends upon the sting of a wasp for its polenization. It has an abundance of nature's sugar, thus requiring very little additional sugar in its preparation.

FIG NEWTONS

Cream ½ **cup butter** with **1 cup sugar.** Add **1 well beaten egg,** ¼ **teaspoonful salt,** ½ **cup milk, 1 teaspoonful vanilla, 3 cups flour** and **3 teaspoonfuls baking powder.** Turn out on board and roll like pie crust. Cut in strips 3 inches wide and spread with the following paste: Pour **1 cup boiling water** in a sauce pan. Add **1 cup chopped figs,** ½ **cup sugar, grated rind of 1 lemon** and **2 tablespoonfuls flour.** Stir and boil five minutes, cool. Spread on one strip and cover with another. Cut in oblongs and bake in quick oven.

FILLED COOKIES

Mix **1 cup sugar** with ½ **cup shortening, 1 egg,** ½ **cup milk, 3½ cups flour** which has had **2 teaspoonfuls baking powder** and **1 teaspoonful soda** added. Add **1 teaspoonful vanilla.** When thoroughly mixed, roll thin and shape. Place cookies in buttered pans. Place a teaspoonful of filling on each, not allowing it to touch the edge. Place another cookie gently on top. Press edges lightly together and bake in usual way. Filling: Mix **1 cup raisins,** ½ **cup sugar, 1 teaspoonful flour** and ½ **cup water.** Cook until thick, stirring carefully, as it burns easily.

A good general rule to remember when storing cookies is: to keep cookies soft, place them (when cooled) in a jar with tight cover. To keep cookies hard or crisp, place them in can with loose cover.

FILLED ICE BOX COOKIES

Mix **2 cups brown sugar** and **1 cup shortening** together thoroughly. Add **3 eggs,** unbeaten, and mix well. Sift **4 cups of flour, 1 teaspoonful cinnamon, 1 teaspoonful soda** and ½ **teaspoonful salt** together and add to first mixture. Cut into 4 sections. Roll each section with the rolling pin. Make a filling by cooking **2 cups chopped dates,** ½ **cup nut meats,** ½ **cup sugar** and ½ **cup water** until well blended. Spread filling on the flat dough and roll as you would cinnamon roll. Place in ice box. Next morning cut into slices and bake on cooky sheet in moderately hot oven until brown.

FRUIT ICE BOX COOKIES

Mix **2 cups brown sugar, 1 cup granulated sugar, 1 cup dates, chopped** fine, **1 cup pecans,** cut fine, **¼ lb. candied cherries** (cut fine), **¼ lb. candied pineapple (cut fine), 1 cup shortening, melted,** and **3 eggs.** Flavor with **1 tablespoonful vanilla flavoring, ¼ teaspoonful walnut extract** and **½ teaspoonful lemon flavoring.** Add **4 cups flour** that has had **1 teaspoonful soda** added. Set in ice box over night, slice and bake.

GINGER CREAMS

Cream **¾ cup shortening** with **1 cup sugar.** Add **3 well beaten eggs** and **1 cup molasses.** Sift **3½ cups flour** with **½ teaspoonful cloves, ½ teaspoonful allspice, 1 teaspoonful salt, 1 teaspoonful ginger, 1 teaspoonful cinnamon** and **2 teaspoonfuls baking powder.** Add flour alternately with **1 cup sour milk** in which **½ teaspoonful soda** has been dissolved. Spread in thin layers on two cooky sheets which have been greased and floured. Bake in 375° F. oven. Ice cakes while still hot with the following icing: Beat the **white of 1 egg.** Add **1½ cups of powdered sugar** slowly and **1 tablespoonful hot water** flavored with **vanilla.** Cut into squares.

GINGER SNAPS

Cream **1 cup lard** with **1 cup sugar.** Add **2 eggs** and beat thoroughly. Add **1½ cups N. O. molasses, 1 tablespoonful ginger, 1 tablespoonful cinnamon.** Dissolve **1 level tablespoonful soda** in **½ cup boiling water.** Add to mixture. Also **1 teaspoonful salt** and **8 cups flour.** Roll thin, bake in moderate oven until beginning to brown from heat. This recipe makes good gingerbread men for Christmas cookies.

SOFT GINGER COOKIES

Sift **6 cups flour** with **1 teaspoonful salt, 1½ teaspoonfuls cinnamon, 2 tablespoonfuls ginger, ½ teaspoonful nutmeg.** Cream **1 cup shortening** with **1 cup sugar.** Add **1 egg.** Beat all together until light. Add **2 cups molasses** and **2 tablespoonfuls vinegar** then sifted dry ingredients. Lastly add **4 teaspoonfuls soda** dissolved in **1 cup boiling water.** If necessary add more flour to make a soft dough. Drop by teaspoonfuls on greased cookie sheet. Sprinkle with sugar. Bake 8 to 10 minutes in a moderate oven (350°). This makes about 100 cookies.

ICE BOX GINGER SNAPS

Sift **2 cups flour** (may need more) with **2 cups brown sugar, ½ teaspoonful soda, ½ teaspoonful baking powder, 1 tablespoonful cinnamon, 2 tablespoonfuls ginger, ¼ teaspoonful cloves, ¼ teaspoonful allspice, ¼ teaspoonful mace, ¼ teaspoonful nutmeg** and **½ teaspoonful salt** together. Beat in **½ cup molasses (New Orleans)** and **½ cup shortening** that have been boiled together 1 minute and then cooled. Add **2** lightly beaten **eggs** a little at a time. Mix together and knead. Shape into a long roll about 2 inches wide and chill overnight in icebox. Cut into ⅛ inch slices. Bake 10 minutes at 375° F.

GRAHAM CRACKERS

Cream **1 cup shortening** and **1 cup sugar.** Add **2 eggs** beaten and mix thoroughly. Add **1 teaspoonful soda** dissolved in **1 cup sweet milk,** then add **5 to 6 cups graham flour** mixed with **½ teaspoonful baking powder.** The mixture should resemble a stiff batter, almost stiff enough to roll. Spread and press smooth to ¼ inch thickness on greased cooky sheets and bake in moderate hot oven (400° F.) While warm, cut into squares. This recipe makes 4 dozen.

GRANGER COOKIES

Mix **1 cup shortening** with **1 cup white sugar** and **1 cup brown sugar,** add **2 eggs** and beat well. Sift **2 cups flour** with **½ teaspoonful baking powder** and **1 teaspoonful soda** and add to first mixture. Add **1 teaspoonful vanilla, 2 cups rolled oats, 2 cups wheaties, 1 cup cocoanut** and **1 teaspoonful salt.** Measure a rounding tablespoonful dough on cookie sheet. They spread slightly when baking. Bake at 375° F. for 12 minutes.

GUM DROP COOKIES

Mix **4 eggs** with **2 cups brown sugar, 1 tablespoonful cold water, 2 cups flour, ½ teaspoonful salt, ½ cup shredded gum drops** (omit **black ones) ½ cup shredded pecans** and **1 teaspoonful cinnamon.** Bake at 325° F. for about 25 to 35 minutes. Bake as a cake in a long pan. Put the following icing on cake while hot, then cut into small squares. Mix **2 tablespoonfuls melted butter** with **3 tablespoonfuls orange juice** and **rind** of **½ orange,** adding enough **powdered sugar** to make thick enough to spread.

HALF MOON COOKIES

Cream 1½ **cup shortening** until like heavy cream. Add dash **salt, 1 cup sugar, 5 egg yolks** and **3 egg whites,** saving **2 egg whites** for dipping. Cream all together. Add **4 cups flour, 1 teaspoonful baking powder** and **1 teaspoonful lemon flavoring.** Roll out about ¼ inch thick, cut cookies the shape of half moons, then dip in egg white and **chopped nuts** mixed with **sugar.** Bake 30 minutes in moderate oven.

If preferred the tops only of the cookies may have egg white spread over them and sprinkled with nuts.

HONEY COOKIES (Lebkuchen)

Mix and warm **2 cups brown sugar, 2 cups molasses, 2 cups honey, 2 tablespoonfuls butter** and **1 tablespoonful lard.** Force **2/3 cup candied orange peel, 2/3 cup lemon peel, 2/3 cup citron** and **1½ cups shelled almonds through the food chopper.** Add **2 teaspoonfuls soda** to **2 cups sour cream.** Add **2 teaspoonfuls cinnamon, 1 teaspoonful cloves** to flour (enough to make a stiff dough). Mix well and let stand over night. Roll out, not too thin. Bake in moderate oven. Ice lightly with simple **frosting** flavored with **almond** or **vanilla,** as preferred.

HONEY DROP COOKIES

Cream ¼ **cup margarine** with ¾ **cup honey** until well blended, then beat in **1 egg** and **2 tablespoonfuls water.** Sift **2 cups flour** with ½ **teaspoonful soda, 1 teaspoonful cinnamon** and a **little nutmeg** together. Mix in **1 cup raisins** with dry ingredients. Add to first mixture and drop on greased cooky sheets by teaspoonfuls. **Nuts** may be added.

LEMON CRACKERS

Mix **1 cup lard, 2½ cups sugar** and **2 eggs** thoroughly together. Dissolve **1 tablespoonful pulverized baking ammonia** (1 square) and **1 tablespoonful oil lemon** in **2 cups sweet milk.** Add to first mixture. Add enough flour to make a stiff dough. Roll to 1/3 inch thickness, cut into 2 inch squares, prick in several places with a fork and bake in greased pans in a hot oven.

MINCEMEAT COOKIES (No 1.)

Cream **1 cup shortening** and **1½ cups brown sugar.** Add **3 eggs** and 2 **cups mincemeat.** Then add **1 teaspoonful sifted soda** and **2 cups flour.** Gradually add more **flour** (¾ **cup**) until the dough is quite stiff. Roll thin and cut in desired shapes. Bake in a hot oven for 10 minutes. Makes 72 2½-inch cookies.

MINCEMEAT COOKIES (No. 2.)

Cream **1½ cups sugar** with **2/3 cup shortening.** Add **3 beaten eggs, 1½ cups mincemeat, 1 teaspoonful soda dissolved** in **2 tablespoonfuls boiling water, 3 cups flour** and **½ cup nut meats.** Beat thoroughly. Drop by teaspoonfuls on greased cookie sheet and bake in moderate oven for 15 minutes. This makes 4 dozen cookies.

SOFT MOLASSES COOKIES

Melt **1 cup bacon drippngs** and add to **1 cup sugar** and **1 cup molasses.** Mix well. Stir in **2 well beaten eggs.** Sift **1 tablespoonful soda** (scant), **½ tablespoonful salt, 1 teaspoonful nutmeg, ½ tablespoonful ginger, ½ tablespoonful cinnamon** and **5 cups flour.** Add these ingredients alternately with **1 cup cold water. Raisins** and **nuts** may be added. Mix well and set in a covered dish in icebox to chill. Drop on a greased cooky sheet and bake in a moderate oven. Press each cookie down in shape with a floured spoon before baking. This cooky dough will keep a week in ice box so only bake as needed.

MOLASSES CRINKLES

Cream **¾ cup shortening,** add **1 cup brown sugar** (packed). Blend **1 beaten egg** with **4 tablespoonfuls molasses.** Sift **2¼ cups flour** with **2 teaspoonfuls soda, ½ teaspoonful cloves, 1 teaspoonful cinnamon** and **1 teaspoonful ginger.** Put all three mixtures together. Set in refrigerator to chill. Remove chilled dough and form into balls the size of large walnuts. Dip tops of balls in **sugar.** Place cookies unsugared side down about 3 inches apart on greased baking sheets. Sprinkle each cookie with 2 or 3 drops of water. Bake 12 to 15 minutes in quick oven (375° F.)

MOLASSES COOKIES

Cream **1 cup white sugar** with **1½ cups shortening** and **½ teaspoonful salt.** Add **2 eggs** beaten and **1¼ cups of dark New Orleans molasses** and beat well. Sift **6 cups flour** with **3 teaspoonfuls soda, 1 teaspoonful cinnamon, ½ teaspoonful cloves** and **½ teaspoonful nutmeg** and add alternately with **1 cup** of **thick sour milk** that has had **1 teaspoonful of soda** dissolved in it. When well mixed roll out with just as little **flour** as possible, sprinkle with **sugar,** roll ½ inch thick and bake in medium oven until brown.

MOLASSES NUT STICKS

Mix **1½ cups of all purpose flour, ¼ teaspoonful soda, 1½ teaspoonfuls baking powder, ½ teaspoonful cinnamon, ⅛ teaspoonful cloves, ½ teaspoonful ginger** and **¼ teaspoonful salt** together well, cut in **¼ cup shortening.** Mix **1/3 cup sugar, ½ cup molasses, 1 egg, ½ cup milk** or **strong black coffee** with an egg beater. Add this to first mixture. Lastly add **½ cup chopped nut meats.** Bake in a well greased and floured square pan 10x10 at 350° F. for 35 minutes. Cut in strips after sprinkling top with powdered sugar.

NORWEGIAN BUTTER COOKIES

Melt **¾ cup butter,** add **½ cup sugar;** cool. Add **1 well beaten egg** and **1 teaspoonful vanilla** and beat until smooth. Add **1 cup flour** sifted with **¾ cup cornstarch** and **1 teaspoonful baking powder** and stir until well blended. Drop from teaspoon onto cooky sheet and bake 16 to 18 minutes at 350° F.

ECONOMY OATMEAL COOKIES

Mix **2 cups quick oats, 1 cup flour, 1 cup brown sugar, ½ cup white sugar, ¼ teaspoonful salt** and **1 teaspoonful cinnamon.** Melt **½ cup shortening** and **1 teaspoonful soda** in **¼ cup boiling water** and mix well. Drop by teaspoon on greased baking sheet. Dip bottom of drinking glass in flour and press each cookie flat. Bake 5 to 10 minutes in 350° F. oven, remove cookies with pancake turner while still hot. **Nuts, dates** and **raisins** may be added if desired. Sometimes these cookies have to be mixed with the hand to make the mixture blend correctly. A little more water may be added if they are too crumbly.

OATMEAL COOKIES

Place **2 cups brown sugar** in a bowl with **1 cup butter** or **other fat, 1 cup cocoanut, 1 cup chopped nut meats, 2 cups flour, 4 cups rolled oats, 1 teaspoonful baking powder, ½ teaspoonful soda** dissolved in **4 tablespoonfuls hot water, 2 eggs** well beaten and a **pinch salt.** Stir until well mixed. Drop from spoon on buttered pan and bake in moderate oven until golden brown. If more moisture is needed add another egg.

BACON FAT OATMEAL COOKIES

Stir together **1 egg, 1 cup sugar part brown, 2 tablespoonfuls molasses, 1 cup bacon fat** or ½ cup bacon and ½ cup other fat, **6 teaspoonfuls milk, 1 teaspoonful cinnamon, 1 teaspoonful soda, 2 cups rolled oats, 2 cups flour, 1 cup raisins** and **½ teaspoonfuls salt. Nuts** may be added. Make into small balls, flatten with a fork dipped in water. Bake in 350° F. oven about 15 minutes.

OATMEAL COOKIES (Whole wheat flour)

Cream **½ cup butter** and **½ cup shortening** (lard may be used) with **2 cups brown sugar,** then add **2 eggs, 2 cups whole wheat flour** and **½ cup all purpose flour** that has been sifted with **¾ teaspoonful soda, 1 teaspoonful cinnamon, ½ teaspoonful cloves,** and **½ teaspoonful salt.** Add **5 tablespoonfuls milk, 2 cups rolled oats** and **1 cup raisins,** lastly add **1 cup chopped nuts** and **1 teaspoonful vanilla.** Drop on slightly greased cookie sheet and bake at 350° F. for 15 minutes.

OATMEAL ICE BOX CRISPIES

Cream **1 cup shortening.** Add **1 cup white sugar, 1 cup brown sugar** and **2 beaten eggs.** Work all together well. Add **1 teaspoonful vanilla.** Beat again. Add **1½ cups flour** sifted with **1 teaspoonful soda** and **1 teaspoonful salt.** Add **3 cups quick oats, ½ cup nut meats** (black walnuts are best) and mix well. Form into long rolls. Chill overnight. Slice ¼ inch thick and bake on greased pans 10 minutes. Remove from pan with spatula.

OATMEAL AND DATE BLOCKS

Mix **1 large cup shortening** (chicken fat is excellent) with **1 cup brown sugar, 2 cups flour** which has had **1 teaspoonful soda** sifted in it and **2½ cups rolled oats. Salt** to taste. Put half into bottom of pan and pat or roll flat. Then cover with **1 package of dates** that have been cooked with ½ **cup sugar** and **1 cup water.** Sprinkle remainder of first mixture over top of date filling. It tastes like nuts on top. Bake slowly, cut in squares while hot.

OLD-FASHIONED SOFT COOKIES

Cream well **1 cup shortening** (drippings will do) with **2 cups white or brown sugar** (use brown sugar if drippings are used). Then add **2 eggs,** one at a time and beat well. Sift flour, **measure 4 cups** and sift again with **1 teaspoonful salt, 1 teaspoon soda** and 3 **teaspoonfuls baking powder.** Add flour alternately to first mixture with **1 cup milk** (either sweet or sour). Flavor with **1 teaspoonful lemon extract** and ½ **teaspoonful ground nutmeg.** When well mixed put in cold place to chill; roll, cut in rounds and bake in a 400° F. (quick) oven for 15 minutes.

ORANGE COOKIES (Rolled)

Cream ½ **cup shortening,** add **1 cup sugar** gradually creaming until light and fluffy. Add **grated rind** of **1 orange** and **1 well beaten egg,** beat again. Sift 3 **cups flour** with **4 teaspoonfuls baking powder** and ½ **teaspoonful salt,** add to creamed mixture alternately with ½ **cup orange juice.** Chill in refrigerator for ½ hour. Roll out on floured surface and cut with a small cookie cutter. Place on greased cookie sheet, sprinkle with **granulated sugar** and bake in moderately hot oven 400° F. 12 minutes. This makes 8 dozen small cookies.

ORANGE ICE BOX COOKIES

Cream ½ **cup butter** with ½ **cup brown sugar,** ½ **cup white sugar.** Continue to cream until very smooth. Add **1 beaten egg.** Sift **flour once** then measure **2¾ cups.** Add ¼ **teaspoonful soda** and sift with flour. Add to creamed mixture. Add **2 tablespoonfuls orange juice** and **1 tablespoonful grated orange rind.** Stir in ½ **cup blanched almonds,** cut in strips. Shape in rolls. Wrap in waxed paper and let stand in ice box until firm. Slice and bake in moderately hot oven (375° F.) for 12 to 15 minutes. This is a soft dough. Chill between bakings if necessary.

PECAN STICKS

Cream **1 cup butter** and add **5 tablespoonfuls confectioner's sugar** while beating constantly. Add **1 teaspoonful water, 1 teaspoonful vanilla,** ½ **teaspoonful salt, 2 cups general purpose flour** and **1 cup pecans,** cut fine. Blend carefully. Roll in pencil-like sticks 4 inches long or shape into crescents. Bake on cooky sheet in a moderate oven (350) until lightly browned, about 20 minutes. Roll in confectioner's sugar while still warm.

PINEAPPLE DROP COOKIES

Cream 1 **cup butter** with **2 cups brown sugar** and **1 cup white sugar,** add 3 **eggs** slightly beaten and mix well. Add **1 cup crushed pineapple** then 4 **cups flour** that has been sifted with ½ **teaspoonful soda, 2 teaspoonfuls baking powder** and ½ **teaspoonful salt.** Mix well again. Drop from spoon on greased cookie sheet. Bake at 425° F. for 8 to 10 minutes. This makes 6 dozen cookies.

PFEFFERNUSSE (Pepper Nuts)

Sift flour before measuring, then sift again three times until you have **1½ cups sifted flour** and add **1 teaspoonful nutmeg, 1 teaspoonful cloves, 1 teaspoonful cinnamon,** and ⅛ **teaspoonful white pepper.** Cream ¼ **cup butter** with **1 cup sugar,** add **an egg** and beat well. Add **another cup of powdered sugar,** and continue adding **an egg** and **a cup of powdered sugar** alternately until you have used **4 eggs** and **1 lb. powdered sugar,** beating well until all are added. **Add 1 cup walnuts** ground fine and flour with spices. Mix well. The dough should be very stiff, so if necessary add a little more flour. Cover, let stand in cool place over night. Flour hands, roll dough into little balls an inch in diameter. Place on greased tins an inch or more apart. Bake in moderate oven for 20 minutes. Cool and store in air-tight tins.

PLAIN COOKIES

Boil together the following ingredients: **1 cup brown sugar,** ½ **cup lard,** ½ **cup raisins 1 1/3 cups water,** ½ **teaspoonful salt,** ½ **teaspoonful cinnamon,** ½ **teaspoonful cloves,** and ½ **teaspoonful nutmeg.** Let cool. Add **1 teaspoonful baking powder** and **1 teaspoonful soda** to 4 **cups flour** and add to the cooled mixture. Drop from spoon onto greased cookie sheet.

PEANUT BUTTER COOKIES

Mix **1 cup shortening, 1 cup white sugar, 1 cup brown sugar, 2 eggs, 1 cup peanut butter, 3 cups sifted flour, 1 teaspoonful baking soda, ½ teaspoonful salt** and **1 teaspoonful vanilla.** Shape into balls and after placing on cookie sheet press each one down with a fork, first one way and then the other. They should look like squares or waffles. Bake in hot oven.

Since eggs vary in size it is often necessary to add an extra egg when they are used for moisture in cookies.

PRETZELS

Dissolve **1 cake yeast** in a small amount of lukewarm **milk.** Scald and cool **1 pint milk,** add **1 pint water, 4 tablespoonfuls soft lard, 1 tablespoonful salt** and **8 pints flour.** Mix dough stiff like bread dough. Do not let rise. Take a piece of dough the size of an egg. Roll in long strip so middle of strip is about thickness of your thumb or a little larger if you wish large pretzels, taper the ends to a small diameter. Then twist into pretzel shape. Cover with a cloth. Let rise until light. It takes about 45 minutes. If one is using a gas oven and the bottom is solid, wash out good so there won't be any grit. If electric stove where there is no solid bottom use cookie sheet for baking. Heat oven as for bread. Into a granite kettle **¾ full of water,** brought to a boiling point, add enough **commercial lye** so that when one touches some of the liquid on tongue it will be biting. Now take raised pretzels, drop in lye water, and as soon as they come up take them out with pancake turner and sprinkle with **salt.** Slide in bottom of oven and bake until they lift easily with a pancake turner. Transfer to broiler and brown. Then they are done. This recipe makes about 48 pretzels.

RASPBERRY COCOANUT SQUARES

Sift **1 cup bread flour** with **1 teaspoonful baking powder** and **¼ teaspoonful salt.** Work in **¼ lb. butter.** Add **1 egg.** Roll and put this in an 8x14 pan turning up edges slightly and spread with raspberry jam. Mix **2 egg yolks** with **1 cup sugar** and **¼ pound dry cocoanut, 1 teaspoonful vanilla** and **butter** the **size of an egg.** Spread this over the jam by crumbling with fingers. Beat **2 egg whites** slightly and spread over top. Bake 30 minutes at 350° F. Cut in squares before removing from pan.

REFRIGERATOR SOUR CREAM COOKIES

Mix 2 **cups sugar** with 1 **cup shortening** and 1 **cup thick sour cream.** Add 2 **eggs** slightly beaten, then 5 **cups flour** which has had **1 teaspoonful soda** and 2 **teaspoonfuls baking powder** sifted with it. Flavor with either **1 teaspoonful grated orange rind** or **1 teaspoonful nutmeg.** Work into a roll using as little flour as possible. Roll up in waxed paper. Put in refrigerator until hardened. Slice and bake on cookie sheet at 350° F. about 15 minutes . They may be baked as needed as the dough will keep in refrigerator.

RICE FLAKE MACAROONS

Beat 2 **egg whites** until stiff, add ½ **cup sugar gradually,** add 1 **teaspoonful vanilla** and fold in 2 **cups rice flakes** and ½ **cup cocoanut.** Drop by tablespoonfuls on lightly oiled cookie sheet. Bake in a slow oven 300° F. for 15 to 20 minutes. Makes 18 cookies.

ROLLED WAFERS

Cream ¼ **cup butter,** add ½ **cup powdered sugar** gradually, then ¼ **cup milk** drop by drop, add ½ **teaspoonful vanilla** and ⅞ **cup of flour** (measure a full cup of flour then remove 2 tablespoonfuls). Turn square cake pan upside down and grease bottom of it. Spread mixture very, very thin over bottom of pan with spatula. Mark in squares 4 or 5 inches and bake in quick oven (450° F.) until a delicate brown. Cut squares apart with sharp knife and roll while hot. May be rolled over a pencil or wooden spoon handle. If squares become too brittle to roll replace in oven until hot again. Fill with whipped cream or icing.

SAND TARTS

Cream 1½ **cups butter** with 3 **cups white sugar,** add 3 **whole eggs** and **1 yolk** (the extra white is reserved for icing). Add **4 cups flour.** When well kneaded roll very thin. Spread with **egg white** and sprinkle **granulated sugar** over top. **Nuts** make a very pleasing addition to the top, both for flavor and appearance. Bake in a moderate oven.

SODA CRACKERS

Mix **1 cup lard, 3 cups sour milk, salt** and **3 teaspoonfuls soda** and enough **flour** to make quite stiff. Roll thin and cut in squares. Prick with fork and bake until brown. When done put back in oven to dry until crisp.

Cookies that have become hard may be softened by adding a cut apple to cookie jar. Remove before it begins to spoil.

SOUR CREAM COOKIES

Cream **2/3 cup butter** or other shortening with **2 cups brown sugar.** Add **2 eggs** beaten and blend mixture thoroughly. Add **1 cup sour cream.** Combine and sift **4 cups flour, 1 teaspoonful salt, 3 teaspoonfuls baking powder, 1 teaspoonful soda, ½ teaspoonful nutmeg** and add to first mixture. Add **1 teaspoonful vanilla.** Drop mixture from teaspoon onto a well greased cooky sheet. Bake in oven (400° F.) until done, approximately 12 minutes. This recipe makes 60 cookies.

SUGAR COOKIES WITHOUT MILK

Cream **2/3 cup shortening,** then add **1¼ cups sugar,** a little at a time, working in thoroughly before more is added. Add **2 well beaten eggs** and mix well. Sift flour, then measure and sift **3 cups flour** with **1 teaspoonful salt,** and **2 teaspoonfuls baking powder.** Add **1 teaspoonful vanilla** or **1 tablespoonful orange juice** and **grated rind of one orange** and mix to a soft dough. Chill. Roll thin, using as little flour as possible to handle. Cut and sprinkle with sugar. Bake 12 to 15 minutes in moderate oven.

GRANDMOTHER'S SUGAR COOKIES

Cream **½ cup butter** and **½ cup lard** with **2 cups sugar.** Beat **2 eggs.** Mix shortening and sugar thoroughly. Stir **1 teaspoonful soda** into **1 cup sour milk.** Add **6 or 7 cups flour** alternately with the milk, stirring in **1 teaspoonful nutmeg** and **pinch salt.** When mixture is firm enough to handle, roll out and cut into figures or designs. Bake in moderate oven 10 to 20 minutes. Be sure to grease pan for baking.

SCOTCH SHORTBREAD

Have ½ **pound butter** very soft. Work in ¼ **pound granulated sugar.** Then work in ¾ **pound flour** a little at a time. Knead thoroughly and roll out. Cut with cutter the shape desired. Bake in slow oven to a delicate brown.

SPRINGERLE OR ANISE COOKIES

Separate 4 **eggs:** beat **yolks** with 4 **tablespoonfuls water** and 1 **lb. sugar** for a few minutes; add beaten **whites of eggs,** then again beat for about 10 minutes, or until very light. Add 1 **lb. flour** (4 cups) sifted with 1 **teaspoonful baking powder;** add about **three drops of anise oil** and mix dough well. If not quite stiff enough to mold add a little more flour. Roll out about ⅜ inch thick. Press in molds, or cut in squares or any desired shape. Lay on board for 3 or 4 hours before baking them. Bake in a slow oven. They should be made about a month before Christmas, placed in a basket between cloths in a cool damp place so they become soft.

WALNUT MARGUERITES

Beat 2 **tablespoonfuls of powdered sugar** into 1 **egg white** that has been beaten until stiff. Fold in ½ **cup chopped dates,** or **figs** and ¾ **cup broken nut meats.** Add ½ **teaspoonful vanilla.** Drop from teaspoon onto 25 **soda or graham crackers.** Top with more **nut meats.** Bake in moderate oven 15 minutes or until slightly brown.

WASHBOARD OR COCOANUT COOKIES

Cream 1 **cup shortening** and 2 **cups brown sugar packed in cup.** Blend in 2 **well beaten eggs,** add 1 **teaspoonful soda** to ¼ **cup hot water, sour milk** or **buttermilk** and add to creamed mixture. Add 1 **cup moist cocoanut** shredded and chopped fine. Add 1 **teaspoonful vanilla.** Sift **flour** then measure 4½ **cups** and sift again with 1 **teaspoonful salt** and 1½ **teaspoonful baking powder,** add to first mixture. Chill thoroughly. Roll into balls, flatten to oblong. Press with tines of fork to look like washboards. Bake on ungreased sheet. Bake 8 to 10 minutes at 400° F. Store in airtight container.

Deep Fat Frying

Slice a raw potato into a kettle of deep fat to clarify.

Croquettes

Croquettes are a good method of using up leftover materials. They are shaped differently but all are dipped in egg then bread crumbs and fried in deep fat.

CARROT CROQUETTES

Make balls with **1 cup mashed cooked carrots** and **1 cup mashed canned peas, 1 diced onion** and **1 teaspoonful minced parsley** which have been thoroughly blended with **1 cup thick white sauce.** Dip in **2 beaten eggs.** Roll in **bread crumbs** and fry in deep fat. The fat should be hot enough to brown a one-inch cube of soft bread in 40 seconds.

CHEESE CROQUETTES

Make a thick white sauce using **4 tablespoonfuls butter, 4 tablespoonfuls flour** and **1 cup milk;** season with **salt** and a pinch of **cayenne pepper.** Boil until thick, stirring constantly. Take from fire, add **yolks of 2 eggs, ½ cup grated cheese** and **1 cup cheese** cut in small bits. Turn out on platter to cool. Make into balls. Dip in **egg** and **cracker crumbs** and fry in **deep fat.** If they break open a little they are at their best.

CRABMEAT CROQUETTES

Melt **1½ tablespoonfuls butter.** Add **2½ tablespoonfuls flour** and smooth; then add **1 cup milk.** Stir until sauce boils and is very thick. Add **1 can crabmeat** and **¼ teaspoonful paprika, 1/3 teaspoonful salt, few grains of cayenne, 2 tablespoonfuls water** or **milk** and **½ teaspoonful lemon juice.** Roll **1 cup dry bread crumbs** until fine. Divide crabmeat into balls and roll in crumbs, **1 egg** and crumbs again. Fry in deep fat until delicately browned.

EGG CROQUETTES

Chop 5 hard-cooked **eggs** until rather fine. Make white sauce of **1 tablespoonful butter, 2 tablespoonfuls flour** and **1 cup milk.** Season with **1 teaspoonful salt, 1 tablespoonful grated onion,** and **1 tablespoonful** finely minced **parsley.** Add black pepper if desired. Form into the shape of a croquette. Roll in fine **bread crumbs** and fry in deep fat until golden brown. Serve on platter with buttered peas and sliced tomatoes.

FISH CROQUETTES

Mix **2 cups left-over fish,** flaked, **2 tablespoonfuls** minced **parsley, 2 tablespoonfuls** minced **celery, 1 teaspoonful orange juice, salt, pepper, 2 tablespoonfuls cold water** and **1 cup thick white sauce.** Chill. Form into croquettes. Egg **(1 egg)** and **crumb,** then fry in deep fat until browned. Serve hot.

HAM CROQUETTES

Mix **2 cups mashed seasoned potatoes, yolks** of **2 eggs** and a pinch of **caenne.** Beat until smooth. Cool. Chop **cooked ham** until there is **1 cup,** mix with **1 egg yolk.** Heat and cool. Make a small ball of ham and enclose it in a larger ball of potato. Dip first in flour, next in beaten **egg,** then roll in **crumbs** and **bake** in moderate oven. This is delicious served with egg sauce. (See sauces.)

HOMINY CROQUETTES

Put **½ cup water** in top of double boiler. When it boils add **½ cup fine white hominy, ½ teaspoonful salt** and **½ teaspoonful paprika.** Put over hot water and cnd cook until water is absorbed, then add **¾ cup milk** and cook 45 minutes or until soft. Add **2 tablespoonfuls butter.** Cool, then shape in round cakes. Make groove in center of each. Dip in **flour,** then in **1 egg beaten** with **2 tablespoonfuls cold water,** and finally sifted **bread crumbs.** Fry in deep fat that will brown a piece of bread in 40 seconds. Drain. Place **a section of orange** in groove of each croquette.

LAMB CROQUETTES

Melt 3 **tablespoonfuls butter.** Add 4 **tablespoonfuls flour,** ½ **teaspoonful salt** and ⅛ **teaspoonful pepper** and stir until smooth. Add **1 cup milk** gradually and bring to boiling point, stirring constantly. Add 1 **teaspoonful** finely chopped **onion** and **2 cups** chopped **cooked lamb.** Cool. Shape as desired. Roll in **crumbs,** then in beaten **egg** diluted with 2 **tablespoonfuls cold water** and again in crumbs. Fry in deep, hot fat until brown (about 5 minutes). Drain on paper. (Other meat may be used in this recipe in place of lamb.)

LIVER CROQUETTES

Use leftover liver or simmer raw liver in boiling water for 20 minutes. Cool and put through food chopper. Make a **medium white sauce,** seasoned with **1 teaspoonful minced onion,** ½ **teaspoonful salt,** ¼ **teaspoonful pepper** and **1 teaspoonful minced parsley.** Add **1 pound** of **beef liver** and allow to cool. Shape into small balls. Dip the balls first into **crushed cornflakes,** then **egg,** thinned with **milk** and again in **cornflakes.** Fry in **hot fat** five minutes. Drain on brown paper and serve hot with white sauce.

MEAT AND POTATO CROQUETTES

Place **1 tablespoonful butter** in sauce pan and add **1 slice of onion,** minced. Let simmer, add **1 tablespoon flour,** stir until smooth and frothy. Add ½ **cup milk,** season with **salt** and **pepper,** let boil for 3 minutes, stirring constantly. Add **1 cup cold (leftover) meat** and **1 cup hot mashed potatoes.** (Reheat potatoes if leftover ones are used). Mix thoroughly, set on plate to cool. When cold shape into balls or rolls, dip in beaten **egg** and roll in **bread crumbs.** Drop into deep fat and fry 2 minutes, or until a golden brown. Remove and serve immediately while hot. Cold **rice** or **hominy** may be used in place of potato, or a cup of **cold fish** minced fine in place of meat.

SALMON CROQUETTES

Make a cream sauce of **1 tablespoonful flour, 1 tablespoonful butter** and ¼ **cup milk.** Put **1 cup cooked salmon** into a bowl and add sauce. Then add **1 teaspoonful lemon juice,** ½ **teaspoonful salt** and ⅛ **teaspoonful pepper,** mix with fork until salmon is well broken. Set aside and when cold mold into desired shapes. Roll in **bread crumbs,** then in **beaten egg** to which **1 tablespoonful of milk** has been added, then in bread crumbs again. Fry in deep hot fat.

SWEET POTATO CROQUETTES

Boil and mash sufficient pared **sweet potatoes** to make a pint. Beat with them while still hot, ¼ **cup hot milk, 1 teaspoonful sugar, 1 tablespoonful melted butter, 1 well beaten egg, salt** and **pepper** to taste. Let cool sufficiently to handle, then shape into small croquettes. Flour or coat with **egg** and **cracker crumbs** and fry in **deep fat** to a light brown. Remove from fat and drain, setting them in the oven where they will keep warm until served.

Doughnuts

Doughnuts are a fried bread or cake dough. Their usual shape is round with a hole in the center. Recipes requiring the least fat on the inside make the best doughnuts, as these do not absorb fat when fried.

Slip a long metal skewer through the holes of your doughnuts to remove them easily from the hot fat.

DOUGHNUTS

Take **2 cups sugar, 2 eggs, 5 tablespoonfuls melted lard, 1 tablespoonful vanilla** or **1 teaspoonful nutmeg** and mix well. Add alternately **2 cups buttermilk, 5 cups flour** sifted with **2 teaspoonfuls soda** and **2 teaspoonfuls baking powder.** It may be necessary to add a little more flour, but keep dough as soft as possible. **Fry in deep** fat and when cool dip in **powdered sugar** or **granulated sugar** mixed with **cinnamon.**

To sugar doughnuts easily and evenly shake them with the sugar in a paper bag.

DROP DOUGHNUTS

Mix in a large bowl **1½ cups milk, 1½ cups white sugar, 2 teaspoonfuls vanilla** and **3 egg** yolks well beaten. Sift **4½ cups flour 3 heaping teaspoonfuls baking powder** (6 level) and **1 teaspoonful salt** into the liquid mixture, stir until smooth add the **3 beaten egg whites** by folding them into mixture. Drop a teaspoonful at a time into **hot fat.** Cook until brown. Roll in either **powdered** or **granulated sugar.** Turn doughnuts while cooking if necessary, they usually turn themselves. 2 tablespoonfuls melted fat may be added to batter, if desired.

POTATO DOUGHNUTS

Mix **1 cup hot mashed potatoes, 1½ tablespoonfuls melted butter** or **lard, 1 cup granulated sugar, ½ cup sweet milk, 2 small eggs, 4 cups flour, 2½ teaspoonfuls baking powder, ½ teaspoonful salt** and **1 teaspoonful nutmeg.** Pour on floured board and roll out as thick as desired (about ¼ inch). Fry in deep fat in a skillet that has rather high sides. The broad surface allows more doughnuts to be fried at one time.

RAISED DOUGHNUTS

Scald **1 cup milk** at night. Add **2 tablespoonfuls melted butter** and **½ teaspoonful salt.** Cool until lukewarm. Add **½ cake yeast** which has been softened in **¼ cup warm water.** Add **¼ teaspoonful** either **nutmeg** or **cinnamon** and **2 cups flour.** Beat well. Let rise over night. Next morning cut down and add **1 cup sugar, 2 eggs** well beaten, and about **3 more cups flour** (enough flour to make a soft dough). Cover and let rise to double its bulk. Turn onto slightly floured board. Roll in sheet ½ inch thick and either cut with cutter or in strips and twist as for twisted doughnuts. Cook in **hot fat** (365° F.). Drain on crumpled paper. The doughnuts should rise to top and begin to brown almost instantly. This makes 48 doughnuts.

SWEET MILK DOUGHNUTS

Sift **2½ cups of all purpose flour** with **1 cup sugar, pinch salt** and **2½ teaspoonfuls baking powder.** Work in **2 teaspoonfuls fat** (either lard or butter). **Beat 1 egg,** add **¾ cup milk** to egg and beat until egg is dissolved. Flavor with either **nutmeg** or **vanilla** or both. Add this to dry ingredients and mix until it forms a dough. Add a little more **flour** if needed to make dough so it can be kneaded, but watch that you do not add too much. Roll out to ¼ inch in thickness, cut with doughnut cutter, slip rings into fat hot enough to smoke but not hot enough to burn doughnuts. Turn several times while cooking. Remove from fat. Drain. Dust with powdered sugar if desired.

To freshen doughnuts sprinkle with powdered sugar, place in oven, reheat and serve at once. They may be reheated in a skillet with a lid, allowing them to steam.

French Fries

FRENCH FRIED CHICKEN

Select very young **chicken** weighing from 2 to 1½ **pounds.** Thoroughly wash and dry and rub with **salt** and **pepper.** Cut in quarters. Dip in plain fritter batter and fry in **hot deep fat** 8 to 10 minutes. Fritter Batter: Sift 1 **cup flour** with 1½ **teaspoonfuls baking powder** and ¼ **teaspoonful salt.** Add 1 **egg** which has been beaten and 2/3 **cup milk.** Beat until smooth.

FRENCH FRIED POTATOES

Pare **potatoes** and cut in strips ¼ inch thick. Soak in cold water or ice water about 1 hour. Drain and dry between towels. Fill sauce pan half full of **vegetable fat** and heat slowly. When fat is hot enough to brown a bread cube in 20 seconds it is ready to fry potatoes. Fill strainer half full of potatoes and lower it into fat. Increase heat as cold potatoes cool fat. When brown, lift potatoes out, shake lightly and drain on unglazed paper. Sprinkle with **salt.**

LATTICED POTATOES

Pare rather **large potatoes** and cut with a potato latticer. Let stand in ice water 1 hour. Drain and dry in a clean cloth and fry in deep **hot fat.** To brown well, take the basket out of the fat after being in for five minutes. Let the air circulate through them well. Return to hot fat for a few minutes and the potatoes will be deliciously browned and crisp. Fry at 390° F.

ONION RINGS

Peel and cut 4 **medium sized onions** into ¼ inch slices. Separate into rings. Add ½ **cup milk** to 1 **beaten egg.** Stir in ¾ **cup cake flour,** which has been sifted with ¼ **teaspoonful baking powder,** and ½ **teaspoonfulful salt.** Dip rings into batter, one at a time. Fry in deep fat hot enough to brown a 1-inch cube of bread in 45 seconds. Drain on unglazed paper or paper towels. Serve at once with steak or broiled liver. Serves six.

POTATO CHIPS

Slice **potatoes** very thin, being sure they are the same thickness on all sides. Bring a pan of **water** to the **boiling** point and drop in potatoes for just 1 minute. Remove and plunge immediately into **ice water,** allow to stand from 2 to 3 hours. Dry chips well, drop **into hot fat** 390° F. and fry until a golden brown.

SWEET POTATO PUFFS

Sweet potatoes may be cooked beforehand. Do not make the mistake of fixing the puffs ahead of time as they will be ruined if they stand after mixing. Cook **1 pound sweet potatoes** until done, drain, put through fruit press or mash with potato masher or food ricer. Season with **cream, butter** and **salt.** When cool, cover a **marshmallow** with the mashed sweet potatoes, then dip in **beaten egg** and **dry crumbs.** Two coatings of egg and crumbs make a firmer covering. Fry immediately in **deep hot fat.**

Fritters

A fritter is a soft batter filled with fruit or vegetables and fried in deep fat.

APPLE FRITTERS

Pare and core 4 large apples, then slice them; add 2 tablespoonfuls sugar and 1 tablespoonful lemon juice. Sift 1 cup flour, 1½ teaspoonfuls baking powder and ¼ teaspoonful salt together; add 1 beaten egg and 2/3 cup milk, beat until smooth. Dip each slice of apple in batter and fry to a light brown in deep fat. Drain well and sprinkle with powdered sugar. These are excellent with roast pork. Serve hot.

BANANA FRITTERS

Mix 1 cup flour with 1½ teaspoonfuls baking powder, 2 tablespoonfuls sugar and ¼ teaspoonful salt. Add to 2 peeled bananas, mashed fine, alternately with 1/3 cup milk. Add 1 egg beaten and 1 teaspoonful lemon juice. Fry in deep fat. Sprinkle with powdered sugar.

CORN FRITTERS

Sift 1 cup pastry flour, 1 teaspoonful powdered sugar, 2/3 teaspoonful baking powder together and stir into 1 beaten egg and ¼ cup milk. Add 1 teaspoonful melted fat, ½ teaspoonful salt and 1 cup corn. Fry in deep fat by dropping off spoonfuls of batter into hot fat. Turn as soon as batter rises to top and cook until brown. The fat should brown 1 square inch of bread in 40 seconds or register 375° F.

ELDERBERRY BLOSSOM FRITTERS.

Mix 2 cups flour, 2 teaspoonfuls baking powder, 1 tablespoonful sugar together, then add 1½ cups milk mixed with 2 eggs. Beat until it makes a smooth batter. Cut off long stems of clean elderberry blossom cluster, leaving cluster whole. Dip cluster in batter and fry in deep hot fat until browned.

PINEAPPLE FRITTERS

Sift **1 cup flour, 1 teaspoonful baking powder, 2 tablespoonfuls sugar** and **¼ teaspoonful salt** together. Stir **1 egg** into **½ cup milk.** Add **2 tablespoonfuls of melted shortening.** Mix the 2 together. Cut **pineapple slices** (which have been well drained) in half. Stir into batter and drop into **hot** deep **fat.** Fry until well browned. Sprinkle with **powdered sugar.** Serve with maple sirup if being **eaten alone.**

Desserts -- Cold

The best apples for cooking in northeastern part of the State of Ohio are: Spring—Yellow Transparent—Early Harvest. Summer—Oldenburg—Red Astrachan (for jelly) —Summer Rambo. Fall—Wealthy—McIntosh—Grimes Golden—Rhode Island Greening—Jonathan—Northern Spy (best cooker of all). Winter—Rambo—Baldwin—Rome Beauty—Stayman Winesap (best winter keeper). The apple recipes may fail if good cooking apples are not available. Grimes Golden and Jonathan hold their shape after cooking so may be used where that feature is desired.

Chill dishes that are to be used to serve cold foods.

APPLE BUTTER ICE BOX CAKE

Whip ½ **pint of heavy cream.** Add ½ **cup apple butter** and mix well. Spread each **vanilla wafer** (use as many as you need for your family) with this mixture, placing 1 on top of the other until all wafers are used. (This recipe used 30.) Cover outside of roll with cream mixture. Sprinkle with ½ **cup chopped nuts.** Place in refrigerator for at least 3 hours. Cut in diagonal slices and serve.

If you like strained apple sauce the apples need not be pared before cooking.

APPLE SAUCE

Wash, pare, core apples. They may be cut into slices or eighths as the size requires. To **2 lbs. apples** add ½ **cup water** and cook slowly (watching that they do not burn) until apples are all cooked to a mush. Add from ½ to **1 cup sugar** according to the apples and cook for 3 minutes longer. If the flavor of **cinnamon** is liked it may be sprinkled over the top after the sauce has been poured into a dish. Early apples often are cored but not pared and cooked as above, but run through a sieve before sugar is added.

APPLE SAUCE ICE BOX DESSERT

Dissolve **12 marshmallows** in **1½ cups** of **heated apple sauce**, add **½ cup sugar, ½ cup cocoanut, juice of ½ lemon,** few **grains salt** and the beaten **whites of 2 eggs.** Stir this mixture and place in refrigerator to chill. (**½ teaspoonful vanilla** may be used in place of lemon juice) Serve in sherbet glasses with or without whipped **cream.**

If apples are to be broken up and kept light in color, cook rapidly.

APPLE SNOW

To **1 cup** of **strained apple sauce** add unbeaten **whites** of **2 eggs** and **sugar** to taste. Beat hard with an egg beater for 20 minutes. Pile in chilled glass dishes and serve at once.

Apricots and dried peaches make an excellent breakfast dish.

APRICOT REFRIGERATOR CAKE

Scald **1 cup evaporated milk.** Add **1 teaspoonful gelatin,** softened in **1 tablespoonful cold water.** Then chill in a freezing tray until almost frozen. Place in a well chilled bowl. Whip until the milk has reached about three times its original volume. When somewhat thick, add **1 teaspoonful lemon juice.** Strain **1 large can** of **apricots** and press through a potato ricer. Add **¼ cup sugar,** stirring occasionally until dissolved. Soak **1 tablespoonful of gelatin** in **½ cup apricot juice,** then melt over hot water. When melted add a little of the **apricot pulp.** Finally, mix with the rest of the apricot pulp. Combine the fruit and whipped evaporated milk. Pour into mold, lined around the sides and bottom with split **lady fingers.** After half filling the mold, more lady fingers may be added. Top with **whipped cream.** Garnish with **maraschino cherries.** Serves 6 to 8.

APRICOT SNOW

Soak **2 tablespoonfuls gelatine** in **½ cup cold water** for 1 hour. Dissolve it in **½ cup boiling water.** Mix with **1 pint apricot pulp** rubbed through a sieve. Place on ice and stir frequently until it begins to set; otherwise the fruit will settle. Stir in lightly **1 pint of whipped cream.** Turn into molds to harden. (It is better to use a porcelain or glass mold as tin discolors.) When firm turn out on deep platter. Pour custard sauce over top and serve. Boiled Custard Sauce: Beat **2 egg yolks** and **2 tablespoonfuls sugar** to a cream, then add **1 cup milk, scalded.** Return to fire to cook eggs. When slightly thickened remove from fire. Add ¼ **teaspoonful vanilla** and beat with wire whip to make it light and foamy. Set aside to cool, beating occasionally. Serve over apricot snow.

BISQUE TORTONI

Heat **1 cup milk,** add **1½ teaspoonfuls plain gelatin** dissolved in **¼ cup cold water,** then add **¼ cup sugar** and **1 egg well beaten.** Heat through but do not boil. Add **pinch of salt** and **1 tablespoonful vanilla.** Cool. Mix with **¼ pint heavy cream,** which has been whipped. Fill glasses in which it is to be served. When ready to serve cover with **grated macaroons** or **maraschino cherries.** Place mixture in refrigerator to set but do not put in freezing compartment.

CHOCOLATE CREAM ROLL

Beat **2 whole eggs** 3 minutes with an egg beater. Add **1 cup sugar** and beat 3 minutes longer. Next add **¼ cup hot water** and **2 squares of melted chocolate (bitter), 2 tablespoonfuls shortening, 1 cup flour,** sifted 2 or 3 times with **1½ teaspoonfuls baking powder** and a **pinch of salt.** Fold the flour in lightly. Bake in a greased pan 350° F. 15 or 20 minutes. Roll while hot in waxed paper, edges trimmed. Open and roll in **¼ pint of cream,** whipped. Reroll and slice, serving with a spoonful of whipped cream on top. This roll may be put away for a day or so until ready to use. Then add cream and serve. Chocolate sauce may also be served over the roll. It may also be iced with chocolate frosting.

CHARLOTTE RUSSE

Soak **1 tablespoonful gelatin** in **¼ cup cold water** and dissolve in **¼ cup boiling water.** Add **1 cup sugar.** When mixture is cold, add **1 pint heavy cream** stiffly beaten, **¼ lb. blanched** and chopped **almonds, 6** rolled stale **macaroons, 12 marshmallows,** cut in pieces, **2 tablespoonfuls** chopped **candied cherries** and **1 teaspoonful vanilla.** Dip square mold in cold water. Place about **14 lady fingers** around side, four on bottom (after they have been split). Turn mixture into mold and chill.

CHOCOLATE ICE BOX PIE

Make a crust of **1½ cups of graham cracker crumbs, 1/3 cup powdered sugar** and **½ cup butter.** Mix all together and pat in pie pan. Place in ice box until hard. Use **1 package of prepared chocolate filling,** following the directions on the box, but adding **1 egg yolk** while cooking. When desired thickness has been obtained, add **¼ cup cocoanut** and fold in the stiffly beaten **egg white.** Put in pie shell and return to ice box until ready to serve.

CHOCOLATE WAFERS WITH WHIPPED CREAM

Buy thin **chocolate wafers** and put them together with a generous amount of **whipped cream,** using as many as you think you will need for the number to be served. Then lay the stacked cookies on their side on a platter. Cover the whole with whipped cream (as if one were icing a cake). Set aside for 6 to 8 hours. Serve by cutting slanting of the loaf. The cross sections are striped brown and white and when lying flat make an attractive dessert complete in itself.

Custard is a combination of eggs and milk. The eggs are a thickening agent and should be beaten only very little so they will perform their duty.

You may prevent the formation of a top crust on custard and other puddings by covering them closely while hot.

CUSTARD BAKED IN CUPS

Beat 4 **eggs** slightly. Add **1/3 cup sugar** and ¼ **teaspoonful salt.** Gradually add **3 cups scalded milk,** stirring constantly. Add **1 teaspoonful vanilla** and sprinkle with **nutmeg.** Pour into custard cups, set in pan of hot water. Bake in slow oven for 30 minutes (300° F.) Do not allow water to boil as custard will curdle. If 30 minutes is not long enough, then bake until custard is firm. It may be tested by inserting a silver knife. When it comes out clean the custard is done.

(SOFT) CUSTARD — Boiled or Baked

Combine 4 **eggs slightly** beaten with ½ **cup sugar** and ⅛ **teaspoonful salt.** Pour 3 **cups scalded milk** into egg mixture, stirring constantly. Add **1 teaspoonful vanilla** or a **dash of nutmeg.** Cook in double boiler (simmering water, and do not have it touching bottom of custard pan) until mixture coats spoon.

This same custard may be baked in 325° F. oven if custard cups are set in a pan of water while baking.

FLOATING ISLAND

Bring **1 quart of milk** to scalding temperature. Beat **4 egg whites** until stiff. Add ¼ **cup sugar** and beat again. Drop egg whites by spoonfuls into scalded milk. Dip milk over tops of egg whites until cooked. (This is cooking the meringue.) Remove cooked meringue to a platter. Drain off any milk that may adhere. Beat **4 egg yolks** with ¼ **cup sugar, pinch salt** and **1 teaspoonful flavoring** (any kind, vanilla is usually preferred). Add to scalded milk and cook in double boiler until it coats a spoon or begins to show thickness. (A tablespoonful flour may be added to the egg yolk mixture if you prefer the custard thicker.) Cool, pour into a glass bowl, cover with heaping spoonfuls of the cooked meringue.

Put a small amount of sugar syrup over fresh fruit that has been cut for serving. It will keep it from turning dark.

FRUIT CUP

Cut **6 slices** of **pineapple** fine, or an equal amount of crushed pineapple. Mash **2 bananas** and add **1/8 teaspoonful salt, 2 tablespoonfuls powdered sugar, 2 tablespoonfuls lemon juice, grated rind of 1 lemon** and **1 egg white,** unbeaten. Place all in bowl and beat with rotary or electric beater until light and frothy. Place in refrigerator tray and freeze. Serve with chilled pineapple juice.

FUDGE WHIFFS

Bake your favorite **chocolate cake** in muffin tins. Scoop out a teaspoonful of inside of cake and fill with **whipped cream** and cover with top. Put **3 tablespoonfuls** of following mixture over each and serve. **Fudge Sauce:** Mix **1 cup sugar, 1 square chocolate, 1 tablespoonful cornstarch, 1/3 cup milk,** and **2 tablespoonfuls corn syrup** together and cook until the soft ball stage, then add **1 tablespoonful butter** and **1 teaspoonful vanilla.** Cover cakes. Scoop out centers and fill with ice cream. This makes another dessert.

Graham flour obtained its name from Sylvester Graham, as he was the first to make flour out of the whole grain of wheat.

GRAHAM CRACKER REFRIGERATOR CAKE

Soak **2 tablespoonfuls gelatin in 1/4 cup cold water** for 3/4 hour. Add **1 cup hot milk** (May use **1 part canned milk** and **2 parts whole milk**) in which **2 tablespoonfuls butter** have been melted. Mix until gelatin is dissolved. Cool slightly. Add **1 1/4 cups light brown sugar** (sifted), **1 teaspoonful cinnamon, 1/4 teaspoonful salt** and enough fine **graham cracker crumbs** to make a stiff batter. Fold in the stiffly beaten **whites of 2 eggs.** Put in mold that has been dipped in cold water. Top with **whipped cream,** sprinkle with fine **graham cracker crumbs** and either fine **grated cocoanut** or finely **chopped nut meats.** Place in refrigerator. Set at medium until firm. Remove from mold onto a chilled serving plate. Garnish with **maraschino cherries** or **fresh firm berries.** Return to refrigerator until ready to serve.

GRAHAM CRACKER ROLL

Roll **8 graham crackers until** very fine. Mix **½ cup chopped dates, ½ cup chopped nut meats** and **½ lb. marshmallows,** quartered, until well covered. Add **½ cup coffee cream** and mix well or until all is moist. Roll **4 extra crackers** to crumb stage, turn other mixture onto crumbs and roll until well coated and a good shape obtained. Set aside for 24 hours. Slice and serve with plain cream or whipped cream.

GRAHAM TORTE

Cream 5 beaten **egg yolks** with **2 cups sugar.** Add **27 graham crackers** which have been put through the finest knife of the food grinder, with **1½ teaspoonfuls baking powder, 1 cup** chopped **English walnuts** and **1 teaspoonful vanilla.** Fold in stiffly beaten **egg whites.** Bake in two 7-inch square pans in slow oven for 30 minutes. Put together at once with a custard made as follows: Blend **½ cup sugar** with **1 tablespoonful cornstarch.** Add to **1 cup milk** and **½ teaspoonful vanilla.** Bring to a boil, add **1 egg** slightly beaten. Cook until thick, set aside to chill. Cut in squares and serve with whipped cream. This recipe serves twelve.

HEAVENLY HASH

Beat **1 cup whipping cream** and add **1½ dozen macaroons,** chopped fine, **1 cup English walnuts,** chopped fine and **6 or 8 marshmallows** cut into quarters. Mix well, then whip **another cup cream** and add to first mixture. Let stand for 2 hours. Serves 8.

LEMON COCOANUT ICE BOX CAKE

Line a mold with waxed paper (an angel food pan or ring mold will do). Split **2 dozen lady fingers** to fit mold using them to line sides and bottom. Remember that the rounded part of the lady fingers must be put down in the mold, for this will be the top when inverted. Cream 2/3 **cup butter.** Add **1¼ cups** sifted **powdered sugar.** Gradually beat in 3 well beaten **egg yolks, 1 grated rind** of **lemon** and **1 tablespoonful lemon juice.** Fold in **1 cup toasted cocoanut** (cocoanut slightly browned in broiler) and **½ pint whipped cream.** Lastly, add 3 well beaten **egg whites.** Turn half of this mixture into the prepared mold, cover with another layer of lady fingers, add the remaining filling and top with more lady fingers. Place in ice box for 24 hours. Unmold, lift off paper and serve garnished with **whipped cream** and **maraschino cherries.**

LEMON DESSERT

Cream **2 tablespoonfuls butter** with **1 cup sugar.** Add **2 egg yolks, 2 tablespoonfuls flour** and **grated rind** and **juice** of **1 lemon.** Beat well. Beat **2 egg whites** stiff and add **1 cup sweet milk.** Blend thoroughly. Add to yellow mixture. Fold well together. Bake in individual glass dishes and serve with a topping of **whipped cream.**

LEMON ICE BOX CAKE

Mix **¾ cup sugar** and **1 tablespoonful flour.** Add to 3 beaten **egg yolks.** Add **1 cup milk** and **1 tablespoonful butter.** Cook over hot fire until thick and smooth. Add **¼ cup lemon juice** and **grated lemon rind.** Remove from fire, cool slightly and add 3 stiffly beaten **egg whites.** Cover bottom and sides of a deep cake pan with waxed paper, then with **24 lady fingers** (in halves). Turn in lemon mixture. Cover with lady fingers and set in ice box for 12 hours or over night. Remove to serving dish. Fill center and cover sides with **1 cup whipped cream.**

LEMON RICE MERINGUE

Cook **¾ cup rice** in **1 quart of milk** in top of double boiler, until tender. While hot, add beaten **yolks** of 3 eggs, **juice** of **2 lemons, grated rind** of **1 lemon, 1 cup sugar, ½ teaspoonful salt,** and **1 tablespoonful butter** which have been mixed together in a small bowl. Mix well, turn into buttered casserole, bake 20 minutes at 350° F. Top with meringue made from **egg whites,** beaten stiff, Add 3 **teaspoonfuls powdered sugar gradually.** Lastly, add **½ teaspoonful vanilla** and a **pinch salt.** Brown slowly in oven 325° F. for 10 or 15 minutes.

STORING LEMONS OR ORANGES

Take perfectly fresh fruit and wrap each one in soft paper. Put in glass jars and cover each lemon with white sand that has been dried thoroughly. Have the top covered with a thick layer of sand. Close jar tightly and keep in a cool dry place. Oranges can be kept the same way.

When grating orange or lemon rind wash fruit, then rub it against the surface of grater, taking care that only the outermost colored portion is removed.

Bavarian cream is the name of a dessert made with gelatin, fruit and whipped cream. It is not frozen, just chilled. One recipe should suffice as the fruit may be changed.

MAPLE NUT BAVARIAN CREAM

Heat **1 cup maple syrup** to boiling. Pour very slowly onto **1 whole egg,** beaten with **2 egg yolks.** Cook over hot water until mixture coats the spoon. Add **1½ tablespoonfuls gelatin** which has been softened in **¼ cup cold water.** Cool until **congealing starts.** Beat **1 cup cream** until firm and stiff. Beat **2 egg whites** until stiff. Add **pinch salt** and **½ teaspoonful vanilla.** Fold egg whites, **½ cup nuts** and maple mixture into cream. Turn into molds rinsed with cold water, and chill until firm. If desired, molds may be lined with vanilla wafers before pouring in the mixture, making an ice box cake type of dessert.

MAPLE CREAM PUDDING

Put in double boiler **1 cup maple syrup.** When hot, add **yolks of 3 eggs,** beaten. Add **2 tablespoonfuls gelatin** which has been soaked in **1 cup cold water.** When well dissolved, let cool until partly jellied. Then add **3 egg whites** beaten and **½ pint cream,** whipped until stiff. Put into mold. Keep on ice until ready to serve.

MAPLE DELIGHT

Separate the **yolks** from the whites of **three eggs.** Place yolks in mixing bowl and beat until foamy. Heat **1 cup** of **maple syrup,** being careful not to let it boil. Pour on beaten yolks. Beat whites of eggs until dry and fold into first mixture. Then add **½ pint of table cream,** beaten. Fold all together. Place in refrigerator tray or freezer and freeze. If the latter is used, use equal parts of salt and ice. Crank very little. This requires a rather low freezing temperature due to the large amount of sugar present.

Junket, a commercial form of rennet removed from the lining of the stomach of a calf. It acts as a coagulating agent, thus solidifying milk without souring it.

MAPLE JUNKET

Make a **package** of rennet powder **(junket)** with **vanilla** flavor, according to directions on the box. Or if you have rennet tablets then dissolve one in small quantity of water. Heat **1 pint of milk** to lukewarm temperature, 110° F. If it reaches beyond that before you notice, then allow to cool to proper temperature before adding **2 tablespoonfuls sugar, 1 teaspoonful vanilla** and the prepared rennet tablet. Work quickly. Pour immediately into molds or sherbet glasses as this forms the same kind of curd that is formed in making cottage cheese. Be careful not to break this curd before serving as the whey will quickly appear, thus making the dessert watery. When ready to serve place 2 tablespoonfuls of maple syrup over each serving.

MERINGUE (Hard)

Add ¼ **teaspoonful cream of tartar** and ¼ **teaspoonful salt** to **6 egg whites.** Beat with rotary or electric beater until eggs stand in peaks. Gradually add **2 cups sugar,** beating all the time. Beat until they stand alone, add **1 tablespoonful vinegar** and beat again. Butter muffin tins generously. Make sure that the butter is soft enough to stay on sides of muffin pans. Fill with mixture within ½ inch of top. Put in slow oven not over 275° F. Let stay for 1 hour or more. Allow to cool before attempting to remove meringues from pans. Then do so by a rotary motion so as to loosen bottoms. Remove tops and fill with **ice cream.** Replace tops and cover with **fresh fruit.**

The orange is the most popular of citrus fruits. It may be obtained the whole year. It is high in vitamin content, equally good for young or old.

Molds for gelatin mixtures oiled with salad oil will give up their contents without dipping in hot water.

MARMALADE PUDDING

Melt ½ **cup butter** in **one small cup milk,** then add **4 tablespoonfuls flour** and boil a few minutes, stirring all the time. Remove from fire. Add ½ **cup sugar** and **yolks** of **three eggs.** Beat **egg whites** stiff and add at the very last. Put **3 tablespoonfuls orange marmalade** in the bottom of the bowl in which the pudding is to be steamed. Cover with the batter mixture and steam for 1 hour. Turn out and serve at once with whipped cream.

ORANGE CHARLOTTE

Soak **1 1/3 tablespoonfuls plain gelatin** in **2 tablespoonfuls cold water,** then dissolve in ¼ **cup boiling water.** Add ¾ **cup sugar, 3 tablespoonfuls lemon juice** and **1½ cups orange juice** and **pulp.** Chill in refrigerator. When quite thick and frothy, but not fully congealed, fold in the **whites** of **3 eggs** beaten stiff. Fold in **1 pint whipped cream.** Pile lightly by spoonfuls into compotes (small glasses). Place in refrigerator about 10 minutes or just long enough to cool charlotte but not make it hard. When ready to serve, garnish with **maraschino cherries,** or if they are in season, whole **strawberries** rolled in sugar.

ORANGE CREAM

Put **1 pint milk** and **1/3 cup sugar** in top part of double boiler. Heat well. Soak **1 tablespoonful gelatin** in ½ **cup orange juice** for 5 minutes. Separate **3 eggs.** Beat **yolks** with **1/3 cup sugar** until smooth. Add hot milk and cook until thick, stirring constantly. Add softened gelatin, **grated rind** of **1 orange** and ¼ **tablespoonful salt.** Stir until gelatin is dissolved. Cool. When mixture begins to thicken, fold in **3 egg whites** stiffly beaten and **1 cup heavy cream,** whipped. Place in freezing tray of automatic refrigerator. Serve with whipped cream or sweetened orange juice.

ORANGE ICE BOX CAKE

Mix ½ **cup sugar, 1 tablespoonful cornstarch** and **3 slightly beaten egg yolks.** Add **1 tablespoonful butter** and **1 cup orange juice.** Cook in double boiler until it thickens. Remove from fire and add at once the **grated rind of one orange** and **3 stiffly beaten egg whites.** Line sides and bottom of mold with **separated lady fingers.** Pour cooked custard in pan, put layer of lady fingers, then more of the custard. Put in refrigerator over night. Before serving, top with **whipped cream.** This recipe requires 18 lady fingers and serves eight.

There are two types of peaches, free stones and clings. It is only a matter of preference which to use.

PEACH KISSES

Peel, halve and remove the pits from **10 large peaches.** Make a sirup of **1 pint sugar** to **½ pint water.** Cook until it strings from the spoon. Dip peaches—on a wire spoon—into this, then set them away to chill. Whip the **whites** of **three eggs** stiff with **5 tablespoonfuls powdered sugar.** Have ready a sauce pan of boiling water and into this drop the meringue by spoonfuls, cooking for 10 minutes and removing carefully with a flat skimmer. Place them in the centers of the peach halves. Sprinkle with chopped **almonds** and set on ice until serving time.

Keep pieces of charcoal in refrigerator to absorb odors.

Pineapple is a peculiar tropical fruit which grows flat on the ground. It has a very tough covering which must be removed before it can be used.

TO PREPARE PINEAPPLE

Slice off top and bottom, then stand upright and slice off sides. Core by quartering apple and cutting out core, or use a regular core remover. Use an apple corer to remove eyes.

PINEAPPLE ICE BOX CAKE

Soak **2 tablespoonfuls gelatin** in **½ cup cold water** about 5 minutes. Dissolve over hot water and add **1 No. 2 can crushed pineapple, ½ cup sugar, ¼ teaspoonful salt** and **1 tablespoonful lemon juice.** Stir until all gelatin and sugar are dissolved. When it begins to thicken, beat and fold in **1½ cups** of **whipped cream.** Line sides and bottom of large square or round mold with **lady fingers.** Cover with pineapple cream mixture, then alternate cakes and cream until mold is full. Place in ice box and let stand three hours. Unmold on a large cake plate and garnish with whipped cream. (When strawberries are in season they add to the garnish.)

PINEAPPLE BAVARIAN CREAM

Soak **1 tablespoonful gelatin** in **¼ cup cold water.** Dissolve by heating over boiling water. Add **1 cup grated pineapple, juice of ½ lemon, pinch salt** and **½ cup sugar.** Set in cold place and stir until it begins to thicken. Whip **1 cup heavy cream** and beat evenly into gelatin mixture, part at a time. When chilled enough to hold its shape, turn into mold.

PINEAPPLE PATTIES

Drain syrup from **2 cups** of **crushed pineapple,** add **½ cup sugar** and **1 tablespoonful butter.** Cook all slowly from 8 to 10 minutes or until a rich amber in color. In gem pans, have small pastry shells that have been baked but not allowed to brown. Pour in the above mixture and bake about 10 minutes. Serve cold with whipped cream.

There are on the market three kinds of raspberries, red, purple and black. The red is very soft, the black rather firm. The purple a cross between the two.

Berries will keep better if spread out on a platter before being put in ice box.

RASPBERRY SPONGE DESSERT

Heap **raspberries** on top of squares of **sponge cake. Cover top** with **whipped cream.** Garnish with a few berries.

RICE FLUFF WITH GRAPE SAUCE

Cook **½ cup rice** in **2 cups milk** with **1 tablespoonful butter** and **¾ cup sugar** in double boiler, then cool. Add **2 tablespoonfuls gelatin** dissolved in **¼ cup hot water.** Stir into rice and when cold add **2 cups whipped cream.** Put into molds. Sauce: Blend **½ cup water** with **2 tablespoonfuls cornstarch,** add **½ pint grape juice** and cook until it thickens.

Strawberries are the most delicious of the berries and are the first to appear. Their brilliant red color should be retained when canned or preserved.

STRAWBERRY SHORTCAKE (Biscuit Dough)

Wash and pick over **1 quart strawberries,** add **1 cup sugar** and set aside. Sift and measure **2 cups flour.** Add **½ teaspoonful salt, 1 tablespoonful sugar** and **4 teaspoonfuls baking powder.** Work **4 tablespoonfuls shortening** into flour. When well mixed add **¾ cup milk** to which **1 beaten egg** has been added. Stir lightly, put out on pastry board. Cut rounds 3 inches in diameter. Place one on baking sheet, brush with melted butter and cover with a second round. Bake in a hot oven, 472° F. When done split open, cover bottom round with berries, put top back on and cover with berries. Serve with cream.

STRAWBERRY SHORTCAKE (Cake Batter)

Cake part: Whip **2 eggs** with Dover egg beater or electric beater until thick. Add **1 cup sugar** and continue beating. Heat **½ cup milk** with **1 tablespoonful butter** until butter melts. Add to egg and sugar mixture, beating constantly. Sift **1 teaspoonful baking powder** with **1 cup flour** and add to other mixture, beating all the time. Pour into greased and floured pan. Bake in 350° F. oven for 30 minutes. Filling: Clean **1 qt. strawberries,** save a few whole berries for top garnish, slice the rest. Add **1 cup sugar** to sliced berries and set aside for at least 1 hour. Cut cake in squares and split for individual servings. When ready to serve cover bottom cake with berries and juice and **1 tablespoonful whipped cream.** Put on top piece of cake. Add more berries and juice. Top with whipped cream and a whole berry.

STRAWBERRY (ICE BOX) SHORTCAKE

Wash, clean and slice **1 qt. strawberries.** Sweeten with **1½ cups of powdered sugar.** Soak **1½ tablespoonfuls gelatin** in **8 tablespoonfuls cold water.** Melt over hot water. Stir into strawberry mixture. Line freezing tray with **sponge cake.** When gelatin mixture is thickened, but not stiff, spread over cake. Add a layer of mousse and freeze. Mousse: To **1 tablespoonful lemon gelatin** add **4 tablespoonfuls boiling water.** Cool slightly. **Whip 1 cup cream.** Add **2 tablespoonfuls powdered sugar, ½ teaspoonful vanilla** and dissolved gelatin. Fold in **white of 1 egg,** beaten stiff. Pour over top of strawberries. Set in freezing unit until frozen.

STRAWBERRY ICE BOX CAKE (Fresh Fruit)

Soak **1 tablespoonful gelatin** in ¼ **cup cold water.** Dissolve over hot water. Strain into **1 cup strawberry juice** and **pulp** with **1 tablespoonful lemon juice** added. Add ½ **cup sugar.** When dissolved set in a pan of cold water, stirring often. When chilled add **1½ cups whipped cream.** Line a deep pan or cake tin with waxed paper and fill with alternate layers of **split lady fingers** or **sponge cake** and the gelatin mixture. Set in refrigerator several hours or over night. When ready to use, invert and remove paper. Spread top and sides with **sweetened** whipped cream to which **crushed strawberries** have been added.

Tapioca is made from starch of the root of the Cassava plant. There are two kinds on the market, the pearl, which is small round balls and requires soaking before using, and the granular, which does not require soaking.

APPLE TAPIOCA PUDDING

Wash ½ **cup pearl tapioca.** Put in double boiler with **1 pint boiling water** in which ½ **teaspoonful salt** is added. **Stir often and** cook until transparent. Pare and core **six apples.** Place halves in baking dish and bake until apples are soft but not broken. Serve hot or cold with **cream** and **sugar** or **lemon sauce.** Lemon Sauce: Boil **1 pint of water** and **1 cup** of **sugar** together for 3 minutes. Mix **2 teaspoonfuls of cornstarch** with enough **cold water** to pour easily. Add to boiling syrup, stirring constantly. Cook 5 minutes. Just before serving add **1 tablespoonful butter** and **grated rind** and **juice of one lemon.** Stir until butter is melted, then **serve at once. One teaspoonful vanilla** may be used instead of lemon and the sauce is just as satisfactory.

CHERRY TAPIOCA DEEP-DISH

Grease baking dish, then add ½ **cup quick tapioca, 1 cup firmly packed brown sugar, 1 teaspoonful salt,** ¼ **teaspoonful nutmeg,** ½ **teaspoonful cinnamon, 2 cups canned sour cherries,** drained, 3 **cups cherry juice** and **water, 1 tablespoonful lemon juice,** and **2 tablespoonfuls melted butter.** Bake in a moderate oven, 375° F., 30 minutes or until done, stirring well every 10 minutes and again when removing from the oven. Serves eight.

DATE AND NUT TAPIOCA

Soak ¾ **cup pearl tapioca** in **4 cups cold water** over night. Cook with ½ **teaspoonful salt** until each pearl is clear. Add **1 cup brown sugar, 1 cup English walnuts** (chopped), ¾ **cup chopped dates.** Cook and stir about 10 minutes. Serve with **whipped cream.**

MAPLE WALNUT TAPIOCA

Heat 1 **pint** of **milk** until hot. Add **1 cup maple sirup** and **1/3 cup quick cooking tapioca, 1 teaspoonful salt.** Cook in top of double boiler for 15 minutes or until tapioca is clear, stirring frequently. Add **1 well beaten egg yolk** and stir for 1 minute. Add **2/3 cup nut meats** and **1 stiffly beaten egg white.** Garnish with **whole nut meats** and serve with **cream.** Serves six.

OLD-FASHIONED CREAM TAPIOCA

Soak 2/3 **cup pearl tapioca** over night in cold water. Bring **1 quart milk** to boiling point, add drained tapioca and stir until clear. Beat 2 **egg yolks,** add **1 cup sugar** and stir into milk and tapioca. Cook until thick. Add **1 teaspoonful vanilla** and **pinch of salt.** Pour over 2 **beaten egg whites.** Stir until egg whites are well blended into mixture. Serve either hot or cold.

PEPPERMINT TAPIOCA CREAM

Mix 1 **egg yolk** with **small amount of milk** in top of double boiler, add the remaining amount of 4 **cups milk,** ½ **cup quick tapioca,** ⅛ **teaspoonful salt** and **2/3 cup crushed peppermint candy** (candy sticks with red strips preferred) Cook over boiling water 10 to 12 minutes. Beat **egg white.** Fold hot tapioca pudding into beaten egg white. Pour into serving dishes and chill before serving.

PINEAPPLE TAPIOCA

Cook in double boiler for 15 minutes 4 **heaping tablespoonfuls pearl tapioca,** ¼ **cup granulated sugar, 1 quart hot water** and a **pinch salt.** Remove from fire and stir in **1 No. 2 can grated pineapple.** Sweeten to taste. Serve with **milk** and **sugar** or slightly sweetened **whipped cream.** Any canned or fresh fruit may be used.

QUICK CREAM TAPIOCA

Put **2 cups milk** in top of double boiler with ½ **teaspoonful salt** and **4 tablespoonfuls quick tapioca.** Cook for 20 minutes. **Beat 1 egg yolk** with ½ **cup sugar** and **1 teaspoonful vanilla** and add to tapioca. Beat **egg white** stiff, fold into first mixture. Chill before serving.

RHUBARB TAPIOCA

Put **1 quart rhubarb,** cut in small pieces, in **2 cups hot water** with ½ **cup quick cooking tapioca** in the upper part of double boiler. Cook over steam for 15 minutes, stirring frequently. Add **1½ cups sugar** and ½ **teaspoonful salt.** Cook 5 minutes longer or until tapioca is clear and rhubarb is tender. Chill thoroughly before serving. Serve with **top milk** or **cream.** This is an attractive pink dessert and requires less rhubarb than a pie.

(ROSE) APPLE TAPIOCA

Soak for 1 hour ½ **cup pearl tapioca** and **3 cups cold water.** Add ¾ **cup sugar,** then cook in double boiler till clear. Add **2 tablespoonfuls butter.** Pare and core **6 apples.** Put them in the following sirup made of ¾ **cup sugar, 1 cup water** and **1 teaspoonful rose coloring.** Turn apples in sirup until all sirup is absorbed if possible. Put tapioca mixture in casserole and place apples in it. Add **1 tablespoonful lemon juice** to any remaining sirup and pour over apples and tapioca. Bake in moderate oven until apples are tender. Serve cold with whipped cream.

Desserts -- Frozen

ANGEL FOOD (FROZEN)

Whip 1 **pint** of **cream** until stiff. Beat 4 **egg whites** stiff. Cook **1 cup sugar** in 1/3 **cup water** until it threads. Flavor with **1 teaspoonful vanilla** and a **pinch salt.** Slowly blend into egg whites, then combine with cream and place in freezer. Pack as for ice cream. Do not stir. Let it stand for 5 or 6 hours and it is ready to use. Quantity 2 quarts. When ready to serve pour a little hot water on can and it will slip out in a round roll. Cut in slices.

CHOCOLATE MINT FREEZE

Place ¼ **cup cocoa** in top of double boiler. Add **1 cup milk** gradually, stirring to make a smooth paste. Add **18 marshmallows** and stir until melted. Add dash of **salt.** Cool and chill. Just before freezing, add **1 teaspoonful peppermint extract** and **½ pint of cream** whipped. Turn into tray of automatic refrigerator and freeze.

CINNAMON APPLE SAUCE (FROZEN)

Add **2 tablespoonfuls red cinnamon candies** to **1½ cups** of hot sweetened **apple sauce** with **⅛ teaspoonful salt.** Stir until dissolved. Chill thoroughly in refrigerator. Fold in **1 cup heavy cream** whipped and **1 egg white** beaten stiff. Pour mixture into freezing unit of refrigerator, and freeze about 1 hour.

FROZEN FIG TAPIOCA

Add **3½ tablespoonfuls quick tapioca, ⅛ teaspoonful salt,** add **1 tablespoonful butter** to **2 cups water** and cook in double boiler for 20 minutes, or until smooth and clear. Stir frequently. Cook **½ pound finely chopped figs** with **1 scant cup sugar** and **2 cups water** for 25 minutes or until well thickened. Add to tapioca mixture. Fold in **1 cup whipped cream, 1 teaspoonful vanilla** and **1 tablespoonful lemon juice.** Pour into refrigerator tray and freeze.

Ices are frozen fruit juices with sugar.

GINGER ALE ICE

Dissolve **1/3 cup sugar** in **1/3 cup hot water.** Add **½ cup orange juice, ¾ cup pineapple sirup, 1 cup crushed pineapple,** drained, and **1 quart** of **ginger ale.** Freeze at quickest temperature. When it is solid for 1 inch from the tray, beat once vigorously with wooden spoon. When frozen, reset to holding temperature according to your refrigerator.

Ice cream is frozen cream with flavor and sugar added. It may or may not have a binder. It may be made in either a freezer or an electric ice box.

CHOCOLATE ICE CREAM

Melt **1½ squares of chocolate** and add **2 cups of scalded milk** slowly. Mix **1 tablespoonful cornstarch** with **2/3 cup sugar** and **¼ teaspoonful salt.** Add to chocolate mixture. Cook 10 minutes, stirring until thickened. Cool, add **1½ teaspoonfuls vanilla, freeze to** a mush. Fold in **½ pint whipped cream** and finish freezing.

FRENCH ICE CREAM

Make a steamed custard (double boiler) of **2 cups scalded milk, 1 cup sugar, 3 eggs** and **½ teaspoonful salt.** Cool, add **1 quart coffee cream** and **2 tablespoonfuls vanilla.** Follow directions under Philadelphia ice cream for freezing.

Maple is the flavor obtained from the sap of the maple sugar tree, which is converted into either syrup or sugar.

MAPLE ICE CREAM

Scald **2 cups milk** in top of double boiler. Combine **2 tablespoonfuls cornstarch, ¼ cup sugar** and add to scalded milk. Cook 10 minutes. Add hot mixture to 2 slightly beaten **egg yolks.** Return to double boiler and cook until thick (about 5 minutes). Cool, then add **¼ cup maple syrup** and fold in **½ pint heavy cream** which has been whipped until stiff. Turn into refrigerator trays and freeze. Nuts may be added before freezing if desired.

STORING MAPLE SYRUP

As soon as purchased from producer, pour into sterile jars until full to the top; put on sterile lids. DO NOT HEAT.

MINT ICE CREAM WITH CHOCOLATE SAUCE

Heat **1½ cups milk** slowly. Add **15 marshmallows,** cubed. Stir until smooth. Cool, add **3 drops peppermint** and a few **drops** of **green coloring.** Add ½ **pint** of **heavy cream** whipped. Freeze in electric refrigerator. Do not stir. Chocolate Sauce: Thin **1 small can** of **commercial chocolate syrup** with **cream.** Serve by placing mint ice cream in sherbet glasses and covering with chocolate sauce.

Marshmallows that have become hard may be softened by placing in bread box for several days, or melted and used in marlows.

ORANGE VELVET ICE CREAM

Dissolve **¾ cup sugar** in **2 cups orange juice.** Add **½ pint whipped cream** and fold in until mixed well with juice. Place in electric refrigerator with dial on high. After it is frozen to a mush, stir once, then smooth out and freeze. Time 1 to 2 hours, according to your refrigerator. A little yellow cake coloring can be used if desired. Another ¼ cup of whipped cream can be added to increase amount of servings.

PHILADELPHIA ICE CREAM

Scald can and dasher of freezer. Adjust and pack with ice (4 parts) mixed with salt (1 part) When inside of can is frosted, fill 2/3 full of coffee cream, using the proportions of **1 quart coffee cream** to **¾ cup sugar, 1½ tablespoonfuls vanilla** and a **pinch salt.** Turn crank slowly at first, then more rapidly. Stop turning when mixture is at its greatest swell. Remove dasher and pack down contents. Fit cork in top of can. Repack freezer with fresh ice and salt mixture. Cover with heavy canvas and let stand to ripen.

Ice cream should not be allowed to freeze until it is too hard before stirring, to obtain smoothest texture. If it gets too hard, allow it to stand at room temperature until soft enough to stir.

PLAIN ICE CREAM

Beat **2 eggs** until light and foamy, add **1 cup sugar** and beat again. Add ¼ **teaspoonful salt** and **1 teaspoonful lemon extract** and **2 teaspoonfuls vanilla extract.** Beat **1 quart coffee cream** until foamy; add **2 cups milk to egg mixture** and combine the two. Put in freezing trays and allow to freeze partially. Remove from tray and beat with electric or Dover beater until smooth. Refill trays and freeze. This makes 2 quarts of delicious ice cream with no cooking — May be frozen in a freezer too.

PUMPKIN PIE ICE CREAM

Beat **1 egg yolk**, slightly, combine with **1 cup cooked strained pumpkin, ½ cup milk, ¾ cup sugar, ½ teaspoonful vanilla, ¼ teaspoonful cinnamon, ⅛ teaspoonful cloves** and **⅛ teaspoonful salt.** Stir at intervals while preparing the **egg** white **and** cream, so that the sugar will be completely dissolved. Beat the **egg white** until stiff and dry, then add **1 tablespoonful sugar** to make meringue. Chill cream **(1 cup coffee cream)** until nearly frozen. Beat until as thick as custard. Add egg white and cream to pumpkin mixture blend, then pour into dessert tray. Freeze without stirring. **Editor's Note:** We used the above recipe freezing in a pyrex pie plate. When about half frozen it was removed from freezing unit long enough to pinch the edges so that it appeared as the crust of a pie. Garnish with **whipped cream** and serve in pie wedges the same as any ordinary pie.

VANILLA ICE CREAM

Soak **1 tablespoonful** of **plain gelatin** in **½ cup cold water** a few minutes. Scald **1½ cups milk** in double boiler. Slowly pour over **2 egg yolks** beaten with **½ cup sugar.** Add gelatin and **⅛ teaspoonful salt.** Return to double boiler and cook until thickened, stirring occasionally. Set aside until cold. Add **1 cup cream,** whipped, **2 egg whites** beaten, and **1 teaspoonul vanilla.** If made in refrigerator have it set for fastest freezing. Pour mixture into trays Let freeze about 40 minutes. Remove to bowl, beat well and return to trays to finish freezing.

VELVET CREAM

Cook **1 cup brown sugar** and **¼ cup water** together until a thread spins from the spoon. Pour over **2** beaten **egg whites.** When cool add **1 teaspoonful vanilla** and **1 pint of heavy cream** beaten until stiff. Pack in freezing mixture or tray of electric refrigerator. If one is using a freezing mixture seal the mold with a strip of muslin dipped in lard (the lard hardens making a good seal). Coffee cans will act as molds while galvanized buckets will hold the ice and salt mixture, using four parts ice to one part salt. Rock salt is best to use.

Mallobets and marlows are names given to desserts made with marshmallows.

BLACK RASPBERRY MALLOBET

Melt **20 marshmallows** with **½ cup water.** Remove from heat; add **1 1/3 cups crushed black raspberries, 2 tablespoonfuls orange juice, 2 tablespoonfuls lemon juice** and **1 tablespoonful sugar.** When cold and beginning to stiffen, combine with **¼ cup egg whites** beaten stiff with **1 tablespoonful sugar.** Put in refrigerator to freeze.

ORANGE MALLOBET

Steam to the liquid stage **20 marshmallows,, ¼ cup water** and **¾ cup orange juice.** Add **1 tablespoonful lemon juice** and **1 cup more** of **orange juice.** Add **2 tablespoonfuls sugar** and set aside until slightly jellied. Add **½ cup sugar** to **¼ cup** of **egg whites** and whip stiff. Combine eggs with marshmallows and juice mixture and freeze without stirring. Requires several hours for freezing.

STRAWBERRY MARLOW

Wash, stem, and crush enough **berries** to make **1 cupful.** Mix with **1 tablespoonful sugar** and **1 tablespoonful orange juice.** Let stand 30 minutes. Steam **20 marshmallows** and **¼ cup water** together over hot water until the liquid stage is reached. Remove from heat. Add prepared berries and set aside to cool. When quite cool and slightly stiffened, carefully combine with **½ pint whipping cream** which has been whipped stiff. Pour into trays and freeze without stirring.

GRAPE MARLOW

Melt **20 marshmallows** in **1 cup grape juice.** Cool and add **½ pint cream,** whipped. Freeze in tray of electric refrigerator or in small freezer.

MAPLE SYRUP SPONGE (FROZEN)

Roll **4 ounces of vanilla** wafers to make crumbs for top and bottom of dessert. If wafers are rolled in waxed paper they can be handled easier. Make a sponge by beating **3 egg yolks** slightly with **1 tablespoonful cold water,** add to **¾ cup maple syrup** scalded in double boiler. Cook over hot water until egg thickens. Cool. Fold **3 beaten egg whites** and **½ pint cream** whipped into syrup mixture. Sprinkle half the cookie crumbs in a freezing tray, pour in mixture. Cover with remaining crumbs. Freeze several hours or overnight with the refrigerator set just a little above normal. Cut in squares and serve. This serves 6 to 8.

MOCK WHIPPED CREAM

Beat **3 egg whites** until almost dry. Add **1 cup sugar** and **1 cup finely crushed apple sauce** and **1 teaspoonful vanilla.** Beat well. Other crushed fruits may be used instead of apple sauce. Apple jelly will do equally well.

Mousse is a delightfully soft frozen dessert using a large amount of whipped cream.

Honey—sugar extracted by bees from flowers.

HONEY PINEAPPLE MOUSSE

Beat the **yolks of 4 eggs** and the **whites of 2** slightly. Heat **¾ cup honey** and pour slowly over the eggs, cooking in double boiler until thick. Cool the mixture, then add **1 cup crushed pineapple.** Beat the other **2 egg whites** until thick. Then beat in **2 tablespoonfuls sugar.** Whip **1 cup heavy cream** and fold all together. Freeze without stirring at the fastest freezing speed your refrigerator has. When frozen, reset temperature to holding point.

PEANUT BRITTLE MOUSSE

Mix **1 cup ground peanut brittle** with **1 cup whipping cream.** Place in tray of electric refrigerator until frozen.

RASPBERRY MOUSSE

Whip 2 **cups heavy cream** until solid, add gradually **1 cup powdered sugar** and fold in **2 cups** of finely mashed **raspberries** (or any kind of berries.) Add a few grains of **salt.** Turn mixture into a mold or refrigerator pan, let freeze from 3 to 5 hours, according to your method. Serve with whipped cream and a red cherry on top.

BUTTERSCOTCH PARFAIT

Combine 2/3 **cup brown sugar** with **2 tablespoonfuls butter.** Heat until melted and boil 1 minute. Add ½ **cup water,** cook until butterscotch is dissolved. Add sirup slowly to **4** beaten **egg yolks.** Cook in double boiler until light and fluffy. Chill. Add **1 pint** of **heavy cream** whipped, **pinch salt** and **2 teaspoonfuls vanilla.** Pour into freezing tray and freeze without stirring. Chopped nuts may be added when served.

GOLDEN PARFAIT

Beat **¾ cups sugar** with **8 egg yolks** until light in color. Then cook in double boiler, stirring constantly. Whip over ice until thick and cold. (Empty hot water out of bottom of double boiler and fill with ice.) Add ¼ **teaspoonful almond extract.** Whip **2 cups whipping cream** until thick but not stiff. Fold two mixtures together. Then freeze without stirring.

MAPLE PARFAIT

Cook **¾ cup maple syrup** until it spins a thread (270° F.) **Pour** syrup over **3 beaten egg whites** and beat until cold. Fold into **1 pint of whipped cream.** Place in freezing tray and freeze until solid.

PEPPERMINT MARSHMALLOW CREAM

Crush ½ **lb .stick of peppermint candy.** Add to **1 cup milk.** Mix with 12 **marshmallows.** Heat sufficiently to dissolve candy and marshmallows, but do not boil. Cool until slightly thickened. Add **pinch salt** and **1 cup heavy cream** whipped. Put into refrigerator pans and freeze. Stir twice during freezing process.

PINEAPPLE DESSERT (FROZEN)

Blend ½ **cup sugar** with 5 **tablespoonfuls flour** and ¼ **cup cold milk.** Cook in double boiler until thick. Add beaten **yolks** of **3 eggs** and cook 2 minutes longer. Remove from stove. Add 12 **marshmallows** that have been cut into pieces. Add **1 cup crushed pineapple** and allow to cool. Fold in 3 **beaten egg whites** and ½ **pint heavy cream** whipped. Place in tray and freeze in refrigerator. This recipe serves 15. This dessert is made still more delicious by topping it with the following: Make a syrup by cooking ½ **cup sugar** with ¼ **cup water** for a few minutes. To this add ½ **cup** finely cut **marshmallows** and ½ **cup crushed pineapple.** If fresh pineapple is used it should be put through a food chopper.

PUERTO RICO COCOANUT ICE

Pour boiling hot water over **1 cup** of freshly **grated cocoanut** (the moist canned will do). Add **4 sticks cinnamon, 1 cup orange juice, 1 cup lemon juice** and **1 cup sugar.** When cool remove the sticks of cinnamon, add 2 well beaten **egg whites** and freeze. It makes 1 quart of the most unusual ice.

A sherbet is a frozen dessert made with water and egg whites besides fruit juices for flavor.

AMETHYST CREAM SHERBET

Scald **1 cup light cream** and combine it with ½ **cup sugar** and 2 **tablespoonfuls of light colored honey.** When cold, add ½ **cup** juice from **canned pineapple** and ½ **cup grape juice.** Beat well. Fold in **2 beaten egg whites** and **1 cup of heavy cream,** whipped. Freeze without stirring for 2 or 3 hours. Serve in footed glasses with sprig of frosted mint, made by dipping mint sprigs in egg white and then in confectioner's sugar.

APRICOT SHERBET

Boil ¾ **cup powdered sugar** with ½ **cup water** for 2 minutes. Pour over **1 package of lemon gelatin,** cool, add **4 tablespoonfuls lemon juice** and **1 small can of apricots** that have been put through a sieve. Beat 3 **egg whites** until stiff. Whip **1 cup heavy cream** until stiff. Then mix egg whites and cream folding together lightiy. Fold in fruit mixture. Place in freezing unit. Stir every half hour for 2 hours or until frozen too hard to stir. Serves 12.

CRANBERRY SHERBET

Cook **4 cups cranberries** in **2 cups boiling water** till skins pop; press through a strainer. Add **1 teaspoonful plain gelatin** that has been soaked in **¼ cup cold water**; add **2 cups sugar**. Stir until dissolved. Cool and add **1 pint ginger-ale**. Fast freeze in refrigerator to a mushy consistency. Turn into mixing bowl and beat well. Freeze until firm in tray.

GRAPE SHERBET

Cook **¾ cup sugar** for 3 minutes with **¾ cup water**. Meantime soak **½ tablespoonful unflavored gelatin** in **3 tablespoonfuls** of **cold water**, then add this to hot sirup. Set mixture in pan of ice and beat until stiff. Next add **¾ cup grape juice, 5 tablespoonfuls lemon juice, ½ cup orange juice** and **½ cup crushed pineapple**. Let this mixture cool, then turn this in freezing unit in refrigerator. When frozen to mushy consistency remove to bowl and beat with beater. Whip **½ cup cream** and fold in. This makes an excellent sherbet.

LEMON SHERBET

To the **juice** of **2 lemons** add **2 cups sugar**. Beat in **2 egg yolks** and add slowly **1 quart of milk**. Beat **2 egg whites** stiff and add to mixture. Put in refrigerator pan and freeze. Stir twice during freezing.

ORANGE SHERBET

Boil **1½ cups sugar** and **1 cup water** together for five minutes, then cool. Add **2 cups orange juice** and **¼ cup lemon juice**. Chill thoroughly. Add **2 egg whites**, thoroughly beaten, with **2 tablespoonfuls sugar**. Freeze at fast freezing point. When frozen 1 inch from the edge of pan, beat thoroughly, right in the pan, using wooden spoon; or turn into a chilled bowl and beat with a rotary or electric beater. Return to the freezing unit and freeze as quickly as possible. When frozen, reset the control to holding point.

PINEAPPLE BUTTERMILK SHERBET

Mix **2 cups buttermilk, 2/3 cup sugar, dash salt, 1 cup crushed pineapple** and **1 teaspoonful vanilla** and freeze to a mush in refrigerator tray. Whip **1 egg white** until stiff, add **1/3 cup sugar**, beating all the time. Fold into well beaten pineapple mixture. Freeze without further stirring.

PINEAPPLE SHERBET WITH MARSHMALLOWS

Put **20 marshmallows** in **1/3 cup water** in top of double boiler. Heat until marshmallows are melted. Stir in **1 cup pineapple juice** and **2 tablespoonfuls lemon juice.** Remove from fire and cool until quite thick. Stir several times to keep the mixture well blended. Fold in **2 well beaten egg whites** which have had **2 tablespoonfuls powdered sugar** added. Whip **¾ cup cream** stiff and add to other mixture. Turn into ice tray and freeze. Serves six.

SUMMER SHERBET

Grate rind of **1 lemon** and **1 orange** and add juice of **3 lemons** and **3 oranges.** Mash **3 bananas** and add to fruit juices and rinds. Boil **3 cups sugar** and **3 cups water** 5 minutes. Allow to cool. Add to fruit mixture. Place in freezing tray of refrigerator and allow to freeze. This makes 8 generous servings.

Desserts -- Hot

Have dishes hot for hot foods.

BAKED APPLES

Select **apples** that are good bakers, those that do not go to a mush, but will stand after baking. Scrub but do not peel. Score around the middle of apple, by that, we mean cut through the skin only to keep it from bursting open. Take out core, fill with **brown sugar, butter** and **a little cinnamon** if desired. Bake in hot oven until done. Top each one with **a marshmallow** and return to oven to brown. Serve hot.

APPLE DUMPLINGS

First make a thin syrup by boiling together for 10 minutes **2 cups white sugar, 1 teaspoonful cinnamon, ¼ teaspoonful nutmeg, 2½ cups water** and **2 tablespoonfuls butter.** Set syrup aside where it will keep hot while **6 tart apples** are pared, cored and sliced. Make a rich dough with **2½ cups flour, 4 teaspoonfuls baking powder ¾ teaspoonfuls salt, ½ cup shortening** and a **scant ¾ cup milk.** Turn out on pastry board and knead lightly for ½ minute; roll ¼ inch thick, cut into 6 inch square. Put a mound of sliced apple in center of each square, add a **spoonful sugar,** a **dash of cinnamon** and a **dot of butter,** bring up the corners of pastry square and pinch together. Place them smooth side up in a large buttered pan. When all dumplings are in pan pour hot syrup over them. Cut a slit in top of each dumpling to allow steam to escape. Bake in 425° F. oven for 10 minutes then lower heat to 350° F. for 30 to 35 minutes. Serve hot with their own syrup as a sauce or with plenty of cream.

The word peel is used when the skin or rind of fruit or vegetable will come off without cutting. The word pare is used when cutting is necessary to remove the outside covering of fruit or vegetable.

APPLE SAUCE DUMPLINGS

Cut and pare **3 pounds apples.** Add **2 cups water,** cook until apples are soft. Mash. Add **1 to 2 cups sugar** and **½ teaspoonful cinnamon.** Cook until dissolved. Apple sauce should be quite thin. Add more water if necessary. Make the following dumplings. Sift **1 cup flour** with **3 tablespoonfuls sugar, 2 teaspoonfuls baking powder** and **¼ teaspoonful salt.** Cut or rub in **2 tablespoonfuls butter** or other shortening. Add **1 beaten egg** and mix with a fork. Add **⅛ to ¼ cup water** or **milk** to dry ingredients until dough will stick together. Drop by teaspoonfuls into boiling apple sauce. Cover tightly and cook slowly 10 to 12 minutes. This may be reheated the next day. Serve with cream. Makes six servings.

BAKED APPLE DUMPLINGS

Mix **4 cups flour, ½ teaspoonful salt, 1 cup shortening** as for pie dough, moisten with **½ cup cold water.** Mix well. Divide into six equal parts and roll to ¼ inch thickness. Pare and core **6 tart** medium sized **apples.** Cut into eighths, place 1 apple on each piece of pastry, drawing the edges together over the apples; press **edges** together and place in pan with pressed edges on bottom. Mix **2 cups water, 2 cups sugar, 1 teaspoonful cinnamon** and **1 tablespoonful butter,** bring to boiling point. Pour over dumplings and bake in moderate oven. May be served with or without cream.

OLD-FASHIONED APPLE DUMPLINGS

Sift together **1 quart flour, 3 teaspoonfuls baking powder, 1 teaspoonful** salt and **2 tablespoonfuls sugar.** Mix in **3 tablespoonfuls shortening.** Pour in about **¾ cup milk** to make pie dough consistency. Roll out ½ of the dough to pie crust thickness, then cut in squares large enough to hold **1 medium sized apple** pared and quartered, **1 tablespoonful sugar** and **a dash of cinnamon.** Fold dough around apples, place dumplings on greased pan. Bake at 450° F. until light brown in color, then continue to bake at 350° F. until done.

Dip for dumplings — Beat **1 egg,** add **1 quart milk, ½ cup sugar** and **½ teaspoonful nutmeg.** Mix well, put in large pitcher and pour over dumplings.

CARAMEL RICE

Cook ½ **cup rice** in salted water. When tender, **drain and rinse** with cold water. Whip 1 **pint of cream** and fold into cooled rice, adding a little more **salt** (if needed). Make a sauce of **1 cup brown sugar** and **1 pint of cream.** Stir overfire. Let boil a **minute or** two. Keep warm to serve over rice and cream.

CHERRY COBBLER

Sift **1½ cups flour, 2 teaspoonfuls baking powder, ½ teaspoonful salt** and **½ cup sugar** together. Cut in **¼ cup butter** or other shortening. Add **½ cup milk** to **1 beaten egg** and **stir** into **dry** ingredients. Pour **1 pint cherries** in baking dish. Drop **batter** over top. Bake in hot oven.

ELDERBERRY COBBLER

Arrange in casserole **1 quart elderberries, 3 apples,** pared and sliced, **4 tablespoonfuls brown sugar, 1 tablespoonful quick tapioca.** Sprinkle with **cinnamon.** Cover with a rich biscuit dough which has been rolled out to about ¼ inch thickness. Make 2 or 3 openings in the cover for steam to escape. Bake about 1 hour. Serve while warm, plain or with milk.

MAPLE CUSTARD (STEAMED)

Beat **6** whole **eggs** until yolks and whites are thoroughly mixed. Add 1 **cup heavy maple syrup, ¼ teaspoonful salt** and **3 cups milk.** Stir until well dissolved. Strain into individual cups, set on rack with **1 cup** of **water** in bottom of cooker, cover and steam for 30 minutes.

PEACHES (Baked)

Pare and halve **peaches.** Place in pyrex baking dish and fill cavity of each with **brown sugar.** Dot with **butter** and sprinkle with **cinnamon.** Put **1 tablespoonful** of **water** in pan. Place in moderate oven and bake 1 hour. Fifteen minutes before taking from oven, place ½ **marshmallow** on each half peach and let brown.

PEACH COBBLER

Beat **1 egg** until light, add ¼ **cup sugar, 3 tablespoonfuls melted butter** and **1/3 cup sweet milk.** Sift **1 cup flour** with **2 teaspoonfuls baking powder** and ½ **teaspoonful salt.** Add to egg mixture. Beat well. Butter a baking dish and half fill with 8 fresh **peaches,** pared and sliced. Mix **2/3 cup sugar** with ½ **teaspoonful nutmeg** and sprinkle over peaches. Then pour batter over peaches. Bake in 375° F. oven for 30 minutes. Serve with milk, cream or whipped cream.

BAKED RHUBARB

Mix 2 **tablespoonfuls flour, 2 cups sugar** and **pinch of salt** together. Stir in **5 cups rhubarb, 2 eggs,** slightly beaten, and **1 tablespoonful vinegar.** Let stand few minutes to draw a little juice to dissolve sugar. Stir well and bake in oven (250° F.) until tender. Stir at least twice while in oven to prevent sticking. Cool.

BAKED RHUBARB DUMPLINGS

Make a **rich dough.** Roll out small pieces of the dough. Fill with **rhubarb** that has been washed and cut in small pieces. To this add a **spoonful** of **sugar** and close dumplings by pressing dough around rhubarb. Place side by side in biscuit pan. Dust over with **dry cinnamon** and cover barely to top with mixture of **1 cup sugar, lump of butter** and as much **water** as needed. Bake in moderate oven for 30 minutes. Serve either warm or cold with **sugar** and **cream.**

Puddings

A pudding is usually a cooked dessert.

APPLE BROWN BETTY

Butter a pan and add a layer of pared sliced **apples,** cover with **sugar,** dot with **butter,** sprinkle with **cinnamon** and **bread** crumbs. Repeat until pan is ¾ full making bread crumbs last layer. Steam for ¾ hour in cooker, or bake, covered, 1 hour **in moderate oven.**

APPLE NUT PUDDING

Chop **2 cups** pared **apples** fine, mix with **½ cup seedless raisins**, **¼ cup sugar, ¼ teaspoonful cinnamon, 1 cup** chopped **nuts** and **¼ cup orange juice.** Turn into buttered baking dish, dot top with bits of **butter** and bake covered, until apples are done. Moisten with a little hot water if apples are not juicy enough. Serve hot with sauce made as follows: Cream **1/3 cup butter** with **1 cup brown sugar.** Heat in double boiler and add slowly **½ cup cream.** Stir constantly to prevent curdling.

Do not store bananas in refrigerator.

BANANA PUDDING

Sift **1 cup flour, 2 teaspoonfuls baking powder, ½ teaspoonful salt** and **¼ cup sugar** into a bowl, add **¼ cup milk** and **1 well beaten egg.** Peel and mash enough **bananas** for **1 cupful.** Mix all together. Grease a baking dish with butter, pour in mixture and bake 30 minutes in a 350° F. oven. Serve warm with **milk** and sugar or **fruit juice.**

BLUEBERRY BUCKLE

Cream **¼ cup shortening.** Add **½ cup sugar** and cream thoroughly. Add **1 egg** and mix well. Mix and sift **1 cup flour, 1½ teaspoonfuls baking powder** and a **few grains salt.** Add alternately with **1/3 cup milk** to first mixture. Pour into greased 8-inch square pan. Spread **1 pint blueberries** on cake mixture. Mix together **½ cup sugar, 1/3 cup flour, ½ teaspoonful cinnamon,** rub in **¼ cup butter** with finger tips. Sprinkle this mixture over berries. Bake in moderate oven 375° F. 45 minutes. This should serve 8 people.

Butterscotch is the name of a flavor produced by adding butter to brown sugar. It resembles the flavor known as caramel which is made by heating plain cane sugar to a degree of heat where it turns to a straw color. Both of these give a pleasing taste to desserts and candy.

BUTTERSCOTCH PUDDING

Cook **1 cup brown sugar, 2 cups** boiling **water** and **1 tablespoonful butter** together until dissolved. Cream **1 tablespoonful butter** and **½ cup brown sugar.** Add **1 teaspoonful baking powder** to **1½ cups flour** and **1 teaspoonful vanilla** to **½ cup sweet milk.** Mix all together. Drop by spoonfuls into the syrup which has been put into a deep baking dish. Bake 20 minutes in moderate oven.

CARROT PUDDING

Mix together **1 cup** grated **carrots** (raw), **1 cup** grated **sweet potato** (raw) **1½ cups melted butter, ½ cup brown sugar, 1 cup raisins, 1 cup flour** and **1 teaspoonful** each of **nutmeg, cinnamon, salt** and **soda.** Grease well and flour two pound baking powder cans. Fill each can about 2/3 full and then steam 2 hours. Half cup suet may be substituted for the melted butter. Reheat before serving. Serve either with whipped cream or pudding sauce.

CHERRY PUDDING

Cream 2 **tablespoonfuls butter** with **1 cup sugar.** Add **1 cup milk** alternately with **2 cups flour** to which **2 teaspoonfuls baking powder** have been added. Beat until smooth. Pour into greased baking dish. Sauce: Mix **2 cups** stoned **cherries** with **1 cup sugar** and **1 cup hot water.** Pour over cake batter. Bake in moderate oven. The dough comes to the top and the cherries and water form a sauce.

CHOCOLATE PUDDING

Dissolve 2 **squares** of **chocolate** in **3 cups boiling water** and add **1 tablespoonful butter.** Mix **½ teaspoonful salt, ½ cup sugar** and **4 tablespoonfuls cornstarch** together. Then pour on a small amount of water and chocolate mixture, keep stirring to avoid lumps. Add remainder and stir over fire until it boils and thickens. Add **1 teaspoonful vanilla** and **½ cup** chopped **nuts.** Pour into molds and chill. Serve with sweetened whipped cream.

CHOCOLATE CUSTARD BREAD PUDDING WITH CHOCOLATE SAUCE

Beat 3 **eggs**, then add 1/3 **cup sugar, 2 tablespoonfuls cocoa, 1 teaspoonful vanilla, pinch** of **salt** and 3 **cups** of **milk.** Cut 4 or 5 **slices** of **bread** in small squares and drop in egg mixture. Place pudding pan in another pan containing a small amount of boiling water. Place in oven and bake until a silver knife inserted in pudding comes out clean. Chocolate Sauce: Mix **1 cup sugar, 2 tablespoonfuls cocoa, 1½ tablespoonfuls corn starch,** and **¼ teaspoonful** salt together. Add **1½ cups water** and **1 tablespoonful butter.** Place on fire and cook until it thickens.

CHOCOLATE RICE PUDDING

Add 1½ broken **squares** of **unsweetened chocolate, 1 cup** cooked **rice,** and more **salt** if needed, to **2¾ cups** of **milk,** and cook in double boiler about 5 minutes, until rice is heated through and chocolate melted. Combine 2½ **teaspoonfuls gelatin** with ¼ **cup milk** and let stand 5 minutes, add ½ **cup sugar.** Add gelatin mixture to hot rice and stir until gelatin is completely dissolved. Chill. When slightly thickened add **1/3 cup nut meats** and ½ **teaspoonful vanilla.** Fold in ½ **cup** of **whipped cream.** Chill until mixture thickens again. Serve in sherbet glasses with additional whipped cream. This recipe serves six.

CHRISTMAS SUET PUDDING

Mix in the following order: 2 **cups brown sugar,** 2 **cups flour, 1 lb. raisins,** 1 **package citron,** 1 **package lemon peel,** 1 **package orange peel** (and anything else in this line such as **candied cherries, pineapple.**) Add **1 teaspoonful cinnamon, 1 teaspoonful nutmeg, ½ teaspoonful salt, 6 eggs, 2 cups** finely **chopped suet, 2 teaspoonfuls soda,** 2 **teaspoonfuls baking powder** and a little **water** or **grape juice** if needed for moisture. Put in glass or tin jars, fill half full. Boil in steamer 3 hours.

Sauce

Blend **2 tablespoonfuls flour** with **1 cup sugar,** then add **2 cups boiling water,** a large lump of **butter** and cook until thick. Flavor with **vanilla** or any other desired flavor.

CORNSTARCH PUDDING

Heat **2 cups milk** in double boiler. Mix in a bowl **¾ cup brown sugar,** a little **salt** and **3 tablespoonfuls cornstarch.** Beat **1 egg** and add to sugar. Add to heated milk slowly and stir until thickened. Remove; add **1 teaspoonful vanilla.** Cool. May be served plain or with cream.

COTTAGE PUDDING

Cream **1 cup** of **sugar** with **¼ cup butter.** Add **2 egg yolks,** beaten, and **½ cup milk.** Then add **1½ cups flour,** sifted, with **2 teaspoonfuls baking powder.** Fold in the **whites** of **2 eggs,** beaten stiff. Bake in moderately hot oven until done.

DATE NUT PUDDING

Mix **1 egg yolk, 2 tablespoonfuls butter** and **1 cup brown sugar.** Add **1½ cups flour, 1 teaspoonful soda, 1½ teaspoonfuls baking powder,** sifted together. Pour **1 cup hot water** over **1 package** of **dates** which should be stoned and cut into small pieces **and added** to batter. Cut **1 cup maraschino cherries** and add to mixture. Add **1 cup** chopped **English walnuts** and lastly, the beaten **egg white.** Bake 10 to 12 minutes in moderately hot oven. Dressing for above pudding: Cook **½ cup dates,** cut in small pieces, **1 cup water** and **1 cup sugar,** add to top of pudding which has been cut **into** squares for serving. Instead of this dressing whipped cream may be put over pieces of pudding and topped with a cherry.

DELICIOUS CHOCOLATE PUDDING

Work the following together with fingers, **¾ cup sugar, 1 cup flour, 2 teaspoonfuls baking powder, 1 tablespoonful cocoa** and **2 tablespoonfuls butter,** then add **1 cup nut meats** and **½ cup milk, 1 teaspoonful vanilla** and **¼ teaspoonful salt.** Mix thoroughly. Put in a ten or twelve inch square pan. Now mix the following: **1 cup brown sugar, 1 cup white sugar, 3 tablespoonfuls cocoa** and **¼ teaspoonful salt.** Spread over top of cake in pan. Over this pour **1¾ cups boiling water.** Bake in moderate oven ¾ hour. Serve upside down with whipped cream.

DUTCH PEACH CAKE

Sift together **2 cups flour,** ½ **teaspoonful salt** and 3 **teaspoonfuls baking powder.** Work in ¼ **cup shortening** and mix to a light dough with **1** well beaten **egg** and ¾ **cup milk.** Spread in greased shallow pan, then imbed either fresh or canned sliced **peaches in** dough having the fruit cut in rather thick slices. Place close together. Sprinkle with **sugar, cinnamon,** and **nutmeg.** Bake 30 to 35 minutes in a moderate oven, 350°-375° F. Makes a 10-inch cake. Serve warm with milk or cream.

ENGLISH PLUM PUDDING

Mix **1 lb. sugar, 1 lb. eggs, 1 lb. butter, 1 lb. flour, 1 lb. raisins, 1 lb. currants, ¼ lb. orange peel, ¼ lb. lemon peel, ½ lb. citron** and **1 tablespoonful baking powder,** well together. Then add enough **sweet milk** to make a stiff batter. Steam 5 hours. Makes 2 large puddings. When ready to serve, pour brandy over **pudding and** light. Serve hard sauce in separate dish.

(REAL) ENGLISH PLUM PUDDING

Mix **1 cup flour, 1½ lbs. bread crumbs, 1½ lbs. beef kidney suet** (ground fine), **1 teaspoonful salt, 1 lb. raisins, 1 lb. sultanas, 1 lb. currants** (well washed and dried), **4 teaspoonfuls** ground **allspice, ½ lb. lemon, orange** and **citron** mixed and chopped fine, **½ lb. blanched almonds,** chopped fine and **2½ cups sugar.** Be sure to mix these ingredients well with the hands. Add **10** well beaten **eggs** and ½ **pint** to a **pint** of **milk.** Stir well again. Put this mixture in bowls that have been greased with butter, tie over tightly with a cloth and then boil 10 hours. This recipe will make 4 puddings.

Directions for Boiling: A wash boiler is the best to boil these in as they may all be boiled together. Be sure water is boiling very fast when the puddings are put in, also see that the puddings are kept well covered with boiling water during the time they are cooking. These will keep two years if necessary. When using one boil again for 3 hours. These should be served with a rich hard sauce. Brandy may be used as the flavor.

Since elderberries grow by the road side they are almost always free for the picking. The blossoms are especially good for wine.

FIG PUDDING (Steamed)

Take **1 lb. figs** soaked in warm water, chopped fine, **1 cup suet** ground, **2 cups bread crumbs, 1 cup brown sugar, 3 tablespoonfuls sweet milk, 2 eggs, salt, 4 teaspoonfuls baking powder** and **flour** enough to make batter as stiff as fruit cake. Steam 2 or 3 hours according to the size of molds used. Dressing for Pudding: Cook **6 egg yolks, 4 tablespoonfuls butter** and ½ **cup sugar** until thick. Add 6 beaten **egg whites.**

GRAHAM APPLE SAUCE PUDDING

Mix either freshly made or canned **apple sauce** with **sugar** to taste. Add little **cinnamon,** then put layer of **graham cracker crumbs** in pudding pan, next layer of apple sauce, then another layer cracker crumbs and apple sauce until apple sauce is used. Whip **1 pint heavy cream,** add **powdered sugar** and **vanilla** to suit your taste. Spread on top graham crackers and apple sauce. It is ready to serve. This is ideal when you are in a hurry or unexpected company arrives, or a small amount of apple sauce is left from the previous meal.

GRAHAM PUDDING (Steamed)

Mix **1 cup molasses** with **1 cup milk.** Add ¼ **teaspoonful cinnamon,** ½ **teaspoonful salt** and ½ **teaspoonful soda** to **2 cups graham flour.** Combine the 2 mixtures, then add **1 cup seedless raisins.** Put in coffee cans and steam 3 hours. If smaller cans are used, such as baking powder cans then 2 hours is all the time required. Serve with the following sauce: Mix **1 cup sugar** with ½ **cup butter,** and 2 beaten **eggs** in double boiler. Cook until it thickens. Cool. Add ½ **pint cream,** whipped.

HUCKLEBERRY PUDDING

Remove crusts from **four slices of white bread** and cut in pieces one inch wide and 2 inches long. **Butter** each piece of bread. Wash and drain **2 cups huckleberries;** crush with **1 cup sugar** and **1 cup boiling water.** Heat to boiling point. Pour enough hot berry mixture into deep glass bowl to cover bottom. Arrange 1/3 of bread in layer and add another layer of the berry mixture. Add another bread layer and another berry layer, being sure to save enough of the berry mixture to completely cover the last layer of bread. Allow to stand in a cold place at least 4 hours, preferably 8. Invert on a platter. Cover with custard sauce. See Sauces.

LEMON RICE PUDDING

In a greased baking dish place **1 cup boiled rice, grated rind of 1 lemon, 6 tablespoonfuls sugar, pinch salt, yolks** of **2 eggs,** well beaten, **2 cups milk,** and **1 cup seedless raisins.** Mix well and bake until brown, using a moderate oven and water bath. (Custards and puddings with a custard base, bake better, that is more even, if put into a pan of water while baking. Frost this pudding when baked with a meringue made from beating **2 egg whites** until stiff with 4 **tablespoonfuls powdered sugar** and **1 tablespoonful lemon juice.** Spread over pudding and brown.

LEMON SNOW PUDDING

Soak 1¼ **tablespoonfuls gelatin** in ¼ **cup cold water,** dissolve in **1 cup boiling water.** Add **1 cup granulated sugar,** stir until dissolved, add **juice of 1 lemon** and set away to cool. When it begins to set, beat with egg beater, add **3 egg whites,** beaten stiff, and beat until smooth. Mold and chill. Serve with yellow custard sauce. Beat 3 **egg yolks** until thick. Add **1 cup sweet milk, 1 tablespoon lemon juice** and a **pinch** of **salt.** Cook in double boiler until creamy. Serve around the white snow which has been unmolded in a suitable container. This is lovely in an old-fashioned cut glass bowl. Individual molds are very attractive.

LOUISIANA RICE PUDDING

Wash ¼ **cup rice** and cook in boiling salted water until tender. Drain and add ½ **teaspoonful salt** and 3 **cups milk.** Moisten **2 tablespoonfuls cornstarch** with ¾ **cup milk** and stir into hot rice and milk. Cook over hot water until creamy, stirring with a fork. Add **5 egg yolks** beaten with ½ **cup sugar.** Stir with fork until egg is set. Add ½ **teaspoonful vanilla** or a **few grains cinnamon.** Turn into baking dish. Cover with meringue made of **5 beaten egg whites,** adding **10 teaspoonfuls sugar** gradually. Set in pan of hot water. Bake at 300° F. until meringue is brown and firm. Chill and serve with cream.

MACAROON PUDDING

Heat **2 cups milk** in double boiler. Add ¾ **cup sugar** mixed with 3 beaten **egg yolks.** Add **1 tablespoonful gelatin** soaked in ¼ **cup** cold **water** and cook, stirring frequently for 20 minutes or until the mixture is velvety. Avoid too hot a fire. Remove from fire and **fold in 3** beaten **egg whites.** Crumble **1 dozen macaroons**—almond **flavor is best.** Put alternate layers of macaroons and custard into the desired mold. Chill. Serve with whipped cream and any desired garnish.

MAPLE NUT ICE BOX PUDDING

Roll enough **vanilla wafers** into crumbs to make **2 cups.** Spread 1 cup of the crumbs into a shallow flat pan. Dissolve **1 tablespoonful** of **gelatin** in **2 tablespoonfuls cold water** and stir into **1 cup scalded milk.** Add **1 cup maple sirup** and **1 cup** chopped **nuts.** When this mixture begins to thicken stir in **2 cups** of **cream,** whipped stiff. Pour over vanilla wafers in the pan. Spread the other cup of crumbs over the mixture and let set about 2 hours in the refrigerator or over night if desired.

ORANGE PUDDING

Dissolve **1 package** of **lemon gelatin** in ½ **cup hot water.** When dissolved add **1 cup orange juice** and the **yolks** of **six eggs,** beaten lightly, with **1 cup sugar.** When this starts to jell beat with electric or rotary beater until light, then add the beaten **whites** of **six eggs.** Place in refrigerator to set. Serve with whipped cream. This makes 8 servings.

PLUM PUDDING (PLAIN)

Mix **1 cup suet,** chopped fine, with **1 cup raisins, 1 cup sweet milk, 1 cup molasses, 3 cups flour, 1 teaspoonful soda, 1 teaspoonful cinnamon** and **½ teaspoonful salt.** When thoroughly blended put in cans and steam 3 hours.

Prunes are the dried fruit of the prune plum tree.

PRUNE PUDDING

Mix the following ingredients: **1 cup** cooked **prunes,** seeded and **chopped fine, ¾ cup** sugar, **½ cup cracker crumbs,** rolled fine, **1 cup** chopped **nuts,** preferably English walnuts, **1 teaspoonful vanilla, 1 teaspoonful baking powder, ½ cup milk** or prune juice or both combined, **1 tablespoonful** melted **butter** and a **pinch salt.** Pour into buttered pan or dish. Place pan in another pan of hot water. Bake in moderate oven 20 minutes or until mixture is firm. Serve hot with either plain or whipped cream.

QUEEN PUDDING

Mix **1 egg, 2 tablespoonfuls sugar, 2 teaspoonfuls melted butter, ½ cup New Orleans molasses, 1½ cups flour,** and **1 cup seeded raisins.** When well mixed add **1 teaspoonful soda** to **½ cup boiling water** and add to other ingredients. Steam 1 hour. Sauce for Queen's Pudding: Beat **yolks of 2 eggs** with **1 cup powdered sugar.** Add **½ pint whipped cream** and beat well. Add any flavoring desired. **Lemon** is probably the best. The pudding is a light brown and the sauce is a golden yellow, which is also pleasing to the eye.

Use left over rice in puddings.

RHUBARB PUDDING

Sift **1 cup flour, 1 teaspoonful salt** and **1 teaspoonful soda,** mix with **1 cup sour cream** to make a smooth batter. Cut **rhubarb** in small pieces **(measure 2½ cups)** but do not peel, put a layer of rhubarb in a buttered baking dish, sprinkle with **sugar,** on top of this put 3 or **4 small spoonfuls** of **batter.** Then another layer of rhubarb, sugar and batter, etc., using batter for the final layer. It requires about **1¼ cups sugar.** Bake uncovered in a moderate oven from 45 minutes to 1 hour, stirring occasionally to get the uncooked batter to the top. Add more sugar if necessary. When done this pudding is brown all through and is delicious served hot with cream.

RICE PUDDING (Old-Fashioned)

Put ½ **cup uncooked rice** in a well greased baking dish with **4 cups milk, ½ cup sugar, ¼ teaspoonful salt** and a **dash of nutmeg** or **grated rind** of ½ **lemon.** Set oven at low temperature (275° F.), stir at intervals of 15 minutes for the first hour. Then let it remain in for 2 hours. It is the stirring and slow cooking that does the trick. A few **raisins** may be added if preferred.

RICE CUSTARD PUDDING

Mix in top of double boiler **2 cups milk, ½ cup sugar** and **¼ teaspoonful salt.** Wash **¼ cup rice** and add to the hot milk. Cover and cook 1 hour. Turn rice into a deep buttered pudding dish and stir in **½ teaspoonful vanilla.** Allow to stand while making the following custard: Scald **1½ cups milk** in double boiler. Break **2 eggs** into bowl, add **3 tablespoonfuls sugar** and **⅛ teaspoonful salt,** mixing thoroughly. Pour scalded milk into mixture, stirring fast while pouring. Add ½ **teaspoonful vanilla** and pour over rice in pudding dish. Place dish in pan of cold water and bake in moderate oven until custard is done.

SAILOR'S DUFF

Mix **2 tablespoonfuls sugar** with **2 tablespoonfuls** melted **butter, ½ cup molasses** and **1 egg.** Dissolve **1 teaspoonful soda** in **½ cup hot water** and add alternately with **1½ cups flour.** Add **½ cup raisins** or **dates.** Pour all into a buttered pan and steam for 1¾ hours. Sauce: Add **½ cup powdered sugar** and **1 teaspoonful vanilla** to a beaten **egg yolk.** Fold in stiffly beaten **egg white.** Add to **½ pint of whipped cream.** The pudding should be served hot. It will serve 8 to 10 persons generously.

SCOTCH ROLY POLY PUDDING

Mix 2 **cups flour, 1½ teaspoonfuls baking powder, ½ teaspoonful salt** and sift together. Rub in 2 **tablespoonfuls butter,** then mix with enough **sweet milk** (about ¾ **cup)** to make a soft dough. Roll out ½ inch thick. Spread with a little **soft butter,** then spread on top of this any **fruit** that has been **sweetened to taste** but not too sweet. Wet edges of dough, roll up and pinch edges together firmly. Steam 1 hour. Cut in slices and serve with sauce.

Sauce For Scotch Roly Poly Pudding

Mix smooth **½ cup butter, 1 cup sugar** and **1 tablespoonful flour.** Add **1½ cups boiling water** and a little **lemon juice.** Stir while cooking. Flavor with either **vanilla, lemon, nutmeg** or the **fruit** used in pudding.

SUET PUDDING

Mix **1 cup raisins, 1 cup chopped suet, 1 cup sour milk** or **buttermilk** with **1 egg, 1 teaspoonful soda** and a **pinch of salt.** Add enough **flour** to make a batter the consistency of cake batter. Steam 1½ hours. Be sure the water is boiling.

Sauce For Pudding

Put **½ cup sugar, 1 tablespoonful flour** and a piece of **butter** the size of a walnut in a sauce pan and mix. Pour **boiling water** on it until it thickens. Add any flavor desired.

ZWEIBACH PUDDING

Mix **2 tablespoonfuls cornstarch** with **a little milk,** which is a part of **2 cups.** Add **remainder of milk, ½ cup sugar** and **4 slightly beaten egg yolks.** Cook until thick. Spread **1 box of zweibach crumbs** on bottom of pan, reserving **1 cup** for top. Add custard, then beaten **egg whites,** with **1 tablespoonful sugar.** Place remainder of crumbs on top and bake in slow oven 30 minutes. Serve cold with **whipped cream.** This same recipe may be baked in a pie plate, thus giving the appearance of a pie instead of a pudding.

Dessert -- Sauces

BRANDY SAUCE FOR PLUM PUDDING

Put 3 **egg yolks** in a stew pan. Add **1 tablespoonful powdered sugar, ½ cup milk,** a very little **grated lemon rind** and stir over the fire until mixture thickens. Do not allow it to boil. Put in **2 small wine glasses of brandy.** Let the sauce stand by the side of the fire to get quite hot. Keep stirring it and serve in a sauce boat or pour over pudding.

BUTTERSCOTCH SAUCE

Mix **1 cup brown sugar, ¼ cup water, 2 teaspoonfuls lemon juice** and **2 tablespoonfuls butter.** Heat slowly until sugar melts, then boil gently to very soft ball stage (232° F.) It thickens if allowed to cool. Keep warm until used, over hot water. This congeals on ice cream. If desired thinner add ½ cup water after sauce has reached 232° F. and cook 1 minute longer.

CARAMEL SAUCE

Melt **1 cup sugar** until it becomes a clear, amber syrup (constant watching is necessary). Add **1 cup boiling water** and simmer 30 minutes. Just before removing add **½ cup marshmallow cream** and beat thoroughly. **Chopped walnuts** added to this sauce, when cold, give a delicious flavor.

CHOCOLATE SUNDAE SAUCE

Add 2½ **squares** of **unsweetened chocolate** to **½ cup water.** Place over low flame. Bring to boil and cook four minutes, stirring constantly. Add **¾ cup sugar** and dash of **salt,** and boil 4 minutes longer, stirring constantly. Serve hot or cold on ice cream, pudding or cake. This recipe makes 1 cup of sauce.

CUSTARD SAUCE

Scald **1 cup milk** in double boiler. Pour over **1 egg yolk, 2 tablespoonfuls sugar, 1½ teaspoonfuls cornstarch** and **⅛ teaspoonful salt** that have been beaten together. Return to double boiler and cook until thickened. Add **1 teaspoonful vanilla.** Allow to cool.

FOAMY ORANGE SAUCE

Beat whites of 2 eggs until stiff and dry. Add gradually ½ cup sugar and ½ cup orange juice, beating constantly. Just before serving, mix in 1 tablespoonful of grated orange rind and pour over dessert to be served.

HARD SAUCE

Beat ½ cup butter until creamy. Slowly stir in 1 cup of powdered sugar. Beat to a cream. Pile on a plate and grate over a little nutmeg. Keep cool. Wine, brandy or flavoring may be added.

HOT CHOCOLATE SAUCE

Melt 3 squares of chocolate in double boiler. Add ½ cup milk and stir well. Mix 1 cup sugar and 2 tablespoonfuls flour and blend with ¼ cup milk. Add to first mixture and cook, stirring constantly until it thickens. Add 1 teaspoonful vanilla. This sauce keeps well and can be reheated.

LEMON SAUCE (No. 1)

Mix ½ cup sugar, 1 tablespoonful cornstarch and a pinch salt, moisten with cold water. Add slowly to 1 cup boiling water, stirring constantly. Boil 5 minutes, then add 2 tablespoonfuls butter and 1½ teaspoonfuls lemon extract.

LEMON SAUCE (No. 2)

Mix 1 cup sugar, 2 eggs, 4 tablespoonfuls flour together. Add juice and rind of 1 lemon, 2 cups boiling water and cook in double boiler until thick. When cold add ½ pint whipped cream. Serve on either angel food or sponge cake.

MAPLE SAUCE

Combine 1 cup maple syrup and ½ cup marshmallow cream. Beat thoroughly, then allow to simmer for 5 minutes. When cool add 2 tablespoonfuls of marshmallow cream and serve.

STRAWBERRY SAUCE

Pineapple, apricots, peaches, cherries or **raspberries** may be used in this same recipe. Combine **¾ cup sugar** with **½ cup water.** Boil 10 minutes. Allow syrup to cool thoroughly, then add **1½ cups strawberries crushed slightly.**

VANILLA SAUCE FOR COTTAGE PUDDING

Mix ½ **cup sugar** with **1 tablespoonful corn starch,** add **1 cup boiling water** gradually, stirring constantly. Boil 5 minutes, remove from fire, and add **2 tablespoonfuls butter,** a **few grains salt** and **1 teaspoonful vanilla.**

Eggs

Eggs are mostly thought of as the product of the domestic hen, however the duck and turkey furnish some of the eggs of commerce. The fish eggs are known as roe and when properly prepared are very delicious. When eggs are used in foods for leaveners they are beaten to incorporate air but when they are to be used as thickeners, such as custards, they are only beaten enough to thoroughly mix the yolk and white. Eggs are protein in character and must be cooked at a low temperature in order to keep from becoming hard and tough.

Cover egg yolks with water and place in a tightly covered jar if you wish to keep them for future use. Place in refrigerator. Salad oil may also be used.

There is no difference in quality between white and brown eggs.

Add a few drops of water to frying eggs and cover to insure the top of the egg being cooked.

To fry an egg—Break whole egg into hot fat. Cover and cook until white has set.

To remove specks or parts of egg yolks from egg white use the edge of an egg shell.

Eggs may be hard cooked a dozen at a time for salads or school lunches and then stored in refrigerator. Leave the shells on to insure freshness.

EGGS A LA GOLDENROD

Make a white sauce of **1 tablespoonful butter, 1 tablespoonful flour, salt, pepper,** and **½ cup milk.** Hard cook **4 eggs.** Separate the yolks from the whites. Chop whites and add to white sauce. Pour this mixture over slices of **toast** and in the center pile yolks which have been put through potato ricer. Garnish with parsley.

EGGS COOKED IN SHELLS

Place **eggs** in sauce pan, cover with **cold water** and bring gradually to boiling point. For a **soft egg** remove the moment the water starts a good boil; for **a hard egg** reduce heat and keep water at a simmering point, remove in 15 to 20 minutes.

In order to have the yolks centered in a hard cooked egg stir the eggs at the beginning of the cooking when the whites are beginning to set. This is especially nice for devilled eggs.

Chill eggs immediately by placing in cold water. This assures easy removing of shells and leaves a smooth white.

Run cold water over plates on which eggs have been served before putting them into hot water. The yolk is then much easier to remove.

EGG FOO YONG

Fry ½ **lb. raw pork** until brown. Remove from fire and fry **1 small onion minced** and **1 cup chopped celery** until tender. Add to cooked pork **2 cups dried mushrooms** crumbled, **4 water chestnuts** and ½ **to 1 cup bean sprouts** and **1 teaspoonful salt.** Mix and cook 4 minutes. Put mixture in bowl. **Beat 4 eggs** and add to it. Drop by large spoonfuls into hot frying pan, using either **butter or oil** to fry. Cook in cake form. Fry until brown on one side, then turn and brown on the other side. If desired they may be served with sauce made by thickening **soy sauce with cornstarch.** The dried mushrooms may be obtained at an Italian importing store and are useful in flavoring many other dishes. The water chestnuts may be buoght at a Chinese restaurant.

FRIED EGGS

Break **eggs** into a skillet containing a **little fat over** low **flame,** either covered or uncovered. If more fat is preferred it can be dipped over the eggs to cook top. Or when eggs begin to set on bottom, add **1 teaspoonful water,** cover tightly and cook until desired doneness. This gives a delicate egg that has the appearance of a poached egg.

Bacon and Eggs—Cook **bacon** until crisp, drain excess **fat** from skillet, break in **eggs** slowly, leave skillet uncovered and baste eggs with bacon fat.

POACHED EGGS

Fill shallow pan 2/3 full of **boiling salted water (½ tablespoonful salt to 1 quart water)** Break each **egg** into a cup and carefully slip into water which should cover the eggs. Do not allow water to boil after eggs are added. When there is a film over top and white is firm, remove to rounds of **buttered toast.**

An egg poacher may be used if desired. A little **vinegar** added to the water sometimes keeps the egg from separating.

SCRAMBLED EGGS

Break **egg** in top of double boiler over boiling water. Add **1 tablespoonful cream** for every egg and just one **dash** of **pepper.** Stir enough to break white and yolk into yellow and white flecks. When well heated add **1 teaspoonful butter** for each egg and season to taste. Eggs go on cooking after they are taken from the heat so take them out of the double boiler while they are still a bit soft. This brings them to the table creamy and rich.

If you have trouble separating eggs use a funnel. The white will pass through, leaving the yolk in the funnel. You may also break egg in palm of hand and allow white to slip between fingers, leaving yolk in hand.

Omelet is a dish prepared from eggs. It may be just beaten eggs and milk or may have additional flavor added.

OMELET (Plain)

Melt ½ **tablespoonful butter** in heavy iron spider (skillet). Separate **5 eggs** and beat whites until stiff but not dry. Beat **yolks.** Add **1 cup of milk,** less enough to smooth **3 tablespoonfuls flour.** Add this to mixture with ¼ **teaspoonful salt** and melted butter. Lastly, add the stiffly beaten egg **whites** and pour into the buttered spider. Cook over very slow fire, not allowing to boil, until it doubles in height and shakes like jelly. Place in oven until nicely browned on top. 1/3 cup chopped ham may be added on top before putting in oven if desired.

CHEESE OMELET

Add **1 cup cooked rice, ½ cup grated cheese,** and **¼ cup milk** to **2** beaten **egg yolks.** Season with **salt** and **pepper.** Carefully fold in **beaten whites.** Melt **2 tablespoonfuls butter** in frying pan and cook omelet slowly until brown on bottom. Place under broiler until delicately brown on top.

MARTHA WASHINGTON OMELET

Warm **1 cup sweet milk** and pour over **1 cup bread crumbs.** Let stand until cool. Then stir (not beat) in **6 eggs,** one at a time. Heat **4 tablespoonfuls butter** until hot in frying pan. Pour in egg mixture. Season with **salt** and **pepper.** When it begins to set, place in hot oven until done. Should be light and fluffy. When ready to serve, fold over in half with cake turner and serve on hot platter.

STUFFED OMELET ROLL

Sift **2 level tablespoonfuls flour** with **pinch salt** and **dash** of **pepper** and **1 teaspoonful baking powder.** Beat **4 eggs** until well mixed but not frothy. Add prepared flour and **1/3 cup hot water. Put 3 tablespoonfuls cooking oil** in skillet and when it begins to smoke turn in omelet. The skillet should be large to let egg mixture spread out as thin as a pancake. If no large skillet is handy then use a baking pan and cook omelet in oven. When cooked dry, spread with **minced ham** or other meat seasoned to taste, or **minced onion** mixed with **buttered bread crumbs.** With 2 broad blade knives carefully roll the omelet like a jelly roll and transfer to hot platter. Serve with creamed potatoes.

Fish

Under fish we are classing all those creatures that swim in fresh or salt water. They are arranged alphabetically rather than by classes.

In selecting fish be sure that the eyes and gills are bright, the scales firm and the fish has a pleasant odor.

Fish may be kept in refrigerator if kept in a tight glass container.

A little vinegar added to pot or pan in which fish was cooked and to the dish water in which fishy dishes are washed, makes it easy to get rid of fish odors.

BLUE FISH PLANKED WITH VEGETABLES

A fish plank should be made of hard wood about 16 inches long and 12 inches wide. Heat plank very hot and grease with butter. Split and clean **fish,** removing head and tail. Place on plank, skin side down. Spread with **melted butter.** Place under the broiler and cook 15 to 20 minutes, depending upon the size of fish. Decorate with creamed **mashed potatoes** around the edge of plank. (Use pastry tube.) Put back into oven and cook until potatoes are browned. Garnish top of fish with chopped **carrots, brussels sprouts** and **beets** cut in fancy shapes, inside border. Serve from the plank.

CLAMS — FRIED

Choose large **clams** for frying. Allow six for each person. Dry them well in a cloth. Roll in **cracker meal, beaten egg diluted with milk,** then in fine **bread crumbs.** Place a few at a time in a frying basket, not allowing them to touch each other. Fry in deep fat. Remove as soon as light brown, as long cooking toughens them. Serve on hot platter with a garnish of **lemon slices** and **parsley sprigs. Tartar Sauce** is a necessary accompaniment to fried clams.

Clams are small shell fish dug on New England shores after the tide has gone out.

CODFISH BALLS

Soak **1 pound** flaked **salt codfish** for 4 hours. Drain. Add fresh water and boil until tender, then drain again. Place equal quantities of mashed **potatoes** and codfish in bowl. Add **2 eggs, 2 tablespoonfuls flour** and mix thoroughly with the fingers. Add **3 tablespoonfuls milk** if the mixture seems dry. Beat with spoon until very light. Taste before adding more salt, as the fish may have retained enough salt. Drop from spoon and fry in deep fat which has previously been heated. They should fry to a golden brown.

CREAMED COD FISH (Old-Fashioned)

Soak ½ **lb. salt cod fish,** drain, add fresh water and cook until salt is sufficiently removed and fish tender. Pull apart with two forks. Make 2 cups white sauce by using **2 tablespoonfuls butter** melted with **4 tablespoonfuls flour,** slightly brown, then add **2 cups milk** and cook until smooth and even. Season with **salt** and **pepper.** Chop 1 hard cooked **egg** fine, add to white sauce. Mix with fish. Garnish with **parsley** and serve with **plain boiled potatoes.**

DEVILED CRABS

Blend **2 tablespoonfuls butter** with **1 tablespoonful flour.** Stir 2/3 **cup hot milk** into mixture. Beat 2 raw **egg yolks** and add to white sauce with a **pint** of **crabmeat, 1 teaspoonful** minced **onions, 2 teaspoonfuls lemon juice, 1 tablespoonful** minced **green pepper,** ½ **teaspoonful salt,** shake of **cayenne** and **2 teaspoonfuls Worcestershire sauce.** Mix well, fill shells or ramekins, buttering them first. Cover with **buttered cracker crumbs** or bread crumbs may be used. Bake in quick oven. Delicious hot or cold and can be prepared completely the day before they are needed. Serves 6 generously.

CRABMEAT WITH MUSHROOMS

Beat **2 eggs** and stir into **1 large can** of **crab meat.** Add **1 cup mushrooms** and **1 cup cream sauce,** which should be well-seasoned. Place in baking dish. Sprinkle over with **grated cheese** and **buttered bread crumbs.** Bake for 20 minutes in moderate oven. This makes a fine dish for bridge luncheons.

CRABMEAT SCALLOP

Pour 1½ **cups scalding milk** over **1 cup** soft **bread crumbs.** Add **2 cupfuls canned** or **fresh crabmeat, ¼ cup melted butter, 2 canned pimentos,** chopped, **2 tablespoonfuls** chopped **green pepper, 1 tablespoonful** chopped **onion, 1 cup** grated **American cheese, ½ teaspoonful salt, ⅛ teaspoonful pepper,** and 3 beaten **eggs.** Pour into a buttered casserole, individual ramekins or ring mold. Set in pan of hot water and bake in slow oven 350° F. for 50 minutes or until a silver knife inserted in the center comes out clean. Serve with fresh peas and mushrooms in cream sauce.

FILLET OF FISH

Roll **fillets** in **flour,** then dip into **beaten egg** to which has been added **2 tablespoonfuls** of **lemon juice** and **2 tablespoonfuls** of **water.** Roll in fine **cracker crumbs** and fry in deep fat about 7 minutes on each side, or until a golden brown. Lay on platter and sprinkle lightly with **salt.** It may be served with **drawn butter, lemon,** or **finely chopped parsley.**

BAKED STUFFED FISH

Purchase **1 shad** weighing 4 to 6 pounds. Clean ready for stuffing by removing head, fins and any scales that may still be on. Wash, dry, being sure that the cavity is also clean. Put **1 tablespoonful butter** and **1 tablespoonful onion,** chopped, in frying pan; cook until onion is partly done. Add **2 cups bread crumbs, 1 tablespoonful** minced **parsley, 1 teaspoonful salt** and **¼ teaspoonful pepper.** Cover closely for a moment, stir well. The **stuffing** is then ready for use (it will be very dry). Rub fish inside and out with **salt** and **pepper.** Stuff with dressing, sew up with strong thread, put in a dripping pan or roaster, with fryings and butter. Dredge with flour. Lay butter or thin **slices** of **pork** or **bacon** across top. Add **½ cup hot water** and baste frequently. Bake 1 hour in moderate oven.

BAKED WHITE FISH

Clean, wash, and bone **whitefish.** Rub with **salt** both inside and out and lay in pan. Slice an **onion** over top and several **stocks** of **celery.** Cover with **milk.** Bake in a moderate oven (350° F.) until milk has been absorbed or evaporated. When all milk is gone the fish is done. This requires about 1 hour. Serve garnished with **parsley** and **lemon slices.**

FINNAN HADDIE

Soak **1 lb. finnan haddie in milk to cover 1 hour.** Bake in moderate oven 30 minutes and separate into flakes. There should be **2 cups.** Cook **½ teaspoonful shallot or onion,** finely chopped, and **1 teaspoonful green pepper** finely chopped in ¼ **cup butter** 5 minutes, stirring constantly. Add **1 teaspoonful salt,** ½ **teaspoonful paprika** and **few grains cayenne** mixed with 4 **tablespoonfuls flour** and stir until well blended; then pour in gradually to a mixture of **1 cup milk** and **1 cup cream.** Bring to boiling point, add finnan haddie. Serve on toast. Garnish with hard cooked eggs and parsley.

To remove fish scales easily, pour hot salted water over fish until scales curl. Then scrape rapidly. Wash in cold salted water.

If you must clean your own fish place it on a newspaper so the waste may be easily gathered and thrown away.

FRIED FISH AND CHIPS

Take **halibut steak** or **fillets** of **haddock** and cut into serving portions. Dip in batter and fry in hot grease deep enough to just cover. Fry until brown, then turn and fry the other side. Batter: To **8 tablespoonfuls flour,** add **2 teaspoonfuls baking powder,** ¼ **teaspoonful soda,** ½ **teaspoonful salt,** and **1 egg.** Mix all together, adding enough water to make a very thick batter. One may serve **potato chips** or **French fried potatoes** with this meal.

HALIBUT WITH CREOLE SAUCE

With a damp cloth wash two slices of **halibut steak** each weighing about ¾ **lb.** Sprinkle **salt** and **paprika** over the steaks. Place one steak in small baking pan, cover with dressing and top with other steak. Add **4 tablespoonfuls butter** and ¼ **cup water.** Cover, bake in moderate oven 45 minutes. Remove to platter and surround with creole sauce. Garnish with **lemon quarters.** Dressing: mix lightly **2 cups** soft **bread crumbs, 4 tablespoonfuls melted butter,** ½ **spoonful salt,** ¼ **teaspoonful pepper,** ¼ **teaspoonful celery salt, 1 tablespoonful** chopped **onion,** and **1 egg,** with a fork. Creole Sauce: Mix **2 cups tomatoes, 2 slices onion, 2 bay leaves, 2 celery leaves, 4 whole cloves, 1 teaspoonful salt,** ½ **teaspoonful sugar,** dash **pepper** and **1 cup water.** Cook slowly for 15 minutes and strain. Melt **4 tablespoonfuls butter,** add **3 tablespoonfuls flour** and blend well. Add strained tomato mixture and cook 2 minutes.

Lobster—the largest crustacean edible. It is dark green when alive, turning to a brilliant red when cooked. We advise the use of canned lobster unless along the shore where they are freshly caught.

Lobster, crab, and shrimp should be stored in a mild salt brine when in refrigerator.

Fresh lobster, and crab are dropped while still alive in boiling water to cook. Usually 20 minutes is sufficient. They should turn from a dark green to a brilliant red.

Since only the tails of shrimp are used, they are dropped into boiling water and cooked 20 minutes before cleaning.

BAKED LOBSTER

Melt 8 **tablespoonfuls butter**—½ cup—in sauce pan. Add **2 cans lobster meat,** broken up, **3 hard cooked eggs,** rubbed through a sieve, **salt** and **pepper** to taste and the **grated rind** and **juice of two lemons.** Add **2 cups bread crumbs.** Mix well together and pour into baking dish. Add 4 **tablespoonfuls cream and** sprinkle over with **bread crumbs.** Bake about 20 minutes in moderately hot oven, or until crumbs on top are brown.

Any leftover fish may be used in the above recipe.

LOBSTER A LA NEWBURGH

If canned **fish** is used, cover with cold water 20 minutes and drain.

Melt **2 tablespoonfuls butter** in sauce pan. Add **1 tablespoonful flour** and stir until smooth. Add slowly **1 cup cold milk** and boil until thick. Rub **yolks** of **2 hard cooked eggs** through a strainer and add, stirring until smooth. Add 1 **teaspoonful salt,** ¼ **teaspoonful paprika** and **cayenne pepper** to taste. Add finely chopped **egg whites** and **2 cups** finely chopped **lobster.** Put all in top of double boiler over fire for 15 minutes. Add ¼ **cup cooking sherry** and serve immediately.

LOBSTER PATTIES

Make a cream sauce by melting **2 tablespoonfuls butter,** add 2 **tablespoonfuls flour** and when well blended add **½ cup milk** and **½ cup thin cream.** Stir until it boils, then cook 5 minutes. Add **1 cup lobster meat,** a slight grating of **nutmeg, 1 teaspoonful lemon juice, salt** and **pepper** to taste. Beat thoroughly. Just before serving, add **yolk of 1 egg.** Fill baked **puff pastry shells** and serve immediately.

SCALLOPED LOBSTER

Boil **½ pint milk.** Rub 2 **tablespoonfuls butter** with 2 **tablespoonfuls flour** and stir into milk when boiling. Boil the **lobsters.** Open and cut meat into dice. Put layer of white sauce into bottom of baking dish, then a layer of lobster, add **salt** and **pepper** and a sprinkling of **parsley** and **bread crumbs.** Then put in another layer of white sauce and so on until all is used. Sprinkle the top with bread crumbs. Bake in a quick oven for 15 minutes until brown. The above method for white sauce is the old style. It is perfectly all right to make white sauce by the modern method of browning butter and flour, then adding milk, and cooking until thick.

FRESH MACKEREL (Baked)

Split the **fish** as for broiling. Then place it skin side down on a well oiled paper in a baking pan. Sprinkle **pepper,** bits of **butter** and minced **parsley** over the fish. Cover bottom of pan with **milk.** Set into hot oven to bake. When milk is absorbed, fish will be tender and well browned. The paper facilitates removal from pan.

BROILED FRESH MACKEREL, MAITRE D'HOTEL

Clean and split 2 good sized **fresh mackerel,** through the **back.** Remove the spine. Score fish slightly and rub with **1 tablespoonful sweet oil.** Season with pinch of **salt** and small amount of **pepper.** Broil them on a brisk fire for 10 minutes on the split side and 1 minute on the skin side. Lay on a dish. Pour over **maitre d'hotel butter** and serve with a **few parsley greens** and **thin slices of lemon.** Maitre d'Hotel Butter: Put **2 tablespoonfuls butter** in a bowl with **1 teaspoonful** of very finely chopped **parsley,** add the **juice** of **½ lemon,** mix well. Keep in a cool place until needed.

Oysters are a shell fish that are very popular. They are very high in flavor but poor in food value.

Oysters may be eaten raw with only salt and pepper.

COOKING OYSTERS

Oysters should first be washed and looked over carefully for bits of shell, or small crabs which hide inside for protection. Remember, they should just be heated through or they will shrink like a bit of wool dipped in hot water. When cooking oysters plan the time accordingly, or the results will be hard, tough, shrunken up mollusks, although they were plump at the start.

OYSTER CASSEROLE

Melt 4 **tablespoonfuls butter** in sauce pan and add 4 **tablespoonfuls flour** with ¾ **teaspoonful salt** and ¼ **teaspoonful pepper.** Blend well. Combine **1 cup vegetable stock** or **water** with **1 cup milk** and add gradually to the first mixture, stirring constantly to prevent lumping. Allow mixture to come to boiling point. Cook three minutes. Grease casserole with butter and arrange **2 cups cooked rice, 1 cup cooked** and diced **celery**, and **1 pint oysters** in layers in the order given. Cover with sauce. Garnish with **paprika.** Bake in quick oven, 400° F., for 25 minutes. Serves six or eight.

ESCALLOPED OYSTERS

Place in a casserole, a layer of broken **crackers,** a few **oysters,** but not a solid layer, dot with **butter** and sprinkle with **salt** and **pepper.** Continue forming one layer on top of the other until dish is nearly full. Pour **milk** over the entire contents until dish is 2/3 full. Bake in moderate oven until crackers brown on top and sides of dish. Serve from the dish in which they were baked.

FRENCH FRIED OYSTERS

Drain liquor from oysters, **salt** and **pepper** well. Take one oyster at a time and roll in **cracker crumbs.** Lay on a meat board until all are so encased and laid in rows. Let remain 15 minutes, then take the one first treated, and dip in **beaten egg,** then the second and so on until all are dipped. Then roll in cracker dust again. Let remain from one-half to three-fourths of an hour. Now drop oysters lightly into **hot lard.** When a light brown, turn on other side. Then put in colander to drain. Serve while hot on a hot platter.

FRIED OYSTERS

Dust **oysters** with **salt** and **pepper.** Roll in **flour.** Beat **1 egg** slightly with **2 tablespoonfuls milk,** coat oysters with this. Roll them in **crumbs.** In the meantime, heat enough **butter** or **substitute** to make it ½ inch deep in the pan used for frying. When melted, heat until bubbling. Put in oysters and fry slowly until a golden brown, turn when brown on one side and cook the other side. Drain on crumpled paper and serve with maitre d'hotel sauce. Serve at once. (See Sauces.)

Salmon is the most used of the canned fish. Although it may be purchased fresh, there are few who buy it that way. There are different grades of salmon ranging from pink to red. Whenever one sees a sale on salmon they should look for quality as the price ranges with the grade. The "sockeye" is best with its blood-red color, the "chinook" next with its deep pink. Next, the "cohoe," varying from a pale to a deeper pink, then the "humpback" which is a soft but pale pink. The last is "dog" salmon which has very little color, rather whitish or pale yellow. The food value may be the same in all classes but the flavor is different.

If a can of salmon or tuna is too large for your family, divide it, putting the part not to be used in a small tightly closed jar in refrigerator. Use it later for a different recipe.

BOILED SALMON

Obtain **1 to 3 pounds of salmon.** To enough **boiling water** to cover fish add **½ cup vinegar, 10 peppercorns, 1 bay leaf, 2 cloves, 1 small onion sliced** and **1 teaspoonful salt.** When boiling fish place it, loosely wrapped in cheese cloth, in the liquid for from 15 to 20 minutes. Lift from water, drain a moment and serve on warm platter with **Dutch sauce.** Dutch sauce: Make the same as white sauce, melt **2 tablespoonfuls butter,** add **1½ tablespoonfuls flour,** when blended, add **1 cup milk** and **1 cup fish liquid, 2 egg** yolks slightly beaten, **1 teaspoonful lemon juice, ½ teaspoonful salt. Pepper** and **paprika** to taste.

SALMON BALLS

Remove skin and bones from **1 lb. can of salmon.** Combine with 2 medium **potatoes** cooked and mashed, **¾ teaspoonful salt, ¼ teaspoonful pepper, 1 teaspoonful onion juice** and **1 egg yolk.** Shape into flat cakes, roll in **crumbs,** then in **egg white,** slightly beaten, with **¼ cup water,** then in crumbs again. Fry in deep fat hot enough to brown a cube of bread in 55 seconds. Drain on paper towels. Serve with **chopped egg sauce.**

CREAMED SALMON

Put a **layer of salmon** and a **layer of medium white sauce** in a baking dish, alternately. Sprinkle with **cracker crumbs,** dot with **butter** and brown in oven. Serve hot.

SALMON LOAF

Remove skin and bones from **1 can of red salmon.** Add **¾ cup rolled crackers, 1 tablespoonful butter, 2 tablespoonfuls cream, 3 well beaten eggs** and **salt** and **pepper** to taste. Place in mold and steam for 1 hour. Sauce for Salmon Loaf: Blend **1 tablespoonful butter** and **1 tablespoonful flour** together until flour is slightly brown, add **1 cup milk** and stir until all is smooth, as for white sauce. Season with **salt** and **pepper.** When cooked add **2 hard cooked eggs, chopped fine.** Place baked salmon loaf on platter, surround with sauce and garnish with tiny sprigs of parsley.

SALMON LOAF

Mix well the following ingredients: **1 can salmon,** either red or pink; **1 cup ground carrots** (raw), **¾ cup cracker crumbs, 1 egg, ½ cup milk, ½ teaspoonful salt,** and **¼ teaspoonful pepper.** Make into a loaf and steam 45 minutes. Serve with white sauce.

SALMON PATTIES

Mix thoroughly **1 can salmon,** equal amount of **mashed potatoes, 1½ cups bread crumbs, ½ teaspoonful salt** and **pepper.** Make into patties, dip in beaten egg and fry in shallow fat.

SALMON AND PEAS

Prepare **2 cups white sauce** (medium). Add **1 cup peas** and **1 can of salmon** (skin and bones removed). Put in greased baking dish and cover with **crumbs.** Bake 20 minutes, in 350° F. oven.

Sardines are a minute fish which are cured in such a way that they may be eaten bones and all. They are packed in oil, mustard sauce or tomato sauce. In buying them be sure to notice which sauce they have as you may get one that you do not wish.

A scallop is a bivalve shell fish with roundish rib shells about 3½ inches in diameter. Only the muscle or hard part used for opening and closing the shell, is eaten, the remainder, called the "rim" being very soft and considered unfit for food.

SCALLOPS (Fried in Deep Fat)

Clean, drain and dry **scallops** with a cloth. Season well, dip in the following batter: Mix and sift **1 cup flour** with **1 teaspoonful sugar, 1 teaspoonful baking powder** and **½ teaspoonful salt.** Beat **1 egg,** add **1 tablespoonful melted fat** and **1 cup milk.** Beat until smooth. Roll scallops in batter then in very **fine bread crumbs** or **fine cornmeal** and fry in **deep hot fat.**

FRYING SCALLOPS

Wash and parboil **scallops** 2 minutes, then drain and wipe dry. Dip in undiluted **canned milk,** then in a mixture of **2/3 bolted cornmeal** and **1/3 flour.** Fry in **deep fat** until a golden brown.

MOCK SCALLOPS

For four people, take **2 pounds** of thick **halibut steak.** Cut in 1-inch cubes. Roll in **corn meal** and fry in deep fat until well browned. Drain on paper. (Use paper towels.) **Salt** and serve piping hot. Serve a sauce similar to tartar sauce. To **one cup** of good **mayonnaise** add **1 dill pickle** diced and **2 tablespoonfuls** minced **onion. Salt** and **pepper** to taste.

SCALLOPED SCALLOPS

Parboil **1 pint scallops.** Drain and cut in slices. Melt **4 tablespoonfuls butter,** add **2 tablespoonfuls onion** and **1 cup mushrooms** chopped. Cook 5 minutes, add scallops, cook 5 minutes, add **½ cup scallop liquor, 1 cup cream** and **salt** and **pepper** to taste. Cook until thick. Place mixture in buttered baking dish, dot with **butter,** cover with buttered and seasoned **crumbs.** Bake until crumbs are brown.

Shrimp is a small, long tailed, salt water crustacean of which only the tail meat is eaten. Fresh shrimp is boiled in salted water until shells turn pink, cool. Remove shell and intestinal vein. Canned shrimp should have intestinal vein removed before serving.

SHRIMP CALIFORNIA

Boil 1/2 **cup rice in salted water** until done, drain. Cut up, and saute separately **1 pound mushrooms, 1 large or 2 small bunches of celery, 2 medium sized onions** and **2 cans shrimp** (be sure the black vein is removed). Mix with rice and **1 small bottle of catsup.** Place in casserole. Pour 1/2 **pint bottle of cream** over all. Place in a moderately hot oven until cream is absorbed. Equally good if warmed over. Will serve 10 to 12.

CREOLE SHRIMP

Cook **2 sliced onions** and **4 chopped celery stalks** until brown, in **2 tablespoonfuls fat. Add 1 tablespoonful flour, 1 teaspoonful salt, 2 teaspoonfuls chili powder.** Slowly add **1 cup water** and cook for 15 minutes. Add **2 cups tomatoes, 2 cups peas, 1 tablespoonful vinegar** and **1 teaspoonful sugar.** Lastly add **1 1/2 cups shrimps.** Continue cooking 10 minutes or until shrimps are thoroughly heated. Mold **3 cups of hot rice** in either ring molds or cones and serve with shrimp creole.

DEVILED SHRIMP

Melt **1 tablespoonful butter,** add **2 tablespoonfuls flour** and stir until smooth. Add **2 cups milk** and when it begins to thicken add **3 hard cooked eggs** that have been put through a sieve. Remove dark veins from **1 can shrimp,** cut in small pieces, add to sauce. Season with **paprika, 1 tablespoonful parsley** and a **few drops onion juice.** Serve on halves of hot tea biscuits or toast.

SHRIMPS A LA GOLDENROD

Make a white sauce of **3 tablespoonfuls butter, 4 tablespoonfuls flour, 3 cups milk, 3/4 teaspoonful salt** and a **little paprika.** Add the contents of **one 5 3/4 ounce can of shrimp** which have been cut in halves, **1/2 cup sliced stuffed olives** and the **shredded whites of 6 hard boiled eggs.** Pour over buttered toast and sift **egg yolks** over the top. Serves eight.

CLEANING SMELTS

Smelts are very tiny fish, which in the early spring just fill the waters of northern Michigan. They are cleaned by scaling and removing the entrails, and heads. They are usually not boned, as the bones are so fine they may be eaten when the fish is fried well done.

FRIED SMELTS WITH PARSLEY BUTTER

Prepare **1 pound of smelts** for cooking; they may be boned or not; wipe dry and coat with **salted flour.** Heat a small amount of cooking oil in a frying pan, and fry fish, turning to brown on both sides. Cook slowly so that fish will not brown before cooking through. Turn out on hot platter. Heat **2 tablespoonfuls butter** gently. Add **juice of 1 lemon** and when combined stir in **1 tablespoonful** of finely chopped **parsley.** Pour over hot fish and serve at once.

Tuna is a large fish of very light meat which resembles that of chicken.

CREAMED TUNA IN BAKED NOODLE RING

Noodle Ring: **Cook 2 cups egg noodles** until tender, then drain. Place ½ of the **noodles** in bottom of well greased baking dish with **¼ cup bread crumbs.** Make a sauce from the following ingredients and pour half over noodles and bread crumbs. **Heat 1 cup milk.** Add **½ package pimento cheese** and let it melt. **Add 1 tablespoonful chopped parsley, 1 tablespoonful chopped onion, salt, pepper,** and **paprika.** Cool slightly and **add 3 well beaten eggs.** Place rest of noodles in mold. Add rest of sauce. Cover with **buttered bread crumbs.** Bake in 350° F. oven or steam until set. Turn ring out on platter and fill center with **creamed tuna.** Make a white sauce with **1 tablespoonful butter, 2 tablespoonfuls flour** and **1 cup milk.** Add **½ cup chopped celery, 1 small can tuna fish, salt, pepper** and a **little sage** if desired. Garnish with **sliced stuffed olives.**

TUNA FISH WITH POTATO CHIPS

Mix **1 small can tuna fish** with **1 can mushroom soup** which has had **4 tablespoonfuls water** added. Heat. Roll **1 small bag of potato chips** fine and sprinkle a layer on bottom of greased casserole. Pour tuna mixture over this. Cover with remainder of potato chips. Bake in moderate (350° F.) oven for 20 to 30 minutes.

TUNA FISH WITH NOODLES

Cook **one 5-ounce package of noodles** in boiling salted water for 20 minutes. Make a white sauce of **1½ cups milk, 3 tablespoonfuls flour** and **3 tablespoonfuls butter,** blending flour and butter together over flame until they take on a slight color. Add milk and cook until thick. Add **¼ inch slice of pimento cheese** to white sauce and **small amount** of **green pepper.** Next add **1 medium sized can of tuna fish** and noodles to white sauce. Place in baking dish, cover with **buttered bread crumbs.** Bake about 45 minutes in hot oven.

TUNA FISH PIE WITH CHEESE ROLL CRUST

Melt **3 tablespoonfuls butter.** Add **½ cup sliced green pepper** and **2 slices onion** (these amounts may be varied to suit the taste). Cook until soft. Add **6 tablespoonfuls flour** and stir until well blended. Add **½ teaspoonful salt** and **3 cups milk** gradually, stirring constantly until thick and smooth. Bring to boil and cook 2 minutes. Add **1 large can tuna fish,** drained, and **1 teaspoonful lemon juice.** Pour into large baking dish and cover with **cheese roll.**

Cheese Roll Crust

Sift together **1½ cups flour, 3 teaspoonfuls baking powder** and **½ teaspoonful salt;** add **3 tablespoonfuls shortening,** mix in thoroughly with a fork or tips of fingers. Add **½ cup milk** to make a soft dough. Toss lightly on floured board until outside looks smooth. Roll out into thin sheet. Sprinkle with **¾ cup grated cheese** and **2 pimentos,** chopped. Roll up like jelly roll. With sharp knife cut into 8 pieces, flatten slightly and lay on top of creamed mixture. Bake in hot oven (450° F.) about 30 minutes or until browned.

MOCK CHICKEN A LA KING

Open **1 can** of **white tuna fish,** rinse with hot water to remove the oil. Shred and mix with **1 can peas, 1 cup cooked diced carrots** and **1 cup medium white sauce.** Season with **salt** and **pepper.** Serve on **hot baking powder biscuits.**

Fish Sauces

DRAWN BUTTER SAUCE

Melt **1/6 cup butter,** add 3 **tablespoonfuls flour, ½ teaspoonful** salt and few **grains pepper.** Gradually add **1½ cups hot water.** Boil 5 minutes, stirring constantly. Add another **1/6 cup butter, a little** at a time. (2 tablespoonfuls butter equals 1/6th cup).

MAITRE D'HOTEL SAUCE

Cream **¼ cup butter** in bowl; add **½ teaspoonful salt, ¼ teaspoonful pepper** and **1 tablespoonful chopped parsley.** Slowly add **1 tablespoonful lemon juice.** This sauce is especially good for boiled fish or broiled steaks.

EGG SAUCE FOR SALMON AND SPAGHETTI LOAF

Melt **¼ cup butter.** Add **2 tablespoonfuls flour** and blend well. Add **¾ cup milk, ½ teaspoonful salt, ⅛ teaspoonful pepper** and **2 egg yolks.** Stir and cook until smooth. Add **4 tablespoonfuls lemon juice** very gradually and **grated rind of ½ lemon** just before serving.

TARTAR SAUCE FOR FISH

Mix together well, **1 cup mayonnaise, 2 tablespoonfuls chopped dill pickle, 1 tablespoonful chopped parsley, 1 tablespoonful chopped olives,** and **1 tablespoonful** finely **chopped chives** or **onions.**

Frostings - Fillings

Frostings and fillings are classed together as they are used so closely with each other.

BOILED FROSTING

Boil **1½ cups sugar** with **½ cup water.** Add **1 tablespoonful syrup** to **2 beaten egg whites.** Then add **4 more tablespoonfuls syrup** one at a time. Continue beating. Let syrup now boil until it spins a thread 4 inches long from the tip of spoon and add to first mixture of eggs and syrup in a fine stream. Beat till of consistency to spread. Any desired flavoring may be added. Spread on cake with the back of a spoon in large swirls.

BROWN SUGAR FROSTING

Cook together **1 cup brown sugar, ½ cup cream** for five minutes. Cool. Add **confectioners' sugar** until of right consistency to spread. **Vanilla** may be added.

CARAMEL FROSTING

Put **1 egg white, 1 cup brown sugar,** packed, **3 tablespoonfuls cold coffee** in double boiler. Beat over hot water 7 minutes. Add **1 teaspoonful vanilla flavoring.** Spread on cake.

CHOCOLATE FROSTING

Pour **2 cups brown sugar into ½ cup cream** (if cream is thick it will take another ¼ cup). Cook until it just starts to form a soft ball in cold water. Remove from fire and cool. Stir in enough **powdered sugar** to make it the consistency to spread. This is a delicious caramel icing. Now melt **2 squares** of **sweet** and **1 square bitter chocolate** and add to prepared frosting. If this makes it too stiff, thin with cream. It gives the color and flavor of milk chocolate.

CHOCOLATE FROSTING AND FILLING — HUNGARIAN

Melt **4 squares unsweetened chocolate** in double boiler. Remove from boiling water, add **1 cup confectioners' sugar** and **2 tablespoonfuls hot water,** and blend. Add **2 eggs,** one at a time, beating well after each addition. Add **6 tablespoonfuls butter, 2 tablespoonfuls** at a time, beating thoroughly after each addition.

This makes enough frosting and filling to cover tops of 2 nine-inch layer cakes or 2 dozen cup cakes.

CHOCOLATE SYRUP FROSTING

Put a **can of chocolate syrup** in hot water to heat. To **¼ cup of hot chocolate syrup** add as much **confectioner sugar** as can be stirred in. Cover top of warm cake with this hot mixture. When it hardens it becomes a glossy black covering.

COCOA FROSTING

Mix **1 cup confectioner's sugar** with **2 tablespoonfuls butter** or **margarine** and **4 tablespoonfuls cocoa** until butter is in small pieces, then add **2 tablespoonfuls hot water** or **coffee, ½ teaspoonful vanilla** and stir until smooth.

MAPLE SIRUP FROSTING

Boil **2 cups maple sirup** until it spins a thread. Pour over **2 egg whites** beaten stiff. Beat until it piles up high, then spread on cake. It may be dropped on waxed paper by spoonfuls and called maple sugar kisses.

MILE HIGH FROSTING

Soak **1 teaspoonful gelatin** in **3 tablespoonfuls cold water** and dissolve over steam. Dissolve **1 cup sugar** in **¼ cup hot water.** Boil until syrup will spin a thread. Strain gelatin into syrup. Pour slowly into stiffly beaten **whites of 2 eggs** beating constantly. Pour into top of double boiler and cook until it is stiff enough to hold its shape stirring all the time.

MOCHA FROSTING

Cream **6 tablespoonfuls butter** with **yolk of 1 egg.** Sift **3 cups confectioner's sugar, 1½ teaspoonfuls cocoa** and **1 teaspoonful cinnamon** together and add butter mixture alternately with **1½ tablespoonfuls strong coffee** (a little more may be needed). Beat until smooth.

UNCOOKED FROSTING

Mix **1 cup powdered sugar** with **2 tablespoonfuls butter** thoroughly. Add **½ teaspoonful vanilla,** then **boiling water** by teaspoonfuls until icing is of the right consistency for spreading.

REFRIGERATOR FROSTING

Cut **four squares** of **bitter chocolate** in small pieces and melt in double boiler. Add 2 **tablespoonfuls hot water** and blend. Add 2 well beaten **eggs** and **1 cup powdered sugar**, remove from fire, but allow mixture to stand over hot water, stirring constantly until thickened. This will take about 3 minutes. Cool quickly until lukewarm. Add ½ **cup unsalted butter** (butter may be washed in cold water to remove salt), 2 tablespoonfuls at a time, stirring and blending after each addition. This makes enough frosting for three large layers. It may be made and kept in a tightly covered jar for several days if stored in refrigerator.

SEVEN-MINUTE FROSTING

In top part of double boiler put **1 cup sugar, 1 unbeaten egg white** and **5 tablespoonfuls water.** Place over bottom part of boiler which is over fire and contains boiling water. Beat constantly with rotary or electric beater until frosting stands in peaks. **Flavor** with **1 teaspoonful** any desired flavoring.

(**12 marshmallows** may be cut up and added or ½ **teaspoonful cream of tartar,** either improves the texture.)

Cocoanut is the meat from a large tropical nut. It may be used fresh or canned. The milk, when served very cold, is a delicious drink.

Stale cocoanut may be freshened by adding fresh milk to it allowing it to stand until some of the milk has been absorbed, then drain.

TINTING COCOANUT

A nice topping for any dessert that needs color is cocoanut tinted any shade to match the color scheme of the meal. This is done by adding a **few drops of color** to **water,** then mixing lightly with **cocoanut.**

Extra pie filling may be put into individual dessert cups and used for dessert.

BUTTERSCOTCH PIE FILLING

Mix **1 cup brown sugar, 2 egg yolks, 2 tablespoonfuls flour** and **1 cup cold water.** Stir over flame until thick. Add **2 tablespoonfuls butter** and **1 tablespoonful vanilla.** Fill baked crust. Beat the **whites** of **2 eggs** to stiff froth, then add **2 tablespoonfuls sugar** and **¼ teaspoonful baking powder** and beat again. Put this on top and bake in slow oven until golden brown.

CHOCOLATE FILLING FOR ICE BOX CAKE

Melt **¼ lb. cake sweet chocolate** in double boiler, add **2 tablespoonfuls boiling water, 2 tablespoonfuls powdered sugar** and stir until smooth. Add the **yolks of 2 eggs,** one at a time, beating constantly. Add **½ teaspoonful vanilla** and 2 stiffly beaten **egg whites.** Use as a filling for **stale cake** or **lady fingers** used in a form mold or in layers. Chill in ice box over night.

ORANGE CHIFFON FILLING

Soak **1 tablespoonful plain gelatin** in **¼ cup cold water** for 10 minutes. Mix **4 egg yolks, ¾ cup sugar** and pinch **salt** and stir in a double boiler until the eggs are cooked and custard is thick. **Add** softened gelatin and stir until dissolved. Cool and add **2 tablespoonfuls lemon juice** made up to **½ cup** with **orange juice** and **1 teaspoonful grated rind.** Cool until gelatin begins to set. Beat **4 egg whites** until stiff. Add **¼ cup sugar** and beat to a fine meringue. Fold into fruit mixture and pour into baked pie shell. Place in the refrigerator to set. Before serving heap whipped cream over the top.

LEMON PIE FILLING

Mix **1¼ cups sugar** with **6 tablespoonfuls flour** (level) and a **pinch salt.** Add **1¼ cups boiling water,** stirring constantly. Cook 2 minutes or until thick. Add **2 egg yolks** slightly beaten, **grated rind** of **one lemon** and **1½ teaspoonfuls butter.** (Caution must be used while adding yolks. If not stirred constantly the yolk will cook and harden, thus giving a stringy or lumpy result.) Replace on fire and bring to the boiling point again, thus cooking the yolks all that is needed. Remove from fire and add **juice of 1 lemon.** (If lemon juice is cooked into mixture it will cause flour to lose its thickening power.)

LEMON CAKE FILLING

Combine **1 cup sugar** and **2½ tablespoonfuls flour.** Add **grated rind** from **2 lemons, ¼ cup lemon juice** and **1 egg** slightly beaten. Cook until thick, stirring constantly. Remove from fire. Add **1 teaspoonful butter.** This makes enough for a rather thick filling or a thin filling for more layers.

LEFT-OVER FOOD

The following suggestions are given for the use of food once prepared but not served.

APPLE SAUCE
Apple Sauce Cake.

ANGEL FOOD CAKE
Angel Strawberry Shortcake. With Chocolate or any Fruit Sauce.

ALMOND MACAROONS
Macaroon Pudding. Heavenly Hash.

APPLE PIE
Reheat, serve in bowl with thin cream.

BACON
Crisp and serve over other foods. — In Sandwiches. — Fat. Cookies and Frying.

BOILED BEANS
Drain, change to Baked Beans. Use in Sandwiches.

KIDNEY BEANS
Chili Con Carne. Mock Sausage.

ROAST BEEF OR STEAK
Meat and Potato Croquettes. Hash. Beef Steak Pie. Casserole of Beef. Italian Spaghetti. Spanish Rice. Potato Layers. Hot Beef Sandwiches.

CORNED BEEF
Corned Beef Patties. Sandwiches.

BEETS
Pickled. Cardinal Salad.

BISCUITS
Reheat, serve under Creamed Meat or Vegetables. Stuffings.

BERRIES (All Kinds)
Make into Jams. Puddings.

BRAINS
Brain Patties.

BREAD
Toast. Croutons. Puddings. Stufflngs.

CEREAL
Fried.

CHEESE
Dry and Grate. Bread and Cheese Squares. Casserole Dishes calling for Cheese.

CHERRY
Same as Berries.

CHICKEN
Salad. A la King. Pie. Stew. Timbales.

CHILI SAUCE
Add to Beans before baking.

COCOANUT
Cookies. Desserts. Decorations.

CORN
Escalloped. Squaw Dish. Fritters.

CRABMEAT
Salad. Croquettes.

CRANBERRY
Add to Plain Muffin Batter.

DATES
Cookies. Puddings.

DUCK
Same as Chicken.

FIGS
Cookie Fillings.

FISH
Creamed. Fish Balls.

FROSTINGS
Candy.

GOOSE
Same as Chicken.

GRAPE
Same as Berries.

HAM

Croquettes. Escalloped Ham and Potatoes. Ham and Noodles. Ham and Rice. Ham Timbales. Ham Tetrazzini. Spaghetti, Ham and Peas.

HOMINY

Casserole. Croquettes.

JAMS

Jam Cakes.

JELLY

Jelly Roll. Tarts.

LAMB

Casserole. Croquettes. Pot Pie. Patties.

LIVER

Croquettes. Patties.

MACARONI

With Cheese, Dried Beef, Tomato Sauce. Croquettes. Ham. Hard Cooked Eggs.

MEAT LOAF

Reheat. Serve with Tomato Sauce, Horseradish Sauce. Make into Hot Sandwiches.

MINCEMEAT

Cookies. Rolls.

NOODLES

Ham and Noodles. Tuna Fish. Chamoisett.

PEAS

May be Added to Any Spaghetti or Vegetable Dish.

PEPPERS

Good Added to Salads and Casserole Dishes.

PORK

Chamoisett. Chop Suey. Chow Mein. California Chicken. Patties. Pork Pie.

POTATOES (Mashed)

Snow on Mountain. Cakes.

POTATOES (Boiled)

Fried. Creamed. Parsley. Casserole Combinations.

RICE

Rice Pancakes. Puddings. Combination Casserole Dishes.

SALMON

Loaf. Patties. Croquettes. Creamed.

SAUERKRAUT
Reheat

SAUSAGE
Sausage with Biscuit. Sausage with Parsnips. Sausage Surprise. With Tomato Sauce.

SOUPS
Reheat.

SPAGHETTI
Combination Casserole Dishes. Chicken Salad.

SPINACH
Spinach Ring with Mushrooms.

STRAWBERRIES
Same as Berries.

SWEET POTATOES
Croquettes. Orange. Puffs.

TOMATOES
Sauce for Other Foods.

TUNA
Noodles. Salad.

TURKEY
Hash. Croquettes.

VEAL
Mock Chicken Stew. Tempting Salad.

Macaroni Products

MACARONI, HARD COOKED EGGS AND MUSHROOMS

Cut 1 **cup** of **mushrooms** into small pieces and add to **1 cup** of **medium white sauce.** Add 2 **cups cooked macaroni** and mix well. Dice 4 **hard cooked eggs** and fold rather than stir into the mixture. Pour into baked dish, reheat in oven. It may or may not be covered with bread crumbs. Parsley adds for a garnish.

MACARONI MOUSSE

Cook **1 cup macaroni** in boiling salted water until tender. Blanch in cold water and drain. Put **2 pimentos, ½ onion, ½ pound sharp cheese** and small **green pepper** through grinder. Pour **1½ cups scalding milk** over **1 cup bread crumbs** and add **2 tablespoonfuls butter,** stirring until butter is melted. Add ground materials and 3 **eggs,** well beaten. Put macaroni in thickly buttered loaf pan and pour the milk and cheese mixture over it. Bake in slow oven 40 minutes or until loaf is firm. When ready to serve turn loaf out of pan and slice. Loaf will make eight large servings. It is extra fine served with mushroom sauce.

Noodles are a paste made of eggs and flour. They are as near as the housewife can come to making material like macaroni and spaghetti.

NOODLES (Home-made)

To an unbeaten **egg** add **¼ teaspoonful salt** and sufficient **flour** to make a very stiff dough. Roll into thin sheets about 12 to 15 inches in diameter. Allow to dry, turning sheet often. When nearly dry place sheets on top of each other (1 egg makes 1 sheet), roll, then slice, according to preference, wide or very fine. One egg makes enough noodles for 2 servings, so judge the amount to make from that.

NOODLES EN CASSEROLE

Cook **1 package** of **fine noodles** until tender in salted water, then drain. Fry **1 pound hamburg** and **1 small onion** together until brown. Blend with noodles, add **1 pint** of **tomatoes,** and **1 green pepper** diced. Put all in buttered casserole and bake 45 minutes in moderately hot oven, 350° F.

ITALIAN RAVIOLI

First make a noodle dough of **2 eggs, ½ egg shell water** and enough flour to make it very stiff. Roll out and cut with cookie cutter (round preferred), folding dough nearly enough to cut 2 at once. This leaves them partly joined on one side. Each round when opened has one edge which is not cut. Place on one round a **small sprig of parsley** and spoonful of meat mixture. Wet edges and press top over tightly. Let dry ½ hour. Drop in rapidly boiling salted water and boil 5 minutes. Remove with slotted spoon and place in roaster or baking dish. Cover with sauce and bake 1 hour. **Bay leaves** on top improve the flavor. Meat Filling: Mix together **½ pound ground pork** and **½ pound ground veal** with **1 small clove of garlic** chopped very fine. Sauce: Brown **3 tablespoonfuls roast pork drippings or oil, 1 green pepper** chopped and **½ clove of garlic together.** Then add **2 small cans of tomato paste** with **sweet basil.** Add 1 **can of water** to make rather thin sauce as this sauce thickens in the oven.

NOODLES WITH FRANKFURTERS AND SAUERKRAUT

Boil 1 **package of noodles** in rapidly boiling water to which 1 **tablespoonful salt** has been added. Boil until tender. Drain well. Grease well a casserole into which put one layer of **sauerkraut.** Season with **salt** and **pepper,** then a layer of noodles. Continue alternately, until **4 cups** of **sauerkraut** has been used and all the noodles, allowing noodles to form top layer. On this place **1 lb. of frankfurters,** each pricked with a fork. Cover casserole and bake in a moderate oven, 350° F., 1 hour.

NOODLES WITH MUSHROOMS

Cook **1 package** of **egg noodles** in boiling salted water until tender. Blanch with cold water. Melt **3 tablespoonfuls butter.** Add **3 tablespoonfuls flour** and brown, then slowly add **1½ cups milk,** stirring constantly until sauce thickens. Remove from heat and add **½ lb. soft cheese** cut in small pieces. Stir well. Put noodles in buttered baking dish and add **1 teaspoonful salt, ½ teaspoonful pepper** and ½ **teaspoonful paprika.** Then add **1 can** of flaked **tuna fish** and **1 small can** of **mushrooms.** Pour sauce over all. Sprinkle with crumbs. Bake in 400° F., oven until a rich brown.

NOODLE RING WITH SALMON

Cook 1¾ **cup uncooked noodles** in boiling water until tender and drain. Put **1 cup grated cheese** and ¾ **cup scalded milk** in a sauce pan and heat slowly until cheese is melted. Pour mixture over 2 slightly beaten **egg** yolks. Add noodles and fold in **2 beaten egg whites.** Pour in greased ring mold, bake in slow oven, about 45 minutes or until a knife inserted comes out clean. Unmold on large platter. Serve creamed salmon in center of ring. To make creamed salmon: add **1 cup** of **thin white sauce** to **1 can** of **flaked salmon.** Heat until salmon is hot. Drain a **can** of **peas,** season with **salt** and **butter.** Put on outside of noodle ring as a garnish.

Spaghetti, one of the many varieties of paste made from durum flour.

SPAGHETTI, HAM AND PEAS

Arrange **2 cups cooked spaghetti,** ¼ **lb. boiled ham slices** and ¼ **lb. grated American cheese,** in alternate layers in casserole. Pour **1 cup medium white sauce** over this and cover with **2 cups green peas** (or **1 can**). Bake in moderate oven about 30 minutes. **Bread crumbs** may be sprinkled over the top if desired.

ITALIAN SPAGHETTI AND MEAT BALLS

Meat Balls: put **1 pound ground beef** and **pork** into a **mixing** bowl, add **1 or 2 eggs,** and enough **bread crumbs** to absorb eggs. Add salt and **pepper** to taste, **a speck of ground cloves** and **allspice, 1 clove garlic,** cut fine, **1 small onion,** chopped fine, **a bit of parsley** and **2 tablespoonfuls grated Italian cheese.** Mix thoroughly. Make into balls the size of an egg. Brown or fry in skillet. Put aside when browned. Sauce: put fryings or drippings from meat **balls** in a large sauce pan. Add **1 small onion,** chopped, and **1 clove garlic,** brown, but be careful not to burn. Add **1 quart tomatoes, salt** and **pepper to taste,** ½ **teaspoonful sugar, sprig of parsley** and **speck of ground cloves** and **allspice.** Cook down until almost dry. Add ½ **can tomato paste** diluted with ½ **can water.** Let boil. Add meat balls. Cover with enough water and cook slowly until meat is done, and the sauce the thickness of gravy. Boil **1 pound** of **spaghetti in salted water** until tender. Put in center of platter with meat balls around.

SPAGHETTI (Spanish)

Brown **1 lb. round steak (ground)** and 2 **onions,** chopped in a **little bacon fat,** add **1 qt. tomatoes,** ½ **can tomato paste, 2 pimentos,** ¾ **lb. American cream cheese,** and **1 medium jar stuffed olives,** cut **in halves, crosswise.** Season to taste. Cook ½ **lb. spaghetti** in **boiling salted water,** add to other mixture and serve.

SPAGHETTI

Fry 1 **pound either ground beef or pork** with **1 large onion** until brown. Place in a kettle with **1 quart of tomatoes, 1 green pepper** cut fine, and a **little tomato paste** if it is on hand. Season with **salt** and **pepper.** Add to this mixture when it is boiling hot, ½ **pound of spaghetti** (or less if it is all you have) and cook until spaghetti is done. Add ½ **can of peas** just before serving, allowing them to get warm through. The cooking of the spaghetti may be done in the oven while you are away. Place it in a casserole with a tight lid.

SPAGHETTI WITH SAUSAGE BALLS

Shape 1 lb. sausage into small round balls and fry slowly. Brown 1 cup sliced mushrooms and ½ clove garlic (minced) in 2 tablespoonfuls sausage drippings. Blend in 3 tablespoonfuls flour. Add 3 cups tomato juice gradually and stir until thick. Add ¾ teaspoonful salt, ⅛ teaspoonful pepper and 4 teaspoonfuls Worcestershire sauce and sausage balls and cook ½ hour. Add ½ cup green pepper the last 5 minutes of boiling time. Cook 8 ozs. of spaghetti in boiling salted water until done. To serve, combine spaghetti and sauce and arrange balls on top. This should serve 6.

How to Cook Meat

Two Methods:

Moist heat — boiling, braising, stewing, pot roasts.

Dry heat — roasting and broiling.

Moist heat is used on tough cuts of meat. Meat high in connective tissue is always tough. The moist heat dissolves the connective tissue thus making the meat fibres free and tender. These cuts come from those parts of the body where the muscles are used the most.

Dry heat is used on tender cuts of meat. These have very little connective tissue and are cooked by slow dry heat for a long time without water, and not covered.

When buying meat, ask what cut it is; if you do not know, then mentally think where that would be on your own body and you will know whether it is a muscle you use every day or not. This will then tell you whether that meat will be tough or tender and which kind of heat you should use.

Beef

The name beef is given to all kinds of meat which comes from the bovine family. The very youngest is called veal. We are making a separate classification for it. Read carefully each recipe, as the way meat is cooked gives it flavor and tenderness. The two methods, moist and dry heat, are carefully referred to in each recipe so there should be no difficulty in preparation of beef.

CORNED BEEF AND CABBAGE

Bulk **corned beef** is best, because the liquid will give a better flavor to the cabbage. However, canned corned beef may be used successfully. Cover corned beef with cold water. Bring to a boil. Remove scum after it has boiled about 10 minutes. Let simmer slowly until tender. Remove from water and set in a warm place. Skim fat from liquor, add **cabbage** cut in rather large pieces **and** cook until tender. **Potatoes, turnips** and **carrots** may be added.

CORNED BEEF PATTIES

Sift 2 **cups flour** with 1 **teaspoonful baking powder** and ½ **teaspoonful salt.** Cut in 6 **tablespoonfuls shortening** thoroughly. Add 1 **egg yolk,** slightly beaten, to 1/3 **cup milk.** Add to dry mixture and make a soft dough. Turn out on floured board and toss lightly until the outside looks smooth. Roll out half the dough to ⅛ inch thickness. Cut in quarters and fit in greased muffin pans. Fill with **corned beef** mixture fold edges of pastry over to center. Pinch edges together on top. Repeat with remaining dough. Bake in hot oven at 425° F. for 20 minutes. Serves 8.

DRIED BEEF AND ASPARAGUS

With scissors cut enough **dried beef** to make ¾ **cup** small pieces. Cook them with 1 **cup asparagus** (cut small) until tender. Make medium white sauce, using what liquid is left after draining dried beef and asparagus. Allow 2 **tablespoonfuls butter,** 2 **tablespoonfuls flour** to each **cup** of **liquid.** Serve on toasted rounds of cracked wheat bread. Garnish with parsley.

DRIED BEEF IN NOODLE RING

Boil 2 **cups noodles** for 15 minutes. Drain well and mix with 3 **eggs,** ½ **cup milk** and 1 **teaspoonful salt.** Place in a buttered ring mold and bake in 325° to 350° F. oven for 45 minutes or until set. Set mold in pan of hot water during baking. Unmold and fill center with creamed dried beef. Make a white sauce of ¼ **cup butter,** ¼ **cup flour** and 2 **cups milk.** Season with **pepper** and chopped **green pepper,** 1 **small can mushrooms** and ¼ **pound dried beef** which has been frizzled lightly in a little hot **melted butter.** Garnish with parsley.

HAMBURG STEAK (Planked)

Mix 2 **pounds hamburg steak,** 1 **egg,** 1 **tablespoonful** chopped **onion,** ½ chopped **green pepper,** 4 **tablespoonfuls milk,** 1 **cup bread crumbs,** 2 **tablespoonfuls** chopped **parsley,** 2 **teaspoonfuls salt** and ½ **teaspoonful pepper.** When well mixed form into a flat loaf. Fry in hot bacon drippings until well browned. Place on a hot well greased plank, laying strips of **bacon** over top, surrounded with border of **mashed potatoes.** Place in moderate oven to brown potatoes and to finish cooking meat. It takes about 15 to 20 minutes.

HAMBURG PATTIES, MUSHROOM, ONION SAUCE

Slice 3 good sized **onions.** Place **2 tablespoonfuls butter** in frying pan and let brown slightly. Add onions, **salt** and **pepper.** Cover and let simmer until onions are cooked through. When done, add **1 can mushrooms, juice** and all. Let fry until slightly browned. Add **½ cup water,** more if desired. Thicken with **flour** or **cornstarch** as preferred. (**1 tablespoonful** cornstarch is usually enough.) When thickened turn fire off and cover. Place another skillet on the fire. When hot, place hamburg patties (made from **1 pound** of **hamburg** and **seasonings)** in it. Make four patties out of a pound, if too thin, the patties will be tough. With pancake turner press patties real hard and turn them immediately. Repeat until patties are done. Salt and pepper each pattie after it is placed on platter. Mix the sauce just made with the meat drippings and pour over hamburg.

HAMBURG STEAK WITH ONIONS

Combine **1 pound hamburg, 1 egg** and **½ cup** moistened **bread crumbs.** Season with **salt** and **pepper** and form into large patties. Roll in **flour.** Brown on both sides in a small amount of fat, then add **3 sliced onions.** Turn flame very low and cook covered for about 30 to 45 minutes.

MEAT BALLS (Swedish)

Grind **1 lb. beef** and **1 lb. pork** together twice. Soak **2 cupfuls bread crumbs** in **2 cups milk** and mix with **1 egg, ½ teaspoonful** salt and **pepper** to taste. Add **1 medium onion** grated. Mix well together. Make into small meat balls about the size of a hickory nut and fry in **butter.**

MEAT LOAF

Have **1 pound** of **round steak** and **½ pound** lean **fresh pork** and **2 slices** of **bacon** ground. Add **1 small onion,** finely chopped, **1 small green pepper** finely cut, **¼ teaspoonful poultry seasoning, 1 egg,** slightly beaten, and **1 cup** fine **bread crumbs.** Shape into loaf. Pour **1 cup canned tomatoes** and **1 cup water** over top. Bake at 375° F. for 2½ hours.

MEAT LOAF WITH DRESSING

Mix 1½ **pounds ground beef** with ½ **pound ground pork, 2 eggs, 1 cup cracker crumbs, 2 tablespoonfuls catsup, ½ cup top milk, 1 tablespoonful butter, 1 tablespoonful salt, ¼ teaspoonful pepper** and ½ **teaspoonful chopped onion** until all is thoroughly seasoned. Dressing: mix ½ **loaf** of **stale bread,** cut into small pieces, with **2 eggs,** a little **sage** and **salt** and **pepper** to taste. Fry in **1 tablespoonful butter.** Divide meat in 2 parts. Place a layer of meat on the bottom of pan, then spread dressing over, add remaining meat. Bake in a moderately hot oven for 1 hour.

ROAST BEEF

Select a **5 lb. boned, rolled roast.** Place meat on rack of roaster fat side up. Start in slow oven (300° F.) and keep at this temperature until done. 25 to 27 minutes is allowed for each pound of meat, for a medium roast and 30 minutes for a well done one. Do not add water or cover. (Dry heat.)

MEAT PIES (Individual)

Either beef, lamb or pork may be used for meat pies. Cut **2 cups** diced cooked **cold meat** into small pieces. Cook ½ **cup** diced **carrots** until soft. Add **carrots,** ½ **cup peas,** cooked and ½ **cup** small button **mushrooms** to meat. Sprinkle with dash of **sugar** and pour **1 cup gravy** over all. Simmer gently for a few minutes. Line patty pans with thin layer of baking powder biscuit dough or plain pastry. Fill and cover with another thin layer of dough or pastry. Make holes in top for steam to escape. Bake in hot oven (450° F.) until dough is baked. Serve individually.

OX JOINTS (Braised)

Cut **1 oxtail** in short lengths for ox joints, roll in **flour** and brown slowly in **1 tablespoonful butter** or **margarine,** about 15 minutes. Add **1 cup water, 1 cup canned tomatoes, 1 teaspoonful salt,** ⅛ **teaspoonful pepper, 1 teaspoonful celery salt, 4 whole cloves** and **1 bay leaf;** simmer about 2 hours or until tender. Brown 3 **cups diced carrots, 2 small onions chopped,** ½ **clove garlic** and ¼ **cup diced turnips** in **1 tablespoonful butter** or **margarine** 3 to 4 minutes; add to meat and cook ½ hour longer. Add ¼ **cup lemon juice** the last 10 minutes of cooking.

SHORT RIBS OF BEEF (Braised)

Place a **5 lb. short ribs** of **beef** in a roaster and put into a very hot oven (400° F.) for 30 minutes. This is to sear it and hold the juice inside. Then reduce the heat. Add **2 cups water,** cover, and bake 1 hour. Add **8 medium potatoes, 4 large onions, 4 turnips, 8 carrots, 3 teaspoonfuls salt** and dash of **pepper.** Cook until they are tender. Serve with horseradish sauce.

Hamburg is ground beef. It usually is made up of the tougher cuts of meat that do not sell so readily.

It is best to buy hamburger from a reliable butcher who has ground it fresh in the morning and stored it in a refrigerator, than to have it ground specially for you late in the day.

When chopped or ground meat is called for in a recipe, have a cheap cut like shoulder, breast or flank ground. Never buy expensive meats for this purpose.

FILET MIGNON

The **tenderloin of beef** is used for **filet mignon.** It is the tender side of the loin and the tenderest part of the beef.

Have **filet** cut into even slices about 1 inch thick. Trim off fat so that all are of same size. Broil 3 minutes with hot fire on one side then that same time on other side. Serve with mushroom sauce.

Each filet may be wrapped in a slice of bacon fastened with a string or toothpick. Fry on sides in pan until bacon is brown, then lay filets flat on broiler and broil until done.

SNOW ON THE MOUNTAIN

Make into cakes the following mixture: **1½ lbs.** good **chopped beef** with **1 cup bread crumbs** soaked in **1 cup milk.** Add **1 egg** well beaten, **2 teaspoonfuls salt, ½ teaspoonful pepper** and **1 tablespoonful minced onion.** Brown well on both sides and remove to warm platter. Make sauce by adding **1 cup tomato juice** to **drippings** in pan. Thicken with **1 tablespoonful flour** mixed with a little cold **water.** Season with **salt** and **pepper.** Pour around meat cakes and top each with a mound of mashed potatoes.

POT ROAST OF BEEF WITH VEGETABLES

Select about 4 **pounds of chuck, rump** or **brisket of beef.** If meat is not in solid piece, skewer or tie into shape. Wash and wipe dry. Roll in flour. Heat 4 tablespoonfuls of fat in old-fashioned flat-bottom iron kettle or deep frying pan. Put meat in and brown on all sides over hot burner. Add **salt** and **pepper.** Turn heat low, cover kettle tightly and let simmer slowly 4 hours. Turn 5 to 6 times during the cooking. Add **2 cups potatoes, 2 cups cubed carrots, 1 cup sliced onions, 1 cup celery,** a little **water** and cook ¾ an hour longer. Remove meat and vegetables and thicken gravy. It should be brown but if not, add a little kitchen bouquet. Arrange vegetables around the meat on platter and garnish with parsley. Serve with a salad and light dessert. It makes a splendid meal.

MOCK DUCK

Select a **flank steak** weighing **2 or 3 lbs.** Make a stuffing of **1½ cups stale bread crumbs, 1 teaspoonful salt, ½ teaspoonful pepper, 1 minced onion, ½ cup chopped celery** and **2 tablespoonfuls melted butter.** Mix all together lightly and spread over steak. Roll steak crosswise and tie it in two or three places with a string. (By rolling it crosswise the meat will be carved against grain and slices will be more tender.) Roll outside of mock duck in **flour,** then sear surface in a small quantity of fat in a baking pan. When meat is thoroughly seared on all sides, add **1 cup of water.** Cover closely and cook until tender. This takes 1½ hours or over. Use liquor from baking dish in making brown gravy.

MOCK FILET MIGNON

Filet Mignon or **beef tenderloin** as it is better known, is sometimes wrapped in **bacon** when prepared for serving. **Mock mignon** can be made from **hamburg cakes,** each wrapped in bacon for cooking. Mix **1 pound hamburg, salt, pepper, 1 egg, 1 small onion** chopped, with **1 cup cracker crumbs** and **½ cup milk** together as for a meat loaf. Divide into six or more patties according to the size of the family. Allow for shrinkage. Wrap a strip of **bacon** around edge of each one, overlapping bacon. It need not be fastened as bacon seals itself. These may be cooked in a skillet or placed in a roaster and baked in the oven.

STEAK WITH MUSHROOMS

Purchase a **porterhouse steak** 1 inch thick. One-half pound is usually the right amount to serve each person. Cut off outside heavy skin and remove surplus suet. **Fresh mushrooms** are more tasty with steak. To prepare them, peel if necessary. Wash thoroughly and slice lengthwise if mushrooms are large. Place skillet on stove with a large **tablespoonful** of **butter** and **one** of **lard.** When fat is hot, add drained mushrooms and **salt.** Fry gently until tender. Sliced onions may be added if desired. When done push to one side of skillet. Place steak in same pan and fry with hot fire 5 to 8 minutes for each side according to taste. Salt steak as you turn it then scoop mushrooms on top of the side that is done first. While steak is finishing, heat the dish on which it is to be served and rush to the table piping hot.

BEEF STEAK PIE

The dough: sift together **1 cup flour, ¼ teaspoonful salt** and **1 teaspoonful baking powder.** Cut or rub in ½ **cup shortening** Add ½ **cup mashed potatoes** and mix to a dough with ¼ **cup water.** Set aside to chill while the meat is being prepared. Cut 1 flank or 1½ lbs. of **round steak** into strings. Dip each into **2 tablespoonfuls flour, 1 teaspoonful salt, 1/3 teaspoonful pepper** and **1/3 teaspoonful cloves** that have been mixed together. Put a small piece of **fat** in the center of each strip. Roll up and place in a deep baking dish or casserole. Half fill the dish with water. Cover closely and bake in a slow oven for 1 hour. After that remove the cover. Roll out the crust and place over meat. Return to oven and bake 25 minutes longer.

STEAK ROLL

Use one or two slices of **round steak** according to the size of the family. Make a filling with **3 cups bread crumbs, salt and pepper** to taste and **1 tablespoonful butter.** Add **onion, parsley, celery** as you desire. Lay steak out flat and spread filling evenly over top, roll it like a jelly roll. May be tied by wrapping cord around several times or held by skewers. Brown in hot lard. Lower flame, add a little water, and cook like a pot roast. Is attractive when sliced. Good hot or cold.

PLANKED STEAK

To prepare it, broil the **steak** as usual. That is, place it on a broiler rack in a thoroughly pre-heated broiler oven, so that the top of the steak is about 3 inches from the flame. When the steak becomes nicely browned on one side, season it with **salt** and **pepper.** Then turn and brown on the other side. Place it on the center of a wooden plank. Place around it **spinach cups** filled with **diced carrots,** and pile a border of **mashed potatoes** around the edge. This is done by forcing mashed potatoes through a pastry tube. Brush the mashed potato border with **egg yolk** and place plank in oven or under broiler flame long enough to slightly brown the mashed potatoes. This requires only a few minutes. When potatoes are browned, remove plank from oven. Season steak with salt and pepper, dot with butter and serve immediately.

TENDER ROUND BEEF STEAK

Take a meat hammer and beat a piece of **round steak** large enough for your family. **Salt** and **pepper** to taste, which means a generous sprinkling on both sides. Roll in **flour** and cook in plenty of **hot fat** in skillet that has a good tight cover. Cook over slow fire until tender and brown. Be sure to have cover on skillet while steak cooks. Turn when one side is brown so other side may cook, too. Remove from pan and make gravy with remaining fat. Add a small amount of **flour,** cook until brown, then add either **milk** or **water** as your taste prefers and perhaps a little bit more salt.

SPANISH STEAK WITH NOODLES

Season **4 lbs. round steak,** cut thick, with **salt** and **pepper.** Dredge in **flour,** then saute in fat until brown. Place in roaster. Cover with **2 pounds** old **onions** sliced, **1 large bottle catsup** and **juice of 1 lemon.** Add ½ **cup water.** Roast in oven from 3 to 4 hours at 250° F. or slow oven. Cook **2 cups noodles** in salted water until tender, drain. Serve by slipping meat from roaster on to a big platter (it will be hard to lift as it will fall apart). Surround with noodles. Sprinkle **grated cheese** over noodles. Garnish with parsley.

BAKED FLANK STEAK

Grease an iron skillet well. Put in a scored **flank steak.** Add **salt** and **pepper.** Pour **juice** of **whole lemon** over steak, then add **1½ cups catsup** over top of steak. Place **1 cup water** around the outside of the steak and slices of **lemon** over the top. It is now ready for the oven. Cook 1 hour in hot oven. When ready to serve pour juice over steak.

SWISS STEAK

Wipe off **3 lbs. steak** cut about ¾ inch thick, pound **flour** into both sides as much as it will take. Melt **3 tablespoonfuls fat in** skillet, sear meat on both sides, allowing to brown. Then add **1 cup** finely chopped **pimentos, 2 cups** diced **celery, salt** and **pepper** to taste. Cover with water and allow to simmer 2½ hours or until tender. This may be done in the oven.

Game

Duck is cleaned and cooked very much as other fowl; roasting being the best method.

ROAST WILD DUCK

Clean, then soak **wild duck** 24 hours in several solutions of **salt water.** Wipe dry and remove all pin feathers. Rub inside and out with **salt** and **pepper.** Stuff with Orange Dressing: Mix **1½ cups bread crumbs** with **1 cup diced orange sections, 1 teaspoonful salt, ¼ teaspoonful pepper, 2 tablespoonfuls butter** or **bacon drippings** and **4 tablespoonfuls orange juice.** Stuff interior of duck. Brush duck with **melted butter** and brown in a very hot oven (450° F.). Add **orange juice** to basting sauce. When brown, baste, reduce heat (300° F.), cover and roast until tender.

Rabbit is the most used of the wild game. The wild taste is removed by soaking or parboiling. The meat is made tender by moist heat.

BREADED PHEASANT

After **pheasant** is cleaned and skinned, cut into serving pieces, making at least four pieces out of the breast. Roll each piece in egg, then in **bread crumbs,** then again in egg and again in crumbs. Season with **salt** and **pepper** and fry slowly in half **lard** and half **butter** until a golden brown on all sides. Remove to a roaster, add a small amount of water and roast in a 300° F., oven for 2 to 3 hours, according to age of bird and amount of meat. (An **onion** may be added to meat when placed in roaster.)

Rabbit may be oven baked in barbecue sauce—See meat sauces.

ENGLISH RABBIT

Joint the **rabbit, lard** each piece with **strips of bacon fat** and season with **pepper** and **salt.** Flour well and brown in very **hot fat.** Place in casserole. Cover with stock or water and add the following: **A sliced lemon, pepper, salt, a bay leaf, 1 tablespoonful chopped parsley, 3 cloves, 1 whole black peppercorn.** Simmer very gently until the meat is quite tender.

FRENCH RABBIT

Joint the **rabbit** and flour it thoroughly, then brown in **seasoned fat.** Add a **cup of stock** and a little **white wine** if available. Simmer for half an hour and add about ½ **pound lean diced bacon** and **1 large onion chopped** with ½ **pound mushrooms** which have both been browned in **butter.** Simmer for another 40 minutes, adding salt and **pepper** to taste. This makes a very rich brown stew.

FRIED RABBIT

Cut up **rabbit,** wash in mild salt water. Roll in **flour,** using all the flour the meat will take up. Place in a heavy frying pan in which **equal parts** of **butter** and **bacon fat** have been melted. Season with **salt, pepper** and a **pinch** of **sage** or **celery salt** as preferred. Brown on all sides, turning often. Then add **1 cup** of **boiling water** with the **juice** of ½ **lemon.** Cover closely. Simmer gently for 45 minutes or until tender. Remove the meat and scrape all the brown crust from frying pan, then add **2 cups cold water.** Stir 4 **level tablespoonfuls flour** smooth in ½ **cup milk** and add, stirring until thickened. Add more salt and pepper if needed.

GERMAN STYLE HASSENPFEFFER

Dress **rabbit.** Soak in **salt water** a few hours, drain off and cover with **2 parts water** and **1 part vinegar.** Let stand over night, lift out pieces of rabbit. Wipe dry and fry brown in part **lard** and **butter.** Return rabbit to vinegar solution, add several **sliced onions** and **2 tablespoonfuls mixed spices** which have been tied in a bag. Boil until rabbit is tender, 1 to 1½ hours. Mix **flour** for thickening and add as for any other gravy. Season with **salt** to taste.

RABBIT WITH SOUR CREAM GRAVY

Clean and cut **2 rabbits** into pieces. **Salt** and allow to stand over night. Wash off salt in the morning. Place over fire in a large kettle without water. Allow meat to sear slightly. **Season** rabbit. Add **1 pint water** and when liquid comes to a boil turn fire low. Place in a cloth bag **2 tablespoonfuls** of **pickling spices,** close securely and toss into liquid. Remove rabbit when tender. Remove spice bag also. Make gravy with **flour** and **water** and **1 pint sour cream.** Dumplings are delicious served with this gravy.

SQUIRREL STEW

Dress **squirrel** and wash thoroughly. Cut in pieces for serving. Put in sauce pan with **½ cup vinegar, 1 teaspoonful mixed spices, 1 small diced onion** and a few **celery leaves.** Cover with water. Let stand about 2 hours. Drain. Place in roaster. Brown in moderate oven (375° F.) Add **salt** and **pepper** to taste. Add **2 diced onions,** and **2 diced carrots.** Cover with water. Cover and cook slowly until tender. Thicken broth with a **flour** and **water paste** until of the consistency of thick cream.

Venison is a tough meat and should be cooked with moist heat. —Use veal recipes.

Lamb

Lamb is the name applied to the meat of the young of the sheep family.

WHAT TO SERVE WITH LAMB

Leg of lamb—Browned potatoes, green vegetables (peas, spinach, turnips, asparagus, broccoli or cauliflower) and relish (currant jelly, mint sauce or mint sherbet). Roast shoulder of lamb—Browned or mashed potatoes, green vegetables and relish as above. Crown roast of lamb—Mashed potatoes, green vegetables, bread dressing and mint sherbet. Saddle of lamb—Rice or mashed potatoes, green vegetables, currant jelly and bread dressing. Rolled breast or shoulder—Mashed potatoes, dressing, green limas or Swiss chard. Broiled lamb—Dumplings, green vegetables. Broiled chops—Creamed potatoes, green peas or asparagus and mint or currant jelly, or French fried potatoes, cauliflower or broccoli and tart jelly. Lamb patties—Potatoes au gratin, green beans. Stew—Boiled potatoes, dumplings, turnips, parsnips or onions.

LAMB AND CARROT BALLS SERVED WITH RICE

Buy **1½ lbs.** inexpensive cut of **lamb** (shoulder cut). **Trim** off waste. Put through grinder. Put **1 small onion** and **7 small carrots** through grinder (makes 1½ cupfuls). Add **1½ teaspoonfuls salt** and **⅛ teaspoonful pepper** and **1 egg.** Mix. Shape into small balls. Roll in **flour.** Melt **4 tablespoonfuls lard** in skillet. Fry meat balls until brown. Add **½ cup water.** Cover skillet. Cook slowly 10 minutes. Remove meat to warm place. Add **3 tablespoonfuls flour** to sauce in skillet. Brown smoothly. Add slowly **1 cup hot stock** or water. Cook until gravy thickens. Pour over meat balls. In meantime, boil **1 cup rice** rapidly in **1½ cups hot stock** or water (salted). When done, drain and arrange around meat. Sprinkle with **paprika.** Decorate with mint jelly.

BROILED LAMB CHOPS

Wipe 6 **lamb chops.** Remove superfluous fat and place in a greased broiler. Place under flame, turning every 10 seconds for the first minute. After the first minute, turn occasionally until well cooked on both sides. Remove to a hot platter and spread with **Worcestershire sauce, salt** and **pepper.**

CROWN ROAST OF LAMB

Have butcher prepare **crown roast.** Rub with **salt, pepper** and add **1 small onion** to pan. Place in oven at 325° F. and roast until tender. Cover ends of ribs with **potatoes** to keep from burning and dress with paper covers when removed from pan for serving. Mint Sauce—Wash leaves and discard stems until there is **½ cup of mint leaves.** Place on board and chop with sharp knife, adding **3 tablespoonfuls sugar** as the leaves are chopped. This is the secret of good mint sauce. Add **½ cup** good **cider vinegar.** Prepare about 2 hours before serving. Any left over may be placed in refrigerator.

LAMB POT PIE

Recipe for left over lamb. Have **1½ pounds** of **shoulder of lamb** cut in 2-inch pieces, if fresh meat is used, otherwise cut the left over lamb in small pieces according to what there is. Dredge in **flour.** Melt **2 tablespoonfuls fat,** add **½ small onion** sliced and cook over a slow fire until tender. Then brown the meat on all sides and place in a greased baking dish. Prepare **¼ pound of mushrooms** and sauté in the fat. Add **1 teaspoonful fat, ⅛ teaspoonful pepper** and stir in **2 tablespoonfuls flour** gradually, forming a paste. Add **1½ cups stock (bouillon cubes** may be used), and stir until smooth and boiling. Remove from fire and add **1 cup** of cooked **peas.** Pare and slice 3 **potatoes.** Place over the meat and pour sauce over all. Cover with a rich pastry. Slit to allow steam to escape. Place in hot oven (450° F.) until pastry is glazed and then reduce heat to moderate (375° F.) Bake from 1 to 1¼ hours.

LAMB LOAF

Grind 2 **pounds lamb shoulder,** and **1 cup bread crumbs, 1 onion,** minced, ½ **green pepper,** minced, **1 egg, 1 cup milk** and **salt** and **pepper** to taste. Mix all together well. Bake in a greased ring mold. Use moderate oven 350° F. for about 1½ hours. Turn out on platter and fill center with buttered **peas** and **carrots,** which have been cooked separately and then combined. Garnish with tomatoes and sprigs of parsley.

LAMB PATTIES

Grind **1 small onion** with enough **leftover lamb** for serving the family. Season with **salt** and **pepper** and **add 1 egg.** Make into patties. Dip in **bread crumbs** and fry in **deep hot fat** until golden brown. Serve with creamed peas and mashed potatoes.

RAGOUT OF LAMB

Brown **1½ lbs. lamb shoulder** thoroughly in **chicken fat** or **butter.** Add **6 carrots,** scraped, **1 Bermuda onion,** cut into fourths, and **10 ozs. tomato juice.** Tie together **2 sprigs** of **celery tops, 1** of **parsley,** and **1 bay leaf.** Place on top of stew. Cover and cook slowly for 90 minutes, adding water from time to time, so that about 10 ounces of gravy is left when stew is cooked. Remove seasoning bouquet. Salt to taste and add a dash of **thyme.** A dash of **curry powder** is also good. Then add **1 cup** of **leftover vegetables** such as peas or green beans. Recover and cook for about 10 minutes longer.

ROAST LAMB (With Moist Heat)

Sear **lamb** in open roaster for 30 minutes at 450° F. Add **half cup boiling water.** Lay **potatoes** around meat and **salt** and **pepper** to taste. Turn oven down to 275° F. and place cover on roaster. Roast is juicy and well browned and broth in roaster makes good gravy. Mint sauce should be served with this meat.

ROAST LEG OF LAMB (Dry Heat)

Select a **5 to 6 pound leg of lamb.** Do not remove fell. Rub all over with **salt.** Place in roaster with **no water** and **no cover.** Roast at 300° F., allowing 30-40 minutes to the pound.

STUFFED LAMB SHOULDER

Bone a **shoulder** of **lamb** or **veal.** Leave knuckle and fill cavity with rich **bread stuffing.** Tie neatly in shape and wrap in buttered paper. Lay in deep pan with **2 tablespoonfuls butter, 2 carrots, 2 turnips,** and **1 onion** stuck with **2 cloves. Put** sufficient water to cover bottom of pan. Put in slow oven and baste every 10 minutes. When nearly done remove paper and brown. Pour gravy over meat and garnish with green peas. This meat may be stuffed with fresh mint leaves.

SHISH KOBABS

Cut **1 lb. of lamb meat** (leg or shoulder) into small squares. Mix it well with **1 medium sized onion** finely chopped, **thyme, salt** and **pepper.** Set aside for 2 or 3 hours. When ready to serve arrange meat pieces on wooden or iron skewers. Broil over strong fire. Serve hot on lettuce leaves. For picnics prepare the day before, allowing to set in refrigerator until ready.

Pork

Pork is the name given to the meat of the pig.

Bacon is the cured side meat from the pork. It has such a pleasing flavor that it combines well with many foods as well as eaten alone. Bacon is economical meat as every bit of both fat and lean is utilized. Left-over bacon may be used in sandwiches or cut up in scrambled eggs, omelets, cereals or stuffed eggs. It can be crushed fine and sprinkled over stewed potatoes or baked stuffed potatoes.

A tiny bit of flour sprinkled over bacon will keep it from spattering while frying.

PAN BROILING BACON

This is the usual method employed. The cold **bacon is placed** on a cold skillet and fried very slowly, removing the excess fat as it appears. Turn up fire at last to crisp bacon.

BACON AND FRIED APPLES

First wash and remove spots from **3 apples per person.** Do not pare apples. Remove core and cut into eighths. Broil ½ **lb. bacon** (4 servings) in frying pan until nearly crisp, then cut into small pieces and leave in pan. Retain fat. Add apples and fry until soft. They should be covered while cooking and stirred frequently as they stick easily. Add **1 cup brown sugar,** stirring it into the apples and bacon. The amount of sugar may vary with individual tastes. Bran muffins, whole or cracked wheat bread seem to accompany this dish.

BACON AND OLIVE ROLLS

Roll a thin strip of **bacon** around **2 olives.** Place on end of a sharp stick and broil over camp fire. Serve in **hot rolls.** If prepared at home, secure bacon around olives with tooth picks and broil.

Ham is the thigh of the pig. It may be either fresh or smoked. Usually the smoked variety is thought of when the word "ham" is used.

Pour melted paraffin or lard over the cut end of a ham or bacon to keep from molding. It may also be wrapped in a cloth soaked in vinegar.

BAKED HAM

Select a **ham** of the desired size. Wipe with damp cloth, and place with skin side up in a roasting pan. Set pan in oven and bake until done. Allow 25 to 30 minutes per pound, using an oven temperature of 250° F. to 325° F., or a slow oven. A **cup of water or cider** may be added at the beginning of the roasting period. Remove ham from oven ¾ hour before it is done. Remove skin. Score the fat top in crisscross fashion with diagonal gashes about 1 inch apart. Insert **whole cloves** at each cross section. Rub the fat with **2 tablespoonfuls prepared mustard,** then cover with a ½ inch layer of **brown sugar** and very fine **bread crumbs** combined in equal amounts and moistened with **vinegar.** Set ham back in oven and bake at moderate temperature, 325° F. to brown the crumb mixture.

BAKED HAM CUTLETS STUFFED WITH PINEAPPLE

For eight servings: Cut **slices** of **uncooked ham** in **16 rounds** about the size of a coffee can cover. Place in baking pan with **16 slices of pineapple**, in double layers. That is, on a round of ham, put a round of pineapple, then another round of ham, then another round of pineapple. In the center of each top slice of pineapple place a cooked prune. This will require 8 **large cooked prunes.** Bake until ham is tender and serve with the following sauce. Sauce: add **2 tablespoonfuls brown sugar, ½ dozen cloves, 1 teaspoonful vinegar,** and **1 cup cream.** Cook in double boiler for ½ hour, then strain out cloves, add **1 beaten egg** just before pouring over ham cutlets. Garnish and serve. Water cress makes a fine garnish with a few carrots for color.

HAM AND ESCALLOPED POTATOES

Cut **slice** of **ham** ½ inch thick and **flour** lightly. Fry eash side until it is brown, then put in baking dish. Cover with **1½ cups thin white sauce** and bake in moderate oven for ½ hour. Turn and bake another ½ hour. Pare **potatoes** and cut into medium thick slices until there are **5 cups.** Boil until tender and drain. Arrange in casserole and lay slice of ham on top. Bake 25 minutes. Serves six.

FRESH HAM AND VEGETABLES

Rub surface of **1 slice** of **ham** or several **pork chops** with **½ teaspoonful Worcestershire sauce, 2 teaspoonfuls brown sugar** and **1 teaspoonful prepared mustard,** mixed together. Place in casserole and cover with layer each of the following; 2 thinly sliced **onions, 3 carrots, 1 turnip** and 3 **potaoes.** Sprinkle each layer with a little **flour, salt** and **pepper.** Add **milk.** Cover and bake in a slow oven for 1½ hours. During last 15 minutes of baking remove the cover and brown.

HAM LOAF

Grind **1½ pounds** of **smoked ham** with **1 pound veal** and **½ pound pork.** Beat **2 eggs** and add to **1 cup milk,** then mix with meat, **1 cup cracker crumbs, 1 tablespoonful sugar** and **½ teaspoonful ground mustard.** Shape into a loaf. Put this mixture over the top: **1 teaspoonful sugar, ½ teaspoonful ground cloves** and **½ teaspoonful ground mustard.** Bake slowly 2 or 3 hours. This recipe serves 15.

HAM LOAF

Mix 2¼ **lbs. ground ham** and 1¾ **lbs.** of **fresh pork** ground twice, with **1 cup bread crumbs, 2 onions** chopped fine, **1 green pepper** minced, **2 eggs** and **1 large can** of **condensed tomato.** Bake either in a large loaf pan or spread out in a flat pan so that it can be cut into squares rather than slices. The time of baking depends upon the form into which it is shaped. Serve with Mustard Sauce: heat **1 pint** of **coffee cream,** mix ½ **cup sugar, 3 tablespoonfuls ground mustard, 2 tablespoonfusl flour** and **1 cup diluted vinegar** with a pinch of **salt** and **2 egg yolks.** Cook until it begins to thicken. It is not very thick. Pour over sliced or squares of ham loaf. This recipe serves 16. It may be divided to serve less. The mustard sauce makes excellent salad dressing if any is left over.

HAM AND NOODLES

Cook **1 package noodles** (6 ozs.) in salt water 5 minutes. Drain. Grease casserole and add alternate layers of noodles and **ham (2 cups).** Beat 2 **eggs** well. Add **2 cups white sauce** and pour over noodles. Cover with **crumbs** and dot with **butter.** Bake in moderate oven about 20 minutes or until brown.

HAM WITH RICE

Sear one thick **slice** of **smoked ham** on both sides, using a little fat in the skillet. Parboil **1 cup rice** until about half done. Do not drain but have moist. Pour over ham. Cover with **1 pint milk** and bake 1 to 1½ hours or until ham and rice are both done. Add more milk during baking, if needed.

HAM TIMBALES WITH BECHAMEL SAUCE

Beat **4 eggs** or 8 **yolks** slightly. Add **1¼ cups milk,** ⅛ **teaspoonful pepper,** ¼ **teaspoonful paprika** and **1 teaspoonful onion juice.** Add **1 cup chopped ham.** Turn into individual molds. Put greased paper over top. Bake or steam until firm in pan of hot water. Serve with Bechamel Sauce. See sauces.

BAKED PORK CHOPS

Roll each **chop** in **flour** that has had **salt** and **pepper** added. Brown in fat. Pack in a roaster. Add **1 cup water** to **fryings in** skillet. Pour over chops. Cover and bake slowly 1 to 1½ hours.

SPANISH PORK CHOPS

Place desired number of **pork chops** in roaster. Slice **onions** over them. Wash a handful of **rice** and sprinkle over this. Pour **small can of tomatoes** over all. Season. Place this, well covered, in oven at 300° F. with scrubbed and greased **potatoes.**

STUFFED PORK CHOPS

Select **6 thick loin pork chops.** Make a pocket in each pork chop by cutting the meat from the outside to the rib. Make a stuffing of **three slices** of **bread,** broken into bits, **pepper, salt, poultry seasoning,** or **onion** and **sage, 1 egg, 2 tablespoonfuls butter** and enough **hot water** to soften. Fill each pocket with stuffing. Put in roaster with **1 cup water.** Place in hot oven until brown, reduce heat and cook until tender.

PICKLED PIG'S FEET

Cover **three pig's feet,** cut in fourths, with boiling water. Add **1 teaspoonful salt** and cook gently until tender. Next add **½ cup vinegar, ¼ teaspoonful allspice, salt** and **pepper** to taste. Place over low fire until hot. Put in jars and seal. It is ready for use in 12 hours.

PORK PATTIES

This is suitable for a quick luncheon. Cut **fresh shoulder meat** in a grinder. Season with **salt, pepper** and a bit of **onion.** Add **1½ cups bread crumbs** soaked in water and squeezed dry, to each pound of meat. Bring ingredients together with beaten **egg,** form into small patties. Fry to a nice brown, serve with apple rings. See apples.

PORK PIE (Cold Roast Pork)

Cut **cold roast pork** into small pieces. Roll in **flour** and brown in hot fat. Add water to cover. Cook slowly for 1 hour. Pour into baking pan lined with pie paste. Add enough diced **raw potatoes, celery, carrots, and onions** for your family. **Season** to taste, using enough **liquid** to moisten. Bake in moderate oven for ½ hour then add a rich pastry crust and bake the pie another half hour.

PORK ROAST

Use one 4 or 5 **pound** cut of **pork loin, shoulder or ham.** Wipe with clean damp cloth, place in roaster, **salt** by rubbing it all over the surface of the roast. Leave uncovered and roast at a regular temperature of 350° F. until done.

Sausage is ground meat of pork. It often has the most choice cuts put into it and therefore should be very excellent food. Before the curing of tenderloin into Canadian bacon it was always ground up for sausage meat. Sausage is sold both in bulk and casings.

Roll sausages in flour before frying. It will hold them together and gives a better flavor.

SAUSAGE WITH BISCUITS

Sift 2 **cups flour** with 2 **teaspoonfuls baking powder,** ½ **teaspoonful salt.** Cut in 4 **tablespoonfuls shortening,** add 2/3 **cup milk** gradually to make a soft dough. Spread 1½ **pounds of bulk sausage** in a shallow pan, cover top with biscuit dough. Score in squares, convenient for serving. Bake in hot oven 20 minutes. Cut crust through scored sections. Serve.

PORCUPINES

Mix 1 **pound sausage** with ½ **cup uncooked rice.** Season with **salt, pepper,** (add **poultry seasoning** if desired) and ½ **cup milk.** Form into balls. This should make 6 nice sized balls. Place in casserole and cover with **tomato soup.** Allow plenty of room between balls as the rice expands. Bake in moderate oven (350° F.) for 2 hours. Serve with either scalloped potatoes or baked potatoes.

SAUSAGE SURPRISE

Use 2 **cups cooked or canned spinach** and combine with 1 **cup bread crumbs,** 1 **medium onion** chopped, 1 **egg,** ½ **pound bulk sausage,** 1 **cup celery leaves,** chopped, or use chopped celery, 1 **teaspoonful salt, pepper.** Mix as for a meat loaf. Put in a deep casserole. Pour a few spoonfuls of **spinach water** over the mixture and cover top with **grated cheese. Bake in moderate** oven, 325° F., for 40 minutes. Serves six. Cover the dish for 30 minutes, then uncover and allow to brown the last 10 minutes.

SAUSAGE AND PARSNIPS

Place **sausage** in roaster. Stand **pared parsnips,** uncooked, around sausage. Season with **salt** and **pepper,** add **½ to 1 cup water.** Cover and cook in moderate oven for 1 hour. Finish in slow oven, until parsnips are soft.

SAUSAGE WITH TOMATO SAUCE

Make **1 lb. bulk sausage** into small cakes. Place in skillet with small amount of water. Boil down and let sausage brown in its own fat. Cover with **1 cup tomato pulp** that has been seasoned with **salt, pepper, cloves, sugar** and **chili powder** to taste. Cook about 10 minutes more.

SCHNITZ UN KNEPP

Soak **1 quart** of **dried apples** over night. Cook **3 pounds smoked ham,** sliced 1 inch thick, until tender. Add apples. Continue cooking 1 hour. Add **¼ teaspoonful pepper** and **2 tablespoonfuls brown sugar.** Sift **2 cups flour, 1 teaspoonful salt, ¼ teaspoonful pepper** and **4 teaspoonfuls baking powder.** Add **1 beaten egg.** Add **¾ cups milk** to make moist but stiff batter. Drop from spoon into **boiling ham broth.** Cover tightly and cook 15 minutes. Arrange ham on large platter, top with dumplings. Border with apples. This should serve 8.

SCRAPPLE

Boil **8 or 9 pounds** of **pork shoulder** till bones drop out. Reserve **4 quarts** of **liquor.** Chop meat fine and add **2 quarts of white cornmeal** to liquor and cook 10 minutes. Then add chopped meat with **3 tablespoonfuls salt, 2 tablespoonfuls ground sage** and **2 teaspoonfuls black pepper.** Stir while cooking, about 30 minutes. Cool in oblong tins. When cold and set, slice off in ½ inch pieces and fry until a golden brown. This is a very good cold weather dish.

STUFFED SPARERIBS

Take a **small loaf** of **bread,** moisten with **warm water,** and mix well. Add **1 or 2 eggs, 1 onion,** cut fine, **salt** and **pepper** to taste. Mix again until thoroughly blended. Spread on spareribs that have not been cracked. Roll up and tie together. Bake in oven until brown.

BARBECUED SPARERIBS

Prepare 3 or 4 **pounds** of **spareribs** by cutting into portions wanted and put into roaster. Make sauce of the following ingredients: **2 tablespoonfuls vinegar, 2 tablespoonfuls Worcestershire sauce, 1 tablespoonful salt, ½ teaspoonful red pepper, 1 teaspoonful paprika, ½ teaspoonful black pepper, 1 teaspoonful chili powder, 1 8-ounce bottle catsup** (¾ cup), and **¾ cup water.** Pour sauce over spareribs. Slice 2 **onions** over the top and bake 1½ hours in moderate oven (350° F.) Remove cover from roaster the last 15 minutes. Turn meat twice during time of roasting.

SOUSE

Clean 4 **pig's knuckles, 1 lb. beef** or **lean pork** or **heart** and **tongue,** thoroughly. Cook all together with plenty of water until tender. Remove bones, cut into small pieces or chop with sharp knife. Strain broth before adding chopped meat. Add **1 cup vinegar, salt** and **pepper** to taste. Boil all together for 5 minutes or until liquid is thick. Pour into enamel or earthen dish. Place in a cool place until set. It will slice easily and will keep 2 weeks if put in a cool place.

TENDERLOIN (Breaded)

Have the butcher "French" the **tenderloin,** that is, cut into 2 or 3 inch lengths and flatten with a cleaver. **Salt** on both sides. Slightly beat 2 **eggs** and add **2 tablespoonfuls water.** Dip meat in egg, then in **bread crumbs.** Repeat so that each piece of meat has two coverings of crumbs. Fry in fat until brown. Remove to roaster, add ½ **cup water,** cover and roast in moderate oven for 1½ to 2 hours.

CALIFORNIA CHICKEN

Combine ¼ **pound ground pork, 1 pound ground veal, 1 teaspoonful salt, ⅛ teaspoonful pepper, 1 tablespoonful** chopped **green pepper** and **¼ cup grated pineapple,** drained. Shape like a chicken leg around a wooden skewer. Roll in **bread crumbs,** then in slightly beaten **egg** with **1 tablespoonful water** and again in bread crumbs. Let stand in refrigerator for 30 minutes. Brown in hot fat, then reduce temperature. Cover closely and let cook slowly for 45 minutes.

CITY CHICKEN

Cut 1½ **pounds** of **fresh ham** and 1½ **pounds** of **fresh veal steak** into 1 inch squares, season with **salt** and **pepper**. Place piece of meat on skewers, alternating first ham then veal until four pieces are in place. Roll in slightly beaten **egg**, then dip in **cracker crumbs** (or bread crumbs). Repeat if a heavier coating is needed. Pat each stick into shape to resemble chicken legs. Fry in deep hot fat until golden brown. Place in roaster and pour **1 quart milk** over all. Bake for 45 minutes. If milk is not available a small amount of water will do.

Poultry

Giblets are the heart, liver and gizzard of a fowl. They are mostly served cut up in gravy. The chicken livers are often served as a dish by themselves, being fried with bacon.

HOW TO CLEAN CHICKEN

Singe over free flame. Remove pin feathers. Cut off head, feet and wing tips. Remove oil sac at base of tail. Slit skin at neck, loosen windpipe and crop; pull out, push back skin from neck and cut neck off close to body. Save neck for soup. Make slit below breast bone; loosen intestines from back bone and pull on gizzard firmly to loosen entrails. Cut around vent so that intestines are unbroken and pull out. Remove heart, lungs, kidneys and clots of blood. Allow cold water to run freely through bird. Wash thoroughly and drain. Cut through fleshy part of gizzard to inside sac and remove sac carefully. Wash giblets (gizzard, liver and heart) to remove blood.

CHICKEN CREOLE

Melt 3 **tablespoonfuls butter.** Add 2 **tablespoonfuls** chopped **green pepper** and saute a few minutes. Blend in **3 tablespoonfuls flour** and ½ **teaspoonful salt.** Add **1 cup chicken broth** slowly. Stir constantly to prevent lumping. Add ½ **cup tomato puree,** and **2 cups cooked** diced **chicken.** Heat thoroughly and add **1 tablespoonful lemon juice** just before serving.

TO CUT UP A CHICKEN

After chicken has been thoroughly cleaned, cut through the hip joint on both sides, removing thigh and drumstick. Bend at knee joint and cut through at this point, severing the thigh from the lower portion. Cut wings off at shoulder joints. Remove tip of wing, then bend back small portion and fasten under other part. In the middle of the back is a joint that can be easily cut through. Work with both hands on back until this point is found then cut through with a sharp knife, pull back apart with fingers of each hand pulling in opposite directions. Cut around vent. Cut through the soft ribs of the breast up to neck, break the joint that holds breast to back. Separate. There now is left only the breast piece with the wishbone attached. At the base of the breast bone there is a soft place that can be cut through very easily, thus dividing the two pieces. If large, the breast pieces may be cut in two lengthwise. There should be **10 pieces** to a chicken when properly cut up.

CHICKEN IN BATTER (Virginia Style)

Cut 2 young **chickens** into pieces and if very tender they may be dipped in batter and fried raw in deep hot fat. If they are not so tender the pieces of chicken may be fried slowly in a little fat until light brown on both sides, then dipped in batter and fried quickly in deep hot fat. To make batter: sift **2 cups flour, 3 teaspoonfuls baking powder, ½ teaspoonful salt** and **pepper** (if desired) together. Beat **2 eggs,** add **½ cup milk,** then stir in dry ingredients. Add more milk if necessary. The batter should be quite thick. Drop one piece of chicken at a time in batter and fry as directed.

CHICKEN A LA KING

Melt 2 **tablespoonfuls butter** add ¼ **lb. fresh mushrooms,** cover and cook about 5 minutes. Dredge with **2 tablespoonfuls flour,** add **1 cup milk** and **1 cup chicken broth** or **2 cups milk, 1 pimento** cut in strips, **⅛ teaspoonful pepper, 1 teaspoonful salt,** and **2 cups cooked chicken, cut in pieces.** Allow to cook until sauce thickens. Serve on toast or in patty shells.

ESCALLOPED CHICKEN NO. 1

Stew a **4-pound chicken** until very tender. Remove bones and cut into small pieces. Put a layer of **cracker crumbs** into a 2-quart baking dish, then a layer of chicken and continue until the chicken is all used. Finish with crumbs on top. Pour over all **hot broth** in which the chicken was cooked. If not enough broth, add **rich milk.** If broth is too fat, use part milk. Bake at 400° F. for 1 hour. Take from oven. Remove cover, and pour over the following: The **whites** and **yolks** of **3 eggs** beaten separately, then lightly mixed with **1 tablespoonful melted butter** and **salt.** Return to 350° F. oven until eggs are set and a golden brown. Will serve 8 or 10 people.

ESCALLOPED CHICKEN NO. 2

Cook **1 large chicken** until it can be easily taken from the bones. The amount of meat should measure **6 cups.** Cook **1½ cups rice** in salted water. This should also measure **6 cups.** Pour **1 cup** of **chicken broth** over the cooked rice. Make a rich gravy by adding 4 **tablespoonfuls** of **butter** that has been browned to **¾ cup flour** that has been cooked in butter with 3 **cups** of **chicken broth.** Season with **salt** and **pepper.** Put a layer of chicken, then a layer of rice in a casserole. Sprinkle with **blanched almonds,** sliced canned **mushrooms** and pieces of **pimento.** Alternate layers until 1 cup of almonds, 2 cups mushrooms and 1 small can of pimentos have been used. Put gravy over all, and cover with **buttered crumbs** that have been browned slightly. Bake at 350° F. until all is cooked thoroughly about 20 to 30 minutes).

FRIED CHICKEN

Clean **fryer** and cut into pieces or fourths as desired. **Salt** and dip well in **flour.** Put 1 cup lard in iron skillet and heat very hot. Put chicken in and have the fire very low. Cover tightly and fry slowly for 15 to 20 minutes, according to size of chicken. Turn chicken over and fry 15 minutes with the lid still tight. It should be nice and brown. To make gravy, add 3 **tablespoonfuls flour** in **fat** and brown. Add **salt** and enough **water** or **milk** to thickness desired.

FRICASSEE CHICKEN

Cut up 1 medium sized **chicken** into the usual number of pieces (10), dredge in **flour.** Dip in undiluted **evaporated milk,** then in ½ **cup flour** and ½ **cup cracker meal** or **bread crumbs** seasoned with **1 teaspoonful salt** and ¼ **teaspoonful pepper.** Fry in 4 tablespoonfuls shortening in deep frying pan until brown. Change to a pan that can be put in the oven. Add **1½ cups evaporated milk** diluted with **1 cup water,** pinch **soda, 3 stalks celery** cut fine, **1 green pepper** chopped fine, **3 sprigs parsley,** minced, **1 bay leaf, 1½ teaspoonfuls salt** and dash of **pepper.** Bake in slow oven, 275° F., until chicken is tender. Arrange pieces of chicken on hot platter. Garnish with toast points or hot biscuits. Pour gravy over all.

JELLIED CHICKEN

Clean 1 large fowl, cut into pieces and cook in water until tender. Soak 2 tablespoonfuls plain gelatin in 1 cup cold water and add to 3 cups of the hot chicken stock. Remove chicken from bones. Have ready a loaf-shaped glass dish. In the bottom arrange sliced stuffed olives, chopped pimento and minced parsley for a bottom layer. Put in a layer of chicken and a little of the gelatin broth, then add more stuffed olives, pimentos and parsley and another layer of chicken meat. Pour over more gelatin liquid. Repeat if necessary to use up all chicken. Chill in refrigerator until set.

CHICKEN LOAF WITH MUSHROOM SAUCE

Melt **3 tablespoonfuls butter** in double boiler, add **5 tablespoonfuls flour** and blend well. Stir in **2 bouillon cubes** and **1½ cups milk.** Cook until thick. Mix with **2 cups chopped cooked chicken, 2 cups soft bread crumbs, ½ teaspoonful grated onion** and **1 slightly beaten egg.** Pack in greased loaf pan and bake in moderate oven about 1 hour. This is a soft loaf. Tuna may be substituted. Serve with mushroom sauce.

MARYLAND FRIED CHICKEN

Cut up **1 chicken** for frying. **Salt** and **pepper** each piece. Dredge with **1 cup flour.** Dip in **2 beaten eggs** and **1 cup** sifted **bread crumbs.** Brown with **¼ cup lard** in heavy iron frying pan. Cover. Cook in moderate oven until tender 30 to 45 minutes. Baste with ¼ **cup butter** after 15 minutes' cooking. Uncover the last 15 minutes to brown. Arrange on hot platter. Serve with cream sauce.

CHICKEN PIE WITH CRUST

Line a deep round pan with **biscuit dough.** Cook **chicken** until it falls from the bones. **Season** well. Remove bones. Cook until done as many **potatoes** as desired. Add a thickening of flour and **water** to some of the **chicken broth** to make enough gravy to cover chicken and potatoes. Place chicken and potatoes in crust lined pan and cover with biscuit dough. Roll edges of dough together to make a seal. Prick top of dough with fork, to let out steam. Bake in hot oven until crust is brown.

CHICKEN PIE FROM LEFTOVERS

Boil **leftover chicken** in a little water until ready to fall from bones. Cook 3 **potatoes** and 2 **onions** in water until done, but not soft. While this is cooking, mix up recipe for **baking powder biscuits** and cut into small pieces. Remove all chicken from bones, cut in pieces, return to broth, add potatoes, onions and any leftover gravy. Pour into casserole. Place biscuits on top very closely together. Bake in hot oven until biscuits are done. We suggest pickles and a canned fruit to complete this menu.

PRESSED CHICKEN

Cook 1 medium sized **chicken** until it falls from bones. Cut into pieces. Add **2 cups chicken stock, juice** of **1 lemon, 1 teaspoonful celery seed, ½ teaspoonful black pepper, 1 teaspoonful salt,** and **½ teaspoonful cayenne.** Mix well. Soak **2 tablespoonfuls gelatin** in **½ cup cold water,** dissolve in hot chicken stock, add **5 hard cooked eggs,** chopped or ground and chicken mixture. Stir all together and pour into molds.

ROAST CHICKEN WITH DRESSING

Clean and dress **chicken.** Place in roaster. Rub salt over the inside and the outside of the fowl. Add water enough to keep the chicken from sticking and browning before it is tender. Roast at 350° F. until tender. Dressing: take **1 loaf** of **corn bread** made with **white meal.** Add **1/3** as much **cold biscuit** or **loaf bread** as there is corn bread. Add 2 **onions,** cut very fine, and **sage** and **black pepper** to taste. Moisten with **chicken broth**, pat into small biscuits, place around chicken and bake until a light brown. This dressing may also be used with a pork roast.

CHICKEN STEW WITH DUMPLINGS

Use either young or old **chickens.** Dress, clean and cut up. Put in stew pan. Cover with boiling water and cook slowly until tender. Add ½ **tablespoonful salt** and dash of **pepper** when chicken is about half done. Dumplings: mix **2 cups flour** with ½ **teaspoonful salt** and **3 teaspoonfuls baking powder,** add **1 cup sweet milk** and make a very soft dough. Roll or pat out to ¼ inch thickness. Cut in squares. Place on top of stew. Cover tightly and cook for 15 minutes without looking.

CHICKEN TETRAZZINI

Simmer slowly in a covered pan, **1 small green pepper** shredded, ½ **red pimiento** shredded, **3 tablespoonfuls butter** and **¼ cup chopped mushrooms.** Add **¾ cup cooked ham** shredded, **1¼ cups cooked chicken chredded,** ½ **teaspoonful paprika** and **1 teaspoonful salt.** Cook together about 3 minutes and add **¾ cup cooked spaghetti** and **2 cups cream or condensed milk.** Boil about 3 minutes. Mix a little more cream with **3 egg yolks** and add to mixture. Take off fire and serve very hot.

CHICKEN VEAL CHOPS

Use the **white meat** from the **chicken** breast and **1 pound veal,** both having been previously cooked. Grind together with **one small onion, salt** and **pepper.** Make into croquettes or patties, and roll in well beaten **egg.** Then roll in **bread crumbs** and fry to a golden brown in deep fat. Place in a heavy skillet or casserole and bake until tender. This takes about 30 to 40 minutes in a moderate oven. If gravy is desired, take ½ to ¾ cup hot water and pour over meat before placing in oven. Be sure to cover.

Goose is another member of the fowl family used for meat. It is particularly fat so should be placed on a trivet when roasting.

CLEANING GOOSE

Since a goose is very hard to clean, it is best to have the poultry man do this for you, if not available, then after goose is killed and bled, pick as many of the feathers off dry, next pour melted paraffin over entire bird. When it hardens it can be pulled off in a sheet, taking the down with it. Clean as described in chicken.

ROAST GOOSE

Prepare **goose.** Wipe with a damp cloth. Place in a roaster. Dust with **salt, pepper** and **flour,** allowing from **1 to 2 tablespoonfuls of flour** to sift on bottom of the pan. Stuff with peanut dressing (if desired). Put in hot oven and brown (15 to 20 minutes). Pour a **little hot water** containing 3 **tablespoonfuls shortening** and ½ **tablespoonful** of **dark corn syrup** in the pan. Baste meat with this every 15 minutes until done. Make a gravy from the drippings in the pan, adding a cup of boiling water to each half cup of drippings. If necessary, thicken the gravy with a little flour blended with cold water.

Turkey is the king of American poultry. It is usually roasted but may be prepared in the same recipes as chicken.

CARVING A TURKEY

1. Use a platter large enough to hold all carved pieces or use an extra plate to hold some of the servings. The carving knife and fork should be the best you can afford. Have the knife absolutely sharp. Place the platter above the plates and before the host. Drumsticks should be at the host's right.

2. The host carves first the side nearest himself. Steady the bird with the fork, tines down, placed in the thigh. Cut close to body of the bird with a long stroke. With the fork, draw leg away from body joint as the knife cuts off the leg.

3. Rest leg on platter. Sever drumstick from thigh, using a clean stroke from outside tip of the joint to the inside bend. Cut

the thigh meat into three or four pieces. Slice meat from drumstick and place to one side of the platter or put on the auxiliary plate.

4. Thrust fork into second joint of the wing. With long stroke, cut off the second joint and lay it to one side. (Do not serve at table.)

5. Next make an incision lengthwise above the wing bone cutting into the breast until the knife strikes the ribs. Withdraw the knife without cutting off any meat.

6. Start to slice the white meat, beginning about 2 inches above the incision and cutting down to it. Slice thin, using long strokes. Lay slices on platter or auxiliary plate.

7. Continue to cut slices of white meat. For each slice start about quarter of an inch higher on the breast. Keep cutting until breast bone is reached, with the slices uniform in thickness.

TURKEY CROQUETTES

Add **4 tablespoonfuls quick cooking tapioca** and **½ teaspoonful salt** to **1½ cups stock** and cook in double boiler 15 minutes or until tapioca is clear, stirring constantly. Add **2 cups cooked turkey,** finely chopped, and cook 5 minutes longer. Chill. Shape into cones. Dip in **egg,** roll in **crumbs** and fry in **deep fat** 390° F. 1 minute or until a golden brown. Drain, serve with **tart red jelly. Garnish with parsley.** Makes 10 to 12 croquettes.

TURKEY HASH

Cut turkey into cubes. If there is left over **gravy** it may be used, if not, make a **white sauce** of **2 tablespoonfuls butter** and **2 tablespoonfuls flour, ½ cup cream** and **¾ cup white stock.** Stir turkey into sauce. Add **grated rind of lemon,** and **white pepper to taste.** Add **¼ lb. mushrooms** sauted and a **little mace** if desired. Allow to simmer gently, until heated through. Do not cook vigorously, nor too long, or it will be tough.

ROAST TURKEY

Dress, stuff and truss an **8 to 10 lb. turkey.** Place in roasting pan, breast up. Sprinkle with **salt, pepper** and brush with **melted non-salted fat.** Rub inside of turkey with **salt.** Put into 300° F. oven, with no water, no cover. Stuffing: **melt ½ cup butter.** Add **4 tablespoonfuls minced onion** and brown slightly. Pour over **8 cups stale bread,** diced. **Add 2 eggs,** well beaten, **2 teaspoonfuls salt, 2 tablespoonfuls parsley** and **½ teaspoonful pepper.** Mix well, then add **1 cup milk** to moisten. **Water** may be used if desired. Rub bird inside with **salt** and **pepper,** and stuff. **A crust of** stale bread fastened over opening with skewers will hold stuffing in place.

Veal, the meat of the very young beef calf. Although it is a young meat, it is a tough meat, and must be cooked with moist heat to break down the connective tissue present.

VEAL LOAF

Mix 2½ **lbs. ground veal** with ½ **lb. ground lean pork, 6 soda crackers** soaked in milk, **1 whole egg, pinch of thyme,** and **salt and pepper** to taste. When well mixed form into loaf. Bake at 375° F. for 2 hours, beating occasionally.

FRICASSE OF VEAL

Cut **1½ lbs. of veal** into pieces for serving. Roll in **flour** and brown in **hot fat.** Add **water** to almost cover and simmer for ½ hour. Make an uncooked sauce by combining **2 tablespoonfuls flour, ½ teaspoonful salt** and a dash of **pepper** with **½ cup chili sauce** and **1 cup water.** Pour sauce over meat. Stir until boiling, then simmer for 30 minutes.

JELLIED VEAL LOAF

Soak **1 tablespoonful gelatin** in **¼ cup cold water** 5 minutes. Dissolve in **1 cup boiling water.** Add **¼ cup sugar, ¼ cup vinegar, 2 tablespoonfuls lemon juice** and **1 teaspoonful salt.** Strain. Cool and when it begins to stiffen add **1½ cups cold cooked veal** cut in small pieces with **1½ pimentos,** cut fine. Turn into mold, first dipping into cold water. Chill. Serve with horseradish sauce.

VEAL BALLS WITH RICE

Mix **1 pound of ground veal** with **½ pound of ground pork.** Add **½ cup bread crumbs, 1 egg, 1 onion,** chopped fine, **1 green pepper** and **2 stalks celery** with **salt** and **pepper** to taste, Then mix with enough **milk** to make soft balls. Fry in rather deep fat slowly enough to be cooked through. Cook **1 cup rice** in rapidly boiling water which has been salted. Keep in double boiler until ready to use. Arrange the rice on a platter. Put meat over rice and cover all with **1 can of hot tomato soup.**

VEAL BREAST OR POOR MAN'S CHICKEN

Get a **3 or 4-lb. veal breast** and ask the butcher to make a pocket for stuffing. Salt inside and out, using about **2 teaspoonfuls salt** and some **pepper** if desired. Grease roaster well with **vegetable shortening.** Stuff breast with favorite **poultry stuffing,** rounding it to an attractive shape. A few stitches will close the opening. Then rub surface with **cooking fat** and dust with **flour.** Set roast on trivet in pan. Set oven at quick. After 20 minutes turn over to hot and in another 20 minutes turn to 350° F. and allow to remain for 2 hours. The last hour baste a few times with a little hot water and drippings from the pan. Do not cover.

VEAL BIRDS

Purchase **2 slices of veal from the leg,** which is the same as round steak in the beef. Season each piece of meat with **salt** and **pepper.** Dredge with **flour** and cut into pieces. Usually four birds can be made from one steak. Make a dressing of **1 cup bread crumbs, 1 egg, 1 tablespoonful butter, ¼ teaspoonful salt, ½ teaspoonful onion juice** and **hot water** to moisten. Place 2 tablespoonfuls or more of the dressing in center of each piece of meat. Roll meat around and fasten with tooth pick or tie with cord to hold shape. Saute birds in fat in frying pan, until golden brown on all sides, then place in a roaster. Add **1 cup water, stock** or **milk.** Cook slowly until done, using a 300° F. oven.

VEAL WITH DUMPLINGS

Brown 2 **lbs. veal** which is cut in about 2-inch squares with **1 cup diced onions.** Add 2 **cups water** and let **simmer about ½ hour.** Add **1 cup diced celery, 3 good sized carrots** and **salt** and **pepper** to taste. Cook 2 hours. To make dumplings: take **1 cup flour, 2 teaspoonfuls baking powder, ½ teaspoonful salt, 1 teaspoonful shortening** and enough **milk** to make soft dough. Now drop in dumplings with tablespoon, being sure there is enough liquid to cover meat and vegetables. Let cook 10 minutes. Do not raise lid after dumplings are put in until ready to take out.

VEAL PAPRIKA

Melt 3 **tablespoonfuls shortening** in a heavy frying pan. Gently brown **1 sliced onion.** Cut **2 pounds veal steak** in individual servings **and coat with flour.** Fry veal in shortening until brown. Season well with **salt** and **pepper.** Lower heat and add **1 cup boiling water** Cover pan, simmer slowly about 1 hour or until veal is tender. Then stir in **¾ cup sour cream** and **1½ teaspoonfuls paprika.**

Variety Meats

The brains of several animals, are used as food, the choicest being those of the calf. They are a soft membrane and require very little cooking.

BRAINS AND EGGS

Use **1 pound brains.** Let soak in cold water about ½ hour then remove all the red membrane from brains as well as the blood clots. Put a small piece of butter and lard in a skillet. When melted, add brains, which have been well drained. Cook over a slow fire until brains are quite dry and nicely browned. They should be watched closely as they burn very easily. Beat 2 or 3 **eggs** slightly, add **salt** and **pepper,** then pour over brains and cook 2 or 3 minutes longer or until eggs are done. This recipe will serve 5 or 6 people.

BRAIN PATTIES

Soak 1 **cup brains** in 2 cups slightly salted water for 15 minutes. Drain and stew in just enough water to cover 10 minutes. Pour off water and chop fine. Add ¼ **teaspoonful salt, dash black pepper,** ½ **teaspoonful** chopped **parsley, 1 egg yolk** and **3 tablespoonfuls cream.** Shape into patties, dip in **cracker meal,** sprinkle with **paprika,** and fry as oysters in shallow fat, turning after the first side is well browned.

FRIED CALVES' BRAINS

Soak **1 lb. calves brains** in salt water for at least an hour. Remove excess blood and membrane. Let simmer for 20 minutes, drain and cool. When cool divide in small pieces. Dip in **1 beaten egg** seasoned with **1 teaspoonful salt** and **1 teaspoonful paprika.** Dredge with **flour** and fry in deep fat to a nice brown. Drain and serve.

The hearts of beef and veal are used as foods. Sometimes the pork heart is used. Heart is usually left whole when prepared for the table.

STUFFED AND BAKED BEEF HEART WITH ONIONS

Soak **1 beef heart** in cold water for 1 hour. Cut away large veins and arteries. In cavity made by removing large veins and arteries put a stuffing made of the following ingredients: Mix **2 cups soft bread crumbs** and **1½ teaspoonfuls salt** and dash of **pepper.** Melt **4 tablespoonfuls butter,** then add to crumbs, mix well. Sew or skewer heart to hold stuffing in place. Sprinkle **2 tablespoonfuls flour** over heat. Heat **4 slices bacon** in frying pan, add heart, and brown the entire surface of heart. Put **3 cups tomatoes, salt** and **pepper** in baking pan. Add browned heart. Put 8 medium cleaned **onions around.** Cover and bake 275° F. 3 hours or 250° F. 4 or 5 hours. Serves 8.

STUFFED BEEF HEART (Boiled)

Wash **1 beef heart** and remove arteries, veins and all superfluous fat from outside. Melt **2 tablespoonfuls drippings** in **¼ cup boiling water.** Add **2 cups bread crumbs, 1 minced onion, ⅛ teaspoonful pepper, 1 teaspoonful salt, 1 teaspoonful sage.** Mix well. Fill cavities of heart with this dressing and sew together. **Salt** and dredge whole heart with **flour.** Melt tablespoonful fat in iron kettle. Brown heart in this, then cover with boiling water and cook slowly until tender. Serve on platter, surrounded by gravy made of the liquid. A cup of chopped ripe olives, 1 tablespoonful minced onion and 1 tablespoonful chopped green pepper added to the gravy gives a pleasing taste, as well as variety.

Kidney is one of the edible organs of the beef or veal.

KIDNEY PATTIES

Use **1 kidney** cut in halves lengthwise. Soak in cold water 10 minutes. Remove from water and dry. Put in food chopper with **1 onion,** alternately, that is, first ½ kidney, then ½ onion and so on until all is ground, Mix with rolled cracker or **stale bread crumbs** until of the consistency to hold together. Add **½ teaspoonfuls salt** and a dash of **pepper.** Make into patties and fry as you would hamburg.

KIDNEY STEW

Soak **1 veal** and **1 beef kidney** in salt water for 1 hour. Drain, scrape and dry. Scrape and clean **1 large carrot.** Peel **1 small onion** and slice. Cook carrot and onion together in **2 cups of water** until tender. Slice kidney and dredge with **flour.** Brown in frying pan. Add **flour** to **fat** and brown. Add to this the 2 cups water in which the carrot and onion were cooked. Boil until thickened. Add onions, carrot and kidney. Season with salt and pepper and cook for 3 minutes.

KIDNEY STEW WITH RICE AND GREEN PEPPERS

Split 3 **beef kidneys,** remove core, skin and hard membrane and cut into sections. Cover with **cold salted water,** bring to a boil and drain. Brown lightly in **3 tablespoonfuls shortening,** add **¼ cup flour** and cook about 3 minutes longer or until brown, stirring well. Add **2 cups water, 1 tablespoonful chopped onion, 2 green peppers cut in rings, ¼ teaspoonful salt** and **⅛ teaspoonful pepper.** Cover and simmer 25 to 30 minutes. Serve on cooked **rice.** This serves 6.

Liver is an edible organ of the beef, veal or pork. It is excellent for the anaemic person.

BAKED CALF'S LIVER

Soak **liver** in salted water 1 hour, then drain. Pour boiling water on it, let stand few seconds, then drain again and peel off the membrane on the edges. Dip each slice into **flour** and lay in baking pan greased with **bacon fat, salt** and **pepper.** Put little dots of bacon fat all over each slice. Put about **2 tablespoonfuls** of **water** into bottom of pan, cover tight and bake ½ to ¾ hour in moderate oven. This comes out brown and juicy. Serve with crisp bacon.

BREADED LIVER

Salt and **pepper 1 lb. liver,** sliced, then dip in **1 beaten egg** and roll in fine **bread crumbs.** Fry in hot fat until brown. If you prefer onion flavor, slice an **onion** in frying pan as liver is browning. Put browned liver in baking dish or pan, cover, add a little water to grease left in pan in which liver was fried. Pour contents over liver. Bake in moderate oven 45 minutes. This dish will give the flavor of fried liver but will be much better cooked than the ordinary way of frying it.

LIVER DUMPLINGS

Put **1 lb. of liver** (baby beef preferred) through a food chopper with 1 medium onion. Add **1 egg, ½ teaspoonful salt, ½ teaspoonful baking powder** and **2 tablespoonfuls flour.** Stir well until all is thoroughly mixed. Drop by spoonfuls into rapidly boiling water (salted) and allow dumplings to cook for 20 minutes. Drain from water and fry dumplings with diced bacon in hot bacon grease. This recipe serves four.

LEFT OVER LIVER PATTIES

Mix **1 cup left over** fried or broiled **liver** that has been chopped, with **1 cup mashed potatoes, 1 egg, 1 medium** minced **onion** and **salt** and **pepper** to taste. Pat into flat cakes. Dip in **bread crumbs** and fry or bake in little oil or shortening.

SMOTHERED LIVER

Liver cooked in this manner is always tender and surprisingly delicious. For this dish **beef liver** is used in preference to calf's liver. To 1 pound of sliced liver add **2 tablespoonfuls** of **prepared mustard.** Sprinkle generously with **salt** and **pepper.** With fork, stir mustard through liver until every piece is thoroughly covered with a thin coating. Dredge pieces in **flour.** Place **4 tablespoonfuls** of **bacon fryings** in heavy skillet and heat. Arrange pieces of meat in skillet and brown lightly on either side. Cover closely, reduce heat and smother for 25 minutes. A **few tablespoonfuls of cream** may be added to liver before it is covered. Serve with gravy made from fryings left in skillet. Slices of crisp bacon give a tasty garnish to the platter of liver.

SWISS LIVER

Season **flour** with **salt** and **pepper.** Dip each serving of **liver** in flour. Sear in both sides in **bacon fat,** then place in casserole and simply cover with water. Place in oven for 1 hour at moderate temperature (350° F.)

Sweetbreads are the thymus and pancreas glands of the young beef.

SWEETBREADS

To cook **beef sweetbreads:** Soak sweetbreads in cold water for 1 hour. Then cook in **simmering water** to which has been added **1 teaspoonful salt** and **1 teaspoonful vinegar** to **each pair** of **sweetbreads.** Drain, dip in cold water and remove membrane and tubes.

TO COOK VEAL SWEETBREADS

Soak sweetbreads in cold water ½ hour. Cook in water just to boiling point for 20 minutes. Plunge immediately into cold water, remove excess membrane. They are now ready for preparing in any way desired.

CASSEROLE OF SWEETBREADS

Soak **1 pound sweetbreads** in salt water for 1 hour. Cook slowly (simmering for ½ hour or until tender). Remove membrane and pull apart. Return to water in which they were cooked. Add **2 cups diced potatoes, 1 cup diced carrots, 2 medium chopped onions, ½ green pepper,** chopped, **4 stalks celery, ½ can peas, sprigs parsley, 1 tablespoonful butter, salt** and **pepper** to taste. Put in greased casserole and bake in moderate oven 1 hour. Add water if there is not enough broth to cover well. Serves six. Add more butter if a richer dish is referred.

CREAMED SWEETBREADS

Cut cooked **sweetbreads** into ½ inch cubes and add to **medium white sauce.** *Editor's Note*: If the sweetbreads are browned in a little butter first they have a better flavor.

SWEETBREAD PATTIES

Put **2 pairs** of **sweetbread** in cold water for 1 hour. Drain. Set on stove in a kettle of salted water. Bring to a boil and parboil 20 minutes. Plunge sweetbreads into ice water until very cold. Trim off all fat and membrane and cut into fine pieces. Saute **½ cup** finely cut **mushrooms** in **3 tablespoonfuls butter.** Heat **1 cup milk** and **1 cup cream** together, thicken wth **3 tablespoonfuls butter** and **3 tablespoonfuls flour**, blended together. Add **salt, pepper** and **paprika** to taste. Cook in double boiler, stirring until smooth and of creamy consistency. Add sweetbreads, mushrooms and **½ cup blanched almonds,** shredded into tiny bits. Serve in puff paste shells.

The tongues of beef, calves and lambs are used as food. They are cooked with the heavy outside coating left on, when done, this heavy skin removes easily.

BOILED TONGUE

Wash **tongue** thoroughly, scrubbing with vegetable brush. Cook in boiling water with **2 thickly sliced carrots, 2 small onions** stuck with **whole cloves, 2 stalks celery** and **salt** to taste. Simmer for several hours until tender. Remove skin while tongue is hot and allow tongue to cool in broth. Serve with mustard sauce. Melt **2 tablespoonfuls butter.** Blend in **2 tablespoonfuls flour** and add **1½ cups tongue broth, 1 teaspoonful dry mustard** and **½ cup of dill or sour pickle**, chopped fine. Serve hot over sliced tongue.

BEEF TONGUE WITH RAISINS

Soak a **smoked, pickled** or **fresh tongue** over night in cold water. Place in fresh water. Add ½ **lemon,** thinly sliced, **1 bay leaf, 3** or **4 cloves, ½ onion, 6 peppercorns** and if possible **1 small chili pepper.** Simmer until tender, at least three hours. Remove from liquor, skin and trim neatly. Set aside while sauce is being made. Boil liquor down rapidly to reduce quantity. Melt **2 tablespoonfuls butter.** Add **2 tablespoonfuls flour** and cook to smooth paste, then add **3 cups strained liquor.** Season to taste and stir in **juice of ½ lemon** and **½ cup raisins, seeded.** Simmer until smooth and slightly thickened. Add tongue and simmer 10 minutes. Remove tongue to platter, skin and trim. Serve sauce separately. This tongue may be served sliced cold. Cold sliced tongue, in alternate circles, on a chop plate with sliced corned beef, makes a nice buffet plate.

Tripe is the fatty inner lining of the stomach of several food animals, that of the calf being the most acceptable.

TRIPE IN BATTER

Mix **1 cup flour** and **¼ teaspoonful salt,** add **½ cup cold water** gradually. When smooth add **1 egg,** well beaten, **½ tablespoonful vinegar** and **1 teaspoonful melted butter.** Cut cooked **fresh honey comb tripe** in pieces for serving. Dip in batter and fry in a small quantity of **hot fat.**

STEWED TRIPE WITH TOMATO SAUCE

Cover **tripe** with cold water. Bring to boiling point, then drain. Cover with **boiling salted water** and simmer until tender. This will take about 4 hours if tripe is cooked whole, or 2 hours if tripe is cut in pieces. Serve with **tomato sauce.** Tomato Sauce: cook **1 sliced onion** and **2 cups tomatoes,** cooked or canned, 15 minutes and strain. Brown **2 tablespoonfuls butter** and **3 tablespoonfuls flour.** When well blended add to tomatoes. Bring to boiling point and serve. Salt and **pepper** to taste.

Meat Accompaniments

Sugar added to apples when they are just starting to cook will make them hold their shape better and give a transparent appearance to the apples.

CINNAMON APPLES

Pare and core **6 apples,** leaving fruit whole. Make a syrup of **½ cup sugar, 1½ cups water** and **½ pound** of **cinnamon candy drops.** Drop apples in syrup and cook very slowly until apples are tender. Serve with syrup on apples or with whipped cream. (If desired these apples make a lovely garnish for roast pork.)

The syrup from cinnamon apples may be saved and used over and over again.

APPLE RINGS

Select firm red **apples** that do not fall apart when cooked—Jonathans are good for this purpose. Remove the core with a corer or sharp paring knife. Slice the apple crosswise making as many rings as the apple will allow, each ring should be ⅛ inch thick—rings that are too thick lose their attractiveness, (do not cut rings until ready for syrup). Make a heavy syrup of **2 cups white sugar** and **1 cup water,** boil until a thread spins from spoon **(red cinnamon candies** may be added for color and flavor). Drop apple rings in syrup (a shallow pan will allow more rings to cook at a time). Cook rings until clear. Remove from pan, place on a large platter until cool. Do not stack one over the other until cool. These rings may be made a day before using.

CELERY — Spiced

Chop together **5 bunches** of **celery, 15 ripe tomatoes** and **1 large pepper.** Add **2 cups sugar, 1½ cups vinegar, 1 tablespoonful salt, 1 teaspoonful mustard, 1 teaspoonful celery seed** and **1 teaspoonful** each of **ground cloves, allspice** and **cinnamon.** Mix ingredients thoroughly. Boil mixture for 1½ hours. Seal in jars while hot. This is delicious with any kind of meat.

Cranberry is a small swamp berry of bright red color. It belongs to the blueberry family.

CRANBERRY JELLY

Clean **1 quart** of **cranberries** and cook with **1 cup water** until each one bursts. Press through strainer. Return to fire, add **2 cups sugar** and stir until dissolved. Pour into a mold and let stand until firm. Cook the sugar only enough to dissolve it; otherwise it will not jell.

CRANBERRY SAUCE

Pour **2 cups boiling water** over **1 quart** of **cranberries.** Let cook until every berry is open. Add **1 cup sugar** and cook 5 minutes more. More sugar may be added if one desires a sweeter flavor.

Dumplings are either a batter cooked in broth or a filled dough, either baked or steamed. They may be plain or have fruit added.

DUMPLINGS (Plain)

Mix **1 cup flour, pinch salt, 2 teaspoonfuls baking powder** with just enough **water** to make a stiff batter. Drop into **boiling broth** and do not cover. After raised, cover tightly and cook 20 minutes without uncovering. These dumplings are light, stay light and may even be warmed over.

POTATO DUMPLINGS

Pare **10 medium sized potatoes** and boil until tender. Put through potato ricer or mash quite fine. Add **3 slices of bread,** diced and browned in butter, **2 eggs,** well beaten and **4½ heaping cups of flour.** Mix well and form into balls. Drop into boiling water and boil 20 minutes. This makes about 14 dumplings. Serve with catsup or chili sauce.

RICE DUMPLINGS

Cook **1 cup rice** in **3 cups** of **milk** in double boiler and let cool. Then mix **1 teaspoonful butter, 4 egg yolks** and **1 teaspoonful salt.** Add rice and stir. Add 4 stiffly beaten **egg whites** and **1 cup flour.** Mix to a smooth dough. Drop by teaspoonfuls into boiling **chicken broth.** Cook for 5 minutes without cover. Serves 10.

Mustard is a small seed used as a spice.

GARNISHES

The following are a few of the foods used for garnishes: lemons, oranges, lettuce, endive, parsley, mint, watercress, radishes, peppers, paprika, hard cooked eggs, olives—plain, ripe or stuffed—pickles, cinnamon apples and sauted fruits. It is always best to choose a garnish that is edible, yet attractive in color. Color is of utmost importance in meal planning. A colorful plate of food is always eaten with better appetite.

PLAIN MUSTARD

Use **2 tablespoonfuls dry mustard, 1 tablespoonful flour** (sifted) and **vinegar** to make a smooth paste. Then add a **few drops** of **salad oil, sugar** and **salt** to taste. This does not require cooking. Horse-radish Mustard: The fresh horseradish root can be bought at the market and should be grated, not ground. Add **½ teaspoonful** grated fresh **horseradish root** to the above recipe.

Syrup left from pickles is good over roasts of meat.

Bay leaves or sage added to pork tenderloin give it a better flavor.

YORKSHIRE PUDDING

Mix **1 pint flour, 2 teaspoonfuls baking powder, 1 scant table-spoonful melted butter** or margarine and a pinch **salt.** Add **1 egg** well beaten and **1 cup milk** to make a batter. Bake 20 minutes in 350° F. oven. Cut in squares and place around roast of beef.

Meat Dressings and Stuffings

Stuffing or dressing is the name applied to the filling used when roasting poultry or game.

BREAD DRESSING

Break up **stale bread** in small pieces until there is about **2 quarts.** Pour **2 cups boiling water** over this and cover tightly, allowing to steam . When cool enough to handle, add **2 whole eggs, ¼ lb. butter, 1 small onion,** cut fine, **salt** and **pepper** to taste. Mix all with the hand until thoroughly blended. This is a good dressing for chicken, turkey, roasts or fish. If too moist from the hot water, drain before adding seasoning.

CORNBREAD DRESSING

About 2 days before you want the dressing make up this cornbread: Mix **1 cup white cornmeal** with **1 cup flour, 2 level teaspoonfuls baking powder, 2 level tablespoonfuls shortening, 1 egg, 1 teaspoonful salt, ¼ teaspoonful soda** and enough **buttermilk** to make the dough like cake dough. Bake at 450° F. until a nice brown, about 20 to 25 minutes. Allow to dry out for a day or two. When ready for dressing crumble bread into pan, add **½ teaspoonful pepper, 1 tablespoonful sage, ½ medium sized onion** minced, **1 teaspoonful baking powder** and enough **water** to moisten. If dressing is to be cooked outside of fowl then add **broth** instead of water. Work well, then stuff fowl or put in a greased pan to bake.

DRY DRESSING

Three medium sized loaves of homemade bread, rolled fine with hands, add **½ pound melted butter, 2 eggs, salt, sage** and **pepper** to taste. Mix well. Enough for a large fowl.

DUTCH DRESSING

Cut **1 potato** into small pieces and boil until soft. Mash and add to this, **1 small onion,** diced and friend in **butter** until tender. Add **½ cup hot milk** and **3 large cups bread,** alternately, beating well all the time. Next add **1 tablespoonful chopped parsley** or **celery leaves,** and **2 hard cooked eggs,** cut in small pieces. Add **salt** and **pepper** to taste.

OYSTER DRESSING FOR TURKEY

Mix **1 lb. bread crumbs, 2 stalks celery** chopped, **½ cup butter** melted, add **salt** and **pepper** to taste. Add **1 qt. oysters,** strained and cleaned. Add **oyster juice** and fill turkey.

PEANUT STUFFING

Break up bread to make **2 qts. soft bread crumbs.** Season with **salt, pepper** and **½ tablespoonful sage.** Brown **1 diced onion** in **¼ cup butter** and add to crumbs. Add **2 cups chopped peanuts** (salted peanuts may be used if they are scalded, then dried and cup up). Moisten the mixture with **1 qt. milk** or **milk** and **water** to bind dressing together. Stuff goose and bake.

RICE STUFFING

Cut **fat salt pork** in tiny cubes to fill **1 cup.** Fry out in **iron** frying pan and strain, reserving both **fat and scraps.** Return **¼ cup fat** to frying pan. Add **1 cup uncooked rice** and stir until slightly browned. Add **4 cups water** or **stock** in which giblets were cooked. Boil 5 minutes. Turn into a double boiler and cook until soft. Put remaining fat in frying pan. Add **1 onion,** finely chopped; cook until yellow. Add to rice with **1½ tablespoonfuls poultry seasoning, 1 tablespoonful chopped parsley, 1½ tablespoonful salt, ¾ teaspoonful pepper, 1 cup chopped celery** and **pork scraps** and **giblets** chopped

Meat Sauces

BARBECUE SAUCE—II

Mix 1 cup catsup, 2 tablespoonfuls Worcestershire sauce, 3 tablespoonfuls vinegar, 1 small chopped **onion, 1 teaspoonful sugar** and **salt** and **pepper** to taste.

(Barbecue Sauce number one—See Spareribs.)

BECHAMEL SAUCE

Melt **3 tablespoonfuls butter.** Add **4 tablespoonfuls flour.** Cook well. Add **1 cup meat stock,** heated (stock may be made by heating **1 bouillon cube** in **1 cup boiling water**), being careful to keep the mixture smooth. Add **½ teaspoonful salt, dash pepper** and **¼ teaspoonful paprika.** Add **¾ cup cream.** To be served with ham timbales.

GRAPE SAUCE FOR ROAST

Dissolve **1 tablespoonful cornstarch** in a little **cold water.** Add **¾ cup hot water** slowly, stirring constantly and cook until thickened. Then add **1 cup undiluted grape juice** (sweetened) and **juice of 1 small lemon.** Serve hot with fresh pork roast. *Editor's Note*: One half of this recipe is sufficient for a 4-lb. roast.

Gravy is a sauce made from meat drippings.

GRAVY

Remove any kind of roast from pan. Mix a thickening of **2 tablespoonfuls flour** and **2 tablespoonfuls water** to a smooth paste. If there is too much **fat** remove some, then stir in flour paste and cook until brown. Thin with **hot water** until the desired consistency is reached. Serve in a gravy boat.

GIBLET GRAVY

Boil **giblets** until tender, then grind. To **3 tablespoonfuls of fat** from roaster, add **3 tablespoonfuls flour, brown slightly.** After taking fowl out of pan add **water** to remaining broth, add browned flour, **salt** and **pepper** to taste, ground giblets and boil a few minutes.

BROWN MUSHROOM SAUCE

Melt 3 **tablespoonfuls butter.** Add **few drops of onion juice** and cook until slightly browned. Add 3½ **tablespoonfuls flour** and continue browning. Add gradually **1 cup cream.** Clean ½ **pound mushrooms,** cut in slices lengthwise, and saute in butter for 5 minutes. Add to sauce and season with salt and pepper or paprika.

RAISIN SAUCE FOR BAKED HAM

1 cup boiling water, 1 cup seedless raisins, 2 tablespoonfuls butter, 2 tablespoonfuls vinegar, 1 cup sugar, ½ teaspoonful salt, ¼ teaspoonful ground cloves, ¼ teaspoonful cinnamon, 1 glass grape jelly. Mix well, bring to a boil, add **1 teaspoonful cornstarch** dissolved in small amount of water. Stir until it thickens slightly.

TOMATO SAUCE

Melt 2 tablespoonfuls butter, add 2 tablespoonfuls flour and cook until straw colored. (The browner the flour the less thickening power it has. Add 1 teaspoonful sugar, 1½ cups tomatoes and salt and pepper to taste. Cook until thick and flour well done.

Meat Substitutes

CARROT LOAF

Cook **10 large carrots** in salt water, drain and mash fine. Add **2 cup fine bread crumbs, 2 tablespoonfuls butter, 3 egg yolks** well beaten, **1 onion** grated, **2 cups milk** and salt and **pepper** to taste. Lastly add **egg whites** well beaten. Pour into a buttered pan and bake in moderate oven 1½ hours.

CHEESE RICE CROQUETTES

Make a thick white sauce of **¼ cup butter, 1/3 cup flour** and **1 cup milk;** season with **1 teaspoonful salt, ⅛ teaspoonful pepper** and **⅛ teaspoonful paprika.** Add **1 cup grated pimiento cheese** and stir until melted. Cool and mix with **2 cups cooked rice.** Shape, roll in the fine **bread crumbs,** dip in slightly beaten **egg** diluted with **2 tablespoonfuls water,** roll in crumbs again and fry until brown in **deep hot fat.** This makes one dozen croquettes.

MEATLESS ROAST

Combine **1 cup cooked rice** with **1 egg, 2 tablespoonfuls** chopped **onion, 1 teaspoonful salt, 1 cup crushed peanuts, 1 cup cottage cheese, 1 tablespoonful fat** and **½ teaspoonful pepper.** Bake in a loaf pan 30 minutes at 350° F. This recipe will serve 6.

NUT CROQUETTES

Make 1 cup heavy white sauce by using **3 tablespoonfuls butter or margarine, 3 tablespoonfuls flour,** blending those two together in a pan over flame until they start to change color, then add **1 cup hot milk** and cook slowly, stirring all the while until smooth. Season with **salt** and **pepper.** When done, add **1 teaspoonful chopped parsley, 1 cup nut meats** chopped fine, **1 teaspoonful lemon juice, ½ teaspoonful salt, pepper** to taste. Add **1 cup bread crumbs** to thickened mixture. Cool. Shape into croquettes and dip in **beaten egg.** Fry in **deep hot fat** until a golden brown. When served, garnish with **lemon** and **parsley.** May be served with **tomato sauce.**

NUT ROAST

Use **2 cups of bread crumbs** (crumbs from French bread are best). Add **2 cups diced celery, 1 cup pecan meats**, finely cut, **1 egg** beaten, **1 teaspoonful onion tops** finely chopped or **chives, 1 tablespoonful minced parsley, 1 teaspoonful** salt, **4 tablespoonfuls butter** or **margarin** and enough milk to mix. When well blended, bake in greased baking dish in moderate oven (350° F.) until a light brown. Serve either with **tomato sauce** or **mushroom sauce.**

SOYBEAN LOAF

To 3 **cups cooked soybeans,** add **1 cup cooked macaroni, ¼ cup tomato sauce, 1 chopped small onion, 1 egg** beaten and ½ **teaspoonful salt** with a **dash** of **pepper.** Bake in a greased loaf pan in a moderate oven (375° F.) for 40 minutes.

Aerial view of Akron's Main Street, July 1941. *Courtesy of Cleveland State University, Michael Schwartz Library, Special Collections.*

Editor's Note

Glenna Snow's Cook Book *was published in 1938 and 1944. The following material is primarily intended to document some of the highlights of that era. In the late 1930s, the United States was finally recovering from the Great Depression and in the early 1940s, the United States was participating in World War II.*

Entertainment

On July 27, 1940, *Billboard* magazine published its inaugural "National List of Best Selling Retail Records." The following songs made the list.

No. 1 – "I'll Never Smile Again," Tommy Dorsey
No. 2 – "The Breeze and I," Jimmy Dorsey
No. 3 – "Imagination," Glenn Miller
No. 4 – "Playmates," Kay Kyser
No. 5 – "Fools Rush In," Glenn Miller
No. 6 – "Where Was I," Charlie Barnet
No. 7 – "Pennsylvania 6-5000," Glenn Miller
No. 8 – "Imagination," Tommy Dorsey
No. 9 – "Sierra Sue," Bing Crosby
No. 10 – "Make Believe Island," Mitchell Ayres

Residential street in a suburb of Akron, Ohio, ca. 1935–1940. *Courtesy The Ohio Historical Society.*

Entertainment *(continued)*

The Oscar Winner for Best Motion Picture

1938 – *You Can't Take It with You*
1939 – *Gone with the Wind*
1940 – *Rebecca*
1941 – *How Green Was My Valley*
1942 – *Mrs. Miniver*
1943 – *Casablanca*
1944 – *Going My Way*

Radio

Orson Welles broadcast his adaptation of H. G. Wells's *War of the Worlds* on October 30, 1938, creating a nationwide panic as listeners believed that aliens had landed in New Jersey.

Top-rated Evening Shows

1938 – *Chase & Sanborn Hour* (Edgar Bergen & Charlie McCarthy), Sundays 8PM
1939 – *Chase & Sanborn Hour* (Edgar Bergen & Charlie McCarthy), Sundays 8PM
1940 – *Jell-O Program* (Jack Benny), Sundays, 7 PM
1941 – *Chase & Sanborn Hour* (Edgar Bergen & Charlie McCarthy), Sundays 8PM
1942 – *Pepsodent Show* (Bob Hope), Tuesdays 10 PM
1943 – *Fibber McGee & Molly,* Tuesdays 9:30 PM
1944 – *Pepsodent Show* (Bob Hope), Tuesdays 10 PM

Entertainment *(continued)*

Bestselling Books (fiction; non-fiction)

1938 – Marjorie Kinnan Rawlings, *The Yearling;* Lin Yutang, *The Importance of Living*
1939 – John Steinbeck, *The Grapes of Wrath;* Pierre Van Paasen, *Days of Our Years*
1940 – Richard Llewellyn, *How Green Was My Valley;* Osa Johnson, *I Married Adventure*
1941 – A. J. Cronin, *The Keys of the Kingdom;* William L. Shirer, *Berlin Diary*
1942 – Franz Werfel, *The Song of Bernadette;* Marion Hargrove, *See Here, Private Hargrove*
1943 – Lloyd C. Douglas, *The Robe;* John Roy Carlson, *Under Cover*
1944 – Lillian Smith, *Strange Fruit;* Bob Hope, *I Never Left Home*

Sports

Baseball

Lou Boudreau was twenty-one years old when he broke into the big leagues on September 9, 1938, with the Cleveland Indians.

Ben Chapman of the Cleveland Indians hit three triples in a game against Detroit on July 3, 1939.

In 1940, Cleveland Indians' Bob Feller pitched a no-hitter on opening day (4/16). He won twenty-seven games that year and was named the *Sporting News* Major League Player of the Year.

Ohio grocery store (1942 or 1943). *From the Library of Congress Prints and Photographs Division, Washington, D.C.*

The Akron Yankees were a class C farm team of the New York Yankees from 1935–1941.

Bob Lemon was born on Wednesday, September 22, 1920, in San Bernardino, California. The future hall of famer was twenty years old when he broke into the big leagues on September 9, 1941, with the Cleveland Indians.

Basketball

The National Basketball League (NBL) was a professional basketball league in the United States from 1937 to 1949. It was created by three corporations—General Electric, Firestone, and Goodyear. The Goodyear Wingfoots won the league championship in 1937 and the Firestone Non-Skids won in 1939 and 1940.

Area League Teams and Years in the NBL

Akron Firestone Non-Skids (1937–41)
Akron Goodyear Wingfoots (1937–42)
Cleveland Chase Brassmen (1943–44)
Cleveland Allmen Transfers (1944–46)

Football

The 1941 Massillon Tigers high school football team, coached by Paul Brown, drew 141,000 fans for its eight home games.

In 1939 and 1940, Ohio State's Donald Scott was named a football all-American. On November 1, 1943, the Ohio State University trustees named the new airport Don Scott Field, in honor of Scott, who died in a bomber crash in England on October 1, 1943.

Ohio State compiled a 9–1 records and won the school's first national championship in February 1940.

Golf

Akron, Ohio claimed the distinction of the most golf clubs in proportion to its size than any other city in America. With a population of 250,000 the rubber center had twenty-four golf courses.

Tennis

Miss Shirley Fry, a fifiteen-year-old from Akron, Ohio, won the Western Pennsylvania Women's Tennis Championship in July 1942.

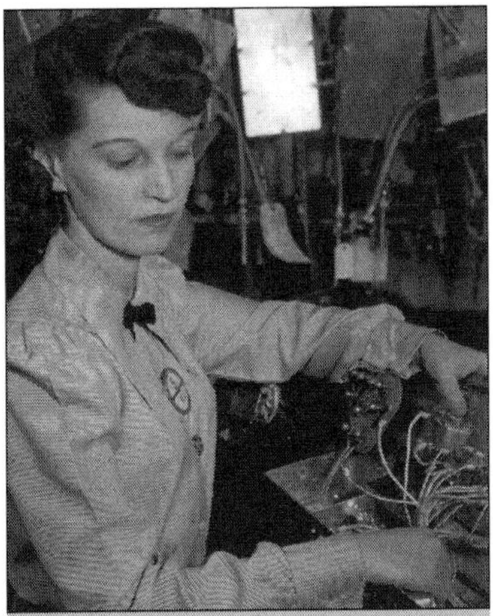

Electronics technician, Goodyear Aircraft Corp., Akron, Ohio (1941). *From the Library of Congress Prints and Photographs Division, Washington, D.C.*

Manufacture of self-sealing gas tanks, Goodyear Tire and Rubber Co., Akron, Ohio (1941). *From the Library of Congress Prints and Photographs Division, Washington, D.C.*

Headlines

Harvey Firestone Dies at His Miami Beach Estate. (2/7/1938)

New Navy Blimp Tested. Airship of 123,000 Cubic Feet Makes First Flight at Akron. (4/14/1938)

Ten Dead As Transport Ship Falls, Burns Near Cleveland. (5/25/1938)

Seven Passengers, Three Members of Crew Burned Beyond Recognition As Plane Wreckage Immediately Becomes Raging Inferno. (5/25/1938)

Cleveland Spurs Torso Killer Hunt. Finding of Victims No. 11 and 12 of Dissecting Maniac Bares Change in His Method. (8/18/1938)

Goodyear Statue Unveiled in Akron. Ceremony Is Climax of Observance of Centennial of Invention of Vulcanizing. (5/23/1939)

Barberton School Wrecked, 44 Hurt in Blast. Three of 40 Injured Children Are Not Expected to Live. (5/31/1939)

Akron-Bound Passenger Train Slams Head on into Freight Train. Nine Passengers Die on Impact, 34 Burn in Flames. (7/31/1940)

Headlines *(continued)*

Detroit Boy Wins "Soap Box" Derby. Thomas Fisher Then Goes on to Win International Race in Annual Program. (8/11/1940)

Blind Man Elected Mayor of Akron, Ohio. (11/5/1941)

Balloons of War Shaped by Women. Their Handiwork at Akron Creates Monsters of Sky for Defense Barrages. (8/30/1942)

Giant Wave Kills 7 on Lake Erie Shore. Wall of Water 60 Miles Long and 4 to 20 Feet High Piles Boats on Ohio Beaches. (5/31/1942)

Bricker, Ohio Governor, Victor for Third Time. (11/4/1942)

Tornadoes Kill 3, Fell Homes in Ohio. 500 Are Made Homeless and 150 Hurt in Cleveland, Akron and Smaller Communities. (4/29/1943)

Akron Transit Strike Ends. (5/14/1943)

Many Die, 200 Hurt in Cleveland Fire. Huge Tanks at East Side Gas Plant Explode and Flames Strike 50-Block Area. (10/21/1944)

Ohio Phone Strike Hits 25th City As Youngstown Operators Quit. (11/19/1944)

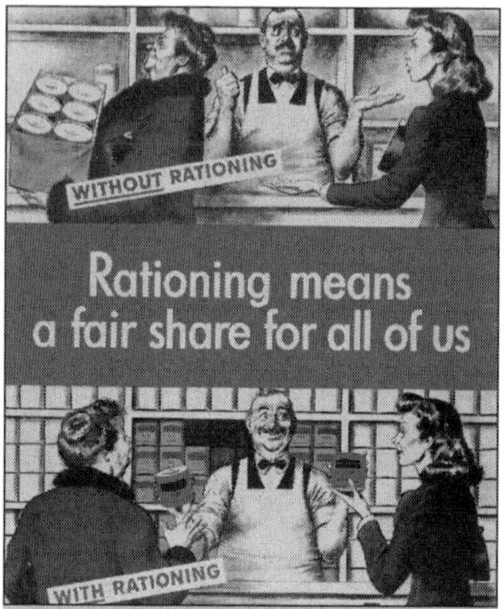

Poster promoting rationing, 1943. *Courtesy The Ohio Historical Society.*

Rationing

After the Japanese attack on Pearl Harbor in 1941, the Office of Price Administration (OPA) was created to begin rationing. Automobile tires led the list of items rationed, which by war's end included automobiles, typewriters, bicycles, stoves, leather and rubber footwear, coffee, sugar, canned and processed foods, meats, fats, gasoline, fuel oil for home heating, and coal. Rationing was undertaken in conjunction with an extensive program of price controls, rent controls, and other restrictions.

From Funk & Wagnalls New World Encyclopedia, 2002.

A Selection of Restaurants and Lunch Rooms, Akron, 1938–1944

- Ann's Sandwich Shop (816 Copley)
- B & B Steak Station (1721 West Exchange)
- B & O Lunch (479 North Arlington)
- The Beanery (54 East Market)
- Blue Cave Restaurant (277 North Howard)
- Black Whale Café (736 South Main)
- Busy Bee Restaurant (47 North Howard)
- China Clipper (769 North Main)
- Cork & Bottle (1720 East Market)
- Dell's Dutch Diner (670 South Arlington)
- Diamond Grill (77 West Market)
- Edison Restaurant (27 North Main)
- Etie's Lunch (90 West Bowery)
- Famous Restaurant (330 South Broadway)
- Friendly Tavern (1078 Kenmore)
- Great Presto Restaurant (204 East Market)
- Gridiron Restaurant (368 South Main)
- Hi-U Food Shoppe (155 South College)
- Hull's Barbecue (1334 Copley)
- Humpty Dumpty (87 East Market)
- Ido Café (1537 South Main)
- Instant Lunch (16 South Case)
- Jake's Sandwich Shop (17 West Exchange)
- Jerry's Steak Station (658 East Cuyahoga Falls)
- Kaase's Dining Room (53 East Mill)
- Kraker's Old Heidelberg (116½ South Main)
- Liberty Lunch & Pool Room (596 South Main)
- Lucky's Chinese American Restaurant (46 North Howard)
- Mary Ann Lunch (2256 Manchester)
- Midnight Lunch (492 Portage Lakes)
- Minute Lunch (376 South Maple)
- New Deal Lunch (60 East Market)
- New Korea Kitchen (706 North Main)
- Oasis Night Club (119 South Martha)
- Old Forge Inn (520 North Arlington)
- Orient Restaurant (216 South Main)
- Pacific Beer Garden (26 North Howard)
- Peppy Service Lunch (1300 East Market)
- Pullman Lunch (2024 Front)
- Rainbow Sandwich Shop (38 South Howard)
- Roadway Lunch (753 Brook)
- Rubber City Café (491 South Main)
- Sand Run Inn (1120 North Portage Path)
- Short Stop Inn (232 East Exchange)
- Silver Goose Café (776 Grant)
- Sky-Haven Sandwich Shop (1543 South Arlington)
- Spotless Spot (1020 South Arlington)
- Texas Steer (19 North Main)
- Tippy Inn (1381 Manchester)
- Von's Nite Club (1307 Grant)
- Union Park Restaurant (166 South Forge)
- Varsity Lunch (663 Portage Lakes)
- Walsh Bros Restaurant (348 South Main)
- White Castle (533 South Arlington)
- Zappion Restaurant (12 North Howard)
- Zissen's Savory Grille (121 South Main)

Swenson's Drive-In Restaurant, Akron, Ohio, 1940–49. *Courtesy The Ohio Historical Society.*

Restaurant Specials, 1938–1944

1938

Ham and Eggs or T-Bone Steak; Home Fried Potatoes; Head Lettuce; Bread and Butter; Drink – 40¢

Restaurant Specials *(continued)*

1939
Breaded Veal Cutlet with Poulette Sauce; Vegetables; Potatoes; Coffee – 35¢

1940
Tomato Juice or Fruit Cocktail; Smothered Chicken; Candied Yams or Mashed Potatoes; Fresh Peas; Homemade Rolls; Jell-O Vegetable Salad; Pie; Coffee – 65¢

1941
Liver and Onions; Wilted Lettuce; Kidney Beans; Potatoes; Bread and Butter; Drink – 35¢

1942
Pork Tenderloin; Chicken Soup; Dressing; Cranberry Sauce; Mixed Vegetables or Sweet Corn; Bread, Hot Biscuits, and Butter; Ice Cream or Cake; Coffee or Tea – 60¢

1943
Victory Vegetarian Dinner; Choice of Side; Ice Cream; Bread and Butter; Drink – 35¢

1944
Fresh Ground Hamburger with Spaghetti; Harvard Beets; Tossed Vegetable Salad; Rolls and Butter; Beverage – 50¢

Food Brands Found Locally in Akron from 1938 –1944

- Akron Pure Milk Company, "Protected"
- Averill's Dairy Products, "It's So Good!"
- Burkhardt's Beer, "Healthful, Delicious"
- Chestnut Ridge Dairy Company, "Milk for Those Who Want the Best"
- City Baking Company, "44 Varieties of Breads Every Day"
- Isaly Dairy Stores, "Ends the Quest for the Best"
- Norka Beverage Company, "And Remember, Norka Spelled Backwards Is Akron"
- Peoples Dairy Company, "Better Dairy Products"
- White Crown Beer, "A Royal Treat"
- X-Cel Dairy, "Your Best Local Dealer

Food Prices, 1938 & 1944

1938
Florida Oranges – 29¢ / dozen
White Bread – 10¢ / 2-pound loaf
Pot Roast – 19¢ / pound
Wheaties – 29¢ / 3 large packages
Bananas – 5¢ / pound
Sliced Bacon – 13¢ / ½ pound

1944
Florida Oranges – 65¢ / 2 dozen
White Bread – 11¢ / 26½ ounce loaf
Pot Roast – 18¢ / pound
Wheaties – 10¢ / 1 small package
Bananas – 25¢ / 2 pounds
Sliced Bacon – 14¢ / ½ pound

National Advertising Slogans, 1938–1944

- Coca-Cola, "With a Taste All Its Own"
- Pepsi-Cola, "The Big Shot"
- Ralston, "Whole Wheat. Ready to Eat."
- Salada Tea, "Still Stimulating & Satisfying"
- Spry, "Mixes like Magic"
- Sunkist Oranges, "Best for Juice and Every Use"

Auto Advertising Slogans, 1938–1944

- Buick, "Buick's the Beauty"
- Chevrolet, "Eye It. Try It. Buy It."
- Chrysler, "Be Modern. Buy Chrysler"
- DeSoto, "The Great American Family Car""
- Dodge, "The Biggest Value at Any Price"
- Nash, "Go Nash and Save Money Every Mile"
- Oldsmobile, "Bigger and Better in Everything"
- Plymouth, "The One for '41'"
- Pontiac, "The Fine Car with the Low Price"

Miscellaneous

HOME MADE SOAP

Slowly add **3 quarts of cold water** to **2½ cans of lye,** being careful not to inhale any of the fumes arising from it. Gather together all waste fat. Melt until it is in liquid form. It is not necessary to remove salt or small particles, as the lye will disintegrate them. Weigh **10 lbs. fat.** Do not guess at this amount as a chemist would not expect even results if he guessed at his measures. Place this fat in a large enamel kettle, add **1 small box borax** and **1 cup ammonia.** Stir until well mixed. Now slowly pour the dissolved and cooled lye into the fat. Stir continually until it begins to have the consistency of whipped cream. Pour into flat enamel pans. Allow to stand over night to set. Next morning cut in bars, spread out to dry.

POLENTA

Pare and cut **8 potatoes** in halves. **Salt** to taste. Let cook in **4 quarts salted water** until done. Mash, return to water they were cooked in. Add **1 quart cornmeal** slowly. Mix well and cook for 20 to 25 minutes, stirring frequently. When done pour into a wet mold for slicing. Fry a golden brown before serving.

PON HOSS

To **six cups boiling water** add **1 tablespoonful salt** and **½ pound liver pudding.** Stir until meat is dissolved or rather separated. Bring to a boil and keep cooking, while slowly adding **1 cup buckwheat flour.** Then **1 cup yellow cornmeal.** Stir constantly and boil 5 more minutes. Pour into molds.

RENDERING LARD

Cup up **leaf fat** in small pieces (about 1 inch square). Place in cold kettle. Add **1 cup water** and cook over moderate fire, stirring often to prevent scorching. When cracklings fry themselves dry when dipped up on a spoon, the lard is ready to pour off and cool.

RASPBERRY VINEGAR

Pick over **3 pints raspberries,** place in kettle and cover with **1 pint vinegar.** Allow to stand overnight. Strain fruit and liquid through a wet jelly bag. Measure, add **1 pound sugar** for **each pint of juice** then boil juice and sugar for 15 minutes. Turn into hot sterile jars or bottles. Cork and seal.

Nuts

Nuts are a delicious food which have separate flavor according to the nut. They are high in protein so may be used as a substitute for meats.

If nuts are kept in refrigerator they will not become rancid.

It is best to make a few jars of peanut butter at a time as the fresher it is ground the better the product.

PEANUT BUTTER

Roast in oven any amount of **raw peanuts** in their shells. Roast to desired brown color. Some people like them darker than others. Shell and remove red skins. Grind peanuts in food chopper using nut butter knife or a very fine knife. Add **salt** to taste and **olive oil** or **salad oil** slightly warmed. Mix to desired consistency.

The amounts are not given as some peanuts make more bulk than others and some people like their peanut butter thinner than others. This may be put into jars and sealed.

SALTED NUTS

Select **raw peanuts, fresh almonds, walnuts** or **pecans.** Remove skins from almonds and peanuts by pouring boiling water over them and allowing to stand 3 or 4 minutes or until skin is loosened. Remove with fingers. Place nuts in a wire basket and lower it into deep vegetable fat, heated to 390° F., or until cubes of bread brown in 40 seconds. Fry until delicately browned. Remove, drain on paper, and sprinkle with salt.

One Dish Meals

One dish meals are preparations of several foods in such a manner that only "one dish" is needed at a meal.

BACON, POTATOES, AND FRIED APPLES

Broil **1 lb. bacon** until crisp. Remove from fat. Place in warming oven or if camping in a bed of coals. Clean, pare and cut 8 medium sized **potatoes** for French frying. Drop into hot bacon fat and fry until a golden brown. Remove to warming oven. In the meantime wash and remove spots from 8 **apples**, slice, fry in the remaining bacon fat. Serve all on one platter. Potatoes in center, apples on outside with bacon over the top.

CHEESE AND CORN SOUFFLE WITH CREAMED MUSHROOMS

Melt 4 **tablespoonfuls butter.** Add **4 tablespoonfuls flour** and mix well. Add **1 cup milk** and cook until thick. Add **1 cup mild cheese, ½ teaspoonful salt, ½ cup soft bread crumbs** and **1 cup corn.** Stir until cheese is melted. Remove from fire. Add **3 beaten egg yolks.** Pour in 3 stiffly beaten egg whites and mix gently. Put into greased casserole and bake until firm. (50 minutes at 325° F.) Serve at once. Creamed Mushrooms: cut **½ lb.** or **1 can** of **mushrooms** in small pieces. Cook in **¼ cup butter** gently for 20 minutes. Blend in **½ cup flour** and stir in **2 cups milk.** Cook over hot water until thick. Season with **salt** and **pepper.**

CASSEROLE DINNER

In a frying pan brown **1 onion,** sliced, in **butter** or **meat drippings.** Add **1 pound** of **hamburg** and brown. Then add **1 can tomatoes, 1 can kidney beans** and **1 pint** sliced **raw potatoes.** Season with **salt** and **pepper.** Place the mixture in a casserole. Cover, place in oven, and cook slowly 1½ hours. In the meantime cook **¾ cup of rice** in a double boiler. When ready to serve, place carefully on a large platter and garnish with small mounds of snowy rice and parsley.

CASSEROLE BEEF

Dredge 3 **pounds of rump beef** with **flour,** mixed with **salt** and **pepper,** until it will not take any more. Brown it in heavy pan. Brown **3 large onions** in fat, and add 3 **tablespoonfuls** mild **prepared mustard,** ½ **teaspoonful celery seed** and **1 cup strained tomatoes.** Pour this sauce over meat. Preheat oven. Place in casserole, bake at 325° F. for 3 to 3½ hours. Moist heat.

CASSEROLE OF HAM AND RICE

Combine **1 egg, 2 cups ham,** cooked and chopped, ½ **cup soft bread crumbs, 2 teaspoonfuls** chopped **green pepper, 1 teaspoonful parsley** (finely chopped), **1 cup tomatoes** (canned), **1 teaspoonful mustard,** ½ **teaspoonful celery salt,** ⅛ **teaspoonful black pepper,** ½ **teaspoonful salt** and **1 teaspoonful onion** (chopped). Have ready **3 cups cooked rice.** Line bottom of casserole with one half the rice. Next put a layer of one half of meat mixture. Repeat and cover with **buttered bread crumbs** (½ cup very fine crumbs). Bake 30 to 40 minutes in a moderate oven (350° F.) Serve hot with tomato sauce.

HOMINY CASSEROLE (No. 1)

Put the contents of **2 cans** of **hominy** in casserole. Season and pour **1 cup top milk** or **cream** over it. Sprinkle with small amount of **grated cheese.** Place in oven and bake for 20 minutes. Take out. Break **6 eggs on top of hominy.** Place back in oven. Let it remain in oven till eggs have set. Serves 6. With a salad or pickle relish and dessert you have a delicious meal, yet very simple to prepare.

HOMINY CASSEROLE (No. 2)

In bottom of casserole put a layer of **cooked hominy,** then a little minced **onion, tablespoonful** of minced **green pepper,** and about **3 tablespoonfuls** of **canned tomatoes.** Add **salt** and **pepper.** Alternate layers of hominy and vegetables, having the last layer of onion, pepper and tomato. Sprinkle a few **bread crumbs** over top, dot with **butter,** and bake in moderate oven until done (about ½ hour).

LAMB WITH VEGETABLES EN CASSEROLE

Cut 2 **pounds shoulder** of **lamb** in small pieces. Remove all bones. Cover bones with water and simmer while preparing vegetables. Roll meat in as much **flour** as it will take up. Brown in frying pan. Put a layer in casserole. Mix **2 cupfuls** diced **carrots, 3 cupfuls** diced **potatoes,** small **onion** and minced **parsley** (about **1 tablespoonful).** Add a layer of this mixture then a layer of meat until all is used, sprinkling with **1½ teaspoonfuls salt, ¼ teaspoonful pepper.** Cover with **broth** strained from bones. Add more water if necessary. Cover and bake in moderate oven 1¾ hours. Ten minutes before serving, add **1 cup canned peas** mixed with **1 teaspoonful Worcestershire sauce** and **2 tablespoonfuls catsup.**

MEAT PIE A LA CASSEROLE

Cover 2 **lbs. beef** or **pork** cut in small pieces with water and boil rapidly for 15 minutes, then simmer until ender. Put meat into baking dish and pour over gravy made by using **2 tablespoonfuls flour** to **each cup** of **liquid** left from meat. Add **1 large onion,** cooked, **1 cup** diced **celery,** cooked, and **1 cup carrots,** cooked. Season to taste. Cover with **baking** powder **crust** rolled ½ inch thick. Directions for making crust: To **1½ cups flour** add **2 teaspoonfuls baking powder, 1 teaspoonful salt, 2 tablespoonfuls shortening.** Work with finger tips until crumbly. Add **¾ cup milk.** Mix well. Roll out as directed. This dish may be baked in the oven or in a heavy aluminum casserole over slow fire on top of stove. Bakes on top of stove in 30 minutes.

SAUERKRAUT EN CASSEROLE

Line bottom of casserole with **kraut.** Sprinkle **rolled oats** and keep alternating kraut and rolled oats until you have used **1 quart kraut** and **3 tablespoonfuls rolled oats.** Cover with layers of sausage **(10 small sausages).** Bake 2 hours in casserole (covered tightly). Remove from oven and cover with **3½ cups** of fluffy **mashed potatoes,** sprinkle with **½ cup grated cheese** and return to oven to brown. This is a delicious "one dish meal."

VEGETABLE CASSEROLE

Combine **1 can peas, 1 cup** diced **cooked carrots, 1 cup** diced **cooked potatoes, ½ cup celery,** with **1 cup** or more of left over **gravy** and **¼ teaspoonful salt.** Put in greased baking dish. Cover top with small biscuits. Bake in moderate oven until biscuits are baked a light brown. By adding **½ cup raw carrots** to biscuits dough, it makes the biscuits more atractive and nutritious.

CHAMOISETT

Combine **1 cup tomatoes, 1 bunch celery,** cut fine, **1 green pepper,** cut fine and **1 onion,** minced, cook until celery is soft. **Cook 1 bag** of **noodles.** Grind and sear **1 lb. lean pork** in a small amount of fat. Add **1 package** of **grated American cheese** and mix with the vegetables. Bake 2 hours in a very slow oven. Can be made the day before and kept in the refrigerator.

Chili is the name given to a small hot pepper, used extensively in Mexico.

CHILI MEXICAN

Soak **2 cups kidney beans** for several hours, then boil until tender, draining off the liquid in which they were boiled. Place in a skillet **½ lb. fresh pork,** ground fine, ½ lb. lean beef, ground fine; **1 green pepper,** chopped fine, **6 tablespoonfuls butter** and **1 large onion,** chopped fine. Simmer until tender. When cooked and brown add **2 cups strained tomatoes** and stir well together. Blend **¾ teaspoonful salt** with **⅛ teaspoonful cayenne pepper, ¼ teaspoonful white pepper,** and **½ teaspoonful dry mustard.** Add this at the very last cooking five minutes before serving. Serve very hot.

Chop suey and chow mein are two Chinese dishes which probably originated in America. They vary with the meat used as a base.

CHINESE CHOP SUEY

Put 3 **tablespoonfuls vegetable oil** in a kettle and brown **1 lb. veal** and ½ **lb. pork** cut in small cubes. Stir constantly. Add **2 bunches celery**, cut into small pieces. Cook. Add **4 onions** cut fine and cook until a rich brown (be sure that this brown is reached as that is the secret of good chop suey). Add ½ **cup water.** Cover and cook ½ hour (it may be necessary to add more water). Make a gravy of **1 tablespoonful flour, 1 cup water** and **2 tablespoonfuls soy sauce** (purchase from grocery) and pour over meat. Serve with boiled rice and Chinese noodles if desired. Bean sprouts may be added to the above recipe.

CHINESE CHOW MEIN

Saute ¼ **lb. mushrooms** cut in pieces, **1 small green pepper** shredded and ¾ **cup chopped celery** in ¼ **cup shortening** for 5 minutes, using a heavy sauce pan. Add **2 cups leftover gravy, 2 cups leftover pork,** cut in cubes, **1 medium sized can bean sprouts** and ¼ **lb. blanched almonds,** shredded. Season highly with **soy sauce**, Cook 20 minutes. Add 2 level **tablespoonfuls cornstarch** (moistened with water) or enough to thicken. Cook 10 minutes longer. Serve on Chinese noodles. When using fresh pork sear it well in fat, then add 2 cups canned chicken broth and then the raw vegetables, cooking this mixture for 25 minutes before adding other ingredients.

CURRY HOT DISH

Fry 3 **medium sized onions** in **butter** until done but not brown. Add ½ **teaspoonful curry powder** and 2 **tablespoonfuls flour.** Mix. Add **juice** from **1 small can of peas** and **1 small can mushrooms** with enough **milk** to make **2 cups liquid.** Place **1 small can tuna fish** in alternate layers with the peas and mushrooms in casserole. Dip sauce over these so as not to disturb. Cover with **1½ cups of rice** which has been cooked and rinsed. Cover with generous coating of **grated cheese.** Cover the dish and bake in oven until sauce boils into rice and cheese is brown.

DEVIL BALLS

Mix **1 pound ground beef, ¼ pound ground pork, 1 small head** of **cabbage,** ground, **1 onion,** chopped fine, **1 pepper,** chopped fine, and **1 teaspoonful salt.** Shape into balls, place in shallow pan about 1 inch apart. Spread **½ cup uncooked rice** between balls and cover all with **1 can of tomato puree** mixed with water if too thick. Bake 3½ hours in slow oven, until rice is cooked. Baste occasionally.

DINNER IN A DISH

Put **4 tablespoonfuls shortening** in a skillet and slowly fry **2 green peppers,** sliced, and **1 chopped onion** for about 3 minutes. Then add **1 pound hamburg** and blend thoroughly. Add **1½ teaspoonfuls salt** and **¼ teaspoonful pepper.** Remove from fire, stir in **2 eggs** and mix well. Put **1 cup fresh corn** in a baking dish, then half of the meat mixture, then a layer of sliced **tomatoes.** Repeat, making another layer. Cover with **½ cup buttered crumbs** and bake in a moderate oven, 375° F., about 35 minutes.

HAM TETRAZZINI

Melt **2 tablespoonfuls butter.** Cook **1 teaspoonful onion,** chopped, **½ green pepper** and **½ pimento,** both chopped fine, **in butter** until soft and brown. Add **½ cup canned mushrooms** and saute until they are heated through. Make a white sauce, using the butter and fried ingredients by adding **3 tablespoonfuls flour** and browning, then adding **3 cups milk.** When cooked add **2 egg yolks.** Mix **2 cups cooked ham** cut into cubes and **2 cups cooked shell macaroni** into the white sauce and other contents. Cook **1 cup new peas** in boiling salted water until tender. Add to first mixture. Put into a greased casserole and bake until hot through. This recipe serves eight.

Hash—a combination of meat and potatoes, usually with left-over materials, but excellent with fresh ones.

HASH

In one pan place **2 eggs** to cook hard. After water boils reduce heat and let simmer for 20 minutes while rest of hash is being prepared. In another pan put 2 cleaned and sliced **onions,** with enough salted water to just a little more than cover. Let this cook until onions are soft and water nearly all boiled away. Cut or chop, but do not grind, enough cooked **meat** for **1 cup** and enough **boiled potatoes** for **2 cups.** When onion is soft, add meat and potato to the onion and water. There should be enough to make it moist, but if not, add **milk.** Heat until potatoes and meat are thoroughly hot. Add **¼ cup butter, salt** and **pepper** to taste. If liquid is thin add a tiny bit of thickening made with **1 tablespoonful flour** and a little **water.** (Only add this when contents of hash are boiling.) If made correctly there is no need of thickening. Fold in one sliced hard cooked egg. Use other one for garnish on top of serving dish. A sprig of parsley also improves the appearance.

BAKED HASH

Put all bits of **leftover meats** of various kinds through the grinder. Add half the quantity of chopped **potatoes** (leftover cooked ones may be used), **one onion,** chopped fine, and **salt** and **pepper** to season. Mix well, then put into a buttered pan. Pour enough **milk** over the ingredients to dampen, or enough so that the milk appears between the openings of the food. Bake until nicely browned, then serve at once. Water can be used instead of milk, but is not quite so good.

RED FLANNEL HASH

Chop 5 **medium cooked potatoes** and 3 **medium cooked beets.** Mix with **1 cup chopped cornbeef** and season with **salt** and **pepper.** Melt **2 tablespoonfuls fat** in a heavy frying pan. Add hash and **2 tablespoonfuls evaporated milk.** Cover and cook slowly until well browned. Cut in sections, turn with spatula and brown on other side adding 2 **more tablespoonfuls fat.** Serve with chili sauce or catsup.

SPANISH HASH

Brown **1 onion** and ½ **pound hamburg** or leftover meat in small amount of fat. Add **1 cup uncooked rice** to **1 quart tomatoes.** Season by adding **3 teaspoonfuls salt, 1 green pepper, pepper,** and **paprika.** Combine the **two mixtures.** Bake in covered dish in slow oven until rice is tender. It takes about 3 hours.

NEW ENGLAND BOILED DINNER

Use a large kettle. Parboil **corned beef** until the desired freshness is reached, then set at lowest heat and boil very slowly for 3 or 4 hours. Prepare medium sized vegetables that may be cooked whole, with the exception of cabbage which is always quartered. If **beets** are used they are cooked separately. When meat has been cooked as above, add the vegetables which require the longest cooking, **cabbage, turnips, onions** and **carrots.** When sufficiently done, add **potatoes, parsnips** and finish cooking. When done, the vegetables are well drained, the beets skinned, meat sliced, and the whole arranged on a huge platter. It is not only tasty but very attractive, too. Use **pepper** if you wish but not salt. The quantities must be judged for the number to be served.

NEW ONE DISH MEAL

Prepare **4 large potatoes** by paring and dicing, **4 large carrots** by doing the same and **2 large onions.** Grease a casserole dish. Put in alternate layers of **1½ pounds hamburg** with potatoes, carrots, and onions, seasoned with **salt** and **pepper** and bits of **butter.** Cover with **1 cup rice** that has been half cooked. Pour a can of **vegetable soup** over all. Dampen with **milk or water** and bake 1½ hours.

POT ROAST DINNER

Wipe off a **2½ lb.** piece of **beef chuck.** Fry in skillet, **1 onion** sliced, in a little fat, until a golden brown, then add meat and cook until 2/3 done. Add **4 carrots,** sliced, **3 sweet potatoes,** sliced, **1 sweet pepper,** cut in strips, and **four stalks celery.** Continue cooking until all can be easily pierced with a fork.

HUNGARIAN GOULASH

Cut **2 lbs. chuck beef** into large cubes and brown in heavy pot. Add **2 pints water, 2 cloves garlic** and **1 bay leaf.** Simmer 2½ hours over low flame. Add **1 teaspoonful salt, dash cayenne pepper** and **6 medium size potatoes,** diced in large pieces. Simmer until potatoes are tender. Cream **2 tablespoonfuls flour, 2 tablespoonfuls butter** or **margarine** and **2 tablespoonfuls paprika.** Mix to a paste with a little of the hot liquid, then add to meat. Cook until thickened. Just before serving add **1 cup tomato puree.**

HUNGARIAN NOODLE GOULASH

Cut **2 pounds** of **beef** in inch cubes and roll in **flour.** Cook **1 cup salt pork,** diced, in frying pan. Add beef and cook until brown, stirring constantly. Add sufficient water to keep from sticking. Cover. Cook until meat is tender. Add **2 cups tomatoes, 1 stalk celery, 1 green pepper,** chopped fine, ½ **cup** diced **onions, 2 cups** diced **carrots, 2 tablespoonfuls** minced **parsley, ¼ teaspoonful pepper, 4 cloves, 1 teaspoonful salt** and 2 **tablespoonfuls flour,** thinned with a little water. Simmer until vegetables are tender. Serve with **2 cups of noodles** which have been cooked in boiling salted water. Add additional seasoning if desired.

HUNGARIAN PIGS IN BLANKETS

Cut the heart out of a **cabbage head** and set the head in a kettle of boiling water. Allow to stand until leaves are soft and come off easily (there should be at least 15 good sized leaves). Part of the leaf rib may or may not be removed. Mix 2 **pounds ground pork, ½ cup uncooked rice, 1 egg, 1 onion,** chopped fine, **salt** and **pepper** to taste. Lay small handful of this mixture on each cabbage leaf. Roll up and stuff end of leaves in toward center. Put ½ of a **large** can of **kraut** (1 pint) in bottom of kettle, next the rolled pigs, then the **remainder** of **kraut** (another pint). Add water to cover. Cook over slow fire 3 hours.

MEAT BALLS IN TOMATO SAUCE

Saute in large kettle **1 cup each of diced onion, celery** and **green pepper.** Add **1 quart canned tomatoes, ¼ cup catsup, salt, pepper** and **a little sugar** to suit the taste. Bring to boil.

Mix together **1½ lbs. ground beef, 2 cups soft bread crumbs, 1½ teaspoonful salt, 2 teaspoonfuls celery seed, 1½ cups milk, 3 tablespoonfuls melted butter or margarine.** Season with **pepper.** Shape into small balls and drop into hot tomatoes. Simmer covered 25 minutes or cook in oven 1 hour. Thicken before serving if needed. Serves 12.

RICE WITH CHICKEN

Clean and cut a **chicken** into small pieces. Fry until a golden brown in **melted butter** with **1 cup** of **uncooked ham** diced. Add **salt** to taste, **1 cup canned tomatoes,** a **little parsley, several small olives** and **Spanish peppers.** To the chicken mixture add **1 pound** of **uncooked rice.** When rice has assumed a golden look add **1 quart of boiling water** and cook slowly, keeping well covered to preserve the aroma.

SAUSAGES, RICE AND PINEAPPLE (Baked)

Put layer of **boiled rice** in bottom of shallow baking dish. Parboil enough **sausages** for the family (15 minutes), then arrange on bed of rice so they radiate from center like spokes of a wheel. Put **spoonful of crushed pineapple** in center of dish and between sausages. Bake in moderate oven, 350° F., for ½ hour, then place under broiler flame for a few minutes to brown sausages, pineapple will brown slightly also, making a pretty and appetizing dish.

SALMON AND SPAGHETTI LOAF

Heat **1 cup milk** and **2 cups stale bread crumbs** together. Stir in **2 egg yolks.** Add **1 cup cooked spaghetti** or **macaroni, 2 cups salmon, 4 tablespoonfuls melted butter, 1 teaspoonful salt** and a **dash of paprika.** Next fold in stiffly beaten **egg whites.** Sprinkle with **paprika.** Set in pan of water and bake 45 minutes. Serve with **egg sauce.**

SCALLOPED POTATOES AND DRIED BEEF

Pare and slice enough **potatoes** to fill a quart dish. Melt **2 tablespoonfuls butter** in a large sauce pan. Add **1/8 lb. dried beef** and stir until slightly frizzled. Add **2 tablespoonfuls flour,** then gradually add **2 cups milk** and cook until slightly thickened. Spread a thick layer of potatoes in a well buttered casserole. Sprinkle with **2 tablespoonfuls onion, salt** and **pepper** to taste (taste dried beef, if salty it may not require additional salt). Add a layer of creamed dried beef and coarse cracker crumbs using **1 cup crumbs for all** layers. Repeat until all ingredients are used, having top layer crumbs. Bake in moderately hot oven 350° F. until potatoes are thoroughly done. This serves 6.

SHEPHERD'S PIE

This dish is made from **meat left over** from a pot roast. **Run** cooked meat through food chopper. **Season** well and moisten with any left over **gravy.** Place in bottom of well buttered casserole and spread with layer of sliced **onions.** Place a generous amount of **mashed potatoes** on top. **Season** well and moisten with **hot milk.** Beat **1 egg** and add a little **milk,** pour over top of potatoes. Sprinkle **salt** and **pepper.** Bake in moderate oven 45 minutes, allowing top to brown slightly before serving.

SPINACH, CHEESE AND BACON

Drain a **No. 3 can of spinach.** Melt **1 package of very fine American cheese** in double boiler, add **1/2 cup milk,** stir until dissolved. Pour over spinach which has been placed in buttered baking dish. Cover with **broken pieces of bread,** small but not crumbs. Cover with **1/2 lb. bacon,** cut into bits. Bake in a moderate oven until bacon is crisp and all thoroughly hot.

TAMALE LOAF

Fry **1 medium onion,** chopped, in **1/3 cup lard** until lightly browned. Add **2½ cups tomatoes** and when hot stir in **1 cup corn-meal.** Cook 10 minutes. Stir to prevent lumping. Remove from fire, add **1½ teaspoonfuls salt, ½ teaspoonful pepper** and **1 tea-spoonful paprika.** Add **2 cups left over** or **ground beef** or **pork, ¾ cup canned corn** and **2 eggs.** Blend thoroughly. Pour into greased loaf pans. Bake 45 minutes in moderate oven until firm and brown. Serve hot or cold with or without tomato sauce.

Pastry

Special Pastry flour is not necessary in making pie crust. Good crust can be made from all purpose flour.

STANDARD PASTRY

Have **1 cup lard or substitute** cold and firm. Work either by cutting with knives or using finger tips into **3 cups flour** and **1 teaspoonful salt.** It need be worked only until it is like gravel and may be coarse at that; but, working must be done before adding liquid. Add **6 tablespoonfuls water,** mix together quickly. Divide into 4 parts. Roll from center out in order to have a round crust. This recipe will make four crusts. Make it all at once then wrap the unused portion in waxed paper, store in refrigerator until another pie is wanted. It really improves with ageing in a cold place. Different flours require different moisture. Study the flour you use then record the amount for the next time.

Cover rolling pin with a small child's white stocking and you will find rolling easier.

Cover pastry board with a piece of heavy duck, work flour into it and the rolling of cookies and pastry is much easier.

To measure a part of a cup of fat fill cup with water, then pour out water equal to amount of fat required, add fat until cup is filled with water. Pour off water and you have the fractional part of cup of fat desired.

The temperature of water has considerable influence on resulting pastry. Ice cold or chilled water does one thing, water at room temperature, another. Choose the temperature according to the results desired, ice water for flaky pastry, warmer water for mealy pastry.

Lemon juice is sometimes added to water for flavor and to make the crust more tender.

PASTRY (With batter)

Sift 2 cups flour and 1 teaspoonful salt together in a bowl. Take out 1/3 cup and blend with ¼ cup water to make a paste. To remainder of flour in bowl, add 2/3 cup shortening and cut in with two knives, a fork or a pastry blender until fat is broken up into pieces the size of peas. Stir flour paste into fat-flour mixture to form a dough. Gather together in a ball and transfer to floured board. This makes enough dough for an 8-inch 2 crust pie.

Salt is vital to pie crust. Allow ½ teaspoonful to 1 teaspoonful per cup of shortening, the amount depending upon your personal taste.

Different fats make different pastry. Oils make pastry rich and crumbly. Butter makes flaky but tough pastry. Lard makes mealy pastry. Hydrogenated fat produces a tender pastry that is flaky.

LIFTING PASTRY

How to lift shortest pastry from board to pie without having it break is sometimes rather difficult. Here is how it is done. Roll pastry lightly. Use but little more pressure than weight of rolling pin. Trim off ragged edges so that no cracks run into pastry. Then lightly place rolling pin near edge of pastry and roll pastry onto rolling pin, rolling toward you, starting pastry on rolling pin with flat of a knife. Roll it all on pin, holding last on with your hand. Lift pin over pie pan, place edge you are holding on edge of pie pan and then quickly unroll pastry onto pie pan.

CHEESE PASTRY

Sift **1½ cups bread flour** with **1 teaspoonful salt.** Cut in **½ cup shortening** and mix in **½ cup grated American cheese.** Add **4 tablespoonfuls ice water** and **1 teaspoonful prepared mustard.** Mix gently. Chill for 5 minutes. Roll lightly. Use only enough water to hold ingredients together.

Mix flour, shortening and salt for pie dough, then store in refrigerator until needed. Add a little water and pie dough is ready.

Be sure to follow directions exactly or cream puffs will not be good.

HOT WATER PASTRY

Pour ½ **cup boiling water** over **1 cup lard** and mix until lard is melted. Sift in 3 **cups pastry flour** which has had ½ **teaspoonful salt** and **1 teaspoonful baking powder added.** Stir with spoon until mixed. Set in ice box and chill.

CREAM PUFFS

Heat **1 cup water** to boiling point, then add ½ **cup butter.** When butter is melted, stir in gradually **1 cup flour.** This makes a smooth paste if beaten well. Cook until dough forms a ball and leaves pan. Remove from fire. When cool, stir in **4 eggs** unbeaten, one at a time, beating after each addition. Add pinch **salt.** Beat until very smooth batter is acquired. Drop with teaspoon onto buttered pan and bake 10 minutes at 425° F., then 10 minutes at 400° F., then 5 minutes at 375° F. This recipe makes 24 cream puffs. They may be filled with whipped cream, plain custard, chocolate custard or ice cream and topped with chocolate syrup.

HUNGARIAN BUTTER PASTRY

Make this pastry in 2 parts: Part 1: Take ¼ **lb. butter** and ½ **lb. flour** and work together quickly. Don't let the butter melt. Roll dough 9 inches in diameter. Part 2: Take 1¾ **lbs. flour** and work together with **6 egg yolks** and just **enough milk** to knead the dough a little heavier than bread. Roll dough out the same size as Part 1. Put the two doughs together, one on top of the other. Fold the top 1/3 of the dough over the other part, bringing it down nearly to the center, then the left edge over to meet the right edge. Lastly, bring the bottom edge up to meet the top of the first folded edge. Put on ice for ½ hour. Repeat rolling out to the 9-inch diameter circle and folding as first described. Chill. Repeat twice again. The last time the dough is folded it is rolled out to ¾ inch in thickness and cut in diamond shape with a knife that has been heated on the fire red hot. Fry in deep fat. Put on waxed paper and sprinkle heavily with powdered sugar.

Small bits of pie dough may be made into tarts or patty shells. Fill tarts with jelly and shells with any creamed meat or vegetable.

Tarts are small desserts made from fancy pastries. Tortes are desserts made with egg white for a foundation.

BANBURY TARTS

Mix 3 **cups flour** with **1 cup lard, ½ cup butter, 1 egg** and **4 tablespoonfuls water,** the same as for pie crust. Roll very thin and cut in squares. Place 1 tablespoonful filling in each square and join corners in center. Bake. Serve cold, with a **teaspoonful whipped cream** on top and a **maraschino cherry. Filling:** Mix **1 pound raisins, 1 cup chopped nut meats, 1 cup sugar, 1 egg** and **1 tablespoonful butter.**

CHOCOLATE TARTS

Melt **2 squares** of **unsweetened chocolate** in double boiler. Add **1 can sweetened condensed milk,** stirring over hot water 5 minutes until mixture thickens. Add water. Stir thoroughly until blended. Pour into baked tart shells. Garnish with **whipped cream.** Chill before serving.

TAFFY TARTS

Mix **1 cup brown sugar, 1 egg, 1 tablespoonful vinegar, dash nutmeg** and **½ teaspoonful vanilla.** Beat until light. Put 1 tablespoonful in unbaked tart shell. Bake in moderate oven 35 to 40 minutes. Serve with whipped cream.

Pies

Pie—The Favorite All-American Dessert.

Pie crust will brown better on bottom if pie plate has been greased.

To form a glaze on pie crust, brush the crust when nearly done with egg yolk mixed with a little water.

Start all pies with a very hot oven until crust is slightiy brown, then reduce heat to 375° F. to finish baking.

If a pie runs over in the oven, sprinkle salt over juice to keep oven from filling with smoke.

Apricots may be purchased either fresh, canned or dried. The dried ones being equally as good for food and flavor as either of the other two.

APRICOT PIE

Wash and soak **1 pound dried apricots** for 3 hours. Cook until tender, then add **1 cup sugar.** Bake the same as apple pie with 2 crusts and ample time to bake thoroughly. It takes about 40 minutes in a moderate oven.

GOLDEN APRICOT PIE

Combine ½ **pound dried apricots,** cooked and drained with **4 tablespoonfuls sugar.** Dissolve 1 **package** of **orange gelatine** in **1 pint** of **warm apricot juice** (adding water to the juice to make 1 pint). Add ¼ **teaspoonful salt** and pour over apricots. Chill. When slightly thickened, turn into cold pie shell. Chill until firm. Cover with whipped cream.

It requires from 1½ to 2 lbs. of apples for a pie according to size of pie pan.

If apples are dropped into a weak salt solution after paring they will retain their white color. The solution does not impair the flavor.

APPLE PIE

Line a pie pan with pie dough, dust the bottom with a little **flour.** Pare, core, and slice enough **apples** to fill the crust to overflowing. Cover with **1 cup brown sugar** and **½ teaspoonful spice,** either **cinnamon, nutmeg** or **allspice** or a little of each. Divide **2 tablespoonfuls butter** into small bits and distribute over the top of the pie. Top with another crust that has had several slits made in it to allow steam to escape. Always wet edge of lower crust before pressing top crust down. Bake in very hot oven for 10 minutes until crust starts to turn brown, then reduce heat to hot or 400° F. and continue baking for 30 minutes.

CRUSTLESS APPLE PIE

Slice as many pared **apples** as will fill an ordinary pie pan about 2/3 full. Mix with **½ cup sugar** or more if apples are very sour. Pack apples down well. Add **¼ cup water.** Cover with a crumb mixture made by mixing together **1 cup brown sugar, ½ cup flour** and **½ cup butter.** Pat down firmly. **Cinnamon** may be sprinkled over the top if desired, but not necessary for flavor, as the brown sugar gives it a butterscotch taste. Bake in a moderate oven until crust is formed on top and apples are done. Serve when cold, by cutting the same as other pies, with a dash of **whipped cream** for garnish. Other fruits may be used in place of apples and the results are very good especially with cherries and peaches.

DUTCH APPLE PIE

Line a pie plate with rich pastry and set aside in cool place until ready to bake. Pare and core enough cooking **apples** to fill crust. Slice or cut into small quarters. Sprinkle **brown sugar** in bottom of unbaked pie shell. Sprinkle with **cinnamon** and dot with **butter.** Fill pie crust with apples, laying them in carefully. Add more brown sugar, cinnamon and butter. Place in a moderate oven to bake apples evenly. When half done pour **½ pint** standard **cream** over all and finish baking. When done, the result is a wonderful caramel filling. When cool, spread **whipped cream** over top just before serving. This is also very good with a meringue topping.

FRIED APPLE PIES

Filling for pies: wash and soak **3 cups** of **dried apples** in **warm water** 1 hour (or use apple sauce). Put in warm water with a **half cup sugar** and cook until tender. Make pastry from the following ingredients: to **2 cups flour** add **¼ teaspoonful baking powder** and **¼ teaspoonful salt.** Then rub in **½ cup lard** and enough **cold water** to make a dough (about 1/3 cup). Roll thin and spread evenly with **butter,** cut the size of a small plate. Put 2 spoonfuls of apple on half of the dough. Fold over and press edges with fork and fry in **deep hot fat.** Remove from fat, cover with **powdered sugar.**

OPEN APPLE PIE

Line a 9-inch pie pan with pastry. Fill with sliced **apples** and cover with the following which have been mixed together: **1 cup brown sugar, 2 tablespoonfuls flour, 1 tablespoonful butter, 3 tablespoonfuls sweet cream, pinch** of **salt** and **¼ teaspoonful nutmeg.** Bake until apples are tender.

The banana is a tropical fruit shipped to the United States while still green. It should not be eaten raw until brown specks appear on the skin. If it is to be used cooked, then select those that are firm and yellow.

BANANA CREAM PIE

Combine **½ cup sugar, 2 tablespoonfuls cornstarch** and a pinch **salt.** Add **½ cup milk** and mix. Add **2 beaten egg yolks,** then another **½ cup milk.** Cook in double boiler. Slice **3 bananas** into baked pie shell. Pour creamed filling over bananas and spread with meringue made from **2 egg whites** and **2 tablespoonfuls sugar.** Brown in moderate oven.

Place a small amount of flour over the hole where juice is running out of a pie, it will help stop the leak.

METHODS TO KEEP JUICE IN PIE

1. The undercrust is left large enough so that it may be brought up and folded over the top crust when it is laid in place.

2. The upper crust is left large enough so that it can be tucked under the lower pie crust.

3. A strip of pie tape is fastened around edge of pie plate.

4. A strip of white cloth is taped around the outer edge of pie plate.

5. A piece of macaroni is put in center of pie to absorb expanding juice which will come down when pie cools.

6. Allow top crust to rest loosely on filling, do not fasten to bottom crust.

BERRY PIE

Fill a pie plate with **one layer of pie dough,** scatter **a small amount of flour** over the bottom, add cleaned **berries** and usually, **1 cup sugar.** Sprinkle **1 tablespoonful quick tapioca** over all and dot with **butter.** Cover with top crust which has been cut larger than bottom one, tuck under and crimp in place. Bake in a hot oven until done. This recipe will fit most any small berry.

BUTTERMILK PIE

Mix **1 pint fresh buttermilk** with **3 well beaten eggs.** Add **½ cup sugar** and flavor with **nutmeg.** Put in **unbaked crust.** Mix **¾ cup flour** with **½ cup sugar, 1 tablespoonful butter** and put on top. Bake in moderately hot oven (350° F.) until pie is set.

BUTTERSCOTCH CHIFFON PIE

Melt **2 tablespoonfuls butter** and **1 cup brown sugar** in skillet. When melted to a thick brown sirup, add **1½ cups milk** and stir until all lumps are dissolved. Then add **3 tablespoonfuls cornstarch** mixed with a small amount of **cold water** and the slightly beaten **yolks of 2 eggs.** Cook until thick. Remove from fire, cool slightly and fold in stiffly beaten **egg whites.** Pour into baked shell. Chill thoroughly and serve with **whipped cream.**

BUTTERSCOTCH SPONGE PIE

Separate **2 eggs**, beat **yolks, 1 cup brown sugar** and **1 tablespoonful butter** together as for a cake. Add **1 tablespoonful flour**, **½ teaspoonful salt** and **1 teaspoonful vanilla.** Add **1 cup milk** and fold in beaten egg **whites.** Pour into pastry lined tin and bake in a moderate oven. There will be a nicely browned meringue over the top when done.

Sour cherries are usually used for pies and puddings, while sweet cherries whether white or black are used for salads and desserts.

CHARLOTTE RUSSE PIE

Soak **1 tablespoonful gelatin** in **1 cup milk,** then heat until gelatin is dissolved. Pour over the beaten **yolks** of **2 eggs** that have been mixed with **1 cup sugar.** Cook until mixture forms a custard. Cool. Beat **whites** of **2 eggs** and add to cooled mixture. **Add 1 pint whipped cream,** a **pinch salt** and **1 teaspoonful vanilla.** Line pie pan with buttered **graham cracker crumbs** and pour mixture into this. Grate **German sweet chocolate** over the top. This is a nice dessert for a party, as it can be prepared the day before.

CHERRY PIE (That Doesn't Leak)

Mix **2 tablespoonfuls flour** with **1 cup sugar.** Add **1 egg,** slightly beaten, and mix with **1 pint** of fresh **pitted cherries** (1 quart unpitted). Put in pastry shell, cover with top crust. Bake at 400° F. until done.

CHERRY CHIFFON PIE

Soak **1 tablespoonful plain gelatin** in **¼ cup water** for 10 minutes. Mix 4 **egg yolks, ¾ cup sugar** and **¼ teaspoonful salt.** Stir in a double boiler until eggs are cooked and custard is thick. Add softened gelatin and stir until dissolved. Cool and add **1 tablespoonful lemon juice** to **½ cup cherry juice** and **½ cup cherries cut in pieces.** Cool until gelatin begins to set. Beat **4 egg whites** until stiff, add **¼ cup sugar** and beat to a fine meringue. Fold into mixture, pour into a baked pie shell. Place in refrigerator to set. Garnish with **whipped cream** and decorate with clusters of **maraschino cherries,** using bits of **green pepper** for stems.

CHERRY TAPIOCA PIE

Line a nine-inch pie tin with pastry. Mix **1 quart pitted cherries, 1¼ cups sugar** and **5 tablespoonfuls quick tapioca** in sauce pan, cook over medium fire for about 15 minutes or until tapioca thickens. Remove from fire. Cool. Sprinkle a little flour and sugar on bottom of pie shell to prevent juice from soaking crust. Place upper crust on filled lower one, dampening the edge of the lower one in order to make top stick. Press edges firmly together. Bake in moderate oven for 25 minutes or until browned.

CHESS PIE

Line individual pie tins (muffin pans may be used) with a rich pie dough. Make the following filling: to **1 cup sugar** add **½ cup butter** and cream well. Add **3 egg yolks** well beaten, **¼ cup milk, ¾ cup** chopped **English walnuts, 1 cup** cooked **raisins** and **1 teaspoonful vanilla.** Pour into unbaked pie shells and bake 20 minutes in moderately hot oven. Serve with whipped cream on top. This recipe makes 15 individual pies.

CHOCOLATE PIE

Stir **½ cup cold water** and **¼ cup cocoa** over direct heat until smooth. Mix **3½ tablespoonfuls flour, 1 cup sugar** and **pinch salt.** Add **½ cup milk,** then add **2 egg yolks** and **1 more cup milk.** Add this to cocoa and water mixture. Cook until thick, stirring constantly. Add **1 teaspoonful vanilla** and **1 tablespoonful butter.** When cool, place in baked pie shell and top with meringue. To make meringue: to the **2 egg whites** beaten stiff, add **2 tablespoonfuls sugar** gradually, beating with egg beater all the time.

CHOCOLATE CHIFFON PIE

Soften **1 tablespoonful gelatin** in **¼ cup cold milk.** Combine **1¾ cups milk** with **¾ cup sugar** and **2 ounces of chocolate** and cook over low fire until chocolate is melted and all is smooth. Pour over **2 slightly beaten egg yolks** and cook 1 minute longer. Remove from fire, pour over gelatin and stir until dissolved. Cool, then fold in **2 stiffly beaten egg whites.** Pour into cooled baked pie shell. Top with **1 cup of heavy cream.**

COCOANUT PIE

Soak **1 cup cocoanut** in **1 cup milk** for 2 hours. Mix **2 tablespoonfuls flour** with **¾ cup milk** and heat until it thickens. Add **2 tablespoonfuls butter.** When cool, add **salt** and **2 egg yolks,** sweeten to taste. Add cocoanut and beat well. Fill crust and bake until firm. Cover with a meringue made from **2 egg whites** and **2 tablespoonfuls sugar.** Brown in oven.

When making custard pies always heat milk to scalding point before mixing it with eggs. This will help to keep undercrust crisp.

Always place custard pies in hot oven to bake crust, then reduce heat to bake custard.

CUSTARD PIE

Have an unbaked pie shell ready. Make the following filling: to **2 cups scalded milk** add 3 slightly beaten **eggs, ¼ cup sugar** (add more sugar if you desire it sweeter) and **¼ teaspoonful salt.** Mix well. Pour into pie shell, sprinkle over top with **nutmeg** or **cinnamon.** (Vanilla may be added to filling in place of spices if desired.) Bake in a very hot oven 450° F. until crust is brown, then reduce heat to 350° F. and continue baking until custard is set.

CUSTARD PIE (Baked in Hot Oven)

Beat 3 **eggs** until yolks and whites are blended. Add **5 tablespoonfuls white sugar, ⅛ teaspoonful salt, ¼ teaspoonful nutmeg** and **½ teaspoonful vanilla.** Mix thoroughly. Add **2 cups scalded milk** slowly, stirring constantly. Pour into pastry lined pie pan. Bake in HOT oven (425° F.) until an inserted knife comes out clean.

BLACKBERRY CUSTARD PIE

Beat the **yolks** of **4 eggs.** Add **1½ cups sugar, 1 cup butter, 2 tablespoonfuls flour** and **2 cups blackberries.** Mix well. Put into pie shell to bake. Bake in slow oven until firm. When done, cover with meringue made from **4 egg whites** and **4 tablespoonfuls sugar.** Set back in slow oven until meringue is brown. This recipe makes 2 pies. For one use only half the recipe.

COCOANUT CUSTARD PIE

Line a deep 9-inch pie pan with pastry. Combine **4 eggs,** slightly beaten, ½ **cup sugar** and ¼ **teaspoonful salt.** Add **3 cups scalded milk,** stirring constantly. Add **1 cup shredded cocoanut** and pour into pie shell. Bake in hot oven 450° F. for 10 minutes, then decrease oven heat to 300° F. and bake 30 minutes longer or until knife inserted comes out clean. Cool before serving.

RHUBARB CUSTARD PIE

Line pie pan with pastry and spread with **1¼ cups diced rhubarb.** Heat **1½ cups milk** in top of double boiler. While heating, break 3 **egg yolks** into bowl and beat slightly. Add **¾ cup sugar, 2 tablespoonfuls flour, 2 tablespoonfuls butter** and **¼ teaspoonful salt** to egg and mix well. Gradually pour hot milk into egg mixture, stirring until cooked. Pour custard over rhubarb in pie shell and bake at 425° F. for 20 minutes, then 325° F. for 25 minutes longer.

SWEET POTATO CUSTARD PIE (Two One-Crust Pies)

Mix **1 cup sugar, 2 cups hot mashed sweet potatoes, 2 tablespoonfuls butter, 1 teaspoonful cinnamon, cloves,** or **allspice** and a **pinch salt,** well together. Add **3 egg yolks,** well beaten, and **2 cups milk.** This makes enough filling for 2 pies. Pour into **2 unbaked pie shells.** Bake in moderate oven until set. Make meringue with **3 egg whites** and **6 tablespoonfuls sugar.** Spread over baked pies and set in oven until brown.

The paper can be removed easier from a package of dates if they are placed in the oven a few minutes before it is to be removed.

Various tricks are recommended to keep pie shell in shape while baking. Dried beans or uncooked rice are sometimes put in the bottom of pastry before baking. Sometimes a slightly smaller pie pan is set on top of crust. The pastry may also be put on the outside of the pie plate and bake in inverted fashion. A properly made pie shell holds its shape without any special treatment.

DATE PIE

To 1 **package** of **dates**, stoned and cut up, add **1 cup water, juice** of **1 lemon, ¼ cup sugar, 1 tablespoonful butter, pinch salt** and **1 cup** chopped **walnut meats.** Put the above ingredients on to simmer for about 20 minutes. Fold in beaten **whites** of **2 eggs.** Pour the above into a baked pie shell and set in slow oven for 15 minutes. Serve with whipped cream. This is a delicious pie, but very rich, and should never be served with a heavy meal.

CARAMEL GLAZE DATE PIE

Mix ¾ **cup brown sugar, ¼ teaspoonful salt,** 3 **tablespoonfuls flour,** and 3 **tablespoonfuls cornstarch.** Stir slowly into **2 cups** hot **milk.** Cook until thick, stirring constantly. Add 2 beaten **egg yolks,** cook 1 minute longer, remove from fire. Add 2 **tablespoonfuls shortening, 1 teaspoonful vanilla** and **1 cup** coarsely cut **dates.** Partly cool, then fold in stiffly beaten **2 egg whites.** Pour into a baked pastry shell. Arrange ½ **cup pecans** on top, cover with a caramel glaze made by melting ½ **cup sugar** slowly in heavy skillet, stirring constantly; when caramelized, add **½ cup hot water.** Stir and bring to a boil. Cool slightly and pour over top of pie filling.

The gooseberry is a small green or pink berry which is very tart. It is seldom eaten raw. It is more popular in England than in America.

GOOSEBERRY PIE

For an 8-inch pie use **1 pint canned gooseberries.** Mix 6 or 8 **tablespoonfuls sugar** with **2 tablespoonfuls flour** and a **pinch** of **salt** and stir into the stewed berries. Let stand while pie dough is being made. Pour into unbaked crust, add ½ **teaspoonful butter,** cover with crust and bake in 400° F. oven until juice runs through slits in crust. Or: thicken 1 pint gooseberries by adding 6 or 8 tablespoonfuls sugar. Bring to boiling point then gradually stir in several spoonfuls of cornstarch mixed with water (the amount of cornstarch varies with the juice of the berries). Cool. When ready to serve place in baked pie shell.

DELICIOUS GOOSEBERRY PIE

Crumb ¼ **cup flour** with 3 **tablespoonfuls butter** until smooth. Place **1 qt.** of cleaned and washed **berries** in bowl, add **1¼ cups sugar** and **crumbs,** and mix well. Pour mixture into lined pie shell. Cover top with pastry and bake about 45 minutes in moderately hot oven, 375° F.

GRAHAM CRACKER CREAM PIE

For crust, combine ¼ **cup sugar, 12 double gaham crackers,** rolled fine, and ½ **cup butter** melted. Line sides and bottom of pie pan, keeping ½ cup crumbs for top. Let stand about an hour. For filling, heat 3 **cups milk** and **1½ cups cocoanut** in sauce pan. Mix together **6 tablespoonfuls flour** and 2/3 **cup sugar.** Beat **4 egg yolks** and add slowly to hot milk. Cook until thick, pour into pie shell. Beat **egg whites** with 4 **tablespoonfuls sugar,** and use to cover top of pie. Lastly, sprinkle with crumbs and bake in slow oven 15 to 25 minutes.

GRAHAM CRACKER LEMON PIE

Roll 12 **fresh graham crackers** until fine, heat ½ **cup butter** and mix with crumbs, add **1 tablespoonful sugar.** Mold in glass pie plate.

Place 3 **egg yolks** in pan used to melt butter. Add ½ **cup sugar, pinch salt, juice** and **rind** of **1 lemon.** Cook over slow fire until thickened. Beat **egg whites** until they stand up, add ½ **cup sugar** and beat well. Fold in lemon mixture and put in pie shell. Place in cold oven, turn on fire, placing regulator at 300° F. Bake 25 minutes. If oven has no regulator, be sure to heat slowly.

GRAPEFRUIT CHIFFON PIE

Beat 4 **egg yolks** and 1 **cup sugar** together until light. Add this slowly to 1/3 **cup grapefruit juice** which has been heated in a double boiler. Cook until thick, beating all the time. Beat 4 **egg whites** until very stiff. Fold half of these beaten egg whites into egg yolk mixture which has cooled slightly. Cut and fold **2 tablespoonfuls** sifted **powdered sugar** into the other half of egg whites, for meringue. Pour filling into a baked pastry shell; cover with meringue and bake in a very moderate oven until delicately brown.

GRAPE PIE

Separate **1 quart** of **blue grapes,** skins from the pulp. **Heat** pulp until soft, then press through a colander or coarse **sieve to** remove seeds. Combine pulp and skins. Add ¾ **cup** of **sugar and 1 tablespoonful lemon juice,** the **yolk** of **1 egg** and **2 tablespoonfuls cornstarch.** Mix all together and cook in double boiler **until** thick. Pour into a baked crust, use egg white for meringue (**made** by adding **2 tablespoonfuls sugar** to beaten **egg white**). Cover **pie** with same. Place in oven until golden brown.

Grapefruit is a fruit grafted to the stock of a rough lemon. It grows in clusters as does the grape, hence its name.

Prepare grapefruit for table by cutting in halves. Loosen each section by inserting a grapefruit knife along one side at the center, bring it back to rind, cut across back of section, and down other side, back to center This allows the grapefruit to retain its whole position and still has each section separated from the skin.

HUCKLEBERRY PIE

Make a rich pastry dough. To **1 pint** of **huckleberries add 1 tablespoonful** of **flour,** tossing the berries about until all have **been** covered. Then add **1 teaspoonful vinegar** and ½ **cup sugar for 1** pint of berries. Fill bottom crust. Cover with top crust and **bake** in hot oven until crust begins to get brown then reduce heat **until** berries appear cooked.

LEMON PIE

Beat **3 egg yolks** and ½ **cup sugar** in double boiler, add **3 tablespoonfuls hot water** one at a time. Cook over hot water till **real** creamy, stirring all the time. Remove from fire, add **juice and grated rind** of **1 lemon.**

Beat **3 egg whites** till very stiff, add ½ **cup sugar,** fold into the above mixture, put into a **baked crust.** Put in a hot oven **400° F.** for browning, as you would meringue.

LEMON CHIFFON PIE

Dissolve ½ **tablespoonful gelatin** in 1/3 **cup cold water.** Place in a double boiled ½ **cup sugar,** a pinch of **salt** and the **rind** and **juice** of **1 lemon.** When hot add soaked gelatin and 3 well beaten **egg yolks.** Cook until thick. Watch water in lower part of boiler; if it gets too hot the egg mixture will curdle. Beat **3 egg whites** until firm, add another ½ **cup sugar** slowly, beating all the time. Pour the hot mixture over the egg whites, stirring constantly. Cool, turn into a well baked crust and let stand until hardened. Serve with whipped cream if desired.

LEMON SPONGE PIE

Cream **3 tablespoonfuls butter** and **1 cup sugar,** add **2 egg yolks** unbeaten, add **2 tablespoonfuls flour, pinch salt,** and **juice and rind** of **1 lemon.** Add **1 cup milk** and finally fold into the mixture, 2 beaten **egg whites.** Pour into a deep pie dish lined with pastry. Bake 30 minutes in a 350° F. oven. (Moderate oven.)

MAPLE SYRUP PIE (No. 1)

Mix **2 egg yolks** with **1 cup maple syrup, 4 level tablespoonfuls flour, 1 tablespoonful butter, 1 pint milk** and **1 teaspoonful vanilla.** Cook until thick. Pour into baked pie crust. Make a meringue of **2 egg whites, 4 teaspoonfuls sugar** and **3 drops of vanilla.** Spread on pie and bake in quick oven until slightly browned.

MAPLE SYRUP PIE (No. 2)

Blend **2 tablespoonfuls flour** and ½ **cup water.** Add **2 tablespoonfuls melted butter** and **1 cup maple syrup,** put in unbaked pie shell and bake slowly for 25 minutes. Nuts may be added if desired. When cold whipped cream may be used over the top or the pie may be served plain.

Meringue is a mixture of egg white and sugar. It may be either soft or hard as the recipe requires.

Allow 2 tablespoonfuls sugar to each egg white used in making meringue for pies. After beating egg whites until stiff, add sugar gradually. Bake 12 minutes in a slow oven. This meringue will not fall or form beads on top.

MERINGUE FOR PIES (Soft Meringue)

Add ½ **teaspoonful salt** and ¼ **teaspoonful lemon extract** or 1 teaspoonful lemon juice to **3 egg whites**, then beat to a stiff foam. Add **sugar** by tablespoonfuls, beating after each addition until **6 tablespoonfuls** have been added. With the last sugar beat until mixture piles well and sugar is dissolved. Spread on pie and bake in moderate oven, 350° F., until delicately browned, about 10 minutes.

MINCEMEAT PIE

Line a pie pan with pastry rolled to ⅛ inch thickness. Fill with **mincemeat**, using a **1 pound can** or jar (1 pint), for an average size pie. Moisten edge of crust with a few drops of water and cover with a top crust, which has been slit in several places to allow the escape of steam. Press edges firmly together and bake in hot oven (450° F.) for 15 minutes. Reduce temperature and bake in moderate oven (350° F.) until done or mincemeat boils. A few drops of cream brushed over the top of the pie helps to make it brown nicely.

PEACH PIE

Make rich pastry and line pie tin. Fill with halved or sliced **peaches**. Add **1 cup granulated sugar.** Cover with the following: **1 tablespoonful flour** mixed with **2 tablespoonfuls milk.** Add **1 egg**, a **pinch** of **salt** and beat thoroughly, then pour over the peaches. Sprinkle with **cinnamon** and bake in hot oven for 10 minutes, then reduce to moderate, and bake approximately 30 minutes or until peaches are well done.

PEACH PIE SUPREME

Line a pie pan with a good pastry. Fill with **peaches** cut in large sections. Blend together with the hand, **1 cup sugar,** ½ **cup butter** and ½ **cup flour.** Spread mixture over peaches and bake 1 hour in moderate oven.

TWO-CRUST PEACH PIE

Select firm ripe freestone **peaches.** Slice **5 cups** (¼ inch slices) for a 9-inch pie. Brush lower crust with an **unbeaten egg white** to prevent soaking. Pack the peaches, when sliced, into the lower crust and sprinkle evenly with **1½ cups sugar** mixed with **1 tablespoonful** of **flour.** Dot with **butter,** and add a few drops of water. Dampen edge of crust, press the top crust down firmly and pinch edges. Top crust must have holes to allow escape of steam. Brush top crust with a whole egg beaten a little with a fork. This gives it a nice finish and will brown evenly. Put pie in very hot oven for 10 minutes to brown crust, then reduce heat to 350° F. until pie is done. Test with a toothpick.

PECAN PIE

This is for a rather large pie; by doubling the recipe it will make three regular sized pies or 15 tarts. Mix **2½ tablespoonfuls flour** with **2/3 cup sugar.** Beat 4 **eggs** slightly. Add **¼ cup** soft **butter, ½ teaspoonful salt, flour** and **sugar, 1 1/3 cups light corn syrup** and 2/3 **cups** broken **pecan meats.** Mix well and pour into unbaked pie shells. Bake at 375° F. for 10 minutes and then reduce heat to 325° F. for 50 minutes.

PINEAPPLE CHIFFON PIE

Soak **1 tablespoonful** of **gelatin** in **¼ cup cold** water 5 minutes. Beat 4 **egg yolks** slightly and add **¼ cup sugar, 1¼ cups crushed pineapple,** drained, **1 tablespoonful lemon juice** and **¼ teaspoonful salt.** Cook over boiling water until of custard consistency. Add softened gelatin, stirring thoroughly. Cool. When mixture begins to thicken, fold in stiffly beaten **egg whites** to which has been added **¼ cup sugar.** Fill baked pie shell and chill. Just before serving, spread over pie a thin layer of whipped cream.

PUMPKIN PIE (No. 1)

Mix **1 cup pumpkin** and **1 cup cream** or whole milk. Add **½ cup sugar** which has had **¼ teaspoonful ginger, ¼ teaspoonful cloves, ½ teaspoonful salt,** and **½ teaspoonful cinnamon** mixed with it to prevent lumping of the spices. Stir until all is dissolved. Slightly beat **2 eggs.** (Do not overheat as these eggs are for thickening.) Add to other mixtures. Pour into unbaked crust. Bake in hot oven for 12 minutes (450° F.) then reduce heat to moderate and continue until pie is set.

PUMPKIN PIE (No. 2)

Mix **¾ cup brown sugar, ½ teaspoonful ginger, ½ teaspoonful cinnamon, ¼ teaspoonful mace** and **1 teaspoonful salt.** Add **2 eggs** and beat only until mixed. Add **1½ cups pumpkin, 1½ cups** rich **milk** and **1/3 cup nut meats** (these may be omitted). Stir until well combined. Line a deep pie pan with pastry and prick a few times with a fork. Bake in a hot oven until lightly browned. Reduce the heat, pour in filling and bake until filling is firm.

PUMPKIN CHIFFON PIE

Add **½ cup** of **sugar, 1¼ cups pumpkin, ½ cup milk, ½ teaspoonful salt, ½ teaspoonful ginger, ½ teaspoonful cinnamon** and **½ teaspoonful nutmeg** to **3 egg yolks,** slightly beaten. Cook until thick in double boiler. Pour **¼ cup** cold **water** in bowl and sprinkle **1 level tablespoonful gelatin** on top. When dissolved add to pumpkin mixture. Mix thoroughly and cool. When it begins to thicken add **½ cup sugar** to 3 stiffly beaten **egg whites** and fold into first mixture. Pour into previously baked pie shell. This pie is delicious garnished with whipped cream just before serving.

RAISIN PIE

Cook **1 cup raisins** until tender. Drain. Mix **1 cup rich cream** with **1 tablespoonful flour, 1 cup sugar** and **1 tablespoonful cocoa.** Cook until it thickens. Add **raisins, 2 well beaten eggs** (reserve whites for meringue). Flavor mixture with **lemon extract** and bake in a rich pastry shell. Cover with meringue made from **2 egg whites** and **2 tablespoonfuls sugar.** By adding sugar gradually, one avoids the water bubbles that often appear on meringue. Brown in oven.

WHITE RAISIN PIE

Cover **1 cup Sultana raisins** with water. Set on to cook until tender and plump. When half cooked, add **1 cup sugar, 2 tablespoonfuls butter** and **pinch** of **salt.** When nearly done add thickening made from **2½ tablespoonfuls flour** and **enough water** to thin it properly. Add **1 tablespoonful vinegar** or **2 tablespoonfuls lemon juice.** Let cool. Bake a pie shell and when done add the cooled filling. **Seeded raisins** may be used also.

RHUBARB PIE

Cut **rhubarb into inch lengths,** without peeling, until there is enough for **2 cups.** Mix with **1 cup sugar, 2 egg yolks, 2 tablespoonfuls butter, 2 tablespoonfuls flour** and cook slowly in double boiler until like jelly or well thickened. Place in a baked pie shell, cover with meringue made from the **whites** of **2 eggs** and **4 tablespoonfuls sugar.** Place in slow oven until nicely browned.

SOUR CREAM PIE

Mix **1 tablespoonful flour, ½ teaspoonful nutmeg** and **1 cup sugar** with **2 eggs** slightly beaten, **1½ cups sour cream** and **1½ cups raisins.** Pour into pie shell and bake 35 minutes.

STRAWBERRY PIE

Dissolve **1 tablespoonful gelatin** in **4 tablespoonfuls cold water.** Heat **2 cups milk** to boiling and add gelatin, **¼ teaspoonful salt,** and **1 cup sugar.** Let partly cool, then stir in **1 cup strawberries** and pour into a baked pie shell. Chill pie and serve with **whipped cream** and garnish with another **½ cup strawberries,** sprinkled with **powdered sugar.**

STRAWBERRY CHIFFON PIE

Add **1 tablespoonful granulated gelatin** to **¼ cup cold water.** Beat **4 egg yolks,** slightly. Add **½ cup sugar, 1 tablespoonful lemon juice** and **½ teaspoonful salt.** Cook in double boiler until thick. Add gelatin. Stir until dissolved. Add **1 cup crushed strawberries** and beat 1 minute. Cool. As it thickens fold in **whites** of **4 eggs** beaten stiff with **¼ cup sugar.** Fill **pie shell.** Chill until set. Top with **whipped cream** and **berries.** Use ½ of recipe for small pie.

STRAWBERRY PIE WITH FRESH BERRIES

Fill **baked crust** with washed and drained **strawberries.** Cover with a meringue made of **3 egg whites** and **6 tablespoonfuls sugar.** Bake in slow oven about 12 minutes until meringue is brown.

TWO-CRUST STRAWBERRY PIE

Hull and wash 1 **quart of strawberries.** Set aside to drain. Have chilled **pie dough** ready and roll bottom crust and put in pie plate. Roll top crust and have ready to use. Preheat oven to (450° F.) hot oven. Add to whole berries: ½ **cup sugar** mixed with **2½ tablespoonfuls cornstarch.** Put over fire, stirring carefully so that berries draw juice slowly and will furnish enough water to dissolve sugar. Increase heat till sugar is dissolved. Do not boil. Pour into bottom crust, quickly putting top crust in place and bake in hot oven until brown. The berries will be only partly cooked and be very whole and firm.

SUNSHINE PIE

Boil 2 **cups** of grated or ground **carrots** until tender. Add 2 **egg yolks, ¾ cup sugar, pinch salt, ½ tablespoonful flour, juice** and **rind** of **1 lemon.** Put all in one pie shell. Bake in moderate oven 350° F. until set or about 20 minutes. Make a meringue of the **2 egg whites** and **2 tablespoonfuls sugar.** Add to pie and return to oven to brown.

SWEET POTATO PIE

Cook 2 or 3 **sweet potatoes,** peel and mash. Add 2 **cups sugar, 1 cup cream, ½ cup butter** and 3 **egg yolks,** well beaten. Add **a dash** of **nutmeg** for flavor. Fold in 3 **egg whites** that have been beaten until stiff. Mix well together. Bake in an unbaked pastry shell, first at 450° F. for 10 minutes, or until edges of pastry are brown, then reduce heat to 350° F. and continue to bake until pie is set

VINEGAR PIE

Beat **1 egg well.** Add **1 cup sugar, 1 cup water, 1 tablespoonful** strong **vinegar** and **1 tablespoonful flour.** Beat until smooth. Pour in unbaked pie shell, sprinkle with **nutmeg** and a little **cinnamon.** Bake until knife inserted comes out clean.

WASHINGTON PIE

Cream ¼ **cup shortening.** Add **1 cup sugar,** 2 well beaten **egg** yolks, 1½ **cups** sifted **flour, 1½ teaspoonfuls baking powder** and **pinch** of **salt.** Adding alternately with **1/3 cup milk** and ½ **teaspoonful vanilla.** Lastly, fold in the 2 **egg whites,** well beaten. Bake in pan 1 inch thick. When cold split and fill with **raspberry jam.** Serve with whipped cream and garnish with cherries.

Canning

Canning is a process we employ to keep perishable food from spoiling. Bacteria is the cause of this spoilage, therefore we must kill both the bacteria and any spore formed by it. These spore formations are the reason some foods require longer periods of processing. Acid foods require less processing time because these spore forming bacteria are not present. Pressure cooker is excellent for the non-acid foods such as peas, beans, corn and meats. However, if the long time is used the water bath will give very good results. In order to avoid botulinus poisoning that often appears in non acid, home canned foods, they should be heated for 10 minutes at boiling temperature, after removing from can.

It would be ideal if we could gather fruits and vegetables from the garden, wash them and pack in jars, seal, and keep until we needed them but that can't be. In the earth in which these foods grow are many tiny things which feed the fruits and vegetables and help in making them good food, but if they're allowed to remain on the food they overdo a good job and cause spoilage. These are bacteria, molds and yeasts.

These minute substances are ever present in air, water and soil, and must be destroyed if we are to keep food. It is not only necessary to see that they no longer exist, but they also must be kept out by a perfect seal. That is why jars used in canning must be sterile (free from bacteria) and kept that way until used. Do not sterilize jars one day and expect them to be germproof the next unless kept in a sterilizer.

Yeasts and molds are easily killed by bringing the food to just below boiling point for various periods of time. In killing bacteria by heat, both the degree of temperature and the length of time that is to be applied must be considered. Too high or too long a period may give a sterile product but at the same time it may cause too great a change in the processed food.

Growing bacteria easily are killed at boiling point of water, but some bacteria go through a dormant stage called spores and these are very hard to kill at boiling temperature. That is why the pressure cooker is used for vegetables and meats.

Flat sour spoilage is caused by bacteria that produce acid without gas. They grow best at temperatures about 130° to 140° F. and sometime cause spoilage in canned foods not properly cooled after processing or held at too high storage temperature. Corn, peas, beans are subject to flat sour. There will be no doubt in your mind about flat sour once you have gotten the odor from a can that has produced it.

Putrefaction is caused by a bacteria that produces gas, a bad odor and the softening and darkening of canned food. Putrefaction usually occurs in foods low in acidity such as meats, peas and corn. When the spores of botulinus bacteria are not destroyed in the canning process they may grow later and produce a toxin in the food.

These bacteria will not grow in salt solutions when more than 9 per cent of salt is present. They are destroyed by processing at 212° F. if the solution is sufficiently acid, but with meat and low-acid vegetable, they may not be killed at boiling temperature unless the food is heated from 6 to 10 hours. The time may be decreased if a pressure cooker is used as it raises heat to 240° F.

Thus unless a pressure cooker is used, be sure to cook over high heat for 10 minutes any home-canned meat or low-acid vegetable.

Authorities on home canning agree that two canners, boiling water bath and steam pressure, are needed to secure uniformly satisfactory results in some canning. However, other methods may be used with good results.

BOILING WATER BATH CANNER

Since this is the most universal method of canning we think every home should have some canner of this type. It need not be expensive, it may be a wash boiler, a deep kettle or a lard can fitted with some sort of a rack that will keep the jars off the bottom of canner and from hitting each other while boiling.

The rack for such canners may be available at your nearest store or you may have to get one made either of wire or wood. The jars should be one-half inch from bottom of canner and the canner should be deep enough to allow at least one inch of water over the top. There have been in the past hot water baths for sale commercially, fitted with racks and lids; but they are too shallow to allow that inch over the top of quart cans. Watch this if you are purchasing a new outfit.

The wash boiler is by far the most satisfactory canner. It will hold eight quarts for processing at one time. This is about the amount one-half bushel of different fruits or vegetables will fill. That gives you an idea about how much to plan on canning at a time. The racks that fit into the boiler are inexpensive and are worth the cost. They have a handle that allows all eight jars to be raised or lowered into the bath at one time.

There are also individual racks for holding just one jar in case you want to process one jar at a time in a bucket. This is very impractical as the amount of heat needed for one jar is very little less than that required for eight jars.

Be sure that any boiling water bath canner you use has a tight lid, to hold in steam. That steam helps to sterilize your canned product.

The water should be steaming, but not boiling when jars are put into canner. The jars should stand at least one-half inch apart and be completely covered with water. Lower jars into the hot water slowly to avoid breakage. Jars that are full of hot liquid will not be so apt to break as those that are hot with cold food inside.

Begin counting processing time when the water is actually boiling. Keep it boiling constantly and at the same rate of speed during the entire time. Remove jars from the canner the moment processing time is up and seal according to direction given for the style jar and closure use. (This will be in a later lesson).

PASTEURIZING

Some fruit juices, (grapefruit) and tomato juice now are processed below boiling to prevent the destruction of vitamins. These jars are placed in a water bath which is kept at simmering temperature for the allotted time.

OVEN-CANNING

The oven may be used for fruits and tomatoes without any questions being asked, but it is NOT RECOMMENDED for low-acid vegetables and meat. However, many women have used this method of canning everything for some time and have had no difficulty. If you have no other way to can, the following is the best way to manage if you are planning to can in the oven.

Remember to reheat every food canned in the oven at least 10 minutes before using.

Oven canning requires very strong jars. Every jar must be carefully inspected for cracks so that it will be sure not to blow up while being processed in the oven. The jars themselves must be of a good material. Do not use jars that commercial food came in for oven canning; save these for foods canned by open kettle, pickling or jams.

In order to use an oven for canning it must have an automatic heat control. Coal, gasoline, oil and wood heated ovens should not be used for this purpose because they are not equipped with the type heat regulators required for canning.

Check heat regulator for accuracy. Preheat oven to 250° or 275° F. whichever you wish to use. Higher temperatures will cause the liquid to boil out of jar.

Do not use tin cans in processing in oven. The steam pressure inside of cans may cause the seams to burst.

Jars with rubber rings must not be tightened while processing in oven. They are finished by sealing immediately upon taking from the oven.

Jars with self-sealing caps are tightened firmly before jars are placed in oven. These, being of metal, will expand if too much pressure collects on the inside of can and contract when cool.

Oven processing has a greater deteriorating effect, as measured by decreased elasticity, upon rubber jar rings than does processing in the boiling water bath or pressure cooker.

Until stoves and methods are better standardized, OVEN CANNING CANNOT BE UNRESERVEDLY RECOMMENDED.

If it has no regulator the oven will be very hard to use as you must get some kind of a cooking thermometer and set inside to get temperature. Each time you look at it, you allow a blast of cold air to enter oven, and it may cause breakage of jars or lower the temperature so you have to count time differently.

Remember the time for processing in the oven is one and one-half the time in the water bath.

Although the heat in the oven is higher than 212° F., the interior of the jar hardly ever reaches any higher than the boiling point of water, as when it reaches that point it forms steam and escapes. Thus for low-acid vegetables and meats a higher temperature is usually required. Pressure cookers are used for that reason.

Preheat oven and count time as soon as all cans are in place.

STEAMERS

Steamers do very much the same work as boiling water baths. Be sure that a good flow of steam is coming from the escape valve before you start to count time. The jars should not touch each other either in oven or steamer and should have space both at sides and top of oven for air to circulate.

OPEN KETTLE

In this method of canning, fruits and tomatoes are cooked directly in an open vessel to kill bacteria. This cooking takes the place of both pre-cooking and processing in the other methods.

The only equipment needed is a large kettle, but not too large, as one should not can more than two quarts at a time. A spoon, a jar funnel, and a jar tightener, as well as a jar lifter make work much easier.

This method should NEVER, UNDER ANY CIRCUMSTANCE, be used for low-acid vegetables and meats.

STEAM PRESSURE COOKERS

All low-acid vegetables and meats should be processed in a steam pressure cooker because it is the only kitchen utensil in which it is possible to raise the temperature much over 212° F.

A steam pressure cooker consists of a metal kettle and cover. The cover, equipped with a safety valve, petcock and pressure gauge, fastens to the kettle with thumb screws or clamps. Pressure cookers will, if properly cared for, last many years. Place jars on rack in a cooker containing one or two inches of water. Leave ample space between jars to permit free circulation of steam. Adjust and fasten lid securely. Do not close petcock until steam has escaped through it in a steady stream from five to seven minutes, depending upon the size of cooker; otherwise the temperature within the cooker may not be as high as indicated by the pressure gauge.

The hand on the pressure gauge begins to rise slowly shortly after the petcock is closed. Begin counting processing time when the pressure reaches the required number of pounds. Keep pressure steady by adjusting heat under cooker. Remove cooker from heat at end of processing time and let it stand until the hand on the gauge falls to zero, then open petcock slowly. Tilt lid, as it is removed, to throw steam away from face. Spread a heavy cloth over top of cooker. Catch handles of rack through cloth and lift out. Seals jars according to directions given for style jar and closure used.

TYPES OF JARS FOR CANNING

Mason Jars: 1. A one-piece cap lined with porcelain, equipped with a rubber gasket between cap and shoulder jar. This kind of a rubber is called a shoulder rubber.

2. A glass cap with rubber ring that fits between the glass cap and the jar top, both of which are held in place with a metal screw band. This rubber is called a top rubber.

3. A metal disc with a flowed-on rubber on the disc. It is held on the jar by a metal screw band.

Types 2 and 3 are sometimes called vacuum or self sealing type. All glass jar—This type is not a Mason jar as its top is held in place with a wire clamp. It uses a shoulder rubber.

Home canning jars may be used repeatedly by providing new rubber and in some cases new lids.

If you are using the metal disc with flowed-on rubber be sure that the screw band fits down tight enough to make the rubber seal properly.

Mayonnaise or other jars which have contained commercial foods may be used for canning if the jar mouth is threaded to take bands and is deep enough to make a perfect seal. They should not be used for oven canning nor long process canning by boiling water bath.

TESTING JARS

All glass jars should be tested for weak spots, chips or other possible means of leakage or breakage before using for canning. If the glass jar has a chipped top it cannot be used for the metal disk type of lid as it will not make a perfect seal. If the chip is small, flowed-on rubber may fill it up, but it is best in such cases to use the shoulder type rubber and a zinc top with porcelain inset.

To use the metal disk it is best to have the top perfectly smooth. Test this by running finger around top or sliding jar over a piece of glass. If there is a chip it will scratch glass. If jars have a chip on side where shoulder rubber goes it is best to use metal disk as shoulder rubber would not make a perfect seal. All jars that have large blisters and cracks should be discarded. They may be used for dried vegetables and fruits.

CHECKING JARS

See that rubbers and lids fit and no jar leaks. Test by filling jars with water half way up and putting on lid and rubber seal as tightly as possible. Turn jars upside down on a table for a half hour to see if they leak. This can not be done well with self-sealing lids. With them the main thing to watch is the smoothness of the top of the jar.

More spoilage is caused by carelessness in jar preparation than any other cause in canning.

If lids used are old they should be scrubbed and thoroughly cleaned by boiling in an alkali solution (usually sal soda), 15 minutes. If you are using the all-glass jars be sure that the wire clamps are tight. A wire clamp that has loosened may be tightened by removing top wire, bending it down in the middle and then bending the sides inward, if necessary to fit the jar.

Do not use 2 rubbers to make a jar fit. A double gasket does not work. It would be better to put a piece of paper or rubber under the top clamp where it fastens onto top of jar.

SEALING JARS

All jars with zinc tops and shoulder rubber should be partially sealed before processing and sealed completely as soon as removed from canner. Never tighten a zinc top after a jar has cooled. Doing so may break the seal. Do not turn any jar upside down to cool.

All vacuum type metal disk tops with flowed-on rubbers are sealed tightly before processing and are not touched until cold and then only to remove screw band.

A glass top, with loose rubber used on top of jar, held in place by a metal band is only partially sealed before processing and tightened upon removal from canner.

Glass top jars, with shoulder rubber, are sealed with the top clamp only in place while processing, the bottom clamp is pulled down as soon as removed.

LOOSE RUBBERS AND FLOWED-ON RUBBER DISCS

Boil loose rubbers in a solution of 1 tablespoon of soda to 1 quart water for each dozen rubbers. Keep hot until used.

Flowed-on rubber discs are just dipped in hot water just before putting in place.

PREPARING JARS FOR USE

Wash jars and tops in hot soapy water and rinse. Place them in a pan of warm water with a rack or cloth in the bottom to prevent bumping. Bring to boiling point and keep hot until required. These jars may also be heated in a 250° F. oven for 30 minutes. Jars and tops for open kettle canning should be sterilized by 15 to 20-minute boiling.

When jars are packed with food and then processed they do not need to be sterilized first, but they should be cleaned and hot when filled.

HEAD SPACE

When food is processed in glass jars a head space is left at the top to permit expansion of the food. Head space is measured from a straight edge laid across the top of the jar. Allow one-half inch of head space in all jars except those containing starchy foods—corn, peas and lima beans—which require one inch because of greater expansion. The solid material in jars should be covered by liquid—water, sirup, or broth as the case may be.

EXHAUSTING AND COOLING

All types of glass jars can be adjusted to allow exhausting or passing out of air from the food during processing. With the Mason jar, the cap is screwed on until it is tight and then turned back one-fourth inch. It may also be put on as tight as you can with thumb and little finger. After processing the cap is screwed down as tightly as possible on the jar. With the lightning type of jar the top clamp is snapped into place and the side clamp left up. After processing the side clamp is pushed down. In both of these jars the actual seal is formed by the pull of the partial vacuum in the jar during cooling. Hence, it is better if these jars are cooled in an upright position.

With the vacuum of self-sealing jars no special adjustment is used for exhausting the air. The screw bands are put in tight or the clamps adjusted. During the processing period the top is held in place by the band or clamp which allows the air to escape but holds the top to the jar. When jar starts to cool after processing, the steam condenses and a partial vacuum is formed within. Greater pressure outside the jar than inside pressed the top down firmly and the seal is formed between top, gasket and jar. The sealing material hardens as the jar cools, making a complete seal. If the screw band should be loose after processing, hold the lid in place so it will not turn and screw the band tight. Jars of this type must be left to cool in an upright position.

When jars have cooled, remove the screw bands and save them to use again. Do not put jars away with screw band on They may rust and be hard to remove. At the same time they would not be fit to be used again. Paraffin these bands by dipping in a hot paraffin solution to keep them fresh until needed again.

Cool all glass jars in air, out of drafts. Special care should be taken to protect jars that have just been taken from a pressure canner as the temperature of the food is still above boiling. This places the glass under considerable strain and breakage may occur if a draft strikes the jars. Leaving the jars in the canner for three to four minutes after the canner has been opened will reduce the danger of breakage. Use a jar lifter or tongs to remove the jars from pressure cooker.

Do not cover the jars with cloths or blankets while cooling as this prolongs the cooking of food. The processing period is adequate to make the food keep and cooling should follow at once. After processing and cooling, all types of glass jars using rubber rings should be inverted and observed for leakage. Tap with a spoon the tops of jars sealed with lacquered metal tops. A clear ringing sound denotes a seal. If the sound is dull a seal has not been formed.

STEPS IN CANNING

Safe canning requires careful attention to every step in the process, from the selection of the raw food to the final check-up of the canned products during storage.

Select good materials—The quality of canned products can be no better than the quality of the raw food that goes into the can. Use only clean, fresh sound foods in prime condition and be sure that the containers in which they are handled are clean. Any unnecessary infection of the raw food increases the difficulty of processing and the liability of the canned products to spoilage.

With fruits and vegetables, grade for size and the same degree of ripeness if a uniform product is desired. Wash thoroughly until every trace of soil is removed. The most dangerous bacteria and those most difficult to kill are in the soil. A wire basket is a help in washing but should not be loaded too heavily. Always lift the fruit and vegetables out of the water rather than pour the water off.

Prepare jars or cans.

Prepare syrup—If fruit is to be canned see that the right syrup is ready when the fruit is, so that fruit will not stand exposed to air.

Pre-cooking—Some foods are pre-cooked for a short time before they are packed into containers. This pre-cooking helps to remove air from the tissues, shrinks them, facilitates packing and speeds up the processing because the foods are already hot when they are placed in the canner. This method is known as the hot pack and is fast replacing the cold pack method.

Packing—When using glass jars, remove one jar at a time from the hot water bath where it has been held. Keeping the jars hot helps to prevent breakage during packing and processing. If needed, place a new wet rubber ring in position, resting flat on the sealing shoulder of jar. Pack containers quickly so that pre-cooked food remains hot. Use a sufficient proportion of liquids to solids to prevent too dense a pack and work out air bubbles with a knife blade or spatula.

Leave the proper head space in containers.

Exhausting and adjusting covers—Glass jars with food are exhausted or the air partially removed during processing, because the jars are not fully sealed. As each glass jar is packed, carefully wipe the rubber ring and sealing edge of jar to remove any particles of food and adjust cap to seal jar partially and permit exhausting. See sealing.

Place the jars as finished in canner or where they will keep hot until processing begins. Many women have found the oven is excellent for this purpose. Set filled jars ready for the pressure cooker or water bath in a 250-degree oven until there are enough filled to fill canner.

Processing—Process at the temperature and time as indicated on table.

Cooling—Cool glass jars in air but protect them from drafts. After they are cool, invert rubber ring jars and observe for leakage. Test lacquer metal top jars by tapping.

Do not attempt to tighten screw caps or screw band after jars have cooled.

Reprocessing — If a container leaks, determine the cause, process food again using another container, top or rubber as needed.

Labeling—Wipe containers clean and label with the name, date and lot number if you wish to designate them from some other canning.

Checking up results—Hold canned products at room temperature for a week or 10 days where they can be examined from time to time to be sure that they are keeping. If any show signs of spoilage examine all that lot carefully.

Storage—Store canned foods in a cool dry place and protect glass jars from the light so that food will not fade in color. The quality is generally better if they are used within the first year after canning. That is why you should can only what you need for the next year.

Loss of liquid—When glass jars are processed in the steam pressure canner there is frequently a loss of liquid. While this may occur to some extent with all types of jars, it is generally less with those of the vacuum sealing type which have a separate rubber ring or sealing composition in addition to the glass or metal cap and screw band. Mason and lightning type jars are partially sealed before they are put in canner and the seals completed as soon as they are taken out. Tight sealing of these jars will not prevent the loss of liquid during pressure processing, and may cause the rubbers to push out, thus making a tight seal difficult to obtain.

Remember, do not open jars after processing to add more liquid. The air inside is sterile and the product will keep. If jars are opened you ruin all the value of the processing and it must be done over again.

CAUSES AND PREVENTION OF SPOILAGE

Plant organisms, too small to be seen without a microscope exist everywhere in the air, water and soil. These organisms are called molds, yeast and bacteria. All of them need food and moisture for growth and reproduction.

When they grow they take a vital part of your food, thus causing it to spoil.

Molds grow where moisture exists and spoil only what they touch. Thus you easily can remove mold from most canned goods and use the part underneath. In severe cases the roots of the mold may extend down into the can, thus spoiling it all.

Yeasts thrive on products containing sugars and acids, thus fruits and fruit products may spoil. A sour jam means yeasts have been living in it. Both of the above molds and yeast are easily destroyed by any method of canning.

Bacteria are the chief cause of spoilage of beans, corn, greens, peas, meats and all other low-acid products which are preserved by canning.

Bacteria exist in two forms, the active organism and the spore. The spores of some bacteria are difficult to destroy by boiling—

that is why it is advisable to use a steam pressure cooker when canning meats and low-acid vegetables.

MANY OF OUR READERS DO NOT HAVE PRESSURE COOKERS BUT WE DO FEEL THAT ALL OF US SHOULD KNOW THAT ALL AUTHORITIES ON CANNING AGREE IT IS THE BEST METHOD FOR THE CANNING OF THESE CERTAIN FOODS.

Since many do not have pressure cookers then we must learn the best way to can without them. We personally recommend the boiling water bath.

The two big factors in either of these two methods of canning are: Freshness of material and cleanliness while working. Those who have their produce fresh from the garden will have very little trouble with the formation of spores. Spores usually form after the vegetable has been pulled from the ground or stalk.

Foods canned by pressure cooker may be eaten right from the can. Foods that are low-acid, such as beans, corn and peas, that are canned by boiling water bath should be cooked 10 minutes on top of stove after opening to insure no ill effects.

Often the toxic bacteria do not have any odor or taste.

Do not pack jars too tight—Jars should be packed loosely to allow the hot water or air to circulate around each piece in the jar.

Sharp knives are essential for efficient canning.

When cans are empty wash and scald. Allow to dry, both can and lids, then put together and either cover with a paper bag or place in a cupboard where they will not get dirty but be ready for next year's canning with very little trouble.

CANNING BUDGET

For each member of the family there should be from **80 to 120** quarts of canned food divided as follows:

30 to 45 quarts of green and yellow vegetables.

Green: Peas, beans, asparagus, brussels sprouts, peppers.

Yellow: Corn, carrots, squash, pumpkin, yellow beans, sweet potatoes and parsnips.

20 to 30 quarts of tomatoes.

30 to 45 quarts of fruit: Apples, cherries, berries, peaches, pears, plums and may have pineapples.

In addition, it would be well to have 10 quarts of meat per person.

CHART FOR CANNING FRUITS

45 Quarts Assorted Fruit and 30 Quarts Tomatoes Per Person Per Year

FRUIT	Amount to be Canned	Yield in Quarts	Minutes in Boiling Water Bath Cold Pack	Minutes in Boiling Water Bath Hot Pack	Min. in 250° Oven Cold Pack	Min. in 250° Oven Hot Pack
Apples	1 bushel	20-22	25	15	75	40
Apricots	1 bushel	20-24	20	15	70	40
Berries	24 quart crate	18	20	5	70	35
Cherries	1 bushel	18-24	20	10	70	35
Cranberries	1 bushel	18-20	10	5	—	—
Currants	1 bushel	18-24	20	5	70	35
Figs	1 bushel	15-18	—	30	90	55
Fruit juices	1 quart	1	20	5	70	35
Grapes	1 bushel	15	20	5	70	40
Peaches	1 bushel	18-24	20	10	70	40
Pears	1 bushel	25-28	20	20	75	45
Pineapple	24 apples	12-16	30	15	90	60
Plums	1 bushel	24-26	20	10	50	35
Quinces	1 bushel	20-24	35	20	75	55
Rhubarb	2 pounds	1	10	5	70	40
Strawberries	24 quarts	12	20	5	70	45
Tomatoes	1 bushel	14-20	35	10	75	50

CHART FOR CANNING VEGETABLES

VEGETABLE	Amount to be Canned	Yields	Amount Needed Per Person	Boiling Water Bath Minutes	Pressure Cooker Minutes	Pressure Cooker Pounds
Asparagus	12 lbs.	8 pints	2½ qts.	180	40	10
Beans, String						
or Wax	1 bushel	14-18 qts.	9 qts.	180	40	10
Beans—Lima	1 bushel	8 quarts	4½ qts.	180	55	10
Beans—Soy	1 bushel	6-8 qts.		210	70	10
Beets	1 bushel	20 quarts	4½ qts.	120	40	10
Broccoli	1 bushel	6-8 qts.	1 qt.	120	40	10
Brussels Spr.	1 bushel	6-8 qts.	1 qt.	120	40	10
Cabbage	1 bushel	10 quarts		120	40	10
Carrots	1 bushel	20 quarts	4½ qts.	120	35	10
Cauliflower	1 bushel	12 quarts		150	35	10
Celery	2 stalks	1 quart	1 qt.	150	35	10
Corn, Cr. style	1 bushel	8 quarts	9 qts.	240	70	15
Whole grain	1 bushel	10 quarts		210	70	10
on the cob	100 ears	15 quarts		210	80	10
Dandelion	1 bushel	6-8 qts.		180	65	15
Egg Plant	1 egg pl	1-2 pints		180	55	10
Greens	1 bushel	6-8 qts.	9 qts.	180	65	15
Hominy	1 quart	1 quart		120	40	10
Mushrooms	1 quart	1 pint		180	60	10
Okra	1 bushel	6-8 qts.	5 pts.	180	40	10
Onions	1 bushel	15 quarts		180	40	10
Parsnips	1 bushel	20 quarts	4 pts.	120	40	10
Peas	1 bu., pod	6-8 qts.	5 pts.	180	60	10
Peppers, green				120	35	5
(pimiento)				40	10	5
Potatos, swt.	1 bushel	20 quarts		240	120	10
new white				150	45	10
Pumpkin			1 qt.	180	70	15
Sauerkraut	1 quart	1 quart	4 pts.	30		
Spinach	1 bushel	13 pints		180	60	10
Squash--						
Summer	1 bushel	20 quarts	1 qt.	180	40	10
Winter				180	60	10
Tomatoes	1 bushel	14-20 qts.	14 qts.	30		
Turnips				150	40	10
Rutabaga				150	40	10
Kohlrabi				150	40	10

Canning Fruits

Did you know that fruit that discolors while paring may be put into a weak solution of salt water (1 teaspoonful salt to 1 quart water) until ready to put into jars? This applies especially to apples, pears, peaches and quinces.

CANNING SYRUPS

1 cup sugar to 3 cups water makes a thin syrup.

1 cup sugar to 2 cups water makes a medium syrup.

1 cup sugar to 1 cup water makes a heacy syrup.

1 cup corn syrup to 2½ cups water makes a thin syrup.

1 cup corn syrup to 1½ cups water makes a medium syrup.

1 cup corn syrup to ½ cup water makes a heavy syrup.

½ cup sugar plus ½ cup corn syrup to 3 cups water makes a thin syrup.

½ cup sugar plus ½ cup corn syrup to 1½ cups water makes a medium syrup.

½ cup sugar to ½ cup corn syrup to 1 cup water makes a thick syrup.

APPLES (Hot Pack)

Wash, pare and core apples. Cut into desired sizes. Drop into slightly salted water to prevent discoloration. Drain and boil three to five minutes in a thin syrup. Pack into clean hot jars to one-half inch of top, put on lid, fasten according to type used, and process in boiling water bath 15 minutes or 75 minutes in a 250° F. oven.

We do not recommend the use of pressure cooker for fruits, although it may be used.

APPLES (Open Kettle)

Pare, core, drop apples in slightly salted water to prevent discoloration. Drop in a **thin syrup** made of **one part sugar to 3 parts water** and cook until tender or transparent. Pack immediately into sterilized jars and seal.

APPLE SAUCE

Make apple sauce as your family likes it for the table. Some like to peel apples, then watch that apples do not cook into mush. Others do not peel the apples at all, but core, and cook, then put them through ricer, thus making a very fine sauce. Take your choice. Season it with sugar according to taste and while boiling hot pour into clean sterile jars, filling to the top. Put on lids and seal completely regardless of the type of lids. Place in a 250° F. **oven for 30 minutes** as an added precaution or 15 minutes in a boiling hot water bath.

BLACKBERRIES (Cold Pack)

Wash berries. Drain, pack into hot jars as tightly as possible without crushing. Cover with medium syrup—**two cups water to one cup sugar**—or berry juice. Process **20 minutes in water bath** or **70 minutes at 250° F. in oven.**

EASY WAY TO CAN BLACKBERRIES

Wash **2 quarts** of berries at a time, picking them over to assure cleanliness. Add **1 to 1½ cups sugar** (according to taste) on top of the berries. Do not stir. Pour **boiling water** over sugar and berries until water can be seen. Place on fire and allow just to come to a boil. Pour into sterilized cans and seal immediately.

BLUEBERRIES AND HUCKLEBERRIES

Place two or three quarts of clean berries in a square of cheesecloth. Hold cloth by corners and dip into boiling water until spots appear, then dip quickly in and out of cold water. Pack into hot jars, adding neither water nor sugar. **Process 20 minutes in hot water bath.** Seal when removed if rubber rings have been used on lids.

CHERRIES (Cold Pack)

Wash, stem, pit if desired. Pack into clean hot jars. Fill to within 1½ inches of top with medium syrup—**2 cups water to 1 cup sugar.** Put on cap, screwing band tightly if it is a metal top with flowed on rubber seal and screw band. If it has a **rubber band,** screw tightly then loosen a fourth of a turn. Process in **boiling water bath for 20 minutes,** or in the **oven at 250° F. for 70 minutes.**

CHERRIES (Hot Pack)

Wash, stem and pit, saving the juice. Cook cherries over low heat in this juice 5 minutes to shrink them. Add sugar to taste. Pack hot into clean sterile jars, cover cherries with boiling hot juice. Seal according to type of lid used. Metal discs with rubber gasket should be sealed immediately, while lids with rubber rings should be loosened a bit and tightened as soon as removed from processing bath. **Process 5 minutes in boiling water bath** or **15 minutes in a 250° F. oven.** If all glass jars are used, fasten the top clamp in place but do not bring down the other wire until processing is finished.

CHERRIES (Open Kettle)

Wash, stem, pit if desired. Sour cherries usually are pitted making them ready for pies while sweet cherries usually have the pits left in as they are clings and do not yield their seed easily. Place in boiling syrup made of **2 cups water to 1 cup sugar** for sour cherries and **3 cups water to 1 cup sugar for** sweet cherries. Boil 20 minutes. Pack boiling hot into sterilized jars. Seal immediately regardless of type of lid used. These jars should be filled to the top, edges wiped off with a clean cloth before sealing.

CHERRY JUICE

This juice does not make good jelly, but is excellent if saved for a winter beverage. Strain any juice not used in canning cherries. **Add 1 to 2 cups of sugar to each gallon,** reheat 5 minutes to simmering temperature—not boiling—in hot water bath. Seal according to type of lids used.

MARASCHINO CHERRIES

Soak **3 pounds royal** or **red Oxhart cherries** in cold water for 2 hours before pitting, then pit and weigh 3 pounds. While pitting keep as whole as possible. Combine **3 pounds sugar** with **1 cup water.** Cook until sugar is dissolved. Add **1 ounce red coloring** and **1 ounce almond flavoring,** then cherries. Cook same as other preserves until cherries are a rich red but not until they fall apart. Seal in fancy bottles and jars.

CURRANTS (Cold Pack)

Wash, stem, pack into clean hot jars. Fill to within 1½ inches of top with medium syrup—**2 cups water to 1 cup sugar or syrup**—or water, put on lids and fasten according to type used—metal discs with flowed on rubber gasket always are partially sealed. Process in **boiling water bath 20 minutes** or in **oven at 250° F** for **70 minutes**, or **275° F. for 50 minutes.** Complete seal if needed.

Editor's Note: We do not recommend pressure cooker for fruits and tomatoes as the time required under pressure is so small that it requires too much time to be bringing the temperature up and down.

CURRANTS (Hot Pack)

Wash and measure firm ripe currants, freshly picked. Drain. Use **½ to ¾ cup sugar to 1 quart currants.** Place layer of sugar and currants in a broad shallow pan. Let stand 2 hours, then cook by simmering, until sugar is dissolved and currants heated through. Pack into clean hot jars. **Process 5 minutes in boiling water bath,** then complete seal as necessary.

CURRANTS (Open Kettle)

Wash, stem and measure 2 **quarts currants.** Put in kettle, add **2 cups sugar** and enough boiling water to just cover. Bring to a boil and pour immediately into sterilized jars. Seal. Do not do more than 2 quarts at a time. They should fill 2 quart jars.

ELDERBERRIES

Wash, stem and pack into hot jars. Cover with thin syrup—**three parts water to one part sugar—process 20 minutes in boiling water bath** or 70 minutes in 250° F. oven, then complete seal if needed. Add lemon juice or vinegar to elderberries when making pies.

GOOSEBERRIES

Wash, drain, stem and measure gooseberries. Add **one-half cup** sugar for **each quart berries.** Heat slowly to boiling, then boil rapidly **15 minutes.** Pour hot into hot sterile jars. Seal at once.

GRAPES

Wash, stem and pulp **1 gallon of grapes.** Cook and strain pulp and add to skins. Add 4 **pounds sugar** and **1 teaspoonful sulphate of lime.** Cook **20 minutes** and seal in sterilized jars.

GRAPE JUICE

Wash and stem grapes. Measure, and to every **4 quarts of grapes add 1 quart cold water.** Boil until soft. Remove from fire. When cool strain through a cloth to extract the juice. Measure juice. To **each quart** add **1½ cups sugar.** Boil 10 minutes. Bottle at once. Seal airtight. Less sugar may be used if desired.

SHORT METHOD GRAPE JUICE

Wash, stem and drain. Place **2 cups grapes in quart jar.** Add **1 cup sugar.** Fill jar with **boiling water** and seal immediately. This is excellent the year 'round and keeps indefinitely. Good for use in about 1 month.

GRAPEFRUIT

Select sound ripe grapefruit. Wash and dry. Cut a circular slice from each end, then remove the peel by cutting it in uniform sections through to the fruit. Tear the peel with all the white section away from the fruit. With a sharp-pointed knife open each section separately and remove the fruit in as large pieces as possible, clean of all membrane and seed. Pack as solidly as possible, without breaking or crushing, into hot jars. Add **4 tablespoonfuls sugar to each quart.** Partly seal and process for **20 minutes in hot water bath.** Remove from canner and seal immediately.

PEACHES (Cold Pack)

1. Select peaches, ripe not soft. 2. Scald, to loosen skins. 3. Cold dip 1 minute (dip in cold water to cool). 4. Remove skin. 5. Pack, half or whole in jars. 6. Fill with syrup, 3 parts sugar to 2 parts water and boiled 5 minutes. Partially seal. (See note.) Process in boiling water **bath 20 minutes.** 8. Remove from canner. 9. Seal immediately.

Instead of partially sealing, the can may be sealed tight and put into a boiler of boiling water, the fire turned out and the jar allowed to remain until the water is cold. Lift out. Invert to test for leaks. Then put away.

PEELING PEACHES FOR CANNING

Use a thin cloth or wire basket. Dip peaches into boiling water just long enough to loosen skins. Dip immediately into cold water to stop heat and make them easier to handle. The skins should just peel back easily and smoothly. Cut peaches in half before removing skin as they will stay whole better. Drop into a salt solution of **1 teaspoonful salt to 1 quart of water** if you wish them to stay their original color and not darken by exposure to air. This is much better and easier than paring a bushel of peaches.

PEACHES (Hot Pack)

Make a thin sirup of 3 **cups water to 1 cup sugar.** Add peeled and halved peaches a few at a time and simmer until hot through, depending upon their ripeness. Usually five minutes is sufficient. Pack in clean hot jars with cut side down, each overlapping the other. Cover with sirup in which peaches were cooked and process in hot water bath 20 minutes or 70 minutes in a 250° F. oven. Seal according to type of lids used.

PEACHES (Open Kettle)

Add 2 **cups sugar to 1 cup water.** Bring to boil. Add **2 quarts of peeled and halved peaches.** Cook until tender. Pack hot into sterilized jars. Fill to overflowing with boiling syrup. Seal at once.

The Bartlett pear is by far the favorite for canning, but other pears such as Duchess or Kiefer may be used for preserves and jams.

PEARS (Cold Pack)

Blanch pears in hot water for a few minutes to loosen skins. Dip in cold water, so as to handle. Halve pear, remove core and stem, then peel or pare as the case may be. Drop immediately into cold salt water made in the proportions 1 tablespoonful salt to 1 quart water (to keep pears white). Make a syrup of **3 parts sugar and 2 parts water.** Boil 3 minutes. Pack pears into hot sterile jars. Cover with syrup, see note, partly seal and process for **30 minutes in a boiling water bath.** Remove from canner and seal immediately. Note. Jars may be tightly sealed, placed in a bath of boiling water and allowed to remain until the water is cold. Usually over night.

PEARS (Hot Pack)

Pears can be packed whole, in halves or slices as desired. They also can be packed raw or pre-cooked as in the case of peaches. Here again we are advocating the hot pack for pears.

Pears may be dipped in hot water, dipped in cold water for handling, and the skin removed as for peaches, but it is not as satisfactory, so we advocate the paring of pears. Then drop them into salt water alone or salt and vinegar—two tablespoonfuls of each to a gallon of water—to keep them white.

Put prepared pears into a boiling thin syrup—3 cups water to 1 cup sugar—and cook from 5 to 10 minutes, according to size and ripeness of pears. The pears are cooked enough when they can be pierced with a straw. Pack in clean hot jars, cover with syrup in which they were cooked and process **20 minutes in a boiling water bath** or 75 minutes at 250° F. in oven. Seal according to type of lids used.

A few slices of lemon adds flavor and helps to keep the pears white.

Do not can pears in water unless for a diabetic person, as they need sugar to give them that delicate flavor they possess.

PEARS (Open Kettle)

Make a syrup of 2 **cups sugar and 1 cup water.** Let syrup boil, then add pears which have been halved, cored and pared or peeled. Cook until tender. Pack carefully, cut side down, into hot jars. Fill jars to overflowing with boiling syrup and seal immediately. Some people like to fill the cavity of the pear with a maraschino cherry.

PINEAPPLE (Cold Pack)

Peel pineapple and remove eyes. When the flesh is firm, cut into small cubes or remove core and slice; or quarter, remove core and slice. Pack cold into hot jars. Fill with a syrup made of **1 part sugar to 1 part water.** Partly seal and process for 30 **minutes in a hot water bath** or 90 **minutes in the oven at 250° F.** Remove from canner and seal immediately.

PINEAPPLE (Hot Pack)

Scrub firm, ripe pineapple with brush. Dry. Twist out top. Cut thin slice from bottom, then cut thin slice from top. Set on a heavy board and slice heavy covering down from top to bottom. Remove eyes with a grapefruit knife. Cut into quarters, remove core and cut each piece into half again, then slice into pieces. If you prefer round slices, then cut pineapple into circles and cut into shape with doughnut cutter. Save all pieces of pineapple to make juice which can be canned separately.

Make syrup of **two parts water** and **one part sugar,** add pineapple, simmer until tender. Pack into hot jars. Cover with hot syrup. Process **10 minutes in boiling water bath** or 75 minutes in 250° F. oven.

PINEAPPLE (Open Kettle)

Prepare as above. Mix pineapple with one-fourth its measure of sugar. Let stand one hour, then cook until tender. Pack boiling hot into hot jars, seal at once.

CRUSHED PINEAPPLE

Use **fresh, ripe pineapple** peel and core, then put through food chopper using medium coarse cutter. Save all juice and add to pulp. Add **1 cup sugar** to **each cup pineapple.** Bring quickly to a boil and boil **20 minutes.** Remove from fire, seal immediately. Use this in cream pies, fruit salad, or dressing for ice cream.

PLUMS (Cold Pack)

Wash, stem, and prick skin with fork to prevent bursting. Pack raw in halves or whole. Cover with a thin hot syrup—**3** cups water to 1 cup sugar. Put on lids, process in boiling water **bath 20 minutes** or in oven **50 minutes at 250° F.** Seal according to type of lids used.

PLUMS (Hot Pack)

Pre-cook plums in a thin syrup for 5 minutes, then pack hot in hot jars, adjusting lids according to type. **Process 10 minutes in boiling water bath** or **35 minutes in a 250 ° F. oven.** Seal according to type of lid used.

PLUMS (Open Kettle)

Make a syrup of **2 cups sugar and 2 cups water for each quart** of plums. Wash plums, prick with fork to prevent bursting and drop whole in boiling syrup. As soon as they are hot through, remove from fire and pack in clean hot jars, boiling syrup over them. Seal.

QUINCES (Cold Pack)

Pack the pared **raw fruit** in jars. Fill with syrup, using 3 parts **sugar** to **2 parts water.** Process for **35 minutes** in **boiling water bath.**

QUINCES WITH SWEET APPLES

Pare and quarter equal amounts of **quinces** and **sweet apples.** To each gallon of fruit, make syrup of **4 cups sugar and 4 cups water.** Boil hard 15 minutes. Add fruit and cook until it is a light red. Seal in hot jars. Makes a delicious dessert and is an excellent fruit salad.

BLACK RASPBERRIES (Cold Pack)

Wash and stem. Pack into clean hot jars. Fill to within 1½ inches of top with thin syrup—**3 cups water to 1 cup sugar.** Put on lid, seal tightly if it is a metallic cap with flowed-on rubber gasket, partially seal if a rubber ring is used. Process for **20 minutes in boiling water bath**—always wait to count time after water boils—or **70 minutes in a 250° F. oven.**

The lower temperature does not cook the berries so much. Remove from processor and seal according to the type of lid. Metallic lids with flowed on gasket should not be touched when removed from canner. They were sealed at the first and if you tighten them again you may break the seal of the rubber compound and injure rather than help the keeping qualities.

BLACK RASPBERRIES (Open Kettle)

Wash berries and pick them over carefully. Use one to two cups sugar for each quart in ordinary times but during the war allow only one-half cup sugar to each quart. Put sugar over berries and allow to stand a while to draw out juice. Stir well. Put on to cook for 20 minutes without water if there has been enough juice drawn out, if not, add a small amount of water. Pack hot into STERILIZED JARS and seal.

RED RASPBERRIES

Since these berries are softer than the black ones, an open kettle does not give good results, as only a little bit of heat will cause the berries to break apart. We advocate different method for their canning.

Make a syrup of one cup sugar and one quart water. Boil for 5 minutes. Fill STERILIZED JARS with clean berries. Set in oven and heat slowly until they wilt down. Have jars heaping full when they are to be put in oven. Fill with hot syrup and seal.

This recipe may be applied to all berries.

RED RASPBERRIES IN HOT WATER

Fill STERILIZED JARS with clean red raspberries, cover with hot thin syrup—three cups water to one cup sugar—seal completely regardless of type of jar used. Set in a water bath of boiling water. Turn out heat entirely and let jars stand in water until cold. Remove from bath and set aside for future use.

Other berries, ripe peaches and pears may be put up by this method but sometimes peaches and pears do not have all the enzymes killed, which changes their color to brown for peaches and pink for pears. They are canned best by other methods.

RHUBARB

This may be done by the following methods:

1—Baked rhubarb—Wash and cut rhubarb into small pieces. Add from one-half to one cup sugar to a quart of rhubarb. Bake until tender. Pack into hot jars. **Process five minutes in boiling water bath,** then complete seal.

2—Cold water canning—Fill sterilized jars with boiling water and set aside to cool slightly. When they reach that stage, cool, empty out water, rinse with cold water from faucet. Wash, trim and cut rhubarb into one-inch pieces, drop into jars, filling completely. Shake down, add more rhubarb if possible, add cold water to overflow jars, adjust rubber rings and sterile caps or metal caps as the case may be. Seal completely. Store in a cool dry place.

3—Cold pack method—Select tender stalks of rhubarb, trim, wash and cut into half inch lengths. Pack into clean hot jars, almost full, cover with boiling syrup or boiling water. **Process 20 minutes in boiling water bath.**

4—Open kettle—Wash, cut in convenient lengths without removing the skin. Boil in a medium syrup until tender. Pack in sterilized jars and seal.

5—May be processed **in oven** at 250° **F.** for **70 minutes.**

6—If rhubarb is heated before packing the time in water bath is reduced to **10 minutes and in oven to 35 minutes.**

7—Additional method—When possible use strawberry rhubarb. Wash and cut unpeeled stalks into one-inch pieces. Place in wide bottom pan with alternate layers of sugar. Using one-fourth as much sugar as rhubarb. Let stand two or more hours. Heat slowly to boiling. Remove pan from heat when contents begin to boil. Let stand several hours. Pack cold rhubarb in hot jars. Cover with syrup reheated to boiling. Process **five minutes in boiling water bath** then complete seal.

SALAD FRUITS

Boil together **2 cups sugar** and **1 quart water** until sugar is dissolved. Pare and halve **2 quarts pears,** cutting into smaller pieces if desired, cook them in the syrup first, remove when cooked. Skin and halve or cut into small pieces **2 quarts peaches.** Cook in syrup, when done remove and cook **2 pounds** of small **white grapes,** now add **1 large can** of **chunk pineapple** and **1 small jar** of **maraschino cherries,** cut fine. Add peaches and pears and heat until hot through. Can while hot in sterilized jars and seal. May be processed 10 minutes in boiling water bath.

STRAWBERRIES

Wash fruit. Pack sterile jars full of berries. Pour on hot syrup made with **3 parts sugar** to **2 parts water.** Seal jars. Completely immerse jars in boiler of boiling water. Let stand until water is cold.

CANNING STRAWBERRIES, COOKED

Cook **2 cups sugar with 2 cups water** together until sugar is dissolved. Add **2 quarts strawberries** which have been carefully washed and hulled. Cook for five minutes. Remove from range, cover with cloth and allow to stand overnight. Then pour strawberries into sterilized jars, filling jars to within ½ inch of top. Screw lid on according to kind used. Process in boiling water bath for 5 minutes or in oven 45 minutes at 250° F.

CANNING STRAWBERRIES, UNCOOKED

Make a syrup of **1 cup sugar to 1 quart water.** Boil for 5 minutes, then skim. Sterilize jars, leaving them in hot water until ready to use. Loosely fill with strawberries that have been hulled and cleaned. Fill jars to neck, not beyond. Pour in hot syrup until each jar is filled. Seal.

Canning Meats

If you do not have a pressure canner it is best to store meat in a frozen locker.

CANNING BEEF

1. Be sure animal heat has left body and meat is well chilled. 2. Do not soak meat in water. This extracts meat juices and renders meat stringy and tough. 3. Wash meat if necessary. Only clean meat and clean utensils should be used. 4. Cut meat into convenient size for packing. *Packing.* 1. Pack loosely into clean hot jars. Arrange the pieces to allow for proper heat penetration. This applies to precooked as well as raw meat. 2. Add 2 teaspoonfuls salt to each quart of raw meat. (By adding this salt to each quart of raw meat enough juices will be extracted during the processing to form sufficient liquid in the jar. It is not necessary to have jar filled with liquid. Lack of it does not affect the keeping qualities of a product.) 3. Do not add water to meat which has been packed raw. Adding water to meat when canning renders it stringy, detracts from flavor and reduces its use to practically soup, stews and hash. Add water for soup and stew. 4. Precooked meat may be seasoned before searing, frying or roasting. 5. Bones, if small, may be packed in the jar with meat, as they add to flavor and aid in heat penetration. *Processing and Storing.* 1. Partly seal jar and process for **3 hours in hot water bath** or for **90 minutes in a steam pressure cooker at 10 pounds,** the latter is the best way. 2. Remove from canner and seal immediately. 3. A thin strip of sealing wax around edge of lid will insure more safety in keeping. 4. Store in a cool dry place. 5. Reheat all canned meats thoroughly before using.

CHICKEN

This procedure may be followed for all poultry, rabbits and squirrels. Again the pressure cooker is the best method of canning chicken or any meat. If you can obtain one, do so, but since there are so few available, we are advocating the hot water bath. If the chickens are in your own possession they should be confined 12 to

24 hours before killing. Give water but no feed. Kill six to twelve hours before canning. Avoid bruising, bleed thoroughly. Pluck, singe and wash with mild soap; rinse. Cut skin between legs and body. Bend legs until hip joints snap. Slip knife under ends of shoulder blades and cut up to wings. Pull back and break apart. Remove entrails. Rinse, dry. Chill. Do not salt. Use feet in broth —do not can liver and gizzard with other parts of fowl.

COLD PACKING CHICKEN ON BONE

Separate raw fowl at joints. Pack into hot clean jars. Add **one teaspoonful salt to each quart.** Add no liquid. Put lids on. **Process in boiling water bath three hours.** Be sure water is boiling all that time. A little longer will not hurt. Some charts call for three and one-half hours. If you use the old-fashioned shoulder rubber the lids are sealed only partly before processing, whether they are zinc tops, spring tops or glass inserts but sealed immediately after taking from canner. If you use the metal tops with flowed on rubber gasket, seal as tight as possible before they are put in canner then do not tighten when removed from canner. Cool all jars in upright position. You may turn them upside down to test for leaks after 24 hours. Jars seal by vacuum and cannot do it as well if upside down.

Chicken will form its own liquid and when cooled it will solidify, showing the presence of gelatin. As long as this gelatin remains firm you have assurance that the chicken has not spoiled. If it should become liquid then be very careful about eating it until it has been thoroughly recooked on top of stove.

All meat canned by hot water bath must be recooked on top of stove for 10 minutes before tasting.

HOT PACKING CHICKEN ON BONE

Cut up chicken as desired, boil or steam until from one-third to one-half done, then pack hot into hot jars. Cover with boiling broth, salt to taste. Process **60 minutes** at **15-pound pressure** or **three hours in boiling water bath.** Remove from canner and complete seal if necessary.

BONED CHICKEN

Steam or boil until about two-thirds done. Remove skin and bones. Keep meat in as large pieces as possible. Salt to taste. Pack pieces upright in clean hot jars. Cover with boiling broth. **Process in boiling water bath three hours** or **60 minutes at 15-pound pressure in pressure cooker.** Remove from canner and complete seal if necessary.

FRIED CHICKEN

This is good for spring chicken and young game. Season with salt and pepper and brown in fat. Do not dip in flour or crumbs. Pack hot in clean hot jars. Add one to two tablespoonfuls fat in which it was fried or make a gravy of the fat and pour this over chicken. **Process in boiling water bath three hours** or **60 minutes at 15-pound pressure if a pressure cooker** is used.

ROAST FOWL, RABBIT AND SQUIRRELS

Prepare and roast until about two-thirds done. Cut meat from bones if fowl is large. If small, leave bones in. Season with salt and pepper. Pack into clean hot jars. Skim excess fat from gravy that is in pan from roast. Reheat gravy or broth to boiling and pour over meat. **Process three hours in boiling water bath or 60 minutes at 15 pounds pressure.** Remove from canner and complete seal if necessary.

SAUSAGE

For **20 pounds pork shoulder** mix up in a separate bowl the following seasoning: **5 ounces salt, 1 ounce pepper, 2 teaspoonfuls ginger** and **2 tablespoonfuls brown sugar.** Cut meat into strips, rub seasoning over it on all sides. Then have meat ground but not with a very fine knife, perhaps a medium one would be better. The grinding does the mixing for you. Fry in small patty cakes, not too thick, until about half done. Pack in clean hot jars. Partially seal and process in **boiling water bath for 3 hours.** This is excellent to have on the emergency shelf.

VEAL

Veal may be partially cooked or left raw to can. If one prefers the brown taste, then cook it until that has been obtained, but remember it requires just as long to process it as if it were left raw. Bleed well and cool meat thoroughly before using. (Approximately 24 hours is required for animal heat to leave the body.) Do not soak meat in water. This extracts the meat juices and renders meat stringy and tough. Wash meat if necessary. Only clean meat and clean utensils should be used. Cut meat into convenient size for packing. Pack loosely into clean hot jars. Arrange the pieces to allow proper heat penetration. Add 2 level teaspoonfuls salt to each quart. Do not add water. (There will be enough natural juices extracted to provide sufficient liquid.) Bones, if small, may be packed in the jar with the meat as they add to flavor and aid in heat penetration. Partially seal jar and **process for 3 hours in boiling water canner.** Remove from canner and seal immediately. Store in a cool dry place. Reheat all canned meats thoroughly before using.

All canned meats and low-acid vegetables should be thoroughly heated before they are eaten.

Mincemeat is a pleasing combination of meat, spices and apples. It fits well into pies, cakes and cookies.

MINCEMEAT

Take 6 **cups chopped or ground meat,** packed down, 3 **cups chopped** or **ground suet, 12 cups chopped** or **ground apples, 2 cups molasses, 2 cups boiled cider, 3 cups meat broth, 4 cups sugar, 3 packages raisins, 2 teaspoonfuls cinnamon, 2 teaspoonfuls nutmeg, 2 teaspoonfuls salt, 1 teaspoonful cloves, 1 teaspoonful allspice and citron, orange and lemon peel,** according to taste. Cook slowly ½ hour until it comes to a boil, stirring frequently. This will fill 7 quart jars. When using, add **1 cup coffee** to each quart and more **sugar** if desired.

GREEN TOMATO MINCEMEAT

Grind 1 **peck green tomatoes** and scald twice with boiling water, allow to get cold and then drain each time. Combine in preserving kettle with equal amount of apples, pared and ground. Add 4 **pounds sugar, 1 tablespoonful salt, 1 cup suet,** chopped fine, and 2 **pounds seeded raisins.** Cook slowly until tender. Stir frequently. Let cool, then add 1 **cup vinegar, juice of 2 lemons, 2 tablespoonfuls ground cinnamon, ½ tablespoonful ground cloves, ½ tablespoonful ground nutmeg.** Put in sterilized jars and seal. Makes about 5 quarts. When opening for use add any fruit juices or leftover jelly. May be seasoned to taste. Two tablespoonfuls brandy to each pie will improve the flavor.

GREEN TOMATO MINCEMEAT WITH HAMBURG

Chop 8 **pounds green tomatoes,** then add 1 tablespoonful salt. Let stand several hours. It is important to drain thoroughly before adding the rest of the ingredients. Then add water enough to cover tomatoes. Also add: **2 pounds seeded raisins, 5 pounds brown sugar, 2 tablespoonfuls ground cloves, 2 tablespoonfuls ground cinnamon, 2 pounds hamburg, 1 cup vinegar, 1 pound chopped suet.** Cook 1 hour. Chop **apples** equal to amount of mincemeat and add to mixture. Cook ½ hour longer. Can while hot.

The syrup from pickled peaches and pears may be used in mincemeat.

Canning Vegetables

ASPARAGUS

Grade freshly cut asparagus for size. Wash and remove scales. Place upright in wire basket or in a square of cheesecloth and hold three minutes in boiling water which reaches just below the tips. Pack upright into clean hot jars. Add **1 teaspoonful salt** to each quart. Cover with boiling water. Process **40 minutes at 10 pounds pressure** or **3 hours in boiling water bath.** If canned by hot water bath be sure to heat 10 minutes on top of stove before tasting.

It is best to freeze asparagus if you have a freezer.

Vegetables that need long processing in hot water bath should not be packed tightly. There should be room for heat to circulate.

GREEN BEANS

Green beans are prepared in the same manner for canning regardless of the processing. They are best processed in a pressure cooker but since there are very few available we are advocating the boiling water bath. If green beans are canned by processing in the boiling water bath they should be heated on top of the stove at boiling temperature for 10 minutes after opening and before tasting.

Have beans freshly gathered and as tender as possible. Wash, string and break if desired. Add enough boiling water to cover and parboil from three to five minutes, depending upon the bean, in an uncovered vessel. Pack into clean hot jars. Cover to one-half inch of top with water in which they were boiled, adding one teaspoonful salt to each quart of beans. Seal according to type of lid used.

Remember all lids that have a loose rubber ring are only partially sealed before processing and tightened as soon as they are removed from the processer, but lids with a flowed on rubber gasket are tightened immediately before processing and are not touched after being removed from the processer. The glass top lids with wire bails are only partially sealed before processing. The top bail is put in place but the bottom bail is left up until after processing when it is immediately pressed into place as soon as removed from the processer.

If green beans—waxed beans are treated the same—are to be processed in the pressure cooker they require **10 pounds pressure 30 minutes for pints** and **40 minutes for quarts.**

If processed in **boiling water bath** they require **three hours** with water boiling all the time.

Green beans are at their best during the months of July and August. One bushel will can from 14 to 18 quarts. Usually one-half bushel makes eight quarts and allows enough extra for the family to have a meal. Since eight quarts is the number one can do in a washboiler it is a good practice to do only that amount at a time.

GREEN OR WAX BEANS WITH VINEGAR AND SALT

Remove tips and strings from **3 gallons of green** or **wax beans.** Place in a large kettle with enough water to cover well. Add **1 cup coarse salt** and **1 cup cider vinegar.** Let all come to a boil in a covered kettle. Boil slowly for 15 minutes. Pack into sterile jars and seal while hot. This will can 6 quarts.

These beans will need more cooking when opened to use. Pour off the water they were canned in, and add fresh water.

LIMA BEANS

Carefully sort and grade for size and age. When shelling beans place the older ones into a separate lot for soup, and the young and tender ones into another assortment for extra fine packing. Boil young beans for five minutes and the older beans for 10 minutes. Pack quickly and loosely into clean, hot jar to within 1 inch of top. Add 1 teaspoonful salt to each quart. Cover with boiling water, partially seal and process for **3 hours in a boiling water bath** or for **55 minutes in a steam pressure c**ooker at **10 pounds.** Remove from canner and seal immediately. Lima beans must be freshly gathered to can well.

BEANS AND PORK

Soak **4 pounds navy beans** overnight in cold water then fill quart jar with beans placing **3 small pieces of fat bacon** through beans. Add **1 teaspoonful salt, 1 teaspoonful brown sugar** and **3 tablespoonfuls catsup** (more if desired) in each jar. Fill jar with **hot water,** adjust lids according to kind used and process in **boiling water bath 4 hours** or **80 minutes** at **10 pounds pressure** in pressure cooker.

BEETS

Select small tender beets with a deep red color. Cook until tender, leaving the steam and root on. Slip skins, trim beets and pack hot into jars. Add one teaspoonful salt to each quart. Cover with boiling water. Process **40 minutes at 10 pounds pressure** or **two and one-half hours in water bath.** Seal according to the type of lids used.

PICKLED BEETS

Cook and skin **one gallon beets.** Add **two cups sugar** to **three and one-half cups vinegar** and **one and one-half cups water.** Simmer 15 minutes. Add beets. Boil five minutes. Pack into hot jars. Cover with boiling syrup. Seal according to type of lid used. Process **five minutes in boiling water bath.**

CABBAGE

Wash, remove outside leaves. Cut into desired sized pieces and pre-cook five minutes. Pack into clean hot jars, add one teaspoonful salt to each quart jar and fill to within one-half inch of top with water in which cabbage was cooked. Put on lid, seal according to type used. Process in **boiling water bath two hours** or **35 minutes at 10-pound pressure** in pressure cooker.

Remove from canner and seal according to types of lids used. BE SURE YOU KNOW DEFINITELY WHAT LIDS ARE TIGHTENED AFTER REMOVING FROM CANNER.

CARROTS

Grade for size, putting all tiny carrots together in one jar, allowing them to remain whole. Wash thoroughly, scrape. Pre-cook 5 minutes in boiling water. Pack in clean hot jars. Add **one teaspoonful salt** to each **quart** of **carrots.** Fill to within one-half inch of the top with water in which vegetable was cooked. Put on cap, according to type of lid used. Remember those with loose rubbers are not completely sealed until after processing, those with flowed-on rubbers are sealed immediately and not touched after removing from canner. Process in **boiling water bath two hours** or pressure cooker **35 minutes at 10 pounds.**

Remove from canner and seal according to type of lid used. DO NOT TURN UPSIDE DOWN TO TEST FOR LEAKS UNTIL COLD.

CELERY

Clean and cut celery into small pieces. Pack in sterilized jars, cover with cold water, adding **a scant teaspoonful salt** to **each quart.** Process in boiling water bath for **2½ hours.**

CAULIFLOWER

Soak cauliflower for 1 hour in a cold brine made in the proportions of **1 tablespoonful salt** to **1 quart water.** This will remove any lurking insects and help to prevent discoloring later in the cooking process. Preheat for 3 minutes. Pack quickly into clean, hot jars. Add **1 teaspoonful salt** to **each quart.** Fill with hot water, partly seal and process for **2½ hours in boiling water bath.** Remove from canner and seal at once.

CORN

Corn is a hard vegetable to can as it produces flat sour even while in the canning process, if it is not canned quickly. Corn also produces spores of bacteria which are very hard to kill. These develop rapidly after the corn is pulled. So we advise that corn to be canned should be pulled and canned within 2 hours of gathering.

Watch the utensils you use in canning corn. Do not allow any of the corn milk to remain on them, rinse often to keep them clean. This is to assure that flat sour does not develop during the process of canning. Here again a pressure cooker is the best method of insuring good canned corn, but if that is not available use the boiling water bath.

CORN (No. 1)

Gather young corn with milk still in the liquid stage. It pops when you burst a kernel.

Husk, clean ear of silks, then cut from cob as close as you like. Some prefer to only cut off the top, then scrape the rest. We like to cut as close to the cob as possible. Put in a large kettle, preparing enough for two quarts at a time. Cover with boiling water. Let come to a boil again and cook for five minutes. Pour hot into clean hot jars both corn and water, add one teaspoonful salt to each quart, put on lids and fasten them according to type used. Remember all lids with flowed on rubber are tightened at the beginning. Process in **pressure cooker, whole grain corn, 10 pounds, 70 minutes** for **quarts** and **60 minutes** for **pints, cream style corn, 80 minutes at 10-pound pressure** for quarts and **75 for pints.**

Boiling water bath—3½ hours for both pints and quarts. Be sure to heat corn canned in hot water bath on top of stove for 10 minutes after opening before tasting. Remove from canner and seal according to type of lids used, in no case turn the jars upside down for leaks until after 12 hours of cooling in upright position.

CORN (No. 2)

Wash corn and cut from cob, three-fourths depth of grain. Scrape out rest of substance from cob. Put corn in stew pan after measuring. For every **quart** of corn add **1 1/3 teaspoonful sugar** and 2/3 **teaspoonful salt**, cover with boiling water. Let boil 8 to 10 minutes. Pack in jars quickly and loosely with hot corn and water to within 1 inch of the top. Seal *tightly* and process 3 **hours in boiling water bath.**

EGGPLANT

Pare eggplant. Cut it into thin slices and boil 15 to 20 minutes. Drain off water and pack in clean hot jars. Fill to overflowing with cold water. Place in **boiling water bath for 3 hours** (count time after it starts to boil) or **55 minutes in pressure cooker at 10 pounds pressure.** After processing remove jars, tighten covers. A teaspoonful salt may be added but it darkens the eggplant.

GREENS

By greens we mean dandelions, swiss chard, spinach, kale, collards, turnip tops, beet greens and other greens that you may enjoy eating. Dandelions should be picked before even the yellow blossoms appear, to have them tender. All other greens are better the younger they are. Remember canning does not improve the product. It will come out of the can no better than when it went into it.

Wash carefully and precook in live steam or place in kettle with just the water clinging to the leaves after the last washing and pre-cook until wilted. Cut with sharp knife to make them of uniform size and pack at once into clean hot jars, being careful not to press too tightly. Add **one teaspoonful salt** to **each quart** and fill to within one-half inch of top with boiling water. Put on cap, tighten according to type of lid—and **process in hot water bath three hours,** or **pressure cooker 65 minutes** at **15 pounds pressure.** Remember to reheat 10 minutes on top of stive if canned by water bath.

BEET GREENS

If the tops of the beets are still tender, do not throw them away, but can them the same as spinach for a winter green. Wash carefully and pre-cook in live steam or place in kettle with just water clinging to leaves after the last washing and pre-cook until wilted. Pack at once into clean jars, being careful not to press too tightly. Add one teaspoonful salt to each quart jar if desired and fill to within one-half inch of top with boiling water. Put on lid and fasten according to type. Process in **boiling water bath three hours** or **65 minutes at 15 pounds pressure.**

DANDELIONS

Pick over and clean dandelions. Blanch 5 minutes in hot water (15 minutes if steam is used). Cold dip 1 minute. Pack into jars. Add water to within ½ inch of top, if needed. Add **1 teaspoonful salt for each quart.** Adjust rubber and partly seal. Place in **boiling water bath** and process for **3 hours after water starts to boil.** Remove from canner and finish sealing.

MUSHROOMS

Wash mushrooms thoroughly. Skin if necessary. Boil for 2 minutes in boiling water or steamer. Pack closely in hot jar but be careful not to crush. Add **1 teaspoonful salt to each quart.** Fill with water they have been cooked in. Process in **boiling water bath for 3 hours or 60 minutes in a steam pressure cooker at 10 pounds.** Remove from canner and seal immediately.

PEAS

Peas must be fresh and young to can. Remember the slogan: "Two Hours From Garden To Can." Wash pods, drain, shell, rinse. Cover with boiling water and pre-cook accordingly to size, small ones three minutes, larger ones seven minutes. Pack loosely to within 1 inch of jar top. Fill to within ½ inch of top with water in which they were pre-cooked.

Add **one teaspoonful salt for each quart** and **one-half teaspoonful sugar** if desired. Put on lid and fasten according to type used. Process in steam pressure cooker **10 pounds for 60 minutes** or **three hours in boiling water bath.**

If processed in water bath be sure to cook for 10 minutes on top of stove at boiling temperature for safety, before eating.

PEPPERS (Hot)

Take long green or yellow hot peppers. Wash. Have **jars** sterilized. Pack peppers in jars and to each quart add **1 teaspoonful salt.** Make a solution of **1 quart vinegar** and **1 quart water**—bring to a boil. Cover peppers and seal at once.

PEPPERS

Simmer for 15 minutes—**1 cup sugar** and **1 pint vinegar.** Cut red or green sweet peppers in strips with scissors. Preheat in boiling water 3 minutes. Dip in cold water. Pack in jars. Pour over the hot vinegar and seal at once.

PIMIENTOS (No. 1)

Since these Spanish pimientos have a thick skin it must be removed before canning. Wash, place in pan without water. Put in moderately hot oven for 10-15 minutes or until skins blister and crack. Be careful not o allow them to become too hot as they will discolor. Remove from oven and remove skins. Remove seeds so that flesh of pimiento is not broken. Flatten pimientos. Pack **dry** into **hot** jars. Partly seal and process in **boiling water bath for 45 minutes.** Remove from canner and seal immediately.

PIMIENTOS (No. 2)

Wash carefully, remove tops and seeds of pimientos. Place in a bowl and pour boiling water over them three times. Let stand in water each time a few minutes. Drain well the last time. Pack in jars and fill with boiling vinegar (not very strong) to which a little salt and sugar has been added. Seal and keep in a cool place. Cut with scissors when needed for a garnish.

PUMPKIN

Cut pumpkin in halves, remove seeds, place on pan, bake at 400° F. until soft—about one hour for average size. Remove from oven, take pumpkin from shell with a big spoon. Put at once through sieve into clean hot jars. Add one teaspoonful salt for each quart, partly seal. Do not cover with boiling water. Put in **boiling water bath three hours or pressure cooker 70 minutes** at **15 pounds pressure.**

SAUERKRAUT

Cut **cabbage** fine and pack solid in glass quart jars. To each jar add **¾ cup warm water** to which has been added **1 teaspoonful salt** and **1 teaspoonful sugar.** Add more warm water, if needed to cover cabbage. Seal tight. This will be ready in three weeks for use.

KRAUT THAT WAS CURED IN CROCK

As soon as kraut is thoroughly cured, pack into clean hot jars, adding enough of the kraut brine to fill jars to within ½ inch of top. (If not enough kraut juice, make a weak brine of 2 tablespoonfuls salt to 1 quart water.) Put on lids. Process in boiling water bath 15 minutes.

SAUERKRAUT JUICE

When **sauerkraut** is ready for use or when kraut has been put into jars or cans out of the crock or barrel in which it was made, take all juice that is left, put through sieve and boil for 5 minutes. Put in sterilized bottles at once and seal securely. Dip tops of bottles in parawax. When bottles are all filled jars may be used. The sealing must be perfect as the sauerkraut is already fermented. Store away the same as other canned goods. When wanted or needed it is ready for use without any further preparation.

SANDWICH FILLING

Grind together, **12 green peppers, 12 red peppers**, **12 green tomatoes,** and **2 medium sized onions.** Drain. Add to **1 quart vinegar** (dilute if too strong), **3 cups sugar, 1 teaspoonful celery salt, 1 teaspoonful flour, 1 teaspoonful salt,** and **1 quart prepared mustard.** Mix together well and boil for 10 minutes. Add **1 quart jar of mayonnaise.** Seal in jars. This is enough for 12 pints.

SUMMER SQUASH

Wash squash, pre-cook by steaming three to five minutes. Pack in jars to within half inch of top, add water in which vegetable was cooked. Add **one teaspoonful salt to each quart jar,** put on cap according to type. Process for **three hours in hot water bath or 40 minutes at 10 pounds pressure.**

HUBBARD SQUASH

In the late fall when some cans are empty, and you cut into a large Hubbard squash, eat some and can the rest. Cut in pieces, steam or bake until tender. Remove pulp from shell. Pack into clean hot jars. Add **one teaspoonful salt for each quart,** process **three hours in hot water bath** or **60 minutes at 10 pounds pressure**

SWEET POTATOES

For canning, select firm, freshly dug, small sweet potatoes of uniform size and color. Wash thoroughly and boil or steam for 15 minutes, peel as soon as they are cool enough to handle. It is advisable not to stick potatoes with a fork as that may cause them to discolor. Pack into clean hot jars. Do not add water. Seal according to type of lids used, and process **4 hours in boiling water bath or 120 minutes in steam pressure cooker at 10 lbs.** Remove from canner and seal if that type of lids were used.

If salt is put in the bottom or center of a jar of vegetables to be canned, it may prevent lacquered tops from rusting.

TOMATO SOUP

Boil together ½ **bushel tomatoes** that have been washed and cut up, **7 good sized onions,** sliced, **14 stalks celery,** chopped, **14 strips parsley, 14 bay leaves, 21 cloves** (whole), and a little **garlic** for 2 hours. Strain through a sieve and boil for 10 minutes with the following: **12 teaspoonfuls salt,** ½ **teaspoonful pepper,** ¼ **teaspoonful red pepper, 1½ cups brown sugar** and ½ **pound fresh butter.** When soup is boiling add a thickening made by mixing **2 cups flour** slowly with **water** until it is rather thin. Cook again for 5 minutes. Seal in jars. When ready to use heat, add a little **soda** and either **water** or **milk** to thin.

VEGETABLE SOUP

Scald and peel **1 peck tomatoes,** cut into pieces the size desired four soup. Clean enough **green beans** that when cut, in 1 inch lengths they measure **1 quart.** Clean and scrap enough **carrots** that when diced, they measure **1 quart.** Cook carrots and beans in water to cover for 15 to 20 minutes. Add to tomatoes then add **2 bunches of celery,** chopped, **2 small heads cabbage** cut fine, enough **onions** for **1 quart, 3 green peppers** and a **small bunch of parsley all** cut. Lastly add **1 pint of shelled lima beans.** Add **½ cup salt.** Cook all together uncovered for 30 minutes then pack in hot jars, fasten lids according to kind used and process in boiling water bath 3 hours.

COLD PACK-BOILING WATER BATH TOMATOES

Remove stems and blemishes. Never use even a small part of a spoiled tomato. Scald to remove skins. Pack in clean hot jars, pressing tomatoes down to form their own juices. **Add one teaspoonful salt to each quart.** Seal according to type of lids used. **Process in hot water bath 30 minutes.**

HOT PACK BOILING WATER BATH TOMATOES

Wash, scald tomatoes just long enough to remove peel. Quarter or leave whole. Heat to boiling. Pack hot, cover with hot juice, add **one teaspoonful of salt to each quart** and process **10 minutes in hot water bath.** Be sure to count the time when water starts to boil.

OPEN KETTLE TOMATOES

Wash, remove stems and blemishes, dip in hot water to remove skins. Quarter, place on stove and heat gently until juicy. Then boil for 20 minutes. Salt to taste. Have jars clean and sterile. Pack hot tomatoes into hot jars and seal each jar immediately as soon as filled, doing only one jar at a time. Add tomato juice if more liquid is needed but it, too, must be boiling hot.

EDITOR'S NOTE—We have been successful in canning tomatoes open kettle by only cooking them five minutes. If yours are fresh from the vines and everything is sterile we think you can too. The less time used in open kettle canning the less loss of vitamins.

TOMATOES FOR SALADS (No. 1)

Wide mouth jars are best as they allow the whole tomato to be canned. Select small, uniform, firm tomatoes. Scald, cold dip and drain. Cut out core, skin. Pack into jars but do not press down. Cover with tomato juice, add **one teaspoonful salt to each quart** or leave without any liquid at all. Process **45 minutes in hot water bath.** Seal according to type of lids used.

TOMATOES FOR SALADS (No. 2)

Remove skins from firm tomatoes by holding them over an open flame until skin bursts, finish removing them. Pack in clean, hot sterile jars with sterile lids. Fill with **boiling tomato juice** and seal thoroughly.

Set in **water bath of boiling water,** allow water to come to a boil again, then turn off fire and allow tomatoes to stay in water until cold.

TOMATOES (Volume of Water)

Skin and quarter medium sized **tomatoes.** Put **1 gallon of water** in large kettle and add **1 heaping tablespoonful salt.** When water boils, drop tomatoes in and boil 5 minutes. Remove from fire, put in sterilized jars and seal. Prepare only enough for **3 quarts** at one time. After cooking **6 quarts** add **another tablespoonful salt.**

TOMATO JUICE (No. 1)

Remove stems and all green or bad spots. Cut into pieces. Simmer until soft. Put through a fine sieve. Add **one teaspoonful salt to each quart.** Reheat at once just to boiling. Fill hot jars immediately, leaving one-four inch head space, **process 15 minutes in hot water bath.**

If jars and lids are sterile, the juice may be canned directly after reheating to boiling and sealed without any processing. But processing gives more assurance that it will keep.

TOMATO JUICE (No. 2)

Remove blemishes and stem ends from enough **tomatoes** to make **2 quarts** when cut into pieces. Do not peel. Add **1 cup water, 2 small onions, 1 stalk of celery, 1 tablespoonful salt, 2 tablespoonfuls sugar, ½ teaspoonful pepper** and **4 whole cloves.** Simmer gently 30 minutes. Force through strainer. Add **2 tablespoonfuls lemon juice** and **2 tablespoonfuls vinegar.** Heat to boiling point. Turn into sterile jars and seal at once.

TOMATO JUICE (No. 3)

Remove blemishes and tough stem ends of **tomatoes.** Cut in pieces. Measure **12 quarts.** (Do not peel.) Add **7 cups water, 13 small onions** (cut fine), **6 tablespoonfuls salt, 6 stalks celery** (cut fine), **¾ cup sugar, 3 teaspoonfuls pepper** and **30 whole cloves** (these may be omitted). Simmer 1 hour. Remove from fire, let cool. Force through strainer. Add **¾ cup lemon juice** and **½ cup vinegar.** Boil 5 minutes and turn into sterile jars. Seal at once. Makes about 15 pints.

TOMATO PASTE

Wash as **many tomatoes as kettle will hold.** Cut in quarters, but do not peel. Remove all blemishes. Add just enough **water** to keep from sticking. Boil for 20 minutes. Strain to remove seeds and skins. Return to kettle and boil until very thick, adding **salt** and **pepper to taste.** Watch carefully while it is reducing so as not to scorch. A slow fire will be best. Pour in jars and seal.

GREEN TOMATOES

Wash and slice (about ½ inch thick) green tomatoes, pack in sterilized jars, add **1 teaspoonful salt to each quart,** fill jars with cold water, place in cold canner in cold water and let come to a boil, boil for 3 minutes. Remove from canner and seal.

When desiring to use them in winter, open, drain off water. Dip slices in flour and fry brown in butter. They will taste like fresh fried green tomatoes.

Drying and Salting

DRIED APPLES

Pare ripe apples and cut into quarters. Slice them lengthwise of the quarter, not too thin. Place them on racks over the stove or in the oven, leaving the oven doors open for air, stirring occasionally to have them dry evenly. Do not let apples get too hot. They should dry in 24 hours.

TO SULPHUR APPLES

Work out of doors. For small amounts of fruit the sulphuring chamber may be simply a tight packing box or a wooden frame covered closely with roofing paper or wall board. It should be high enough to cover a stack of trays and wide enough to allow about a foot of extra room for the sulphur pan. At the bottom of the sulphuring box allow a small space for air to enter—otherwise sulphur may not burn. Two blocks of wood laid on the ground will form a support for the loaded trays. Stack the trays one upon the other with pieces of light lath between. The lowest tray should be six to seven inches from the ground.

Measure out one level teaspoonful sulphur for each pound of prepared fruit. Don't use too much sulphur. Wrap the sulphur in a small piece of paper and place in a shallow tin can. Set the can of sulphur on the ground in front of the loaded trays. Light paper and quickly place the sulphuring chamber over trays and can. It should cover the trays completely to prevent loss of sulphur fumes. Apples are sulphured 20 to 30 minutes, if cut in slices. If in larger pieces, it would require a longer time. Apples tre then dehydrated after being sulphured.

SULPHUR APPLES

Quarter apples, place in open basket, hang in an air-tight barrel. Put a can of hot coals resting on a brick in the bottom of the barrel first. Then throw a handful of sulphur over hot coals, cover quickly and tightly with a heavy blanket to keep fumes in. Let smoke three to four hours. Put in a covered crock in a cool place and use these apples for sauce and pie during the winter. You will notice that these apples are not dried after being sulphured.

DEHYDRATING GREEN BEANS

Before drying, vegetables should be pre-cooked in steam or boiling water. The steaming process seems to allow more of their valuable material to remain inside. They also keep better, require less soaking before they are cooked for the table and have a better flavor and appearance.

During wartime, we use what we have in the way of equipment. If you have an old-fashioned steamer, that is fine. If you haven't, then put a thin layer of vegetables in a colander and set it over boiling water. The vegetables should be just over the top of boiling water.

However, pre-cooking in boiling water is quite satisfactory if directions are carefully followed. Work with small amounts of food at a time so the water will not be cooled more than necessary.

The beans are then drained and placed on the dryer racks. Any kind of a dryer may be used. If you do not have a dryer, then use cookie sheets in your oven. The oven should not be higher than 150° F. Most stoves do not have a regulator that reduces the heat to that temperature. If your electric stove does not, perhaps you can turn it to the lowest pont, place an oven thermometer inside of oven and with the door open keep it at near 150° F. as possible. With a gas oven, reduce flame until it is small enough to keep oven at 150° F. Also leave door open, as this allows air to circulate through and that is as necessary as heat in drying vegetables. A small electric fan may be placed in front of the stove to reduce heat of oven and with the door open keep it as near 150 as possible. and aid in air circulation.

Dehydrated vegetables require less room and keep very well.

Vegetables should be rigid and brittle before removing from dryer.

They may be stored in chipped glass jars. This keeps them free from dirt. Save the cracked and chipped jars for these beans.

DEHYDRATING CARROTS

This is the latest method of keeping these young carrots for next winter. They are gathered, washed, scraped if desired. Slice not too thin, cook for five minutes in steam. Drain, spread on cheese cloth in drying racks and dry in oven at 150° F., allowing the door of oven to remain partly open for circulation of air. This requires about six hours drying time. The slower they are dried, the more color remains. They should have a bright carrot color. Store in cracked or nicked jars. You can store in one jar dried, what would require a dozen jars if canned.

DRYING CORN

Corn to be dried should be just as fresh as to be canned and it should be hurried through to the drying stage just as rapidly. Steam or cook as for roasting ears as much corn as you will want dried and your racks will handle. A dozen ears will dry to make a quart of dried corn. Usually a gallon of dried corn is sufficient for a family of four for the winter. Cut from cob as soon as cooked. Pour cold water over if you can't handle it hot. Spread out on drying trays and begin drying at once at 150° F. Dry until it is crisp and firm but not brown. It requires watching so that one side or a certain part does not get too dry. Corn to be dried may be cut from cob, seasoned with sugar, cream and salt, heated on top of stove for about five minutes, watching very carefully to keep from burning, then spread out on trays for drying. We do not think it is worth the extra trouble, as seasoning can be accomplished just as well when it is prepared for the table.

Dry both celery tops and parsley for use in winter.

DRYING PEACHES

Use ripe peaches that are still firm. Wash, then dip into boiling water for a few seconds to loosen skin. Peel. Let the peeled peaches stand for a few minutes in cold water to which 2 tablespoonfuls each of salt and vinegar have been added to prevent discoloration. Halve the peaches or cut them in slices, discard the pit and spread in a single layer in the tray. Halved peaches should be placed cut side up. For oven drying, start the temperature at 130 and gradually increase to 165° F. They are done when still pliable and leathery and a cut piece shows no moisture when pressed with fingers.

DRYING PEARS

The Bartlett and Kieffer varieties are best for drying. Use firm ripe pears. Wash, pare and remove core, cut into quarters or rings or slices ¼-inch thick. Let pears stand in a weak salt solution—3 tablespoonfuls salt to 1 gallon water—for a few minutes. Then steam for 5 to 7 minutes. Place in trays in single layers. For oven drying let temperature start at 130° F. and gradually increase to 150° F. The pears are done when the pieces are elastic and leathery and you cannot press any moisture out of a cut piece.

DEHYDRATING PEAS

The same care should be exercised for peas that are to be dried as for canning. Blanch for five minutes in boiling water, drain, then place on drying rack and dry slowly with a temperature of about 150° F. for six hours, shaking ever so often to prevent sticking.

This may be done in an oven if the temperature can be controlled to this low degree. Let door of oven remain partly open to allow air to circulate.

DRYING GERMAN PRUNE PLUMS

Pour boiling water over German prune plums. Let stand 20 minutes or slightly less. If very ripe take out on towel to drain. Prick with fork and put on enamel pan in oven or close to a fire to dry. They require a rather warm place, but not too hot. Dry them until they are very hard. Put in clean bag to hang up for the winter.

Use salting as the last possible means of preservation.

OLD-FASHIONED SALT CORN

Boil fresh tender **corn** five minutes, cut from cob. Measure corn and mix with ¼ its measure of pure **salt.** Pack tightly to within ¼ inch of top of quart glass jar. Smooth a spoonful of salt over top of corn. Partly seal and store in cool, dry place. The corn is freshened for use by parboiling two or three times. The freshened corn usually is stewed with sweet milk, butter and pepper for serving.

SALTING GREEN BEANS

Wash, dry and weigh beans. Cut intoone-inch lengths. Pack green beans loosely into a stone jar leaving space for brine to cover them.

To make brine, use 3¼ cups of picking salt to six quarts water. Pour brine over vegetables and cover jar with plate weighted down with a gallon jug full of water or a heavy clean stone. Next day, add one pound of salt for every 10 pounds of vegetables used. This is to bring the brine up to its original strength. At the end of the week, add one-fourth pound salt and repeat the process every week until five weeks have been marked off on the calendar. The beans should now be cured.

Remember, when adding salt to place it on top of plate and allow it to be absorbed gradually so that it does not touch the vegetable. Remove scum as it forms.

To freshen vegetables that have been salted, place them in a large kettle, cover with water, heat slowly to lukewarm, stirring frequently. Pour off water and repeat process several times until vegetables are only slightly salty or soak several hours in different waters until they taste just right, then cook.

SAUERKRAUT

Select firm **heads of cabbage** and cut or shred. Put in a barrel or large jar (stone) a layer of cabbage, then sprinkle with **salt.** Pack each layer down tight or better still, mix a small portion of cabbage at a time. Salt it just to suit taste, not too salty, but just as for cooking. Pack each portion down tight. Then add more until barrel is filled. Place outside cabbage leaves over top of cabbage and weight down. Cover top with a cloth. The reason for the weight is so brine will come up to top.

Use ¼ lb. salt to 10 lbs. cabbage for sauerkraut.

Freezing

Fruits may be packed for the locker by one of two methods:

(1) Sugar syrup pack.

(2) Granulated sugar pack.

Fruit mixed with dry sugar.

Fruits that have plenty of their own juice and do not brown easily may be packed by the latter method, but the syrup method is preferred.

Prepare fruit as if it were going to be eaten fresh.

SUGAR SYRUP

30 percent	— 2	cups sugar	— 4 cups water
40 percent	— 3¼	cups sugar	— 4 cups water
45 percent	— 4	cups sugar	— 4 cups water
50 percent	— 4⅔	cups sugar	— 4 cups water
60 percent	— 7	cups sugar	— 4 cups water

CHERRIES

Steam and sort cherries. Wash, drain and pit. Mix well with **1 pound sugar** to **3 or 4 pounds fruit.** Pack in containers. **Freeze.** Sweet cherries may be packed with or without pits. Stem, wash, pack and cover with a 30 per cent syrup.

PEACHES

Wash in cold water and scald peaches for **10** seconds to make peeling easier. Cool immediately and peel. Do not let peeled fruit accumulate for it will discolor. Pour **½ cup of 50 per cent syrup** in **each pint container** and slice **fruit directly** into that. Be sure syrup completely covers fruit. Cover or heat seal and **freeze immediately.**

RASPBERRIES (Red and Black)

Sort and wash berries. Pack in **45 per cent syrup.** Cover or heat seal. **Freeze immediately.**

STRAWBERRIES

Hull, sort and wash berries. Slice or leave whole. **Pack** in containers and cover with **45 per cent syrup.** Cover or heat seal. **Freeze immediately.**

FREEZING MEATS

Meat, freshly killed, should be chilled before freezing. Cut carcass up into pieces suitable for cooking. Wrap each piece closely in paper waxed on one side only. **Label each package** with a **description of the meat, weight, date, locker number. Freeze immediately.**

FREEZING VEGETABLES

There are 3 steps in the processing of vegetables for the frozen locker.

First, they must be washed and sorted, just as though they were going to be cooked immediately instead of stored until next winter.

Second, they are scalded for a brief time and cooled the same length of time (the time depending upon the vegetable.)

Third, they are packaged (usually in a weak brine.)

Scalding is very important in the preparation of vegetables for the locker. The time varies for different vegetables. Follow directions exactly.

Use a **4-gallon kettle of boiling water.** Not more than **one pint of vegetables** should be scalded **at a time** in this kettle. The vegetable is placed in a mesh basket, or colander with a handle or in a cheese cloth bag. Drop the basket or bag of vegetable into the rapidly boiling water. Count scalding time from the time water resumes boiling again.

Cooling. This is **very important.** Remove vegetable from boiling water and submerge immediately in a pan of cold water. **Ice water is best.** It takes as long or longer to cool the vegetable than it does to scald it.

The vegetable must be **cold** when packed,

Brine solution. Dissolve **4 teaspoonfuls salt** in **1 quart water.** Make this brine the day before and chill in refrigerator so that it will be cold when needed.

Packaging. Put prepared vegetable in container, fill to within ½ inch of top for pints, (¾ inch for quarts,) with brine. Put covers on containers, or heat seal tops according to packages used. **Rush immediately to locker for quick freezing.**

ASPARAGUS

Wash and **cut up** or use **straight stalks whole.** More may be packed in container when cut. Scald for 2 minutes. Cool thoroughly and pack in containers. Cover with brine. **Freeze immediately.**

BROCCOLI

Divide into **small pieces. Use only tender parts.** Scald 3 to 4 minutes, depending upon size. Cool thoroughly and pack in containers. Cover with prepared brine. **Freeze immediately.**

CORN (On Cob)

Select **corn** which is just right for table. Scald 6 to 8 minutes. **Chill thoroughly.** Drain and wrap each cooled ear separately in either waxed paper or cellophane, twist ends of paper to seal. Pack in boxes. **Freeze immediately.**

CORN (Cut Off)

Large, uneven ears may be used for cut corn. Scald the corn on the cob for 4 minutes, cool in **ice water,** cut from cob and pack dry in containers.

No brine is needed for corn.

GREEN BEANS

Wash and cut before scalding or scald and pack whole. Scald for two minutes if cut, three minutes if left whole. **Chill immediately** and pack in containers. Cover with **brine.** Seal. **Freeze immediately.**

LIMA BEANS

Harvest while young and tender. Shell. Scald **small sized beans 1 minute, larger beans 2 minutes. Chill immediately.** Pack in containers and cover with a **2 percent brine solution.**

PEAS

Shell before scalding. Scald for 1 to 1½ minutes. **Cool immediately.** Pack in containers and cover with **brine.** Seal. **Freeze immediately.**

Preserving with Vinegar--Pickling

Catsup is another form of a relish. It is served mostly with meats and baked beans. It makes an excellent seasoning for many dish preparations.

CARROT CATSUP

Use 1 quart carrots either chopped or ground. Cook them in water until tender. Chop **1 cup of celery** very fine, also **1 red pepper** and **1 medium onion.** Combine with carrots and add **2 cups vinegar, ½ cup sugar, 2 teaspoonfuls salt, ½ teaspoonful paprika.** Cook mixture until thick. Pour into hot sterile jars and seal tightly.

CUCUMBER CATSUP

Pare, quarter and remove seeds from enough **ripe cucumbers** to make 1 quart. Put through food chopper with **1 cup of white onions** and **2 medium sized green peppers.** Add a **small amount of water** to prevent sticking and boil until cucumbers are tender. Heat **2 cups vinegar, 1 cup sugar** and **2 tablespoonfuls white mustard seed. Salt** and **cayenne** are added to taste. Add **cucumbers** and cook until thick and clear. Can and seal.

GRANDMA'S OLD-FASHIONED CATSUP

Put **1 heaping peck of ripe tomatoes** into a large preserving kettle with **1 large onion, 1 large green pepper** with seeds removed. Cook slowly for 1 hour. Then put mixture through a sieve and return to kettle. Add **1½ cups vinegar, 1 cup sugar, 3 tablespoonfuls salt, 1 tablespoonful ground cloves, 1 tablespoonful black pepper, 1 tablespoonful cinnamon.** Cook slowly for 3 hours. Stir often. Seal while hot in bottles.

TOMATO CATSUP

Cook **1 gallon of tomatoes** that have been cleaned and quartered the night before. Next morning, remove all excess water that comes to the top. Put pulp through sieve. This does not spoil the flavor and does help to reduce time of cooking. Place **3 tablespoonfuls whole cloves** and **1 small onion** in a bag. Add to tomato juice with **1 quart vinegar, 3 cups sugar, 3 tablespoonfuls salt, 2 tablespoonful black pepper** (less if desired) and **3 tablespoonfuls ground cinnamon.** Cook until when tested, no clear vinegar appears around edge of saucer. Keep over a low fire while bottling. Seal immediately.

LIGHT RED TOMATO CATSUP

Do not peel tomatoes. Remove blemishes and hard parts from **½ bushel tomatoes,** boil until soft but not mushy, run through a sieve without pressing. Put liquid on fire, adding **1 cup of mixed spices** tied in a bag. Cook away half. While boiling, rub remainder of tomatoes through sieve. When liquid is ready, put in pulp, adding **1½ cups of sugar, 1/3 cup salt, ½ pint good vinegar** and **2 tablespoonfuls red pepper** (this amount is optional). Boil until thick when tried in a saucer. Bottle and seal.

CHILI SAUCE

Chop fine **18 tomatoes** that have been blanched, cold dipped and peeled. To these tomatoes allow **2½ cups cider vinegar, 1 stalk fine cut celery, 1½ cups sugar, 1 cup chopped green pepper, 1 hot pepper chopped, 3 onions chopped fine, 1 teaspoonful cinnamon, 1 teaspoonful cloves, 1 teaspoonful ginger** and **1 teaspoonful dry mustard.** Add **2 scant teaspoonfuls salt.** Boil all together until a rich sauce is formed. Stir occasionally to avoid scorching. Pack in jars and seal.

WINTER CHILI SAUCE

Mix together **4 quarts of canned tomatoes, 3 onions sliced, 3 green peppers chopped, 1¼ cups sugar, 2 cups vinegar, 1 tablespoonful salt**—more if canned tomatoes are not salted—**1 teaspoonful cinnamon, ½ teaspoonful allspice.** Boil steadily about 2 hours in six-quart kettle, stirring frequently. When nearly done, taste, and add more sugar and salt if needed.

Then boil hard, stirring all the time for 10 or 15 minutes until the chili sauce has some body. The best test is to put a little in a cool sauce dish. When very little liquid separates from the sauce it is done. Pour into sterilized pint jars and seal. This makes exactly **4 pints** and **1 cup.**

CHOW CHOW (No. 1)

Cut up **1 head of cauliflower** and boil in salted water until nearly done. Cut **1 stalk of celery** and cook in salted water. Cut **3 red** and **3 green peppers** and cook in separate water until nearly done. Cut **1 quart of wax beans** and prepare them the same as other vegetables. Clean **100 small pickles, 3 large green cucumbers** and **1 quart of small silver skin onions.** Do not cook onions or cucumbers. Make a dressing of **1 cup flour, 1 cup brown sugar, 2 quarts diluted vinegar, 1 teaspoonful tumeric powder, ½ cup dry mustard, 2 tablespoonfuls salt.** The tumeric powder and the dry mustard should be moistened with a little vinegar to insure a smooth product. Boil 5 to 10 minutes. Now add all vegetables and let come to a boil. Can and seal.

CHOW CHOW (No. 2)

Mix together **1 gallon chopped cabbage, 12 sliced onions, 12 green peppers, diced, 12 red peppers, diced, 2 quarts chopped green tomatoes** with **½ cup salt.** Let stand overnight. Drain. Tie the following spices in a bag: **4 tablespoonfuls ground mustard, 1 tablespoonful tumeric, 1 tablespoonful ground ginger, 4 tablespoonfuls mustard seed, 3 tablespoonfuls celery seed** and **2 tablespoonfuls mixed whole spices.** Add **5 cups sugar** and spice to **1 gallon vinegar.** Simmer 20 minutes. Add chopped, drained vegetables and simmer until hot and well seasoned. Remove spice bag. Pack hot chow-chow into hot jars and seal at once.

CHUTNEY

Chutney, a relish typical of England.

Chop 8 **small tomatoes** and 8 **apples** together with **4 onions, 1 green pepper** and **1 cup seeded raisins.** Tie ¼ **cup of mixed pickle spices** in spice bag and add **4 cups brown sugar, 4¼ cups vinegar** and **1 tablespoonful salt.** Simmer for 1½ hours. Remove bag of spices and seal in hot, sterilized jars.

TOMATO CHUTNEY

Chop **4 pounds ripe tomatoes** and **3 large onions.** Chop **1 pound pared apples.** Combine these with **1 pint strong vinegar, 2 tablespoonfuls salt, 2 cups brown sugar, 1 cup seeded raisins, 1 teaspoonful cinnamon, 1 teaspoonful dry mustard** and **½ teaspoonful cayenne pepper.** Cook until chutney is clear. Seal in clean hot jars. Makes about 4 quarts. If a hotter, more highly flavored chutney is desired, add to the above recipe **½ teaspoonful cayenne pepper, ½ teaspoonful allspice, 1 teaspoonful cloves, 2 teaspoonfuls dry mustard** and **12 cloves garlic.**

GRANDMA'S MANGO PEPPERS

Wash peppers and cut off tops. Save tops to put on again. Remove seeds and pith. Lay in salt water until ready to fill. For **6 large peppers** use **3 pounds cabbage** chopped fine. Add **1/3 cup celery seed** and (same of **corriander seed** if preferred). Sprinkle with **salt** and let stand 2 hours. Squeeze out as much water as possible. Stuff peppers with this dry cabbage mixture. Replace tops and tie in place. Make a vinegar solution of **2 cups vinegar, 2 cups brown sugar, ¼ cup, whole cloves** and **¼ cup stick cinnamon** (cloves and cinnamon should be put in cloth bag). Bring to a hard boil, then let cool. Pack stuffed peppers in crock and pour vinegar over them. Repeat for three mornings, pouring the vinegar off, bringing it to boil, letting it cool then covering the peppers again. After third morning cover crock with muslin and plate and weight down. Let stand 2 weeks before using.

Pickling—the art of preserving in vinegar.

Do not use iodized salt in making pickles.

AN EXCELLENT MIXED PICKLE

Grind **2 dozen large green or yellow cucumbers** coarsely, **2 small or 1 large head cabbage, 3 green sweet peppers** and **12 large onions.** Soak vegetables separately in salt water over night. (Use **3 tablespoonfuls salt** to **1 quart water.**) In morning drain well. Place in kettle, a layer of vegetables, cabbage first as it takes longer to cook, then a layer of seasoning composed of **2 ozs. white mustard seed, 1 oz. black mustard seed, 2 ozs. celery seed, 1 oz. tumeric powder** and **2½ pounds brown sugar** (moisten with vinegar), then more vegetables until all are used. Cover well with vinegar. Boil 30 minutes.

BREAD AND BUTTER PICKLES

Slice **24 medium cucumbers** and **10 onions.** Sprinkle **3 tablespoonfuls salt** over them and allow to stand 3 hours. Drain off accumulated liquid. Add **1 teaspoonful celery seed, 1 teaspoonful mustard seed, 1 teaspoonful ginger powder, 1 teaspoonful tumeric, 3 cups sugar** and **1 quart vinegar.** Cook until mixture is boiling. Put into sterilized jars and seal while hot.

CALIFORNIA STATE PICKLES

Take **17 cucumbers, 12 small onions, 2 green peppers** and **½ cup salt.** Cover with cracked ice and let stand 3 hours. Drain thoroughly. Slice cucumbers and onions on cabbage cutter. Make syrup of **5 cups sugar, 1½ teaspoonfuls tumeric, ½ teaspoonful ground cloves, 2 tablespoonfuls mustard seed, 2 cups water** and **3 cups vinegar.** Bring to boil and add sliced cucumbers, onions and peppers cut into bits. Bring to boil. These will keep without sealing but is best to do so if one expects to keep them over winter.

CHERRY LEAF PICKLES

Heat **1 cup vinegar** slightly. Pour over **1 cup salt.** Add **1½ gallons cold water.** Pack in crock a layer of **whole pickles,** a layer of **clean cherry leaves,** then more pickles. Finish with cherry leaves. Pour liquid over all. Put plate on top to hold pickles down. Let stand ten days. Drain, discard leaves, wash well and heat to boiling point in equal portions of **water** and **vinegar.** Drain again. Slice ¼ inch thick into jars. Add the following syrup and seal: Mix **1 cup vinegar** with **1½ cups sugar, 2 tablespoonfuls mixed spices** with red peppers taken out. Boil 5 minutes, pour over pickles and seal. These are ready to eat in two weeks.

AROUND THE GARDEN PICKLE

Start these pickles in the evening and finish the next day. Put **1 cup salt** in **1 gallon water** to make a brine. Add **1 peck cucumbers,** large ones cut in pieces, and small ones left whole. Let stand overnight. nI the morning take out cucumbers, rince in cold water and put in large container. Put **4 gallons water** and **1 quart vinegar** over cucumbers and let stand. Cook separately 2 **large heads cauliflower** — cut in pieces — **1 quart small onions** — pickling size, 2 **quarts shelled lima beans, 2 quarts celery** cut in pieces and **1 quart string beans** broken in halves. When cooked through, but not soft, rinse each vegetable in cold water and put in container with cucumbers. Soak 20 minutes, **10 green** and **10 red sweet peppers** cut in strips, in 1 tablespoonful salt and boiling water to cover. Soak 20 minutes **2 quarts cut green tomatoes** in 1 tablespoonful salt and boiling water to cover. Rinse these in cold water and add to others.

Cook in large container the following syrup: **1 gallon vinegar, 16 cups white sugar, ½ cup salt, 4 tablespoonfuls mustard seed, 2 tablespoonfuls whole cloves, 4 tablespoonfuls broken stick cinnamon, 2 tablespoonfuls celery seed.** Bring to a boil and put in all and seal. This makes 16 quarts. One-fourth of the recipe is enough vegetables. When all are steaming, not boiling, put in sterilized jars for the average family.

CHUNK PICKLES

To **2 gallons of large cucumbers** add **1 cup salt** and enough water to cover. Keep in brine 3 days. Then soak in clear water 24 hours. Cut in chunks and simmer 2 hours in water with **1 tablespoonful powdered alum.** Drain and place in jars. Make a syrup of the following: **Three pounds brown sugar, 3 pints vinegar, 1 ounce cinnamon, 1 ounce allspice, 1 ounce celery seed, 1 ounce mustard seed** and **1 tablespoonful cloves.** Boil together 20 minutes. Pour over pickles and seal.

DILL PICKLES

Scrub **medium-sized cucumbers** with brush and pack into hot sterilized jars. To each quart add: **Two heads dill, one piece alum** the size of a small pea and **one teaspoonful mustard seed.** Fill jars with hot brine, **one cup vinegar, 4 cups water** and **one tablespoonful coarse salt.** Seal.

GERMAN DILL PICKLES

Bring 3 1/4 **quarts** of **water, 1 cup vinegar** and **1 cup salt** to a boil, then cool. (Best done the night before.) Fill quart jars with fresh crisp **cucumbers** about 3 inches long. Add 1/2 **teaspoonful of powdered alum** to each quart, also **one big bunch of dill** and **one small clove of garlic.** Add pickling syrup and seal.

KOSHER DILL PICKLES

Use 2 quart jars. Pickle the smaller **cucumbers** about 4 or 5 inches long. Put in cucumbers, add **2 tablespoonfuls salt, 1 clove garlic, 1 teaspoonful mixed spices, 1 stalk dill** and **1 hot pepper** to the can. Fill can with cold water. Seal.

DILLED GREEN TOMATOES

Soak **100 small green tomatoes** in salt water, **(1 1/2 cups salt** to **4 quarts water)** over night. Drain. Wipe dry, put in jars with layers of **dill** and diced **horseradish.** Boil 4 **quarts water** with 1/2 **cup salt** and 1/4 **cup vinegar.** Pour boiling hot over tomatoes being careful not to crack jars. Put a piece of **alum** the size of a pea on top of tomatoes in each jar and seal.

END OF THE GARDEN PICKLE

Clean the following vegetables, cut into small pieces and then cook separately in salted water: **1 qt. celery, 1 qt. small onions** (left whole), **1 qt. green beans, 1 qt. lima beans** (left whole), **1 qt. carrots, 1 qt. cauliflower.** When done, drain. When cold, put all together. Add to these cooked vegetables **1 quart peppers,** cut in small pieces, **1 qt. sliced cucumbers** and **1 qt. small pickles** cut in small pieces. Mix thoroughly. Make the following dressing. To 2 **qts. vinegar** add **2 cups sugar** and bring to a boil. Mix 3/4 **cup flour** and **1 tablespoonful tumeric** with a little **cold water.** Add this to boiling vinegar and let come to a complete boil. Add vegetables. Let them come to a boil, then seal in sterilized jars. If some of these vegetables are not available, they may be omitted, however, it is best to have celery as it gives a distinctive flavor.

GREEN TOMATO PICKLE

Slice rather thick **1 peck of green tomatoes.** Clean **2 quarts of small onions** and mix with **1 cup salt.** Let stand over night. **In the** morning drain well. Put on stove with **2 quarts water** and **1 quart vinegar** and **2 dozen red sweet peppers,** sliced; let come to boiling point. Drain again. Make a fresh sirup of **vinegar sweetened** to taste. Let boil a few minutes. Fill jars with pickle, cover with sweetened vinegar and seal.

OLD-FASHIONED GREEN TOMATO PICKLE

Slice **½ bushel green tomatoes** about **¼ inch thick.** Sprinkle with **1 cup salt** and let stand over night. Drain. Combine **1 qt. vinegar, 2 cups water** and boil tomatoes in this for 15 minutes. Drain. Make a mixture of **1 quart vinegar, 4 cups sugar, 1 tablespoonful whole cloves, 1 tablespoonful whole allspice** and **1 tablespoonful stick cinnamon.** Add this to tomatoes and boil 5 minutes or until tender. Pack in jars and seal.

SPICED GREEN TOMATO PICKLES

Slice **½ peck of green tomatoes.** Cover with **1 quart water** in which has been dissolved **1 cup salt.** Let stand 2 hours and drain. Boil together **1 quart vinegar, 1 tablespoonful pepper, 1 tablespoonful cinnamon, 1 tablespoonful whole cloves, 1 tablespoonful celery seed** and **1 lb. brown sugar** for 2 minutes. Then add drained tomatoes and cook very slowly for 45 minutes. Keep these in a crock weighted down with a plate.

MILLION DOLLAR PICKLES

Chop **one quart of cucumbers, one quart onions, two quarts cabbage, four green peppers, four red peppers.** Combine with **one-half cup salt.** Let stand two hours and then drain thoroughly. Make a dressing of the following: **one teaspoonful tumeric powder, two tablespoonfuls dry mustard, two tablespoonfuls mustard seed, one tablespoonful celery seed, two and one-half cups sugar, one-fourth cup flour, three cups vinegar** and **one cup water.** Heat the above, stirring to give a perfectly smooth mixture. Add vegetables. Heat thoroughly and turn into sterilized jars and seal.

Pickles shrink if sugar is added too quickly. Add small amounts at a time.

NINE-DAY SWEET PICKLES

Soak **cucumbers** three days in a brine that will bear up an egg. (This usually requires **1 cup salt** to **1 gallon water.)** Soak 3 days in cold water. Put in **weak vinegar** (half water) and boil slowly for 2 hours or until tender. Drain, pack in sterilized jars. To **1 gallon pickles,** pour over mixture made by cooking, **3 pints vinegar, full strength,** with **3 pounds brown sugar, 1 ounce cinnamon cubes, 1 ounce whole allspice, 1 ounce celery seed** and **1 teaspoonful powdered alum** until sugar is dissolved. While hot pour over pickles in jars and cover. The second day drain off liquid from pickles. Reheat and pour over pickles in jars. Cover. The third day proceed same as second day only seal the jars tightly. *Note*: Do not have pickles too large. If too long cut in pieces 1 inch thick.

OLIVE OIL PICKLES

Wash and slice thin **4 dozen small cucumbers.** Pour over the following mixture: **One quart vinegar, ½ cup black mustard seed, ½ cup celery seed, ½ cup sugar.** Let stand over night. Seal in jars. No cooking.

SACCHARINE PICKLES

Soak **1 peck pickles** all night in a brine made of **½ cup salt to 2 quarts water.** Next morning mix together **¾ cup salt, 1 cup sugar, 2 teaspoonfuls saccharine** and **6 tablespoonfuls dry mustard.** Add to **2 quarts vinegar** and **1 quart water.** Put pickles in large crock or jars, cover with liquid and seal.

SPANISH PICKLE

First prepare a sweet-sour vinegar which will keep all year.

To make this vinegar take **1 quart cider vinegar** and **2 quarts sugar,** boil to a thick syrup. Slice as much **cabbage** as desired allowing the cabbage to be ¼ of the whole pickle made. Add sliced **red pepper, green peppers, carrots, onions** and **celery.** Salt all this and allow to stand for a few hours then squeeze dry. Add the sweet-sour vinegar.

These pickles may be kept in earthen jars on an outside porch. Freezing doesn't harm them.

SPICED CRAB-APPLES

Wash **six pounds of crab-apples.** Do not pare, core or stem. Tie **3 teaspoonfuls whole cloves, 3 teaspoonfuls whole allspice** and **3 teaspoonfuls ginger** in a bag, put in preserving kettle, add **4 cups vinegar, 2 cups sugar** and apples. Bring to boiling point and simmer 20 minutes. Watch, if apples begin to break apart, they are done.

SPICED CURRANTS

Stem and wash fruit carefully and for every **4 pounds of currants** take **2 pounds of brown sugar, 1 pint cider vinegar, 1 tablespoonful each of ground cinnamon, cloves, mace, nutmeg,** and **allspice.** Boil all together for one-half hour. Seal and store.

SPICED GOOSEBERRIES

Cook **five pounds of gooseberries** with **four pounds of brown sugar, one pint vinegar, two tablespoonfuls cloves** and **two tablespoonfuls cinnamon** until quite thick. It may require as long as two hours.

SPICED PEACHES

Prepare fruit for three or four quarts as follows, using fairly firm hard fruit: Wash, scald and peel **peaches.** Clingstones are best although freestones are very good. Leave whole, if not too large, put a few peach pits in to add flavor. Prepare syrup as follows: Mix **three cups sugar** all white or **part brown, one pint cider vinegar, one pint water, three short sticks cinnamon, one teaspoonful whole cloves,** and a **piece of ginger root** if desired. Bring to boil, drop in fruit, part at a time to not overcrowd. When barely tender, remove. Let stand in syrup overnight. In morning pack fruit closely in jars. Strain syrup to remove spice, heat and pour over fruit to fill jars. Seal. Amount of sirup used per quart averages about one cup depending upon how closely fruit is packed. This is excellent for the small Seckel pears which are pickled without peeling.

SPICED PEARS

To **½ peck of pears,** use the small pears that do not have to be peeled, add **1½ pounds brown sugar** and **1 pint vinegar** and enough **water** to cover pears. Cook until pears are tender and juice looks like syrup. Seal while hot in sterilized jars, adding **1 teaspoonful of mixed spices** to each quart.

SPICED SWEET APPLES

Pare and quarter **3 quarts sweet apples.** Cover with cold water until ready to use. Heat **1 quart vinegar** and **1 quart sugar** together. Add **1 tablespoonful cinnamon, 1 tablespoonful cloves** and **1 tablespoonful allspice,** either whole or ground, which have been tied loosely in a thin white bag (salt sacks are good). When vinegar boils, pour over drained apples and let stand until next morning. Drain off syrup and bring to a boil, skim, add apples and boil until apples are tender. Seal in hot jars.

SOUR PICKLES

Mix **one cup salt, one cup dry mustard, one cup sugar** and **one gallon vinegar** until dissolved. Soak pickles overnight in **salt water.** Wipe dry, place in crocks or glass jars and pour the above mixture over them adding **one cup horseradish.** This will take care of between **three** and **four hundred pickles.** Cover crock tightly with a cloth and lid.

SWEET PICKLES

Soak ½ **bushel cucumbers** over night in salt water, using for brine 1 cup salt to each gallon water. Next morning boil together for ½ hour, **1 gallon vinegar, 2 quarts water, 1 package mixed spices, 2 tablespoonfuls salt** and **4 cups sugar.** After vinegar solution has been boiled, drain pickles from salt water, place them in solution, heat until cucumbers are heated through. Pack pickles in jars. In each jar, put a little **alum** the **size of a pea,** and the same amount of **saccharine.** Pour over pickle solution and seal.

SWEET LIBERTY PICKLES

Boil **1 gallon water** with **1 pint salt.** Pour over **2 gallons small cucumbers** while still boiling hot. Let stand 5 days, pour off, cover with boiling water and let stand 24 hours. Then boil **1 gallon water** and a **lump of alum the** size of two walnuts and pour over pickles boiling hot. Let stand 48 hours. Drain off. Split the larger pickles. Cover with the following mixture: boil **5 pints vinegar, 4 pounds sugar, 2 pieces cinnamon bark, 2 ounces mustard seed** and **1 ounce whole allspice.** Pour over pickles boiling hot and let stand 24 hours. Drain off and bring to boil again. Pour over pickles.

These do not need to be canned as they will keep in crock summer or winter.

SWEET MIXED PICKLES

Slice **2 pints cucumbers** and **1 pint onions.** Cut fine **1 pint string beans, 1 pint cauliflower, 1 pint green tomatoes, 1 pint green peppers, ½ pint red peppers** and **2 hot red peppers.** Cook together for 45 minutes. Drain and fill jars. Cover with the following pickling solution which has been boiled 5 minutes: Mix **3 cups vinegar, 1 cup water, 2 cups sugar, 1 teaspoonful mustard seed, 1 teaspoonful celery seed, 5 teaspoonfuls whole allspice** and **6 bay leaves.** Boil 5 minutes before pouring on pickles. Fill jars and seal.

PENNSYLVANIA DUTCH SWEET PICKLES

Take **8 lbs. pickles** (whole), make a salt brine strong enough to float an egg. Put pickles in this brine for 2½ days. Take out and put in fresh water for 2½ days. Take out and cut in small pieces or leave whole if pickles are small. To **1 quart of cider vinegar,** add **3 quarts water.** Add pickles and simmer for 2 hours. Stir often, do not boil. Drain. Let stand until cold. Place in jars and cover with the following syrup: Boil **3 pounds sugar, 3 pints vinegar, 1 ounce celery seed, 1 ounce whole allspice** and **1 ounce cinnamon bark** until it makes a very thin sirup. Drain to remove spices. Cool. Pour over pickles and seal.

PICKLED GREEN BEANS

Prepare **1 peck of green beans** as for table use. Boil ½ hour, **salt** to taste. Make a pickling liquid by boiling **3 pints of cider vinegar** not too strong with **3 pounds of brown sugar.** Add **½ cup dry mustard, 1 cup flour** and **2 tablespoonfuls tumeric** mixed to a paste with **cold vinegar,** then add beans and boil a few minutes, seal while hot.

PICKLED RED CABBAGE

Shred cabbage, then place it on a platter in layers, **salting** each layer as formed until all cabbage has been used. Let stand over night. In the morning drain through a colander. Tie **1 tablespoonful of pickling spice** in a cheese cloth bag and put in the bottom of the jar. Fill jar with cabbage, then fill with **cold vingear** to the top. Seal tightly and it will keep all winter.

PICKLED ONIONS

Peel **1 peck of small pickling onions** and cook in salted water until transparent. Be careful not to cook until they fall apart. Pack onions in jars and drain water out of the jars after packing. To **3 pints vinegar add 1 pint water, 7 cups sugar.** Put in kettle. Put **1½ ounces of pickling spice** in bag and tie onto kettle, allowing it to be immersed in the vinegar solution. Let syrup boil until spices have permeated the vinegar. Pour over onions while syrup is hot and seal. These onions may be peeled by covering with boiling water, allowing to stand 3 minutes, then draining and covering with cold water.

In cleaning peppers it is best not to get the hands covered with the pepper sting. Rubber gloves are best, dry cleaning next; that is removing the seeds without water. Some use milk to wash their hands in while others use rubbing alcohol, a solution of baking soda in warm water, equal parts lime water and linseed oil, or wash hands in strong vinegar.

MEDIUM HOT PEPPERS

Wash and cut peppers, remove seeds and drain. Pack in sterile jars. In each jar put a **sprig of dill** and a **clove of garlic.** To **1 quart of weakened vinegar** add **¾ cup sugar, 2 teaspoonfuls salt, ¼ teaspoonful ground mustard** and **1 teaspoonful mixed spices.** Bring this to boiling point. Pour over peppers and seal. They are ready to eat in 2 weeks.

PICKLED SEMI-HOT PEPPERS

Boil together **1 cup vinegar, 4 cups water** and **4 tablespoonfuls salt.** Cool. Wash **semi-hot peppers** which have been cut in halves or fourths and seeds removed. Pack closely in 2-quart jar or two 1-quart jars. Add either dry **dill** or freshly grown dill to the jar. Cover with the solution and seal. A small piece of **alum** may be added to each jar. Also a **kernel of garlic.**

The rind of the watermelon being thick and firm lends itself very admirably to the making of pickles or preserves.

WATERMELON RIND PICKLES (Dark Color)

Pare and cut into slices the rind of **one watermelon.** Soak over night in **salt water,** made from **3 tablespoonfuls salt** and enough **water to cover.** Drain and rinse. Cook rind in clear water until transparent. Drain again. Make syrup of **2 quarts vinegar, 7 pounds sugar (granulated),** and **4 sticks cinnamon** and **4 teaspoonfuls whole cloves** tied in a bag to keep pickle lighter in color. Cook syrup 30 minutes after coming to a boil. Add rind and boil 40 minutes after coming to a boil. Remove from stove. Add **1 quart maraschino cherries.** Let stand over night. Next morning boil 20 minutes after coming to a boil. Remove spices before putting in jars. Does not have to be sealed airtight. Use ¾ the amount of sugar and vinegar if one does not like them so sweet.

WATERMELON RIND PICKLES (Light Color)

Remove green and all pink from **watermelon rind.** Cut in cubes. Weigh **7 pounds.** Cover with **boiling water** and cook until very tender. Drain thoroughly. Make a syrup of **3½ pounds sugar, 1 pint vinegar, ½ teaspoonful oil of cloves** and **¼ teaspoonful oil of cinnamon.** Bring syrup to a boil and pour over rind. Let stand over night. In morning drain syrup off, bring to boiling point and pour over rind. Repeat this second day. On third day heat both syrup and rind and put in jars, seal. Using oil of spices instead of the ground or whole spices makes a very clear pickle.

WINTER PICKLES

Slice **1 dozen dill pickles** (medium size best) in round slices. **Mix 1 cup brown sugar** with **1 cup white sugar, 1 tablespoonful white mustard seed** and **1 teaspoonful celery seed,** sprinkle this between each layer of sliced pickle, add **½ cup raisins** among the layers as they are being formed. Put weight on top. Set in cool place for 24 hours.

Relishes

A relish is a combination of vegetables chopped fine and mixed with vinegar and spice to be used as an accompaniment for meat courses.

BARBECUE RELISH

Grind **8 carrots, 12 green peppers, 2 red peppers, 2 large heads cabbage, 12 large onions** in food chopper. When ground, sprinkle with **½ cup salt** and let stand 1 hour, then add: **3 pints cider vinegar (strong), 6 cups white sugar, 1 tablespoonful mustard seed, 1 tablespoonful celery seed.** Mix thoroughly and seal in sterilized jars. Use medium sized jelly jars that have lids. Dip each top in hot paraffin. This is not cooked but keeps beautifully and is delicious for sandwiches or as a relish with a meat dinner.

BEET RELISH (No. 1)

Mix **1 tablespoonful dried horseradish** or **½ cup grated horseradish** with **1 pint chopped boiled beets, 1 pint chopped cabbage, ¼ teaspoonful white pepper, pinch red pepper, ½ teaspoonful salt, 1 cup chopped celery, ¾ cup sugar** and **1 cup vinegar.** Let heat through. When boiling point is reached, pour into sterilized glass jars and seal.

BEET RELISH (No. 2)

Cook **12 red beets** until tender. Remove from fire and cover with cold water. Remove skins. When cold, grind in food chopper together with **3 red hot peppers, 1 small head cabbage, 6 medium onions** and **½ cup grated horseradish.** Boil **1 quart vinegar** with **2 tablespoonfuls mixed spices, 1 teaspoonful celery seed, 4 tableepoonfuls salt** and **sugar** to taste. Boil 12 minutes. Pour over ground mixture and let boil six minutes more. Seal in sterile jars while hot.

CELERY RELISH

Chop **1 pint celery, 1 pint cabbage, 1 small onion, 1 green pepper.** Combine with **2 tablespoonfuls salt** and let stand ½ hour. Combine **1¼ cups vinegar, ¼ cup sugar, 2 teaspoonfuls mustard seed, ¾ teaspoonful celery seed, ⅜ teaspoonful cinnamon, ⅛ teaspoonful cloves** and a **few grains cayenne pepper.** Boil 5 minutes. Press out juice from vegetables and pour over them the hot vinegar solution. This will keep without sealing but it is best to seal everything possible.

CORN RELISH

Cut corn from **2 dozen ears of corn.** Grind **4 large onions, 4 green peppers** and **1 red pepper.** Add **1 quart vinegar** and put on to boil. Mix **3 cups sugar, ½ cup salt, ¼ cup dry mustard, ¾ cup flour** and **1 teaspoonful tumeric.** Blend with **another quart of vinegar** and add to boiling relish. Boil ½ hour and seal in hot jars.

GOLDEN RELISH

Chop **4 cups carrots, 4 cups** celery, **2 large green peppers, 2 pimentos** and **4 tart apples.** Add **2 cups** sugar, **2 cups vinegar, 2 tablespoonfuls salt** and **2 tablespoonfuls celery seed.** Cook gently until carrots and celery are almost tender. Seal while hot. Excellent with pork roast.

INDIA RELISH

Put **1 peck green tomatoes** through a food chopper, add **1½ cups salt.** Let drain in cloth over night. Next morning grind and add to tomatoes **6 sweet green peppers, 3 sweet red peppers, 1 head cabbage, 6 good sized onions,** then add **6 sticks cinnamon,** tie **½ box of cloves** in a bag and add **2 tablespoonfuls celery seed, 2 tablespoonfuls mustard seed, 3 pints cider vinegar, 1 pint water** and **8 cups sugar. Boil together 30 minutes. Seal while hot.** This makes 8 or 9 pints.

MUSTARD BOUQUET

Cut **6 green peppers** and **3 red peppers** in strips. String **1 quart of green beans** and break each bean into 3 pieces. Slice **2 bunches of carrots** and **1 quart green tomatoes.** Separate **2 large heads cauliflower.** Boil all together until tender, but not mushy. Drain and soak in brine overnight. Use **1 cup salt** to **1 gallon water.** Make a sauce as follows: scald **2 quarts vinegar** and **2½ cups sugar.** Add **1 cup flour, 6 tablespoonfuls dry mustard** and **1 teaspoonful tumeric** mixed with a little water. Boil carefully for a few minutes. Add vegetables and cook until heated through. Put in clean hot jars and seal.

MIXED RELISH

Chop **1 quart green tomatoes, 1 quart cucumbers, 1 quart cabbage** and soak in salt water **(4 tablespoonfuls salt to 1 quart water)** over night. Drain and add **1 cup red peppers,** chopped, 1 cup **green peppers,** chopped, **1 pint white onions,** chopped, **4 cups vinegar** diluted with **2 cups water, 1 cup sugar, 5 tablespoonfuls** white **mustard seed, 1 tablespoonful celery seed** and **½ teaspoonful tumeric.** Let stand for 2 hours. Bring to boil, boil 10 minutes. Pack in hot sterilized jars and seal immediately.

PEPPER RELISH (No. 1)

Grind **6 red peppers, 6 green peppers, 3 hot peppers** and **4 onions.** Pour boiling water over above mixture, let stand 5 minutes, then squeeze out all moisture possible with the hands. Add **3 cups sugar, 1 pint vinegar** and **1 tablespoonful salt.** Heat and cook 5 minutes.

PEPPER RELISH (No. 2)

Chop or run through a food chopper **1 peck green tomatoes, ½ peck ripe tomatoes, 3 heads of medium cabbage, 1** dozen green **mangoes** and **½ dozen red mangoes** (peppers). **Salt sparingly.** Put in bag to drain over night. Next morning put in large kettle. Add **3 pints brown sugar, ½ dozen onions,** chopped, and enough **vinegar** to cover. Boil 1 hour. Just before removing from the stove, add **1 tablespoonful black pepper, 1 tablespoonful ground mustard, 1 tablespoonful white mustard seed, 1 tablespoonful celery seed** and **1 cup horseradish** ground. Boil for five minutes and seal.

RUBY RELISH

Grind **1 peck of ripe pimientos** saving all the juice. Add **1 quart vinegar,** bring to a boil, then add **6 cups sugar.** Simmer about 45 minutes or until juice becomes thick like syrup. This recipe makes 16 pints.

Preserving With Sugar -- Butter

APPLE BUTTER (Baked)

Quarter **7 pounds of apples,** core and cook as for apple sauce, adding a very small amount of water. Cook till tender. Force through a strainer. Stir in **3 pounds brown sugar, 1 teaspoonful nutmeg, 3 tablespoonfuls cinnamon** and **1 cup vinegar.** Pour into flat pans and bake in moderately hot oven for 3 hours, stirring occasionally. Turn into sterile jars and seal at once.

GRAPE BUTTER

Add **2 cups water** to **2 cups grape pulp** and **2 cups apple pulp.** Cover and simmer 20 minutes. Press through a coarse strainer to remove seeds and skins. Add **2 cups brown sugar, 1 teaspoonful cinnamon, ½ teaspoonful mace** and **¼ teaspoonful cloves.** Cook slowly until thick, about 30 minutes. Seal immediately in sterilized jars.

PEACH BUTTER

Scald, peel and stone peaches. Cook to pulp using very little water. To **each cup of pulp,** add **half** as **much sugar.** Cook until thick and clear. Spices may be added. Pour into sterilized glass jars.

Note — This is a good place for the using of commercial glass jars.

PEAR BUTTER

Pare and core **½ bushel pears,** without adding water, place on fire to cook. Cover with lid. To hasten the process, as pears soften, use a wire potato masher. In another large kettle, place **2 quarts fresh apple cider** with **1 can (1½ lbs. net) of white corn syrup** and cook several minutes. When pears are softened to butter consistency, add **2½ lbs. brown sugar** and the **cider syrup.** Cook at simmer temperature, stirring frequently to prevent sticking and scorching. If spice is desired, add **ground cinnamon** to taste. When butter thickens to spattering stage, place in a roaster and finish cooking in oven at 350° F. for 2½ to 3 hours.

PLUM BUTTER

Wash plums. Do not peel, but remove stones. Cut into small pieces. **Add small amount of water to start cooking.** Cook until very soft. Press through colander. To **each cup pulp,** add **½ cup sugar.** Spices may be added. Cook to a paste, stirring frequently to prevent burning. Pour into sterilized jars and seal.

TOMATO BUTTER (No. 1)

To every **1 pound of ripe tomatoes,** use **½ pound sugar.** To 2 gallons of tomato butter add **juice of 3 lemons or 3 lemons sliced thin** and **1 tablespoonful cinnamon.** Mix tomatoes and sugar with lemon juice. Cook until thick. Add cinnamon, remove from stove and can in clean hot jars. Seal if desired, but, it will keep with a paraffin cover.

TOMATO BUTTER (No. 2)

Cook **10 quarts** of **tomatoes** until thick. Add **6 lbs. sugar** and cook until mixture is of desired thickness. Add **1 tablespoonful cinnamon** and cook a few minutes longer. Seal in jars.

Conserves

The small red currant is the one we refer too most frequently. There is a small dark currant that is dried and used as fruit in cakes and cookies.

CURRANT BAR-LE-DUC

Boil **8 cups sugar** and **1½ cups water** until it spins a **thread,** then add **4 cups cleaned currants.** Boil six minutes. Pour in sterilized jars and seal with paraffin.

A conserve is a spread made from more than one fruit.

RED CURRANT CONSERVE

Cook **5 quarts of red currants** by almost covering them with water and boil them until they are white looking. Drain overnight in jelly bag. To **5 pints of red currant juice** add the rind **of 3 oranges** which have been boiled until tender and then put through a food chopper, together with the **pulp of the oranges** and **1 pound of raisins.** Add sugar in proportions of **1 cup sugar** to **1 cup pulp** and **juice.** Boil until it jells.

GOOSEBERRY CONSERVE

Wash and stem **six cups gooseberries.** Grate the **peel of one orange.** Chop to pulp. Mix with gooseberries and **four cups sugar,** then add **one cup raisins.** Mix well, heat slowly until sugar is dissolved. Boil rapidly to jelly stage. Pour into hot jars and seal at once.

PINK GOOSEBERRY CONSERVE

Cook enough **red currants** and drip the juice until there is **1 pint.** Add **4 lbs. sugar** and stir until dissolved. Boil for 5 minutes, skim well. Now add **4 lbs. cleaned gooseberries.** Cook for 30 minutes, keeping it clear by constant skimming and stirring. Set aside and when cool, add 2 **cups of chopped nuts.** Finish by pouring it on platters and sun cooking it as thick as desired.

GRAPE CONSERVE

Cook 3 **pints grape pulp** and juice of **2 oranges** until quite thick. Cook **grape skins** with **2 pounds seedless raisins** until tender. Add 3 **pounds sugar** and grape pulp. Cook until quite thick. Put in cans. When opened, add **chopped nuts** if desired.

HARLEQUIN CONSERVE

Put 25 **peaches,** peeled and sliced, **10 pitted red plums** and **1 pound seedless grapes** through a food chopped, add **1 No. 2 can crushed pineapple.** Weigh and use **¾ as much sugar as fruit.** Cook over hot fire until thick (about 1½ hours). Seal in sterilized jars.

Plums are a most delicious fleshy fruit being tart near skin and seed.

PLUM CONSERVE

Seed **four pounds of blue plums,** cut in pieces. Add **one cup seeded raisins, juice of two oranges,** juice of **one lemon** and **three-fourths cup sugar** to each cup of fruit mixture. Cook fruit and sugar slowly 45 minutes then **add half-pound of English walnut meats.** Pour into glasses and seal like jelly.

PLUM PINEAPPLE CONSERVE

Skin and stone enough very **ripe plums** to make **4 cups plum pulp.** Add **2 cups canned crushed pineapple, 1 cup raisins,** white preferred, and **10 cups sugar.** Boil until syrup is very heavy—about 10 minutes. Take from fire and remove any scum which rises to top. Add **1½ cups nut meats** and immediately pour into sterilized glasses. Seal with paraffin when cold. This quantity makes 15 ordinary jelly glasses.

The quince is a very hard fruit which is seldom eaten raw. It does have a very distinctive flavor which blends well with apple. It makes lovely jelly either by itself or combined with apple.

QUINCE, APPLE AND CRANBERRY CONSERVE

Mix **2 cups quince pulp, 2 cups apple pulp, 2 cups cranberry pulp,** juice of **1 orange** and **grated rind** with **4 cups sugar** and boil rapidly until thick. Add **¾ cup English walnuts,** remove from stove, put in glasses and seal.

RHUBARB-PINEAPPLE CONSERVE

Cut unpeeled **rhubarb** into quarter-inch pieces until there are **six cups.** Cut **pineapple** into small pieces until you have **two cups.** Pineapple should be cooked separately if not canned. Combine rhubarb and pineapple with sugar and boil rapidly until thick. Pour while boiling hot into clean glasses, seal at once.

STRAWBERRY-PINEAPPLE CONSERVE

Hull and slightly crush **four quarts strawberries.** Pare, cup up and put a **large pineapple** through a **food chopper,** using the coarsest wheel. Mix, add **one-half cup water** and bring to boil, then add **three pounds sugar** and cook slowly until very thick, stirring frequently to prevent scorching. **Blanched almonds** also may be added.

Honeys

CARROT HONEY

To **1 quart grated raw carrots,** add the rind of **2 lemons** and the **juice** of **4 lemons.** Add **4 cups sugar** and mix well. Heat slowly and simmer until thick and clear. Place in hot sterilized jars and seal.

PEAR HONEY

Peel **1 peck pears** and put through food chopper. **Weigh pears and add equal pounds of sugar.** If you do not have scales, then measure the pulp, use **2/3 as much sugar as pulp.** Cook until it begins to look clear then add **1 small can crushed pineapple, 1 can grated cocoanut, 1 large orange** ground fine. Cook until syrup thickens almost to jelly. Pour into glasses and seal. A **few maraschino cherries** give added color and help to make the marmalade more attractive.

PINEAPPLE HONEY

Grind **1½ cups pineapple,** add **6 cups sugar** and **2 cups water.** Cook slowly until thick and clear. Pour into clean hot jars and seal at once.

QUINCE HONEY

Peel, core and grind **5 large quinces** through a food chopper. Have syrup made of **10 cups sugar** and **1 pint water** boiling and add quinces to syrup just as fast as they are ground. After all have been added to syrup, boil 15 minutes longer. Put in glasses while hot. Quince honey should not be too stiff when made as it naturally gets thicker when cool and upon long standing it will have crystals of rock sugar if too heavy at the start.

QUINCE AND APPLE HONEY

Pare **six large quinces** and **4 large sweet apples,** chop or grind, measure the pulp, use **2/3 as much sugar as pulp.** Pour **6 cups of boiling water** over the sugar. Stir until dissolved. Add fruit pulp and the **juice of 2 lemons.** Boil until mixture is clear and thick, then turn into sterile jars. Seal with paraffin.

Jams

Jam—a combination of one or more fruits with sugar, cooked to a spreading thickness.

BLACKBERRY JAM

Clean and wash **blackberries,** crush, then measure and for **each cup** of **berry pulp** add **one cup sugar.** Put on stove and cook until **thick** enough for jam. The jelly test will work for jam as well as jelly or you can remove a bit from kettle and cool in refrigerator to see how thick it will become when cold.

Blackberry jam and jelly may be made with commercial pectin if desired, but it is not necessary. Blackberries usually can be had for the picking, so their cost is small. Their flavor does not extend as raspberries.

CARROT AND PINEAPPLE JAM

Take **10 pounds of carrots** and **one large can of crushed pineapple, six lemons ground, two oranges ground,** and **16 cups sugar.** Cook carrots until tender, then grind and add to other ingredients. Mix thoroughly, and boil until thick enough for jam. Pour into glasses and seal as for jelly. This is a very large recipe. Most families will find half of the recipe sufficient for their needs.

CHERRY AND RED RASPBERRY JAM

Mix **1 cup red cherries** pitted, **2 cups red raspberries** and **3 cups sugar** together, cook slowly at first, then gradually faster until the jelly stage is reached (two drops of liquid run into one when one is dropped from edge of spoon).

ELDERBERRY JAM

Mix **1 cup elderberry juice** with **2 cups sieved apple sauce** and **3 cups sugar.** Boil about 20 minutes. Seal with paraffin in jelly glasses.

GRAPE JAM

Select **large, dark, thick, pulp grapes.** Remove from stems and weigh 5 **pounds.** Wash carefully. Drain well. Place grapes in deep enamel kettle. Add 5 **pounds sugar.** Stir constantly until dissolved. Increase heat and when mass comes to rolling boil, cook 20 minutes. Stir all the time. Remove from fire, put through sieve. Pour in jars and cover with paraffin.

HEAVENLY JAM

Clean and wash 1 **quart red cherries,** 1 **quart red currants,** 1 **quart red gooseberries,** 1 **quart red raspberries thoroughly.** Measure **equal parts fruit and sugar.** Put in preserving kettle. Do not add water as there are enough fruit juices. Cook slowly. When it begins to set or thicken, put in clean pint jars and seal. Use test of two drops running into one from edge of spoon, if you are not sure any other way.

MULBERRY JAM

Take equal parts **sour cherries** or **rhubarb** with **mulberries** and weigh, using the same amount of **sugar.** Let stand 5 to 6 hours or until sugar is dissolved, then boil slowly for 30 minutes or until it jells. Put in glasses and seal with paraffin.

ONE-TWO-THREE-FOUR JAM

Clean 1 **pint red currants,** 2 **pints pitted cherries,** 3 **pints red raspberries** and boil together with 4 **pounds sugar** for 1 hour. Seal while hot in clean sterile jars. Unless a large kettle is available, it is advisable to halve the recipe for cooking.

PEACH JAM

Choose 5 pounds soft peaches, those that are not desirable for canning. Remove stones and cut in slices. Put 1 cup water in preserving kettle, then add peaches. Cover and cook until soft, stirring to prevent sticking. Add 6 cups sugar and cook until thick and jelly-like. Pack in clean hot **jars and seal.**

RASPBERRY JAM

Wash and crush **berries.** Add ¼ **cup water** for each quart berries. Cook until soft. Press berries through a strainer and remove seeds (or leave them in as preferred). Add from **¾ to 1 cup sugar to each cup of berries.** Boil until thick. Pour while hot into clean hot jars. Seal at once.

Jams made with a low sugar content should be processed for 5 minutes in a boiling water bath to insure their keeping.

RASPBERRY BLUFF

Boil **4 cups sugar** and **1 cup water** until it spins a thread. Pare and chop **3 cups harvest apples** and **1 cup raspberries** (any color), add to syrup, cook 20 minutes.

RHUBARB JAM

Cover **2 quarts of rhubarb,** cut in small pieces, with **2 pints of sugar** and let stand over night. Add the **grated rind and juice of 1 orange.** Add **1 cup chopped raisins,** or **1 cup nuts,** or half of each, or omit both if you wish. (Add **raisins,** but **no nuts** if to be stored.) Cook until thick.

STRAWBERRY JAM (No. 1)

Mix **1 quart box of strawberries,** early ones preferred, washed, hulled and sliced with **4 level cups sugar,** the **juice and pulp of 1 lemon,** a pinch **salt** and ¼ **teaspoonful butter** to prevent scum, together in a large kettle. Bring to a boil and boil fast for a little more than 5 minutes, stirring frequently. Then try it, when jam drips in three or four heavy drops at a time from the edge of a large spoon, and then slits off in thin sheets it is done. Remove from fire and stir for 1 minute to keep the fruit slices from floating to the top. Pour into sterile glasses and seal with paraffin. This makes a clear, bright colored jam, almost the consistency of jelly, with the transparent slices of berry evenly distributed throughout.

STRAWBERRY JAM (No. 2—Boiling Water Method)

Blanch **2 qts. of strawberries** (pour boiling water over berries, then drain). Put in kettle and cook for 3 minutes. Add **3 cups sugar,** cook 3 minutes more, add another **3 cups sugar** and cook for 5 minutes. Pour into crock and let stand about 24 hours, uncovered. Stir occasionally. Fill sterilized glasses and cover with paraffin.

STRAWBERRY JAM, PART SUGAR (No. 3)

Boil together for 5 minutes **3 cups corn syrup** and **3½ cups sugar.** Add **5 cups of cleaned whole strawberries** and cook 3 minutes more. Remove from heat, add **½ cup commercial pectin** and set aside for about 1 hour, stirring occasionally. Pour into clean jars and seal with paraffin.

STRAWBERRY SUNSHINE

Select 3 **pounds of large firm home grown berries,** wash and stem, add 3 **pounds sugar,** set aside for 2 or 3 hours. Pour juice into preserving kettle. When it boils, add as many berries as will float and boil for 5 minutes. Skim out berries onto platter. Boil remainder of berries in the juice and skim out as before. Boil juice 10 minutes longer and pour over berries in platter. Set inside a window in the sun, (where there is no dust,) until thick enough. It will take 12 to 14 hours. Turn berries over occasionally.

SUNSET JAM

Pare, core and crush completely, fully ripe **pears** until **3 cups** are prepared. Add **1 cup crushed pineapple, ¾ cup maraschino cherries** cut fine. Measure **7½ cups sugar** and mix with the prepared fruit in a large kettle. Add juice from **1 lemon** and mix well. Bring to a full rolling boil over hottest fire. Stir constantly before and while boiling. Boil hard 1 minute. Remove from fire and stir in **1 bottle of commercial pectin.** Stir and skim for five minutes to cool and prevent floating fruit. Pour quickly into sterile glasses and seal with paraffin.

YELLOW TOMATO JAM

Use **1 lb. sugar, ½ cup water** and **½ sliced lemon** to each **pound** of **tomatoes,** also a little **ginger root** or **powdered ginger.** First put water, sugar, lemon and ginger on to boil. Add tomatoes that have been skinned and cut into quarters. Boil about 2 hours or until it assumes a jelly-like consistency. Pour into jars or glasses and seal.

Jellies

Jelly is a solidified solution of fruit juices and sugar.

GENERAL DIRECTIONS FOR JELLY MAKING

1. Extraction of juice: for soft fruits, use ¼ as much water by weight as fruit; for hard fruits, use equal amount of water. 2. Cook fruit in covered vessel until soft. 3. Strain. 4. Second extraction may be made adding equal water and pulp. 5. Proportion of sugar, ½ to ¾ that of weight of fruit, depending upon acidity of fruit. 6. Better results are obtained when a small amount of jelly is made at one time. Hard fruit juices should be reduced to ½ and soft fruit juices 1/3 their original volume. 7. Addition of sugar to concentrated juice; rapid cooking necessary. Slow cooking results in a dark syrupy mass. 8. Test by dipping a spoon into the product. If two drops form, then gradually blend into one, or like a sheet which breaks loose at one end and shears itself off, the jelly is done. 9. Fill glasses. 10. Cover with paraffin. 11. Cover with paper or tin lids. 12. Label and store in a cool dry place.

APPLE JELLY

The red Astrachan apple, that bears about August 1, is the best for jelly, although practically all apples, if tart, will make good jelly. Many people make jelly from the parings of apples they have used for apple sauce.

Cut up **apples** — cores removed, but not pared — cover with water and cook until fruit is quite done. Strain twice. Add **three-quarters cup sugar** to **one cup boiling juice.** Boil rapidly to jelly stage—when two drops of liquid run into one on the edge of a spoon that has been dipped into the jelly. Pour into sterilized glasses and seal at once.

Apple furnishes pectin for many jellies, therefore it is good to use apple juice with fruits that will not jell by themselves. It also helps to stretch the flavor of expensive fruits.

BLACKBERRY JELLY

Wash, clean **berries,** mash, add very little water to start them cooking, cook until berries are very soft. Drain. To **each cup of juice** measure **three-fourths cup sugar,** but do not add until juice has been cooked down for about 10 minutes. Add sugar and cook until jelly test appears. When two drops run into one on the edge of the spoon jelly has formed.

BLACK RASPBERRY JELLY (No. 1)

Black raspberries will jell on their own accord but their flavor is so strong that the addition of more sugar and commercial pectin gives you more jelly for fruit and flavor.

Wash, clean berries, mash, add very little water to start them cooking, cook until berries are very soft. Drain. To **each cup of juice** measure **¾ cup sugar** but do not add until juice has been cooked down for about 10 minutes. Add sugar and cook until jelly test appears. When two drops run into one on the edge of a spoon dipped into the liquid the jelly has formed.

BLACK RASPBERRY JELLY (No. 2)

Pectin Added

To prepare juice, remove stems from about **four pounds of ripe berries;** place in kettle and crush. Heat gently until juice starts to flow, then simmer, covered, 15 minutes. Place in jelly cloth or bag and squeeze out juice. Squeeze and strain juice from **4 lemons.** Measure **7½ cups sugar** and **3 cups berry juice** and ½ cup lemon juice. Bring to a boil over hottest fire and at once add **1 bottle of commercial pectin,** stirring constantly. Then bring to a full rolling boil and boil hard ½ minute. Remove from fire, skim, pour quickly, paraffin at once. This should make about 10 glasses.

BLUE GRAPE JELLY

Wash and stem **1 peck grapes.** Drain and mash to get juice started before cooking. Let cook until grapes are done. Pour in bag and let drain over night. After juice is ready, measure **5 cups juice** and cook for 20 minutes in a medium sized pan, by the clock. After juice is cooked, remove from fire and add **5 cups of sugar,** stirring constantly until all is dissolved, but do not cook sugar in juice. Pour in glasses and let stand until set. This jelly cannot be made with grapes that are over ripe. They are best to be a trifle under ripe.

Crab-apples are small red apples, very tart, excellent for jelly. Rarely ever eaten raw or made into sauce.

CRAB-APPLE JELLY

Select ripe crab apples. Wash and cut out imperfections. Place on stove and cover with water. Cook slowly until soft enough to strain. Drain through jelly bag. To every **4 pints juice,** use **3 pints sugar.** Heat sugar very warm in oven. Boil juice 14 minutes. Stir in warm sugar and boil together for 5 minutes. Pour into jelly glasses and seal. It is always best to use the jelly test before pouring into glasses as the size of the kettle will make a variation in the cooking time of the jelly. Remember when 2 drops run into one from edge of spoon dipped into jelly the proper stage is reached.

Keep an old coffee pot for pieces of paraffin for covering jelly. Wash paraffin as it is removed from jelly and drop into pot, keeping it for another time.

CURRANT JELLY

Crush **currants** and cover with ¼ by weight of water. Cook until soft. Drain overnight in a bag made of outing flannel to collect juice. Measure, boil juice for 4 to 5 minutes. Add **¾ cup sugar** for each **measured cup of juice** before it was boiled down, **continue** boiling until jelly point is reached—when 2 drops run into one and drop from spoon.

ELDERBERRY JELLY

Use **equal portions elderberry and apple juice.** To prepare elderberries: wash, remove from stems and cook until soft in the water that adheres to them. Strain juice through heavy jelly bag. Cut apples into 8 pieces each but do not peel. Add water to almost cover. Cook until apples are soft. Strain. **Measure apple and elderberry juice cup for cup.** Boil juice five minutes, then stir in **1 cup of sugar to 1 cup of juice.** Boil to jelly stage. Pour into sterile glasses and seal at once.

MINT JELLY

To **5 cups apple juice** add **5 cups sugar, 2 tablespoonfuls green sugar** or **green coloring,** drop by drop until the right color is reached, and **1 tablespoonful mint extract.** Bring to a boil for 1 minute, then add **1 bottle of commercial pectin** and boil 1 minute longer. This makes 9 glasses.

Editor's Note: The above jelly would have jellied without the aid of commercial pectin, but it would have made only 5 glasses instead of 9. We are telling you this because you may have plenty of apples but not pectin.

PARADISE JELLY

Cut up **20 sour apples.** Remove seeds and cook in small amount of water until soft. Remove seeds from **12 quinces.** Cut into small pieces. Cover with water and cook until soft. Clean and sort **1 quart of cranberries.** Cover with water and cook until soft. Drain all in same bag overnight. To **each cup of liquid,** add **1 cup sugar.** Cook only until it gives the jelly test. Pour into glasses and seal. Jelly test: When two drops run into one when poured from side of spoon.

Red raspberries are hard to make jell without the aid of commercial pectin. Follow the directions on the bottle or box.

RED RASPBERRY JELLY

These berries will not make jelly without additional help such as commercial pectin or currants.

Pectin Added

To prepare juice, crush thoroughly or grind about **3 quarts of fully ripe berries.** Place in jelly cloth or bag and squeeze out juice. Measure **7½ cups sugar** and **4 cups juice** into a large sauce pan and mix. Bring to a boil over hottest fire and add **1 bottle of commercial pectin** at once, stirring constantly. Then bring to a full rolling boil and boil hard ½ minute. Remove from fire, skim, pour quickly into glasses, paraffin at once. This makes 11 glasses.

RED RASPBERRY AND CURRANT JELLY

Cook equal parts of **currants** and **red raspberries** about **1½ quarts each.** Mash, heat slowly with little or no water, stirring often. When it comes to boiling point it should be thoroughly softened and ready to pour into jelly bag. If desired, squeeze it through a cheese cloth bag. Let the juice drip through a flannel bag if you wish clear jelly. To each cup of juice, add **2/3 cup sugar,** boil until two drops form one from the edge of a spoon. Pour into hot sterile glasses.

ROSE GERANIUM JELLY

Prepare the **pulp** of **apples** as far as plain jelly. Boil juice thus obtained 20 minutes. To **each pint of juice,** add **1 lb. of sugar** (2 cups). Place in preserving kettle over fire. Stir until all the sugar has melted, then add **2 or 3 rose geranium leaves,** bring to boiling point and boil rapidly for 2 minutes, removing any scum which may rise to the surface. Turn into jelly glasses, removing the leaves, but place a **fresh leaf** in each glass.

TOMATO JELL

Peel **6 cups scalded tomatoes** and cut fine. Add **6 cups sugar, juice of 3 lemons** and **diced peel of two.** Cook until thick. Pour in glasses and seal.

Marmalades

Marmalade is a sweet spread usually containing some citrous fruit such as lemon or orange.

AMBER MARMALADE

Peel **1 large grapefruit.** Remove seeds and run through the food chopper. Remove seeds from **1 large orange** and **1 large lemon** and run through the food chopper. Add **3 times as much water** as there is **pulp and juice.** Let stand 24 hours. Cook slowly until tender. Add 5 **pounds sugar** and let stand 24 hours. Cook slowly until it jells.

CARROT MARMALADE

Grate **12 large carrots fine,** add **1 cup sugar** for each cup carrots. Let stand over night. In morning, add **juice of 3 lemons, 1 teaspoonful cinnamon, 1 teaspoonful cloves,** and **1 teaspoonful allspice.** Cook mixture slowly for 1 hour. Seal while hot.

CARROT, APPLE, PEACH MARMALADE

Combine **two cups of diced carrots, two cups of diced tart apples** and **one cup diced peaches** with **juice of one lemon** and **three cups sugar.** Boil rapidly until mixture is clear. Pour into sterile jars and seal. This makes about six glasses.

CARROT AND ORANGE MARMALADE

Scrape **carrots** and wash. Put through food chopper. To each **quart of pulp,** add **juice** and **grated rind of 2 lemons** and **2 oranges.** For each quart of mixture add 3½ **cups sugar.** Let stand over night and in morning cook until carrots are transparent.

CHERRY MARMALADE

Use from **¾ to 1 pound of sugar** to **each pound of pitted cherries,** depending upon sourness of fruit. Mix cherries with sugar. Let stand overnight. Heat slowly to boiling. Boil rapidly 15 to 20 minutes or until cherries are tender. Let stand until cold. Pack cherries into clean hot jars. Boil syrup until thick. Pour hot syrup over cherries; seal at once.

CHERRY SUNSHINE MARMALADE

To **1 quart of seeded sour cherries** use 4 **cups sugar** and **¾ cup light corn syrup.** Place a cup of cherries in a sauce pan and cover with a cup of sugar, alternate layers of cherries and sugar, mix thoroughly after each addition. Thoroughly mix in corn syrup and bring fruit to boiling point. Boil 15 minutes, shaking pan occasionally. Pour into a crock or enamel vessel and let stand 24 hours, stirring occasionally. These will be much improved, if the crock is covered with glass and set out in the hot sunshine for a day, stirring once or twice to turn the cherries over. Pour into sterilized jars without further heating and seal.

GREEN TOMATO MARMALADE

Wash **green tomatoes,** put through a food chopper. Grind 1 **orange** and **1 lemon** for **every quart** of **ground green tomatoes.** Boil 20 minutes, then add sugar to taste, usually **¾ cup sugar** to each **cup** of **pulp.** Boil 20 minutes, then seal in glasses. One quart of green tomatoes makes 6 glasses of marmalade.

ORANGE MARMALADE

Slice 5 **oranges** and 2 **lemons** very thin, add 3 **cups water** to **each cup fruit.** Let stand 24 hours. Boil for ¾ hour. Let stand 24 hours again. Measure and add **equal parts sugar.** Boil again for ¾ hour. Pour into hot glasses and seal. Makes 9 or 10 large glasses of marmalade.

PEAR MARMALADE

Pare, slice and grind ½ **peck pears.** Grind 4 **whole oranges** and 2 **whole lemons,** saving the juice. Add **equal amounts of sugar to the fruit, about** 8 **cups.** Boil 1 hour or until thick. Watch to prevent burning. Turn into sterilized glasses or jars and when cold cover with paraffin.

PINACOT

(Made with dried apricots and canned pineapple.) Soak **1 lb. dried apricots** over night, **grind 1 orange,** and apricots in food grinder. Add **1 can crushed pineapple.** Put all together in stew pan and cook 15 to 20 minutes, stirring constantly. Add 3 **cups granulated sugar,** cook until thick, about 15 minutes more. Pour into small glass jars and seal.

PINEAPPLE-PEACH MARMALADE

Grind or chop **24 peaches,** add **one No. 2 can of crushed pineapple, one-half teaspoonful salt, one and one-half cups sugar, one and one-half cups corn syrup.** Cook, stirring often until it thickens, for about half an hour. Pour into sterilized glasses and seal.

PEACH MARMALADE

Slice **24 peaches** and **3 large oranges** cutting rind in strips or put all through grinder. Add **3½ pounds sugar** and let stand over night. Next morning boil rapidly for 20 minutes. Remove from fire and add **½ cup nut meats** (broken), if desired. Pour into jam glasses and seal.

RHUBARB AND ORANGE MARMALADE

Mix **3 oranges, ground, 3 pints rhubarb,** cut fine, **3 pints sugar, 2 tablespoonfuls lemon juice** all together and boil 20 minutes.

Preserves

CANDIED CITRON

Clean **citron** and cut into small strips. Cover with cold water, cook in sauce pan until tender. Change water three times while cooking. Allow 20 minutes between each change. Drain. Measure, peel, add **equal amounts of sugar** and enough **boiling water** to just cover. Stir until sugar is dissolved, then let it boil hard until syrup is all cooked away. Watch carefully the last few minutes to prevent burning. Be sure every bit of syrup is gone. Turn out on a platter covered with granulated sugar, shake over it more sugar and toss about with finger tips until each piece is well covered with sugar. Place on paraffin paper with pieces separated to dry.

CITRON PRESERVES

Pare rind of citron and remove seeds. Cut into thin slices. Put fruit into a preserving kettle with enough water to cover. Boil for 1 hour. Measure **7 cups citron** and add **as much sugar as** there is **fruit.** Boil until thick, add **1 slice lemon.** Boil 20 minutes longer. Seal in pint jars.

CHERRY RASPBERRY PRESERVES

Stone **1½ pints of cherries** and put them through a food chopper, cutting quite fine. Let stand and drain for a few minutes. The drained juice may be used for jelly or canned juice for iced drinks. Measure cherries. To each 1½ pints of cherries add **1½ pints** of washed and drained **raspberries.** Put **3 cups sugar** and **¼ cup water** in a preserving kettle and heat. When boiling point is reached, add cherries and raspberries and boil 20 minutes. Pour into sterilized jars and seal while hot.

CURRANT PRESERVES

Wash and pick over berries, let cook slowly until juice is extracted, add **pound of sugar** for **each pound of currants** used. Boil rapidly for 20 minutes. Pour into sterilized jars and seal.

ELDERBERRY PRESERVES

Boil **7 pounds elderberries, 3 pounds brown sugar** and **½ pint vinegar** until quite thick. Keep in crock or jar as it isn't necessary to seal. May be thinned when needed for pies.

PEAR PRESERVES

Pare and halve **½ peck pears.** Drop into a bowl of cold water to which the **juice of 1 lemon** has been added. Put **3 lbs. sugar** and **3 pints water** into preserving kettle and bring to a boil. Drain pears and add carefully to boiling syrup. Cook pears until they can be pierced with a clean toothpick. Lift pears out with a skimmer ladle and pack in hot jars. Fill jars to overflowing with boiling hot syrup. Seal at once.

PINEAPPLE PRESERVES

Mix **two pounds of chopped unsweetened pineapple** with **three cups sugar,** let stand over night. Boil until tender and clear. Pour into hot jars and seal.

PLUM PRESERVES

Take **2 pounds plums,** quartered, **1 pound almonds,** blanched and chopped, **grated rind of 3 medium oranges, pulp of oranges, pulp of 2 lemons.** Weigh these ingredients and add **equal weight in sugar.** Put over fire, stirring until sugar dissolves. Cook until liquid jells. Pour into sterilized glasses and seal. If red plums are used, this preserve has a clear, rich Burgundy color.

QUINCE CHIPS

Pare **6 large or 7 small quinces.** Core, cut into quarters, then slice as thin as possible. Take **10 cups sugar** with **1½ pints water,** bring to a boil and drop in quince slices. Boil hard for 15 to 20 minutes. The last 5 minutes drop in a **lump** of **alum** the size of a pea.

RHUBARB PRESERVES

Boil **3 cups sugar** and **1 cup water** together until syrup becomes brittle when dropped into cold water. Drop **1 quart rhubarb,** cut in pieces, into boiling syrup and cook until mixture is thick and clear. Pour into clean hot jars. Seal at once.

STRAWBERRY PRESERVES

Boil **2 cups sugar** and **½ cup water** until syrup spins a thread. Add **1 quart** of **cleaned strawberries.** Cook for 20 minutes or until 2 drops run into one when dropped from a spoon.

Rice

Rice is a small grain used extensively by the people in China, India and Japan as their main diet. It is used here either in the polished state or as brown rice having part of the hull left on.

RICE COOKERY

Wash **1 cup rice** thoroughly in several waters until all the loose starch is removed. Drain. Have ready **2 quarts of boiling water** in deep sauce pan. Add **3 teaspoonfuls salt.** Slowly drop in the rice and allow to boil for about 12 to 25 minutes, or until a grain when pressed between the thumb and finger is entirely soft. In order to prevent the rice from sticking to the pan, lift if necessary from time to time with a fork, but do not stir it. When sufficiently cooked, turn the rice into a colander or sieve. A little hot water may be run through the rice to wash off extra starch. After water has drained off, cover with cloth and set over pan of hot water on the back of the stove or in oven for a short time. Treated in this way, the grains swell and are kept separate.

FROZEN RICE

Scald **2 cups milk** in top of double boiler. Pour over **2 egg yolks**, slightly beaten, with ½ **cup sugar.** Return to double boiler and cook until spoon coats, then add **1 cup cooked rice** and **2 cups of crushed pineapple,** drained. When cool, fold in **1 cup of cream,** whipped. Set in refrigerator pan to freeze or in mold to set.

GLORIFIED RICE

Dissolve **2 tablespoonfuls gelatin** in ½ **cup cold water.** Add to **1½ cups** of **hot pineapple juice.** Add ½ **cup sugar.** When mixture begins to thicken, whip with a wire egg beater until almost white. Beat in **1 can crushed pineapple,** drained, and **2 cups boiled rice.** Lastly, fold in **1 cup of whipped cream.** Mold in cups. Serve with a little whipped cream topped with a **cherry.**

JAMBALAYA

Mix **1 tablespoonful flour** and **1 tablespoonful lard** together in a sauce pan. Add **1 slice** or **1 cup ham,** chopped, **1 can shrimps,** cleaned, and **1½ cups tomatoes.** Cook for a few minutes. Add **1 small sliced onion, 1 chopped green pepper,** a bit of **minced parsley, 1 bud garlic, salt, pepper, tabasco sauce** and **Worcestershire sauce** to taste. Add **4 cups water.** Let simmer 10 minutes. Add **1 cup rice** and cook until rice is done. Do not stir mixture too much or it will become gummy. This recipe serves 6.

MEXICAN RICE

Wash and drain **1 cup rice.** Wash **2/3 cup raisins** in hot water and drain. Heat **2 tablespoonfuls cooking oil** in frying pan. Add washed rice and fry to a light brown, stirring constantly to prevent burning. Remove rice. Add **2 tablespoonfuls more of cooking oil** and fry **1 pound raw hamburg** for about 10 minutes with **1 small clove of garlic,** chopped, **1 small onion,** chopped, and **1 tablespoonful green chili pepper,** chopped. Add **2 teaspoonfuls salt, 1 cup tomatoes** and **1 tablespoonful chili powder,** dissolved in ¼ **cup cold water.** Allow mixture to cook a few minutes, then mix with rice and raisins. Pour into baking dish. Add **1½ cups water** and lay **2** slices of **bacon** over the top.. Bake 45 minutes at 375° F.

MEAT BALLS AND RICE

Mix 2 **cups uncooked rice** with ½ **lb. ground pork and** ½ **pound ground beef (hamburg)** or 1 pound of either. Season with **fresh celery** or dried celery leaves, **salt** and **pepper.** Add **2 tablespoonfuls chopped onion.** Mix thoroughly and form into balls about the size of walnuts. Boil or bake in **1 pint of tomato juice** for about 2 hours.

RICE LOAF

Cook **1 cup rice** in a double boiler with **4½ cups water** for 10 minutes. Add **1 teaspoonful salt.** Stir it several times, then drain. Dice **1 large onion, 3 sweet peppers** and add to **1/3 cup butter** which has been melted in a pan over a slow fire, stirring for several minutes. Add to peppers, onions, and butter, 1 pint of **strained tomatoes.** Cook 15 minutes. Stir. Add **1 teaspoonful salt** and **1 tablespoonful sugar.** To this, **add rice and mold in a loaf pan. Sprinkle** ½ **cup grated cheese** over the top of loaf. Serve hot.

SAVORY RICE

Put ½ **cup rice** in a **quart of cold water** over a quick fire. Heat to boiling, drain and rinse in cold water. Return to fire in a double boiler, add **1 cup broth** or a **bouillon cube** dissolved in **1 cup boiling water, 1 cup tomato puree,** ½ **teaspoonful salt, 1 onion** cut in halves, **2 sprigs parsley.** Cover, let cook until tender, adding more broth if needed. Remove the onion and parsley. Add **2 tablespoonfuls butter** and **1 cup grated cheese.** . Mix with 2 forks.

SPANISH RICE

Melt 3 **tablespoonfuls butter in a pan,** add **2 small onions,** sliced, and **1 green pepper,** cut in strips, fry until brown, remove from pan, add ½ **pound hamburg** to same fat and fry until brown. Mix all with ½ **cup uncooked rice** and **1 pint canned tomatoes.** Season with **salt** and **pepper.** Put in a casserole, cover, bake at 350° F. for 30 to 40 minutes or until rice is done. A small amount of **sugar** may be added to tomatoes if they are sour to the taste.

Salads

Lettuce is a leafy vegetable used as a salad or as a garnish for salads.

Salads may be served first, with or after the meat course.

A salad may be a combination of fruits or vegetables or both, served with an appropriate dressing. Be sure and serve the dressing designated in the recipe, otherwise the salad will have a different flavor.

Try serving hot buttered toast with any cold salad.

Shredded grapefruit is a nice addition to any fish salad.

Crab is a salt water crustacean. It is best when living inland, to use canned crab for preparing dishes.

BALTIMORE CRAB SALAD

Cut firm red **tomatoes** which have been scalded, skinned and chilled into four sections, laying each tomato flat on a bed of shredded **lettuce.** Fill center with **crab flakes** and pour over this a dressing made as follows: **½ cup chili sauce, ½ cup mayonnaise, dash Worcestershire sauce** and **½ cup small sweet pickles** cut very fine.

LOBSTER SALAD

Mix **2 cups lobster meat, 1 hard cooked egg,** finely chopped, **1** large red **tomato,** sliced, and **2 stalks celery,** diced. Season with **salt** and **pepper, 1 tablespoonful vinegar** and **1 tablespoonful mayonnaise.** Mix thoroughly and garnish with crisp, white leaves of head lettuce. Serve with salad dressing. Serves eight.

SALMON SALAD

Shred **1 can salmon** (bones and skin removed), add **1 cup chopped celery, 1 small onion,** chopped fine, and **2 small sweet pickles.** Add **salt** to taste. Then mix with **½ cup cooked salad dressing.** Serve in lettuce cups or beds of shredded lettuce. Garnish with **hard cooked egg.** Cooked salad dressing for fish salad: Mix **2 tablespoonfuls flour, 2 tablespoonfuls sugar, ½ teaspoonful salt, ½ teaspoonful dry mustard and ¼ teaspoonful pepper.** Beat **1 egg** and add to **¼ cup vinegar** which has been diluted with **¾ cup water.** Mix with dry ingredients and cook until thick. Add **2 tablespoonfuls butter,** remove from stove.

SEA SHELL SALAD

Cook until tender, **¼ lb. shell macaroni** in boiling salted water, without stirring, then drain. Add **1 onion,** chopped fine, **1 cup chopped celery** and **1 small can salmon.** Mix thoroughly with **1 cup mayonnaise** that has had **½ cup cream** added. Chill. Arrange on crisp lettuce. Garnish with **hard cooked eggs.**

Shrimp salad may be served alone on lettuce.

SHRIMP SALAD IN TOMATO ASPIC

Aspic: Soak **2 tablespoonfuls gelatin** in **½ cup cold water** for five minutes. Mix **1 cup tomato pulp, 1 tablespoonful chopped onion, 2 bay leaves, 3 cloves, ½ teaspoonful salt** and **½ cup water.** Cook slowly for 5 minutes, strain into gelatin mixture. Stir until well dissolved. Cool. Pour in small moist ring molds and chill. Salad: Clean **1 cup shrimp.** (Be sure to remove intestinal vein which is the dark line down the back.) Reserve a **few whole shrimp** for garnish. Cut remainder into small pieces. Mix with **1 cup diced celery, 2 tablespoonfuls diced onion, 1 green pepper,** chopped, **2 hard cooked eggs,** and **1 small pickle** or **several olives,** chopped. Mix with **ravigote dressing.** Unmold tomato aspic onto bed of lettuce. Fill center with shrimp salad topping with ravigote dressing and a whole shrimp for garnish.

TUNA FISH AND TOMATO SALAD

Scoop out insides of **6 ripe tomatoes,** sprinkle inside with **salt** and chill. Mix **1 can tuna** with **7 tablespoonfuls mayonnaise** and the **tomato** that was scooped out. Fill tomato shells, top with **whipped cream** and **nuts.** Serve on crisp **lettuce** leaf on **green** plates if possible.

Fruit Salads

AVOCADO SALAD

Remove **pulp** from as many **avocados** as needed. Cut into small cubes. Cut finely **1 medium onion** for **each avocado** used. Mix well with small amount of **French dressing.** Add generous amount of **lime juice** until the salad has a tart taste. Add **salt** and **paprika** as needed.

BANANA SALAD

Dressing: Cook **juice of 1 can of pineapple, ½ cup sugar, pinch salt, 1 egg, 1 tablespoonful flour** and **juice of 1 lemon** in double boiler and cool. Thin with **1 cup whipped cream.** Slice or cut **6 bananas** in cubes, quarter **¼ lb. marshmallows** and chop **1 cup nuts** and **1 can shredded pineapple.** Mix altogether very lightly, then add dressing. This recipe serves seven. In order to keep the bananas from turning black, either sprinkle with lemon juice or lay in salt water until needed. Use one teaspoonful salt to 1 quart of water. Serve on lettuce.

HAWAIIAN BANANA SALAD

Cut **bananas** into slices and squeeze **lemon juice** over them to keep from turning brown. Open 1 **can of pineapple slices.** Put banana and pineapple in refrigerator for an hour or two. Shred several large **lettuce leaves** with scissors and chill. Just before dinner, arrange a thin bed of lettuce on individual salad plates. Place a slice of pineapple on top and encircle it with slices of banana. In the center of the pineapple, place a **ball of cream cheese,** which has been mashed to a paste with **cream** and rolled in **chopped nuts.** Serve with **French dressing** mixed with **orange juice** and melted **currant jelly.**

CINNAMON APPLE SALAD

Heat **1 cup sugar, 1 cup water** and **1 cup red cinnamon candies** in sauce pan over low heat until candy is dissolved. Pare and core **6 small apples,** place in syrup, cover and cook slowly until tender but not broken. The apples should be bright red. Turn once during cooking. Remove carefully from syrup and chill. Fill centers with 1 **cup cottage cheese** that has been mixed with ¼ **cup walnuts** and 2 **tablespoonfuls mayonnaise.** Arrange on lettuce and serve.

CRANBERRY SALAD

Dissolve 1 **package** of either **lime** or **lemon gelatin** in 2 **cups boiling water.** Let cool, mix **1 cup sugar** with **1 cup stewed cranberries, ½ cup diced celery,** and ½ **cup** diced **pineapple.** Chill until firm. Unmold and serve on lettuce with mayonnaise.

CRANBERRY SALAD

Grind 1 **pound cranberries,** mix with **18 marshmallows** cut in small pieces and **1 cup sugar.** Chill in refrigerator for about 2 hours. Add 1 **cup finely chopped apples** and **1 cup finely chopped celery.** Serve on **lettuce** with or without **salad dressing.**

CRANBERRY AND ORANGE SALAD

Grind 1 **quart raw cranberries** and 2 whole **oranges,** saving juice. Dissolve **1 package** of **orange gelatin** in **1½ cups hot liquid,** using the **juice** as far as it will go then filling the amount **with water.** Add **1 cup** or more **sugar** (to suit taste). Add berries and oranges. Set in refrigerator until firm. Serve either with or without mayonnaise.

FROZEN SALAD

Put 4 **egg yolks, 4 tablespoonfuls mild vinegar** and 4 **tablespoonfuls sugar** in a double boiler and cook until thick. Cool. Add **1 pint whipped cream, ¼ pound marshmallows** cut in quarters. **1 large can pineapple** cut into pieces, but no juice, and **1 cup nuts.** Freeze in ice box. Will serve from 10 to 12.

FROZEN FRUIT SALAD

Mash **1 package of cream cheese** and blend with ½ **cup cooked salad dressing.** To this add **1 cup shredded pineapple** and ½ **cup maraschino cherries** cut in pieces. Chop ½ **green pepper and** ½ **cup pecan nuts.** Fold all into **1 cup of cream** that has been whipped. Turn into tray and place in chiller. When frozen, serve on crisp **lettuce leaf.** Do not freeze too long as it will become icy.

FROZEN PINEAPPLE SALAD

Drain **1 can crushed pineapple** and **2 cups of pitted white cherries.** Add to **1 cup of cream** which has been whipped and blended with ¾ **cup mayonnaise.** Stir in ¼ **cup chopped pecans.** Mix well Turn into refrigerator tray to freeze. If one does not have a mechanical refrigerator, this salad is equally as good, if chilled in an ice box.

FRUIT AND PECAN SALAD

Dissolve **1 package of cherry flavored gelatin** in **1 pint water.** Add ½ **raw apple** chopped fine, the **pulp** from **1 orange,** ½ **cup crushed pine apple,** ¼ **cup cooked raisins** and ¼ **cup chopped pecans.** Allow to solidify. Serve on **lettuce** with or without **mayonnaise** dressing. A dash of **Angostora bitters** helps this salad.

PREPARING GRAPEFRUIT FOR SALAD

With a sharp knife, cut off rind in a circular sawing motion, cutting deep enough to remove white membrane with the peel.

Perfect sections may be removed from the peeled grapefruit by cutting along the side of each dividing membrane to the core. Sections then may be easily lifted out.

GRAPEFRUIT SALAD

Remove sections from small **grapefruit,** freeing them from membrane. Arrange five sections in petal fashion on crisp **lettuce** having the sections meet in center. Between sections, close to the center place a rosette of softened **cream cheese.** In the very center place a spoonful of red **jelly.** Garnish with a sprig of parsley **and** serve with French dressing for grapefruit. See dressings.

ICE BOX SALAD

Dice 1 **large can of sliced pineapple.** Stone 1 **large can of Royal Anne cherries.** Place in colander and drain for 8 hours or more. Add **1 cup of chopped nuts, pecan preferred,** and 2 **dozen diced marshmallows.** Mix with dressing made from the following ingredients: 4 **egg yolks** thoroughly beaten, ½ **teaspoonful salt, juice of 1 lemon, scant ½ teaspoonful dry mustard** and ¼ **cup cream.** Cook in double boiler until thick. When cold, add ½ **pint of whipped cream.** Mix with salad ingredients and put in ice box for from 4 to 8 hours before serving. This will make 12 generous servings.

MINTED PEACH SALAD

Use **six large peaches**—allow 1 peach to a serving if the salad is the main dish, but if served with a dinner then ½ peach is sufficient. Place each peach half, rounded side up, on crisp **lettuce.** Sprinkle each half peach with a small amount of **lemon juice** and finely chopped **mint.** Serve with a dressing made by folding **2 tablespoonfuls whipped cream, 2 tablespoonfuls lemon juice, dash salt** and **2 drops almond extract into ¼ cup** of **mayonnaise.**

MOLDED PEAR SALAD

Mix **1 package** of **cream cheese** with a little **lemon juice.** Make balls just the size to fill the cavity of a pear and roll in **ground nuts.** Put **pears** in individual molds. Soak **1 tablespoonful plain gelatin** in ¼ **cup cold water.** Add **1 package of lemon flavored gelatin.** Heat to boiling: **1 cup fruit juice,** either pear, pineapple or orange, and pour over both gelatins. Cool. Add **1 cup ginger-ale** and a dash of **yellow coloring** to give it an amber appearance. Pour over pear in mold and let set in refrigerator until firm. Serve with Sweet Dressing.

SWEET DRESSING FOR PEAR SALAD

Boil **2 cups sweet pickle juice** with **1 cup water.** Mix **6 tablespoonfuls cornstarch, 1½ teaspoonfuls prepared mustard, 1 cup sugar, ½ teaspoonful salt** and **2 whole eggs.** Add to boiling liquid and cook until thick. Cool, beat again, then add ½ **pint of heavy cream,** whipped.

RECEPTION SALAD

Boil the juice from **1 large can pineapple** and add to **1 package of lemon gelatin.** When it begins to jell, add **crushed pineapple** from can, **2 packages of cream cheese, 1 small can pimientos, ½ cup celery** diced, **2/3 cup walnut meats** cut fine, **⅛ teaspoonful salt** and **½ pint of heavy cream** whipped. Pour into individual molds and allow to stand in cold place until set.

SNOWBALL SALAD

Mix **1 package of cream cheese, ¼ cup mayonnaise,** and **½ cup chopped walnut meats.** Fill cavities of **canned peaches** with mixture, then put the 2 halves together with toothpicks. Roll each peach in **cocoanut.** Serve on a bed of **lettuce** with **mayonnaise** that has been mixed with **whipped cream.** If rolled in **macaroon crumbs,** it makes a different salad.

TWENTY-FOUR HOUR SALAD

Chop **1 large can of pineapple** into small bits, but do not use crushed pineapple. Chop **½ pound blanched almonds** and cut **½ pound marshmallows** into fourths. Mix together, cover with following dressing: mix **4 tablespoonfuls flour, 1 teaspoonful mustard, ½ teaspoonful salt, dash pepper** and **½ cup sugar** together, add **1 tablespoonful melted butter.** Add **1 cup hot water** and **½ cup vinegar.** Add **1 egg,** well beaten. Cook until smooth. Whip **½ pint heavy cream.** Add it and salad dressing to other ingredients. Let set twenty-four hours in cold place or refrigerator.

WHITE MOUNTAIN SALAD

Dissolve **1 tablespoonful gelatin** in **½ cup pineapple juice** by setting in bowl of hot water. Cool. Scald **1 cup milk** with **½ cup sugar.** Cool again. When two mixtures are sufficiently cold, combine and beat hard. When mixture starts to thicken, add **½ pint whipped cream.** Beat until stiff. Fold in **1 small can diced pineapple, 1 bottle maraschino cherries, ½ pound white grapes** (seeded) and **½ pound chopped nut meats.** Pour into oblong pan and set in refrigerator until stiff.

YUM YUM PINEAPPLE SALAD

Heat 2 **cups crushed pineapple, juice** of **1 lemon** and ¾ **cup sugar.** Stir until sugar is dissolved. Soak 2 **tablespoonfuls gelatin** in ½ **cup cold water** for 10 minutes, add to first mixture and continue heating until gelatin is dissolved. Cool. When cool and beginning to set, add ¼ **cup** grated **American cheese** and ½ **pint of cream** whipped. Mix thoroughly. Mold in a deep narrow pan (bread size). Set in ice box until firm. Remove from mold, slice and serve on lettuce leaves with the following dressing: mix ¾ **cup sugar** with 2 **tablespoonfuls flour,** add to **juice** of **1 lemon** and 1½ **cups pineapple juice** (drained from crushed pineapple) and 2 whole **eggs** slightly beaten. Cook in double boiler until thick. When ready to serve, add **1 cup cream** whipped, 2 **tablespoonfuls** chopped **green pepper** and 2 **tablespoonfuls** chopped **celery.** This dressing is absolutely a part of the salad, be sure to plan to use them together.

Meat Salads

Aspic is the name for the jelly formed from cooking meat that contains a large amount of connective tissue. Usually pig's feet, veal shank or chicken are used for the foundation. Other stocks will jell with the addition of 1 tablespoonful gelatin to each pint of stock.

ASPIC SALAD

Melt 2 **cups chicken aspic** over warm water. Add 4 **tablespoonfuls mayonnaise,** ½ **cup grated** or chopped **cucumber,** ½ **cup** cooked **green peas, 1 teaspoonful grated onion, 1 canned pimiento** cut in strips, **1 tablespoonful** chopped **celery, 1 tablespoonful parsley, 1 tablespoonful** unpeeled **radishes.** Turn into small ring molds and chill almost to freezing. Unmold on water cress and fill center with stiff mayonnaise to which a little chili sauce has been added. **Chicken aspic is the jelly formed by cooking chicken in water and allowing it to cool. It may be made by adding gelatine to chicken broth.**

CHICKEN ASPIC

Chicken aspic in a quantity sufficient for salad making may be made from the **back, neck,** tips of **wings** and **feet** of a good sized **chicken,** purchased for stewing or frying. These parts are not especially desirable for serving and are particularly high in gelatin. Prepare feet, which are a splendid source of gelatin, by covering them with boiling water. Let stand a few seconds, then dip in ice water. The skin with toenails intact may then be peeled from the feet, leaving them pink and clean. Add them to the other parts named above and cover with **1 quart water,** add **½ teaspoonful salt** and a **slice** of **onion.** Simmer until meat falls from bones, then strain through a double thickness of cheese cloth, slightly dampened. Set aside to cool and form a jelly.

CORN BEEF ASPIC

Dissolve **2 tablespoonfuls plain gelatin** in **1¾ cups hot water.** When partly congealed, add **1 cup mayonnaise, cup cup corned beef** shredded, **2 cups celery, 1 small onion** cut fine, **1 green pepper** cut into strips, **3 hard cooked eggs** diced and **½ cucumber** diced. Add **salt** to taste. Mix all together and let stand a few hours or over night.

TOMATO ASPIC

Put **1 No. 3 can of tomatoes** (1 quart), **1 cup celery, ½ cup** diced **carrots, 1 slice onion,** 1 minced **pepper, 1 sprig parsley, 3 whole cloves, pinch cayenne,** and **1 teaspoonful salt** into a deep sauce pan. Simmer 30 minutes and strain. There should be about 3½ cups of liquid. Soften **2 tablespoonful gelatin** in **¼ cup cold water.** Dissolve in boiling tomato stock. Pour into moistened ring mold and chill. Crab meat, shrimp or tuna fish salads go very nicely into the center of this ring for a luncheon dish.

CHICKEN SALAD

Mix **2 cups** of **cooked chicken,** diced, **2 cups celery,** diced, **1 small onion,** diced, **6 sweet pickles,** diced, together with enough **mayonnaise** to sufficiently flavor. Add a bit of **lemon juice** if needed for tartness. Lastly fold in **2 hard cooked eggs** that have been diced. Serve on lettuce. Garnish with **radish roses, quarters of tomatoes** or **watercress.**

CHICKEN SALAD DRESSING

Cook chicken stock down until there is a ½ **cup of thick stock.** Add ½ **cup vinegar; 5 egg yolks,** slightly beaten, 2 **tablespoonfuls prepared mustard, 1 teaspoonful salt, ¼ teaspoonful pepper** and a **dash of cayenne.** Cook in double boiler until mixture begins to thicken. Strain. Add **1/3 cup butter** and ½ **cup heavy cream.** Allow to cool before using.

CHICKEN SALAD WITH CUCUMBER TOPPING

Cucumber Top—Mix **1 12-ounce jar** of **creamed cottage cheese** or **1 pound** of **dry cottage cheese, 1 large cucumber,** ground, ½ **teaspoonful salt, 2 tablespoonfuls plain gelatin** soaked in ½ **cup cold water** then dissolved over hot water, a few drops of **green coloring** and a dash of **Worcestershire sauce.** A little **chopped onion** may be **added.**

Chicken Salad—Soften **1¼ tablespoonfuls plain gelatin** in **1 cup cold water,** dissolve over hot water, cool; add **¾ cup mayonnaise** and ½ **cup heavy cream** whipped. Mix with **¾ cup diced chicken, ½ cup cooked rice, ½ cup** cooked diced **green beans, 2 tablespoonfuls minced pepper, ½ cup** finely diced **celery, 1 tablespoonful** minced **parsley, ½ teaspoonful salt,** and **1/3 teaspoonful paprika.** Place in a large glass dish or flat aluminum pan and spread until even. Set in refrigerator until firm. Remove and spread the cucumber combination over top. Return to refrigerator to set. Cut in squares, serve on lettuce garnished with radish roses and black olives.

CHICKEN SALAD AND SPAGHETTI

Cook ½ **lb. spaghetti (elbow)** until tender. Drain and chill. Add **2 cups diced cooked chicken, 1 cup celery, 1 tablespoonful grated onion, ½ cup mayonnaise, 2 tablespoonfuls chopped green pepper, 1 tablespoonful minced red pepper or pimento, 1 tablespoonful capers** and **1 teaspoonful salt.** Serve on **watercress. Salmon** or **tuna fish** may be used in place of chicken.

LEFTOVER MEAT SALAD

Mix and chill before serving the following materials: **1½ cups diced cooked meat (cold chicken, pork, beef or lamb** may be used), **1 cup diced celery, 2 hard cooked eggs** diced, **2 tablespoonfuls pimiento** diced, **2 tablespoonfuls sweet pickle** chopped, **1 tablespoonful onion** finely chopped, **½ teaspoonful salt, ¼ teaspoonful paprika,** and **½ cup salad dressing.** Serve in a huge bowl lined with **lettuce** leaves, with a salad fork and spoon.

Vegetable Salads

BRIDE'S SALAD

Shred **1 quart of cabbage,** crisp in ice water, drain. Mix cabbage, **1 quart diced marshmallows, 1 cup chopped almonds, 1 cup diced pineapple,** and **1 diced apple.** Combine with the following dressing when ready to serve. Mix together **2 tablespoonfuls flour, 1 cup sugar** and **¾ cup lemon juice.** Beat **4 egg whites** and fold into above mixture. Cook slowly in double boiler until thick. Cool. Just before serving fold in **1 cup** of **heavy cream,** whipped.

Gelatin may be unmolded easily by dipping the pan in hot water, if mold will not allow dipping then wring a towel out of hot water and place over mold which has already been inverted on the plate it is to be served upon.

CARDINAL SALAD

Dissolve 1 **package of lemon gelatin** in **1 cup boiling water.** Add **¾ cup beet juice,** 3 **tablespoonfuls vinegar, ½ teaspoonful salt, 2 teaspoonfuls onion juice** and **1 tablespoonful horseradish.** Chill. When slightly thickened fold in **¾ cup diced celery** and **1 cup of cooked, diced, beets.** Turn into mold and serve with mayonnaise. Chill until firm. Serves eight.

Separate head lettuce by cutting out core, then allow water from faucet to run into the hole. The leaves should separate themselves.

CARROT, PINEAPPLE SALAD

Dissolve **1 package** of **lemon** or **orange gelatin** in **1 cup boiling water,** add **1 cup pineapple juice.** When cool add **1 cup grated pineapple** and **1 cup grated carrot.** Pour into molds, set aside to harden. Serve on lettuce with mayonnaise. Use **canned pineapple** as fresh pineapple has an enzyme that liquifies gelatin.

CHEF SALAD

Break **iceburg lettuce** in coarse pieces. Slice **radishes** and **cucumbers** thin. Cut **fresh green onions** and quarter **tomatoes.** Place in a bowl which has been rubbed with **garlic.** Season with **salt, pepper** and **vinegar.** Drain all liquid from bowl and fold in **mayonnaise.** When serving the salad, line bowl with crisp lettuce **and** garnish top with **watercress** and **hard cooked eggs.** This salad must be prepared at the last minute and served ice cold.

DEVILED EGG SALAD IN TOMATO CUPS

Cut 8 **medium sized tomatoes** in fourths without cutting **all the** way through. Press back to form petals. Sprinkle with **salt, pepper** and **French dressing.** Let chill. Now chop **8 hard cooked eggs, 1 cup minced celery** and **8 teaspoonfuls minced onion,** add **8 teaspoonfuls French dressing, 1 teaspoonful salt, ¼ cup lemon juice, 4 teaspoonfuls prepared mustard, ½ cup mayonnaise** and **dash of paprika** or **cayenne.** Mix well and heap in center of cut tomatoes which have been placed on beds of lettuce.

If no celery is available for salad, add a bit of cabbage and some celery salt.

FLUFFY SALAD

Mix **1 cup chopped cabbage, 1 cup pineapple, ½ cup celery** and **¼ cup nuts** with a good **salad dressing.** Chill thoroughly. Serve on individual plates on a leaf of crisp lettuce topped with **1 tablespoonful whipped cream.**

GREEN SALAD

Soak **1 tablespoonful gelatin** in **½ cup cold water 5 minutes.** Dissolve in **½ cup boiling water** and add **½ cup mild vinegar, ½ cup sugar** and **a pinch salt.** When it begins to stiffen and set, add **½ cup sliced stuffed olives, ½ cup diced pineapple, ½ cup diced pickle, ½ cup diced celery** and **½ cup chopped nuts.** Add **green color** to obtain the desired shade. Turn into wet molds. Chill until firm and ready to serve. Unmold on crisp lettuce leaves and top with mayonnaise.

JELLIED SUPPER SALAD

Soak **2 tablespoonfuls gelatin** in **¼ cup cold water** 5 minutes. Dissolve in **2 cups** of **hot chicken broth.** Cool. Dip loaf pan in cold water and decorate bottom with slices of **hard cooked eggs** and **pimientos.** Cover with thin layer of broth and let stiffen. Then add **1½ cups of mixed vegetables (peas, carrots, string beans, etc.)** and **2 cups chicken** cut in small pieces. Place in alternate layers, pouring a little broth over each layer and allowing it to harden before adding another. Letting the pan stand in ice water will hasten the congealing. Chill. Remove from mold and cut in thick slices. Serve in individual portions in nest of crisp **lettuce** leaves with **mayonnaise dressing.** Do not hurry as you will spoil the appearance.

LUNCHEON SALAD

Shred **cabbage** until there is **2 cups.** Cook **½ cup alphabet noodles** and cool. Dice **1 bunch celery** and **1 small cucumber.** When noodles are cold, add vegetables. In the meantime, dissolve **1 package of lemon gelatin** as directed on package and let cool. Just before it is ready to set, add the first mixture. Mold and place in refrigerator. When ready to serve, unmold, slice, place on a bed of **lettuce** and cover with **chopped nuts.** Serve **salad dressing separately.** (Either cooked or mayonnaise.)

MOCK SALMON SALAD

Mix **2 cups grated carrots, 1/3 cup chopped English walnuts, ¼ cup stuffed Spanish olives** sliced, **1 green pepper** chopped, **¼ cup chopped sweet onion** or a **few drops of onion juice,** and **¼ cup of your favorite salad dressing.** Serve in nests of salad greens to suit your own ideas. Garnish with **slices of olives.**

OLD-FASHIONED SOUR CREAM SLAW

Cut fine **1 medium sized head of cabbage.** Use only finer portions of cabbage. Sprinkle with **salt.** Beat **1 cup sour cream, 1/4 cup vinegar, dash** of **black pepper** and **4 tablespoonfuls sugar** until stiff. Combine this thoroughly with cabbage and let stand in cool place before serving. Serve garnished with lettuce. We suggest you add a dash of **celery seed.** You will be surprised at the improvement in flavor.

PERFECTION SALAD

Soak **1 teaspoonful gelatin** in **2 teaspoonfuls cold water.** Cut or slice **cabbage** until there is **1 cup.** Chop **celery,** measure **1 cup,** dice **1 pimiento.** Add **1/4 cup boiling water** to gelatin. Add **1 teaspoonful salt** and **1 teaspoonful sugar.** Pour gelatin in custard cups which have been dipped in cold water. Add celery, cabbage, **1 small onion,** chopped, and pimiento. Set aside to cool and harden.

PICKLED BEETS AND EGGS

Wash and cook until tender **6 to 8 medium sized beets.** Peel off outside covering and pickle in **1 pint vinegar** and **1/2 cup sugar** (add more sugar if you like the pickle sweeter). When cold, add **6 to 8 hard cooked eggs,** let stand until eggs are flavored with the beets and vinegar.

POTATO SALAD

Dice **6 cold boiled potatoes,** add **1 large onion,** chopped, **salt** and **pepper** and **celery seed** to season. Add **hot cooked salad dressing** and mix thoroughly. Add **2 hard cooked eggs** chopped fine. Stir lightly. Set in refrigerator to cool.

Remember red cabbage stays red only as long as it is in an acid solution. An alkaline reaction will cause it to turn blue. Add vinegar to water used for crisping.

RED CABBAGE SALAD

Shred **cabbage** and crisp in **ice water,** then dry with a towel. Arrange on salad plate a layer of **shredded lettuce** and **white cabbage** and place in center, a mound of **red cabbage** that has been mixed with **chopped apples** and **black walnuts,** moistened with **boiled dressing.** Garnish salad with additional dressing and sprinkle with **minced green pepper.**

ROSE TOMATO SALAD

Select **small uniform ripe tomatoes.** Dip in scalding water to loosen skins. Peel and hollow out stem end slightly. Turn upside down on a plate to chill and drain.

Mash 4 **packages of cream cheese** to a paste, tint with **red coloring** and add a **small amount of salad dressing.** Keep mixture stiff enough to hold shape. Take teaspoon half full of cheese mixture, level off top and press on side of tomato with downward stroke so that each teaspoonful of cheese forms a petal. Two rows of petals are sufficient. Chill tomato roses and serve on lettuce. Fill centers with salad dressing. Garnish with riced **hard cooked egg yolks.** This gives the appearance of pollen.

SPRING SALAD

Prepare the following vegetables: **1 tomato** cut fine, **1 onion** chopped, **2 radishes** sliced thin, **1 cucumber** sliced thin, **½ cup celery** chopped, **½ cup cabbage** shredded. Marinate with **French dressing** and serve on **lettuce leaves,** shredded fine. **Watercress, endive, escarole, raw spinach, raw carrots,** and **raw cauliflower** may all or part be added.

SPRING HEALTH SALAD

Dissolve **1 package lemon gelatin** in **1 cup boiling water.** Add **1 cup pineapple juice, 1 tablespoonful lemon juice** and **½ teaspoonful salt.** Set aside to chill. When slightly thickened, add: **1 cup raw grated carrots, 1 cup crushed pineapple, ½ cup finely shredded cabbage** and **1 cup celery** cut very, very fine. Put in refrigerator or very cold place to set. This may be put into a loaf pan and sliced or into a flat pan and cut in squares, or put in individual molds. Serve on **crisp lettuce** with favorite **salad dressing.**

TEMPTING SALAD (For Use With Cold Veal)

Chop **3 hard cooked eggs** and combine with **2 cups of cold diced veal, 4 tablespoonfuls olive oil** or **vegetable oil, 1 cup cold Lima beans, ½ teaspoonful salt, pepper** to taste, **1½ teaspoonfuls vinegar.** Let stand ½ hour to marinate. Moisten thoroughly with **mayonnaise.** Arrange salad in a mound on platter. Spread thinly with mayonnaise, border with **lettuce** and surround with **tomatoes** sliced and overlapping.

TOMATO CUCUMBER SALAD

A whole tomato may be used, cutting slits in the top to allow slices of cucumber to be inserted or, the tomato may be hollowed out and diced cucumber used to fill the cavity or the tomato and cucumber may both be sliced and alternated on the lettuce, or the cucumber may be cut lengthwise, the center scooped out and filled with choped tomato. If this is done, the tomato must be firm. Serve on beds of lettuce with French dressing. Mayonnaise is too heavy for this salad.

TOMATO SOUP SALAD

Divide **1 can of tomato soup,** to one half, add 2 **tablespoonfuls gelatin** which has been soaked in **½ cup cold water** and heat to boiling, cool. To **2 packages of cream cheese,** add other **half of soup,** adding it gradually to assure smoothness of cheese. Combine the two. Add **1 cup mayonnaise, 1½ cups chopped celery, ¼ cup chopped green pepper, ¼ cup chopped onion** and **¼ cup chopped olives** or **¼ cup chopped nuts** may be added. Mix well. Put into square pan or individual molds. Serve on lettuce with no additional mayonnaise.

VEGETARIAN SALAD

Mix **3 cups cooked macaroni** with **2 red peppers** or **2 canned pimientos,** cut in pieces, **1 onion** sliced thin, **2 dill pickles** cut fine, **2 cups shredded cabbage** and **salt** and **paprika** to taste. When well blended, add **½ cup or more** of **mayonnaise** and stir again. Serve cold. This is one of those salads one serves from a large salad bowl. It is excellent for a buffet supper.

WHITE SALAD

Shred **1 quart cabbage,** add **1 small can pineapple, 1 cup blanched almonds, 2 cups marshmallows** (quartered), **1 cup cocoanut** and **1 cup white grapes** (seeded). Make a dressing of **4 eggs,** beaten separately, then mix together. Add **1 cup sugar, 1 tablespoonful flour, juice of three lemons,** and **4 tablespoonfuls vinegar.** Cook in double boiler. Add **½ pint whipped cream** just before serving.

Salad Dressings

Different salads require different dressings. Be sure you use the right one for the best results.

BOILED SALAD DRESSING

Mix together **1 teaspoonful salt, 1 teaspoonful mustard,** 2 **tablespoonfuls sugar, 1 tablespoonful cornstarch, pinch cayenne.** Add well-beaten **yolks of 3 eggs, 1 cup of cream** or **milk** gradually and **2 tablespoonfuls melted butter, ½ cup hot vinegar.** Cook over low fire until it thickens, stirring constantly. Add **well-beaten whites of 3 eggs.** For fruit, add 1 cup **whipped cream** and omit mustard.

PLAIN FRENCH DRESSING

Put **9 tablespoonfuls salad oil, 3 tablespoonfuls lemon juice** or **vinegar, 1 teaspoonful salt, 2 teaspoonfuls sugar** and **⅛ teaspoonful paprika** into a jar or bottle. Close tightly and shake vigorously for 3 minutes. A bit of **lemon juice, tabasco, chili sauce,** or **catsup** give added piquancy.

FRENCH DRESSING (With Tomato Soup)

Mix in a bowl with a Dover egg beater the following ingredients: **1 can tomato soup, 1 tablespoonful Worcestershire sauce, ¾ cup vinegar, 1½ cups salad oil, ½ grated onion, 1 tablespoonful dry mustard, ½ cup sugar, 1 teaspoonful salt** and **1 teaspoonful paprika.** Put in bottles, shake well before using. Makes about 1 quart of dressing.

FRUIT SALAD DRESSING

Cook **1½ cups maple syrup, 2 eggs,** slightly beaten, **juice of 1 lemon** and **1 teaspoonful sugar,** in double boiler until mixture thickens. Let cool. When cold and ready for use, **whip ½ pint heavy cream** and fold into dressing.

GRAPEFRUIT SALAD DRESSING

Grate enough onion for 1 tablespoonful, add ½ cup sugar, ½ teaspoonful salt, 1 teaspoonful celery seed and ½ teaspoonful paprika. Mix well. Put in ice box for 1 hour. Remove from refrigerator, add 1 cup salad oil and 2 tablespoonfuls vinegar, beating all the time. Pour over sections of grapefruit that have had membrane removed.

HONEY SALAD DRESSING

Mix three eggs slightly beaten with ½ cup strained honey, ½ cup lemon juice, grated rind of 1 lemon and 1 tablespoonful sugar. Cook in double boiler until thick and creamy. Add 2 tablespoonfuls of above dressing to ½ pint whipped cream and serve on mixed fruit.

MAYONNAISE

Beat 1 egg, 2 tablespoonfuls vinegar or lemon juice, 1 teaspoonful dry mustard, 1 teaspoonful salt, 1 teaspoonful sugar, dash pepper together. Add 1 pint salad oil very slowly at first then faster towards the end of the making. This may be made with an electric beater, Dover beater or a regular mayonnaise mixer.

MAYONNAISE (With Filler)

Place 1 egg, 2 tablespoonfuls sugar, 1½ teaspoonfuls salt, 2 teaspoonfuls dry mustard or prepared mustard, ⅛ teaspoonful paprika, ¼ cup vinegar and ¾ cup vegetable oil in a mixing bowl. Mix 4 tablespoonfuls cornstarch with 1 cup water and cook over slow flame until clear. Add hot mixture to contents of bowl, and beat with a Dover or electric beater, until all are well blended. Makes more than a pint and keeps indefinitely.

LEMON MAYONNAISE

Break 1 egg into bowl. Add 1 teaspoonful salt, 2 tablespoonfuls sugar and a dash paprika. Beat slightly with Dover egg beater. Add 1½ cups oil very slowly at first to the first mixture, beating all the time with the egg beater. Add 1/3 cup lemon juice and beat until smooth.

OLD-FASHIONED SALAD DRESSING

Heat to boiling point **1 cup sour cream, 1 cup sugar, 1 cup vinegar** (diluted if too strong.) Add **2 eggs** well beaten, **1 teaspoonful mustard, ½ teaspoonful salt, pepper** to taste and **1 tablespoonful cornstarch** thinned with enough water to mix into above mixture. Let boil a few minutes, then take off the stove and cool. Put into pint cans and store in refrigerator. This will keep 2 or 3 months.

PLAIN COOKED SALAD DRESSING

Mix **½ cup sugar** with **¼ cup flour, 1 teaspoonful salt** and **1 teaspoonful dry mustard** until well blended, add **⅛ teaspoonful black pepper.** Beat **1 or 2 eggs** with **½ cup water** until well mixed then add **½ cup vinegar** and another **½ cup water.** Add this to first mixture and stir until smooth. Then place over slow fire and stir constantly until smooth and thick. Let cook a minute or so after it bubbles. If this is thicker than desired it may be thinned with **hot water** or **condensed milk.**

RAVIGOTE DRESSING

Mash yolks of **3 hard cooked eggs** until smooth. Mix with **4 tablespoonfuls of salad oil, 3 tablespoonfuls cream, 1 tablespoonful vinegar** and **1 teaspoonful salt, dash pepper,** a little **paprika, 2 tablespoonfuls chopped chives** or **onions** and **2 tablespoonfuls** of very finely chopped **hard cooked egg whites.** This is an excellent dressing for any fish salad.

RICH SALAD DRESSING

Beat **4 egg yolks** until thick and lemon colored. Melt **1 tablespoonful butter** in top of double boiler and rub in **1 scant tablespoonful flour.** Mix **½ cup sugar, ¼ teaspoonful dry mustard** and **¼ teaspoonful salt.** Add **egg yolks** to butter and flour and beat until smooth, then add the dry ingredients that have been mixed together and beat until smooth. Add **5 tablespoonfuls water** and **3 tablespoonfuls vinegar** and cook in double boiler over low flame for ½ hour. When cold, add **1 cup whipped cream.** This dressing would be excellent on any fruit salad.

ROQUEFORT SALAD DRESSING

Cream **piece of butter** the size of walnut. Into it, cream **1 triangle of Roquefort cheese**, add 2 **tablespoonfuls cream**, either coffee **or** condensed. Keep stirring or beating all the time. Then add **6 tablespoonfuls olive oil** and 3 **tablespoonfuls vinegar, salt, paprika** and **pepper** to taste. Finally, add **1 teaspoonful Worcestershire sauce** and beat.

RUSSIAN DRESSING

Mix ½ **cup mayonnaise,** ¼ **cup chili sauce, 1 tablespoonful chopped celery, 1 tablespoonful chopped pimiento, 1 tablespoonful chopped green pepper** and a few **drops Worcestershire sauce** well together. Excellent on head lettuce.

THOUSAND ISLAND DRESSING

Combine 1 **teaspoonful minced green pepper, 1 teaspoonful grated onion, 2 tablespoonfuls chili sauce,** ¼ **cup minced pickle** and **1 hard cooked egg** chopped fine. Fold into **2/3 cup cooked** mayonnaise. Keep chilled, ready for use. Will serve about six salads.

Use syrup left from pickles for salad dressings.

Do not add salad dressing to a salad until just ready to serve.

Sandwiches

The sandwich was originated when the Earl of Sandwich not wanting to stop playing cards to eat, ordered a piece of meat between two slices of bread. That is still our main idea of a sandwich, but they have had a wide change in many directions since then.

COTTAGE CHEESE USED IN SANDWICHES

Cottage cheese and **olives.**
Cottage cheese and **pickles.**
Cottage cheese and **black raspberry jelly.**
Cottage cheese and **chopped peppers.**
Cottage cheese and **nuts.**
Cottage cheese and **onion.**
Cottage cheese and **pimiento.**
Cottage cheese and **burnt butter.**
Cottage cheese and **peanut butter** with **mayonnaise**.

CLOSED SANDWICH FILLINGS

1. **Cream cheese** and **ground nuts.**
2. **Pimiento cheese** and **browned butter.**
3. **Cream cheese** and **onion.**
4. **Egg** and **onion** ground together and mixed **with mayonnaise.**
5. **Salmon, tuna, lobster, crab meat** or **sardines** mixed **with mayonnaise.**
6. **Creamed cheese, dried beef** with a small **amount of garlic.**
7. **American cheese** and **pimiento, olives** mixed with **mayonnaise.**
8. **Ham** and **egg** groufid together with **mayonnaise.**
9. **Chicken salad.**
10. Canned **sandwich filling.**

Sandwiches may be kept moist for two days if wrapped in a damp cloth, packed in a tightly closed container and placed in refrigerator. If container is not available, use heavy waxed paper.

EGGS IN SANDWICHES

Hard cooked eggs—Sliced **chopped pickles** may be added.

Egg yolk, hard cooked, mashed with a little seasoning **and celery.**

Fried egg.

Devilled egg.

Egg white, hard cooked plus **minced pepper, chopped pickle** and **mayonnaise.**

Hard cooked eggs—Tomato catsup.

Hard cooked eggs—Walnut meats, salad dressing.

Hard cooked eggs—Chopped cucumber and **1000 Island dressing.**

Hard cooked egg and **crabmeat** with **mayonnaise.**

Hard cooked egg and **spinach** moistened with **lemon juice.**

Hard cooked egg and **watercress.**

Scrambled egg.

Scrambled eggs and **chopped ham.**

Sliced tomato and **fried egg** with hard cooked yolk.

Hard cooked eggs and **stuffed olives.**

HOT SANDWICHES

1. **Roast beef** and **gravy** served hot over one **slice of bread** then another placed on top.
2. Same with **roast pork** or **lamb.**
3. Sliced **baked ham** with **raisin sauce.**
4. **Toasted cheese sandwiches** with **tomato** and **bacon.**
5. **Hamburger sandwiches.**
6. **Cubed steak sandwiches.**
7. Hot **creamed chicken** sandwiches.

MUSHROOM SANDWICH FILLING

Clean **1 lb. of mushrooms.** Chop stems, then cook in **2 cups water** with **½ teaspoonful salt** for 15 minutes. Drain, add **4 tablespoonfuls tapioca** to stock and cook 15 minutes longer or until tapioca is clear. Stir frequently. Chop mushrooms very fine. Cook **2 tablespoonfuls onion** in butter until slightly browned. Add mushrooms, cover and simmer until tender. Uncover and cook 2 or 3 minutes until dry. Add **⅛ teaspoonful paprika, ½ teaspoonful Worcestershire sauce** and **dash of tabasco.** Add tapioca mixture and combine thoroughly. Cool. Makes about 1½ cups filling.

OPEN SANDWICH IDEAS

1. Cut **bread** into fancy shapes, spread with **butter** then with **red jelly** and pipe with **cream cheese** around edges.
2. Cut bread in fancy shapes, spread with **goose liver** and decorate with bits of **pimiento.**
3. Cut bread with crescent cutter. Spread lightly with **softened butter** then with chopped **salmon** and **mayonnaise** or use **orange marmalade** with **maraschino cherry.**
4. Cut bread with star shaped cutter. Butter and spread with **sardine butter,** edge with **riced egg** or **parsley** chopped fine.
5. Cut bread oblong in shape, spread with **soft cheese** and garnish with an overlapping layer of **stuffed olives** sliced, placed down the center of the sandwich.

Dice and toast the edges of bread cut for sandwiches and use in soup.

ROLLED CHEESE SANDWICH

Spread a **slice of bread** (crusts removed) with **soft cheese.** Form into a small roll. Wrap a **thin slice of bacon** around the center. Toast until bread is brown and bacon cooked. These sandwiches resemble an hour glass when finished. They may be eaten with the fingers.

ROQUEFORT CHEESE SANDWICHES

Cream ½ **pound Roquefort cheese** and combine with **1 teaspoonful Worcestershire sauce** and **2 cups finely chopped celery.** Spread between thin slices of **buttered white bread** and cut attractively. These are excellent with Waldorf salad.

SARDINE SANDWICHES

One cup sardines boned and minced very fine, **1 tablespoonful oil, 1 tablespoonful lemon juice, 2 tablespoonfuls mayonnaise dressing.** Mix well and spread between slices of buttered bread or serve on buttered saltines, or serve on thin slices of whole wheat bread.

TOASTED CHEESE SANDWICHES

Use as many slices of **bread** as you wish. **Six slices** for **3 sandwiches,** etc. Cut slices **of cream cheese** (or any other favorite cheese) the size of the bread. Place cheese between 2 slices of bread. Spread the outer sides of sandwiches evenly with softened butter. Place in a skillet without grease. Brown on both sides. Place lid on skillet to hold heat to melt cheese. Sometimes these are served with tomato sauce. They make a nice luncheon dish.

Sauces

A sauce is very much like gravy. It is poured over a food preparation to give added flavor.

CHOPPED EGG SAUCE

Combine **1 cup medium white sauce** with **1 tablespoonful of** finely minced **green pepper, 1 chopped hard cooked egg,** ¼ **teaspoonful salt** and **few grains pepper.**

ENGLISH CHUTNEY SAUCE

Chop ½ **lb. ripe tomatoes.** Add **2 teaspoonfuls salt** and mix. Chop **1 lb. tart apples, 12 small onions, 1 1/3 cups seeded raisins** and **three large green peppers,** add **½ cup chopped mint leaves.** Scald and cool **3 cups vinegar,** add **2 cups sugar** and **2 teaspoonfuls dry mustard.** Mix all together and allow to stand 10 days before using. Does not require cooking. Shake jars occasionally.

HOLLANDAISE SAUCE

Melt **2 tablespoonfuls butter.** Add **1 tablespoonful flour** and **½ cup boiling water.** Boil well, then add **2 egg yolks** and **2 tablespoonfuls lemon juice** and **½ teaspoonful salt.** Bring to boil. Serve hot. The addition of flour to this sauce keeps it from curdling.

Horseradish is a root which is ground for seasonings.

HORSERADISH HOLLANDAISE

Divide **½ cup butter** in thirds. Put 1/3 in small sauce pan with the **yolks of 3 eggs, ½ teaspoonful vinegar** and **½ teaspoonful salt.** Place sauce pan in larger sauce pan containing boiling water and stir constantly until butter is melted. Then add second piece of butter, and as mixture thickens, third piece of butter. Remove from fire and add **4 tablespoonfuls grated horseradish root** and **2 tablespoonfuls heavy cream,** beaten until stiff.

HORSERADISH SAUCE

Whip **½ pint cream** until stiff. Add **1 tablespoonful powdered sugar** and **½ teaspoonful paprika.** Then add as much **horseradish** and **salt** as suits your taste. This is delicious served with all kinds of meats, especially meat loaves.

MUSHROOM SAUCE

Blend **¼ cup butter, 1 cup flour** and **¼ teaspoonful salt,** and cook over fire until it starts to brown. Add **3½ cups chicken broth** or **milk** and **½ cup cream.** Cook until thick and well done. Add **1 pound mushrooms** that have been washed, sliced and sauted in butter. Add more salt if needed. Cook about 3 minutes longer or until mushrooms are heated through.

NUTMEG SAUCE

Bring **1 pint of water** to a boil. Mix **3 teaspoonfuls flour** with a **little water** to make a smooth paste. Stir it into the boiling water. Add **2 cups sugar** and **2 tablespoonfuls butter.** Just before serving, add a **grating of nutmeg.** A little bit of lemon juice or vinegar improves the flavor of the nutmeg sauce.

DEPENDABLE WHITE SAUCE

There are three kinds of white sauce:

1. Thin, this requires **1 tablespoonful butter, 1 tablespoonful flour** and **1 cup milk.**

2. Medium, this requires **2 tablespoonfuls butter, 2 tablespoonfuls flour** and **1 cup milk.**

3. Thick, this requires **3 tablespoonfuls butter, 3 tablespoonfuls flour** and **1 cup milk.**

In each case, blend flour and butter together in a pan over a flame until flour takes on a golden cast. (Do not allow to get too brown as flour loses its thickening power when overcooked). Add milk and stir constantly until cooked. Season with **salt** and **pepper** to suit your taste.

All measurements in these recipes are level.

Cook flour and butter well before adding liquid in making sauces and gravies. It not only keeps it from becoming lumpy, but gives a better flavor.

Soups

Soup may be divided into two classes: Clear—Bouillons and consommes. Thick—Creams (purees), bisque and unstrained.

BEEF STOCK (Foundation Recipe)

Use **6 pounds of beef shin, meat** and **bones.** Wipe with a damp cloth. Crack bones open to free marrow. Add **6 quarts cold water** (cold water brings out juices). Add **2 carrots diced, 2 onions** diced, **2 turnips** diced, bits of **celery leaves, parsley, cabbage** or other **green vegetables.** A **sprig of thyme** and a **bay leaf** with **2 whole peppercorns** and a **bit of salt** to suit the taste completes the seasonings. Cover and bring to a boil slowly. Skim off scum as it rises to top. After it reaches boiling point, simmer gently about 3 hours. Keep covered to prevent evaporation. Do not add too much salt at first as some of the meat juices will not extract in the presence of salt. When done, strain through a sieve, then allow the stock to stand a while to settle. Pour off clear liquid from sediment. Cool and store in refrigerator until ready for use. Remove fat if desired.

Cool soup or meat broth uncovered, otherwise it may sour.

BARLEY BROTH

Use **1 soup bone** with **2 quarts water** or **1 quart of soup stock.** Cook **2 teaspoonfuls pearl barley** in meat stock to which has been added **1 cup tomatoes** and **1 small onion,** cut fine. Cook slowly until barley is soft. Season with **salt** and **pepper.**

CELERY SOUP

Place **1 pint of milk** in a double boiler. Use leaves and coarse stems, chopped fine, from **one small bunch of celery.** Steam celery leaves and milk ½ hour. Press through a sieve, leaving milk tinted with strong celery flavor. Then thicken milk with a **small amount of flour** dissolved in milk. Season with **salt** and **pepper** and **small lump of butter.** Reheat and serve. There can be added to this a small quantity of **stewed chopped celery.** This makes a more nourishing soup than the milk soup alone.

CORN CHOWDER

Boil **1 quart diced potatoes** in **1 pint boiling water** for 15 minutes. Fry **2 tablespoonfuls diced bacon** and **1 chopped onion** for 2 minutes. Add **1 can** of **corn** with bacon and onion to potatoes. Continue cooking until potatoes are done. Add **1 pint milk, salt** and **pepper** and a little **celery salt.** Bring to boiling point, add **3 crushed crackers** and serve very hot.

FISH CHOWDER

Cook **2 lbs. haddock** filet in boiling, salted water until done, 15 to 20 minutes. Remove fish from water and set aside, but save fish water. Fry ½ **lb. fat salt pork,** which has been sliced thin and diced. when pork is crisp and dry, remove from fat and set aside. Simmer **4 medium sized onions** sliced, in pork fat, until light brown. Dice **6 raw potatoes;** put potatoes and onions in **3 cups fish water,** simmer slowly until tender. Add more water if necessary. Add to vegetables, fish skinned and flaked, **4 to 6 cups light cream and milk, salt** to taste and the fried salt pork. This should serve 10-12.

HAMBURG SOUP

Cook **1 pound hamburg** in **1 quart water** for 10 minutes, then add **1 quart of cooked vegetables**, assorted, **1 onion,** sliced, and **1 quart can of tomatoes. Salt** and **pepper** to taste. Cook 20 minutes. This amount serves 10.

LENTIL SOUP

Soak **1½ cups of lentils** overnight, add **1 carrot** diced, **1 small onion** sliced, **½ cup** minced **celery, 2 quarts water, 1 teaspoonful sugar, 1½ teaspoonfuls salt, ¼ teaspoonful pepper.** Simmer 2½ hours or until lentils are soft. Add **3 tablespoonfuls butter** and serve. This soup may be thinned with hot milk if desired.

MUSHROOM SOUP

Clean and if necessary peel **½ pound mushrooms.** Cut into as fine pieces as possible (they may be ground). Melt **4 tablespoonfuls butter** in frying pan, add mushrooms and saute until a golden brown (some turn quite black) add **4 tablespoonfuls flour** and cook until it too, is brown. Add **milk** necessary for number to be served, **allowing 1 cup per person.** This can be stretched to serve six but is very excellent for four. A garnish of **whipped cream** may be added when serving.

ONION SOUP WITH CHEESE

Slice **4 medium sized onions** and cook gently in **3 tablespoonfuls butter** until perfectly tender, but not browned. Add **1 quart meat stock** (either **chicken** or **veal)** and simmer for five minutes. Cut **American cream cheese** in ¼-inch slices and place on **slices of toast (one for each serving).** Set in oven or place under broiler until cheese melts. Put a slice in each soup plate, pour soup over and sprinkle with **little finely grated cheese** and **dash of paprika.** This recipe serves four.

ONION SOUP (French)

Peel and slice **3 onions** very thin. Melt **2 tablespoonfuls butter** in frying pan and slowly cook onions until tender, stirring frequently to prevent burning. Add **1 cup water** and simmer for 5 minutes. Combine with **1½ cup beef stock** and simmer for five minutes longer. **Toast 1 piece of bread** for each person to be served, place in bottom of soup plate, sprinkle with **grated cheese** (American or Parmesan) and cover with hot onion soup. **Top with paprika.** The toast comes to the top. Serve at once.

OYSTER STEW

Heat 1 **quart of milk** to scalding, add ¼ **cup butter** with **salt and pepper** to taste. Drop 1 **pint of cleaned oysters** into the hot milk. As soon as they rise to the top, remove from fire and serve. If you want an extra rich soup use coffee cream in place of milk.

OXTAIL SOUP

Divide the ox tail into joints, remove fat, and cook with **1 quart tomatoes, 2 medium sized onions, 1½ cups celery,** ½ to **1 cup diced parsley roots** slowly for 2 hours. Soak **1 cup rice** for 3 to 4 hours, wash well, add rice and **2 or 3 cups diced potatoes** then cook for 1 hour more. Mix **2 tablespoonfuls flour** with **1 cup milk,** add, cook a few more minutes more, stirring all the time.

PHILADELPHIA PEPPER POT

Cook ¼ **cup sliced onion,** ¼ **cup chopped celery,** ¼ **cup chopped green pepper, 1½ cups chopped potatoes** in 3 **tablespoonfuls butter** 15 minutes. Add 3½ **tablespoonfuls flour** and stir until well mixed. Add 5 **cups hot white stock,** ½ **lb. honeycomb tripe** (fresh) cut in cubes, ½ **teaspoonful peppercorns** finely pounded, ¾ **teaspoonful salt.** Cover and let cook 1 hour. Just before serving add ½ **cup heavy cream** and remaining butter.

Salt may be removed from soup by adding a slice of potato, remove before serving, but may be saved for use later. Repeat if necessary to remove more salt.

POTATO SOUP

Boil ½ **cup celery,** cut fine, **1 medium onion,** cut fine, **1 pint water, 1 teaspoonful butter** and **salt** to taste. There will be about ½ pint stock. Add **1 cup leftover mashed potatoes** and **1 cup top milk.** Reheat until hot through. Buttered toast squares are better than crackers with this soup.

RIVEL SOUP

Take **1 pint of broth** from veal, pork, beef or chicken bones. Add ½ **pint water, 1 tablespoonful fresh onion** and **1 tablespoonful chopped celery,** ½ **cup rice** and cook until rice is done. Add **salt** and **pepper** to taste. Take the **yolk** of **1 egg** and slowly add **flour** until rivels are made about the size of a small pea. Add these to boiling broth slowly. Let simmer about 10 minutes.

SPLIT PEA SOUP

Wash and pick over 1½ **cups** of **dried split peas** and soak overnight. Drain. Add 1½ **quarts water** and **1 sliced onion.** Cover and simmer for 2 hours or until peas are soft. Press through sieve, add **2 cups milk, 2 tablespoonfuls butter** and **salt** and **pepper** to taste. Reheat and serve.

The peas may be cooked with a ham bone for flavor in place of butter.

TOMATO SOUP

Clean enough **tomatoes** for **1 quart** or use **canned ones.** Cook tomatoes until soft then run through a sieve. Return to kettle, add **salt, pepper** and **sugar** to taste. Add ½ **teaspoonful soda.** Brown 4 **tablespoonfuls flour** with 4 **tablespoonfuls butter,** add tomato mixture to this and cook until it thickens. Thin with **milk, cream** or **water** as desired.

TOMATO BISQUE, WHIPPED CREAM

Heat contents of **1 can** of **tomato soup** and an equal quantity of fresh **milk** separately. Bring almost to boiling point, then mix just before serving, pouring soup into milk to prevent curdling. Serve in bouillon cups. Top with **whipped cream** that has been seasoned with **paprika** and **celery salt.**

VEGETABLE SOUP

Obtain **1 large soup bone** with about **2 pounds of shank meat** attached. Cut meat from bone and brown in little fat in soup kettle. Add bone and plenty of cold water, bring to a boil. Add **1 onion**, sliced, **½ cup diced carrots, ½ cup diced turnips, ½ cup chopped cabbage, ½ green pepper** cut fine, **1 cup tomatoes, 1 tablespoonful chopped parsley, ½ teaspoonful celery seed** and **2 tablespoonfuls salt.** Cook slowly for about 3 hours. Add water if necessary. Add **1 cup diced potatoes** about 1 hour before serving. Vegetable soup is always better the second day. If you do not cut the meat from the bone it can be used the next day for hash.

To make your own kitchen bouquet melt a teaspoonful of granulated sugar until browned in a skillet or if for soup, in the soup kettle before adding meat.

Use clean white blotting paper to remove fat from hot soup, if allowed to cool it will harden and may be removed easily.

Soup meat should be chopped and used in making meat loaves, patties, croquettes and hash.

To make meat stock quickly run the meat through a food chopper.

Croutons, an accompaniment for soup.

CROUTONS

Cut ordinary slices of day old bread into ½ inch cubes, crusts may or may not be removed. Have ready a kettle of deep fat. When hot, drop bread cubes into it and fry until a golden brown. Serve with soup.

Stews

A stew is a dish prepared from a tough piece of meat, which requires long cooking. It may or may not have vegetables or dumplings.

BEEF STEW

Cut **1 lb. of beef into cubes** about 1 inch thick. Mix **4 tablespoonfuls flour** with **1 teaspoonful salt** and **⅛ teaspoonful pepper**. Roll meat in **flour** mixture. Brown meat in hot fat. Put in stew kettle and cover with boiling water. Add **6 slices onions, 4 carrots sliced, 3 turnips diced** and **6 potatoes diced** or all of these may be quartered. Simmer for 1½ hours or until done. May have **dumplings** cooked on top 12 minutes before ready to serve.

MOCK CHICKEN STEW

Wipe **1½ pounds of breast of veal** with a damp cloth and cut into cubes. Place in top of double boiler with **1½ cups milk, ½ cup water, ½ teaspoonful salt,** and **1 small onion** into which **2 cloves** have been inserted. Cover tightly, and cook over boiling water until tender. When done blend **2 tablespoonfuls flour** and **2 tablespoonfuls butter** and add to stew. Cook until thick. Remove onion.

IRISH STEW WITH DUMPLINGS

Cut **2 lbs. of lamb** in cubes. Roll in flour and brown in **hot fat.** Place in kettle, cover with **boiling water** and when same is boiling add a bouquet made out of **bay leaf, parsley** and **celery** tied together. Add **salt** and **pepper** to taste. Boil for 40 minutes, then add **5 carrots** diced, **2 onions** sliced, and **4 Irish potatoes** cubed. When vegetables are just about done then add dumplings. Dumplings: Sift **2 cups flour** with **1 cup milk** until a soft batter is formed. Drop by spoonfuls on top of broth, place cover on pan and boil exactly 12 minutes. Place stew in center of platter, dumplings around the edge and sprinkle with parsley.

ITALIAN STEW

Mix thoroughly and form into small balls **1 lb. hamburg, 6 tablespoonfuls bread crumbs, 4 tablespoonfuls grated cheese, juice of 1 onion, 1 tablespoonful parsley, 1 teaspoonful salt, ¼ teaspoonful paprika** and **1 egg yolk.** Cook in **2 tablespoonfuls suet** until brown, then cover balls with **2 tablespoonfuls flour** and brown again. Add **1 cup boiling water** and **1 cup tomato juice,** simmer 1 to 2 hours. Before done add **1 cup cooked macaroni, 2 tablespoonfuls broken cheese** and **1 teaspoonful salt.**

VEAL STEW

Take **1 lb. stewing veal,** cut in small pieces and fry in **lard** until brown. Add **water** to cover and boil 15 minutes. Put this in a large kettle and add **4 cups potatoes** cut in large pieces and **4 cups carrots** cut large. Add a **quart of canned tomatoes, a dash of marjoram** and a **small onion sliced.** Cover and cook until vegetables are done.

Substitutes and Recipes

Dates are a tropical fruit very heavy in their own sugar. They make an excellent substitute for candy.

Vegetable fat may be used to good advantage for a butter substitute when making a cake, but do not forget that it does not have salt, therefore always add salt when this substitution is made. ½ tea poonful salt for each cup of unsalted fat.

BUTTER EXTENDERS

1. Blend half butter and half margarine together, adding coloring from margarine.

2. Mix together **½ lb. butter and 1 lb. margarine** then gradually **add 1 large can evaporated milk.** Add **coloring** from margarine package and a little more **salt.**

3. Mix 2 pints sweet cream and 1 pint sour cream in an electric mixer until butter is formed. Mix 1 lb. butter and 1 lb. margarine until coloring is blended thoroughly. Add this butter to butter in mixer. Mix until color is the same throughout. Be sure to use the color tablet that comes with the margarine. Pour off buttermilk to drink. Put butter in large bowl and rinse with water until all the milk is washed out and water is clear. Work in as much salt as you like. Mold into a roll just as the country people do. This makes 3 pounds of delicious butter.

BUTTER STRETCHERS

Soften **1 tablespoonful plain gelatin in ¼ cup cold water.** Set over hot water and stir until dissolved. Cut **1 pound of butter** into small pieces. Place in a dish over hot water and stir until butter is quite soft but not melted. Remove from heat. Gradually whip one **14-ounce can of evaporated milk,** and dissolved gelatin into butter with a rotary or electric beater. After milk is thoroughly beaten into butter add **salt** to suit the taste. If milk separates a little, keep on beating until all has been mixed in. **Yellow coloring** may be added. Pack in jar and put in refrigerator to harden.

This is excellent for spreading sandwiches at any time, but not advisable for baking or buttering vegetables as the milk content gives a different result than all fat.

If 1 teaspoonful gelatin is added to 1 tablespoonful cold water and soaked for a few minutes, dissolved over hot water, then added to cream, to be whipped, it may be whipped early in the day and need not be whipped after the guests arrive. Store in refrigerator.

CHART FOR BUTTER SUBSTITUTIONS IN CAKE

½ cup margarine equals **½ cup butter.**

6½ tablespoonfuls lard equals **½ cup butter.**

7 tablespoonfuls lard substitute equals **½ cup butter.**

1½ cups thick sour cream equals **½ cup butter.**

If lard or lard substitute is used in a cake add **1 tablespoonful more liquid** and **¼ teaspoonful salt.**

If cream is used omit liquid called for in recipe.

CHART FOR SUBSTITUTION FOR SUGAR

When recipe calls for 1 cup granulated sugar use—

Molasses—1 cup—but it is not as sweet as cane sugar.
Maple syrup—1¼ cups, reduce liquid by one-half.
Honey—1 cup, reduce liquid one-fourth.
Corn syrup—1 cup, reduce liquid by one-third.

For comparative sweetness—to 1 cup granulated sugar:

1½ cups molasses
1½ cups maple syrup
¼ cup honey
2 cups corn syrup.

If sugar substitutes are used add the following regardless of what other leavening agent is used.

Molasses—½ teaspoonful soda for each cup.
Maple syrup—¼ teaspoonful soda for each cup.
Honey—⅛ teaspoonful soda for each cup.
Corn syrup may or may not have ⅛ teaspoonful soda.

CHOCOLATE CREAM SUGARLESS CAKE

Add 2¾ **teaspoonfuls baking powder** and ¼ **teaspoonful** salt to 2½ **cups sifted flour** and sift three times more. Cream ½ **cup shortening,** add **1 cup white syrup,** beating well. Add **half of the flour** and beat until smooth. Add **2 eggs unbeaten,** one at a time, add remaining flour in thirds, alternating with 2/3 **cup milk.** For best results beat cake well at each stage of mixing. Add **1 teaspoonful vanilla.** Bake in 2 greased layer pans at 375° F. for 30 minutes.

DARK CORN SYRUP SPICE CAKE

Mix **1 cup dark corn syrup** with **1 egg** and ½ **cup melted shortening,** add ½ **cup buttermilk,** 2½ **cups flour** sifted 2 or 3 times with **1 teaspoonful baking powder, 1 teaspoonful soda, 1 teaspoonful cinnamon,** ½ **teaspoonful cloves,** ½ **teaspoonful allspice** and ¼ **teaspoonful salt.** When well mixed bake in a greased tube pan 1 hour at 350° F.

We have found that by starting these cakes at 325° F. for the first 15 minutes then raising the temperature to 350° F., the results are better.

LIGHT CORN SYRUP CAKE

Sift 3 **cups cake flour,** measure again and sift with **4 teaspoonfuls baking powder** and ½ **teaspoonful salt.** Cream ½ **cup shortening,** add **1 cup light corn syrup** gradually and cream until fluffy. Add **3 egg yolks** one at a time, beating after each addition. Add sifted dry ingredients alternately with **1 cup milk,** stirring well after each addition. Add **2 tablespoonfuls grated orange rind.** Beat **3 egg whites** stiff, add ½ **cup corn syrup** gradually, beating until mixture stands in stiff peaks. Fold into batter until well blended. Bake in 2 greased and floured 9 inch layer cake pans in moderate oven (375° F.) for 25 to 30 minutes. Frost with corn syrup frosting.

SUGARLESS BROWNIES

Cream ½ **cup shortening** well, add **1 cup white corn syrup** gradually, stir in **2 squares of melted chocolate,** add 2 well **beaten eggs** then add ¾ **cups flour,** ½ **teaspoonful baking powder,** ½ **teaspoonful salt** and ½ **cup chopped nuts.** Pour in a greased pan 9 x 9 x 3. Bake 30 to 35 minutes at 350° F. Cut in squares as soon as baked. This makes 2 dozen brownies.

CHOCOLATE CHIP COOKIES WITH HONEY

Cream ½ **cup butter or margarine** and ½ **cup honey** until light and fluffy. Add **1 small egg** and beat well. **Sift 1 cup flour, 2 teaspoonfuls baking powder** and ½ **teaspoonful salt twice.** Add flour mixture to butter mixture and then add **1 teaspoonful vanilla** and blend well. Fold in ½ **cup semi sweet chocolate chips** and ¼ **cup chopped nuts.** Chill. Drop by teaspoonfuls on greased cooky sheet. Bake at 375° F. for 12 to 15 minutes.

CORN SYRUP FROSTING

Combine **2 egg whites** with **1 cup white corn syrup.** Place in a bowl and beat with electric mixer starting at low speed and working up to a high speed until the mixture stands in peaks. Add **1 teaspoonful vanilla** and ½ **teaspoonful almond flavoring.** This requires 15 minutes with the electric mixer.

COFFEE STRETCHING

Purchase whole grain wheat, put in a corn popper and shake it all the time to keep from burning. Roast until real brown but not burnt. Put through a coffee grinder, electric grinder or roll with rolling pin. Either use with coffee as half and half or use by itself.

HONEY BUTTER

Measure **2½ cups honey** and **2/3 cups butter.** Let stand at room temperature until soft enough to blend. Add honey and stir until it is thoroughly blended. Put in a jar with a tight cover and let it remain in refrigerator two or three days before using.

MAPLE SYRUP (Synthetic)

Shell corn from **12 good sized cobs.** Boil cobs in **1 gallon water** for 3 hours (more water may be added if it boils away). Then strain through a clean cloth. Add 2½ **pounds light brown sugar** and boil to ½ gallon. Discard cobs after first boiling.

SUGARLESS LEMON PIE

Mix in double boiler **1 cup light corn syrup, 2 beaten egg yolks, 2 tablespoonfuls cornstarch** and **2 tablespoonfuls flour.** When well mixed, add slowly **1 cup boiling water** and cook over boiling water until thick. Stir often. Take from fire add **1 tablespoonful grated lemon peel** and the **juice** of **1 small** or **½ large lemon.** Cool, then pour into a ready baked crust. Beat **2 egg whites** until stiff. Slowly drizzle **2 tablespoonfuls honey** on egg white and beat again. Cover pie. Brown in oven.

A teaspoonful of cold water added to white of egg causes it to whip more quickly and increases the quantity of egg white.

If cake flour is used where bread flour is called for, add 2 tablespoonfuls flour, but remember that cake flour does not have the necessary ingredients for making bread.

If bread flour is to be used in a cake where cake flour is called for, reduce the amount by 2 tablespoonfuls and add 1 tablespoonful cornstarch.

Three level tablespoonfuls cocoa may be substituted for 1 square of chocolate. It is best to add a tablespoonful butter as the cocoa has had its fat removed.

One tablespoonful vinegar added to 1 cup sweet milk will make it sour enough to be used in recipes requiring sour instead of sweet milk.

To make sour milk from evaporated milk, dilute milk in ratio of 1 part milk to 2 parts water and add 1 tablespoonful vinegar to each cup of diluted milk.

Vegetables

Vegetables are a classification of food plants which are green and succulent and raised for table use. Most vegetables have been given their own heading such as asparagus, cabbage, etc.

All liquor drained from cooked vegetables should be saved for soup or added to tomato juice for a beverage.

VITAMINS

Vitamins are sparks that start off the body engine, if the fuel is good it will be utilized to give the body the right build up, both for energy and tissue building.

Vitamin A—

1. Protects against night blindness.
2. Keeps skin soft and moist.
3. Looks after respiratory tract.

Vitamin B-1—

1. The nerve vitamin.
2. Overcomes that tired feeling.
3. Protects against fatigue.
4. Protects upset nervous systems
5. Peps up morale.

Vitamin B-2—

1. Promotes growth.
2. Promotes good digestion.
3. Promotes good eyes.

Vitamin C—

1. Protects against disease.
2. Protects teeth and gums.
3. Lack of it causes scurvy.

Vitamin D—

1. Prevents rickets.
2. Governs the amount of calcium and phosphate in the blood.

Vitamin K—The blood clotting vitamin—

Prevention of death.

ARTICHOKES

The artichoke is a plant resembling a large thistle. It is cultivated for its flowering head and gathered before the flower expands.

The chief edible portions are the fleshy part of the calyx, the bottom or basin of the blossom and the bases of the leaves of the flower.

To eat artichokes, pull leaves away from base, dip thick white end in butter or sauce and gently pull it between the teeth, thus removing its delicate "meat" and leaving it where it belongs in the mouth.

The choicest part of the artichoke is the heart. This is cut and carried to the mouth with a fork after removing the choke or hairy growth upon it.

Select medium sized **artichokes uniform** in color, allowing one to each person to be served. Remove all dead or dry leaves. Wash and soak 20 minutes in **salted water,** then drain and boil slowly in salted water until the leaves can be torn apart easily. Serve hot with **butter,** melted if desired or **mayonnaise.**

Asparagus is a very delicate vegetable as only the young sprouts are eaten. It should be steamed with the heads up so as to avoid the tips being broken. There are two different colors, white, and green, the food value is the same in both. It is only a matter of color preference which one to use.

BUTTERED ASPARAGUS

Clean and cut **stalks** of **asparagus** to an even length. Tie in bundles and place in a deep pan or double boiler, in a small amount of boiling water, which has been salted and cook for 12 to 15 minutes. (The asparagus cookers that are on the market now are very handy.) Drain, and serve hot with **melted butter.**

ASPARAGUS AND EGGS

Boil **asparagus** in salted water for 20 minutes. Use **tips** only, canned or fresh. If you use canned ones, boiling is not necessary. Lay in a deep buttered pie dish. Dot with **butter.** Add **pepper** and **salt** to taste. Beat 4 **eggs** for 1 minute. Add ¼ **teaspoonful salt** and pour over asparagus. Bake 12 minutes in 375° F. oven. Garnish with **pimiento** and serve at once.

ASPARAGUS AND MACARONI CASSEROLE

Cook **½ pound macaroni** in boiling salted water for 20 minutes. Drain and rinse in cold water. Cook **1 large bunch asparagus.** Make a white sauce of **3 tablespoonfuls butter** and **3 tablespoonfuls flour** browned together, then **1½ cups milk** added with **1 teaspoonful salt.** When smooth and thick, add **macaroni, asparagus, 3 hard cooked eggs** sliced, **4 tablespoonfuls** of **crisp cooked bacon** diced, **1 small onion** minced and **2 tablespoonfuls green pepper.** Turn into a buttered casserole, cover with **buttered crumbs.** Bake in moderate oven 20 to 30 minutes.

ASPARAGUS AND HARD COOKED EGGS

Cook **1 pound of asparagus** until tender or purchase **1 can.** Cut tips into 1 inch lengths. Remove seeds from **1 cup ripe olives** and mix with **2 hard cooked eggs** chopped. Alternate asparagus with egg and olive mixture in layers in a casserole. Pour over enough well seasoned **white sauce** to cover. Sprinkle with **bread crumbs** and bake 10 minutes.

ASPARAGUS SOUP

Take **one large can asparagus.** Cut in inch lengths. Cook this in **1 quart of water** until very tender. Rub through a colander and return to the water. Add **1 pint milk, 1 teaspoonful butter,** rubbed with **1 teaspoonful flour,** and cook three minutes. Season with **salt, butter** and **pepper.** Serve with **white crackers.**

ASPARAGUS SUPERIOR

Arrange four slices of toast on platters. Put **four** or **five** hot buttered **asparagus tips** (either canned or fresh) on each. Pour over this a sauce made by melting **1 tablespoonful butter** in sauce pan, adding 1½ **tablespoonfuls flour** and 2 **tablespoonfuls cold milk,** stirring well. Put in **1 cup milk.** When hot, add ¼ **cup grated American cheese.** Cook to a creamy thickness. Season with **salt** and **pepper.** Sprinkle with **paprika.** Garnish with **hard cooked egg** pressed through sieve and sprigs of **parsley.**

Beets are a root vegetable which bleed if pared before cooking. They are washed, tops removed, and boiled until tender. The young tops make excellent greens, being served in much the same ways as other greens. They may also be canned the same as dandelions.

PREPARATION OF FRESH BEETS

Wash well, cut off tops to about 1 or 2 inches from the beet. Do not cut off the long root at bottom or beet will bleed while cooking and a pale vegetable will result. Cook until tender in plenty of water, about ½ hour is required. Do not test often as each hole made in beet allows the red juice to escape. When tender, place in a pan of cold water and remove skins, tops and roots by pressure of fingers. The tiny stalks at the top are often tender enough to include in the serving.

BUTTERED BEETS

Season cooked **beets** with **salt** and **butter,** a small amount of **sugar** adds to the flavor. Serve while hot.

CREAMED BEETS

Season **cooked beets** with **salt, butter, sugar and cream.** Heat well in seasonings. (Omit pepper as a seasoning for beets, as it seems to detract from the flavor.)

BEET GREENS

Clean the young plants, by washing thoroughly, allowing the small beet to stay on. Or just the leaves, if the root is large enough to eat. Cook in salted water until tender. Season with a cooked salad dressing.

HARVARD BEETS

Use **2 cups beets** either freshly cooked or canned. If young beets are used, cook in boiling water until tender, chill in cold water, slip skins and halve, dice or slice according to size and desire. Make a sauce by cooking **¼ cup water, ¼ cup vinegar, ¼ cup sugar** and **1½ tablespoonfuls butter** together, thicken with **2 teaspoonfuls cornstarch** blended with **¼ cup cold water.** When sauce is done, add beets and cook 10 minutes more. **¼ teaspoonful** of either **cloves** and **cinnamon** gives this recipe a good variation.

Broccoli is a variety of cabbage produced by cultivation. It is the original form of the Cauliflower and is similar to it, except that the heads are coarser and take longer to form their flower buds. Broccoli is not bleached, the flower buds are very tender and for that reason should be cooked quickly with very little handling.

Vegetables such as broccoli and cauliflower should be soaked for at least 30 minutes in salt water after they have been prepared for cooking to bring out any hidden worms or bugs deep down in the vegetables.

BROCCOLI, WITH HOLLANDAISE SAUCE

Cut off tough ends of **broccoli** and cook buds in as small amount of water as possible. When ready to serve pour **Hollandaise sauce** over it.

BROCCOLI WITH CHEESE

The **stems** and **buds** of **broccoli** are edible. Remove all dead and wilted leaves. Soak in slightly salted water to remove dirt and insects. Drop broccoli in boiling salted water having just enough water to cover. Cook rapidly in open kettle until tender (10 to 15 minutes). Drain. Measure **2 cups broccoli** and place in an oiled baking dish, cover with white sauce made of **1 tablespoonful butter, 1 tablespoonful flour, ½ teaspoonful salt, pinch pepper** and **1 cup milk.** Sprinkle **½ cup grated mild cheese** over surface. Place in moderate oven until cheese melts. Serve immediately.

BUTTERED BROCCOLI

Broccoli is the flower of the plant. Its stems are sometimes very tender and they are used with the small leaves. Separate heads into pieces small enough for individual servings. Drop into boiling salted water and cook for not more than 15 minutes. If **broccoli** is very tender, 10 minutes will suffice. Drain, add **melted butter,** cook in this butter for a few minutes, tossing broccoli around in butter very lightly so as not to injure the heads.

BRUSSELS SPROUTS

Remove outer leaves and wash thoroughly. Cook by dropping into boiling salted water (1 teaspoonful salt to 1 quart water). Drain. Season with a **little pepper** and **plenty of butter** allowing the sprouts to reheat in the butter.

BRUSSELS SPROUTS CREAMED WITH CELERY

Cook in uncovered sauce pan 15 minutes or until tender, **1 qt. of brussels sprouts, 1½ cups diced celery,** 4 **cups boiling water, 1 teaspoonful salt.** Drain and save the liquid. Melt in top of double boiler **2 tablespoonfuls butter.** Blend in **2 tablespoonfuls flour, 1 teaspoonful salt, ⅛ teaspoonful pepper** and then add **¾ cup evaporated milk,** diluted with **¾ cup vegetable liquor.** Cook 20 minutes stirring constantly. Add vegetables and heat thoroughly. This will serve 6 persons.

BRUSSELS SPROUTS AND MUSHROOMS

Clean, and cook in boiling salted water, **1 quart of brussels sprouts.** When tender, drain. Saute **½ lb. fresh mushrooms** (caps and stems) in **4 tablespoonfuls butter;** when mushrooms are slightly browned, add **4 tablespoonfuls flour** (level) and cook until brown. Add **1½ cups milk** and cook until smooth, season with **salt** and **pepper.** Add brussels sprouts to mushroom sauce. Serve very hot. (Do not cut mushrooms unless they are exceptionally large.)

Cabbage is a green vegetable which is very economical to use. It ranks next to potatoes in consumption. There are about 70 varieties. The more expensive types of cabbage do not give better food value, they only give a change in flavor and appearance.

CHINESE CABBAGE AND TOMATOES

To 5 **cups of shredded Chinese cabbage** add **salt** and **pepper, ½ cup tomatoes,** cooked or canned, **1 small onion,** finely chopped. Cook cabbage 10 minutes in boiling salted water. Drain, add **tomatoes** and **onion** and season. Cook until tender (about 20 minutes).

CABBAGE COOKED IN MILK

Shred 2 **quarts of cabbage** very fine, add **2 cups milk** and **salt** and **pepper** to taste. Cook slowly until cabbage is done, do not boil, just bring to boiling stage. When cabbage is done, add **4 tablespoonfuls butter,** reheat and serve.

CREAMED CABBAGE

Chop coarsely **1 small head cabbage.** Cook rapidly, uncovered in boiling salted water 10 to 15 minutes or until tender. **Drain.** Add 1 to 1½ **cups white sauce** to cabbage.

NEW CABBAGE

To 2 quarts of boiling water add ½ **teaspoonful soda** and 1 **tablespoonful salt.** Cut a medium sized head of new **green cabbage** into eighths and remove outer leaves and heart. Drop cabbage into boiling water and boil for 15 minutes. Drain well and add a generous amount of **butter,** a little **pepper** and more salt if needed. Cabbage prepared this way retains its green color and has a fine flavor.

SCALLOPED CABBAGE

Soak and wash a **half head of firm cabbage** in salted water. Boil, changing water 2 or 3 times during cooking. Allow to cool and cut fine. Season cabbage with **salt, pepper** and **2 tablespoonfuls lemon juice.** Into a well greased baking dish, alternate layers of cabbage and **medium white sauce.** Cover with **bread crumbs,** sprinkle with **grated cheese.** Bake until crumbs are brown and cabbage is hot.

CABBAGE SLAW

Shred **small head of cabbage.** Mix with **6 marshmallows cut fine. 1 ring pineapple shredded, 4 tablespoonfuls pineapple juice, 1 tablespoonful vinegar** and **4 tablespoonfuls thick cream.** Mix all together and chill.

HOT SLAW (No. 1)

Beat **2 egg yolks slightly.** Add **½ cup cold water** and **¼ cup vinegar,** then **1 tablespoonful sugar, ¼ teaspoonful mustard** and **1 teaspoonful salt** mixed together. Add **1 tablespoonful butter** and cook in double boiler until thickened. Add **2 cups cabbage** and heat thoroughly. Makes about 6 servings.

HOT SLAW (No. 2)

Melt **1 tablespoonful butter** and **1 tablespoonful lard** in iron frying pan. Add **½ head** of medium sized **cabbage** sliced fine. Stir often, season with **salt** and **pepper** and add a **little water,** if necessary. Keep covered most of the time, about 15 minutes to steam tender. Then add **1 tablespoonful flour** by sprinkling it over cabbage or mixing it with **½ cup water** and **2 tablespoonfuls vinegar** (add more vinegar if you wish.) When tender, add **1 beaten egg** and stir in well and serve. **Sour cream** may be used in place of **water.**

STUFFED CABBAGE

Select a **medium sized head of cabbage,** cut center out, stuff with **1 lb.** of well seasoned **sausages,** then, **sprinkle salt** and **pepper** over cabbage. Cook in roaster with **1 cup water** for 45 minutes in oven or until cabbage is cooked enough so that it won't fall apart. When ready to serve, slice in as many pieces as desired.

Carrots are a year round vegetable. They are high in mineral salts and vitamins. Because some of the best food value is next to the skin they should be cooked with skins on or scraped.

To make a ring mold when a regular one is not available, place a small glass jar in center of a pan having the height necessary for the mold. If used for a gelatin preparation, fill center contained with ice to hurry solidification.

BUTTERED CARROTS

Pare or scrape **small carrots,** cook whole in salt water until almost tender. Remove from water, roll in **cracker crumbs** and fry brown in butter.

CANDIED CARROTS

Scrape **carrots** (this need not be done if carrots are young and fresh). Cut in halves lengthwise. Wash, put into a buttered skillet, season with **salt** and **pepper,** allow to brown slowly. When nicely browned all over, sprinkle **brown sugar** over top. Cover with water and cook slowly for ¾ hour.

CARROTS AND CELERY

Clean and cut crosswise, **4 carrots,** clean and cut into small pieces **6 to 8 stalks of celery.** Cook together in a small amount of water. When well done, season with **salt, pepper** and **butter.**

CARROTS DELICIOUS

Take **1 cup bacon** and cut into small pieces. Fry out and remove from pan. Have about **3 cups carrots** to **1 cup celery** and **4 medium onions** cut into small pieces, diced if possible. Fry in bacon fat, add **2 tablespoonfuls flour,** season and cover with boiling water. Put in casserole and bake 1½ to 2 hours in moderate oven. **One bay leaf** or **1 green pepper** may be added. When ready to serve, sprinkle crisp bacon over top.

The carrot scraper is a handy tool to have in the kitchen.

MINTED CARROTS AND PEAS

Clean **carrots** by scraping and cutting lengthwise into fine strips. Drop into salted boiling water and cook 15 minutes. Drain. Shell **peas.** Drop these into salted boiling water and cook 10 minutes if very tender and longer if needed but not too long as they will lose their pretty green color. Put the two together in a sauce pan. Add **butter** and **1 tablespoonful** of **fresh mint** finely minced.

CARROT RING WITH PEAS

Put **2 cups** of **cooked carrots** through the ricer. Beat **3 eggs** until light. Add **½ teaspoonful salt, ⅛ teaspoonful pepper, 1 small onion** chopped fine, **2 tablespoonfuls melted butter, ¾ cup milk** and carrots. Mix well. Place in a well buttered ring mold and set in pan of boiling water. Place in moderate oven, bake until carrots begin to leave edge of pan. Remove to hot platter. Use care when inverting the ring mold. Loosen with knife first, then place platter over top and hold firmly while turning the mold upside down. Fill ring with **buttered peas,** being sure they are rather dry.

BOUQUET OF CAULIFLOWER, CARROTS AND PEAS

Scrape **carrots** and allow to remain whole. Cook in a small amount of salted water. Clean a **head of cauliflower,** allowing it to stand head down in warm salted water for ½ hour to draw out insects, if present. When ready to cook, place the whole head into boiling salted water and cook until soft but not mushy. If **peas** are canned, drain, **butter** and just heat until they are hot throughout. If green fresh peas are used, shell, wash, cook in salted water until done. If peas are dropped into boiling water they will retain their brilliant color. When vegetables are all done, place cauliflower in center of a large chop plate. Cover with a **thin white sauce.** Stack carrots that have been buttered, around cauliflower and fill in the spaces with peas. More white sauce may be served from a bowl, but avoid too much.

BUTTERED CAULIFLOWER

Clean a **head of cauliflower**, break into **flowerettes. Let stand** in warm salted water for ½ hour to remove insects. Remove, drop into **boiling salted water.** Cook from 20 to 30 minutes, or until done. Drain. Pour **melted butter** over flowerettes which have been placed in a serving dish. Season with more **salt** and **pepper** if needed. Garnish with dash of **paprika.**

Celery is a vegetable of which we eat the stock or stem. It is usually bleached so that when we obtain it, it is very white in color. This vegetable is a good winter keeper and is obtainable almost the entire year. Green celery contains more vitamins.

STUFFED CELERY HEARTS

Clean **celery hearts** thoroughly. Fill hollow side with mixture of **2 parts cream cheese** and **1 part mayonnaise** and **1 part crushed pineapple.** Sprinkle stuffed section with **paprika.** Chill before serving.

Another novelty made with stuffed celery hearts is to partly fill the hollow of the celery with **pimiento cheese** (the soft kind) or **blue cheese;** then press all celery back into place as if it were a whole stalk. Chill and cut crosswise before serving. This gives the impression of pinwheels.

Corn, a native of North America is good fresh, canned, dried or made into meal.

Corn on cob should be cleaned, dropped into boiling salted water and cooked until milk is set and no longer. Test by inserting a prong of fork in a grain of corn, if no milk appears, corn is done.

BAKED CORN

Mix **1 can golden bantam sweet corn** with **1 tablespoonful flour, 1 egg** beaten, **1 cup milk, 1 teaspoonful sugar,** with **salt** and **pepper** to taste. Pour into buttered baking dish, sprinkle well with **cracker crumbs** and dot with **butter.** Bake slowly for at least 45 minutes.

CORN CASSEROLE

Combine **1 can corn, 3 beaten eggs, 1½ cups milk, teaspoonful salt.** Arrange in layers in greased baking dish. Cover each layer with **grated cheese.** On top lay a **few strips of bacon** and cover with **bread crumbs** and more grated cheese. Bake in moderate oven for ½ hour.

CREAMED GREEN CORN

Cut **corn** from **6 cobs.** Cook in small amount of water 5 minutes, then hurriedly evaporate the remaining water. Add **2 tablespoonfuls butter, salt** and **pepper, 1 teaspoonful sugar** and **½ cup heavy cream.**

CORN OYSTERS

Purchase the fine corn canned, or run your own canned corn through a sieve. Beat **2 egg yolks** and add to **2 tablespoonfuls flour, 2 tablespoonfuls butter.** Season with **salt** and **pepper.** Fold in the beaten egg whites. Drop batter from spoon into hot fat and fry light brown. Drain on soft paper. Serve hot.

CORN PUDDING

Take 3 **large ears of corn** (or 2 cups). Cut off top of corn, then scrape the cob to get all the sweetness. Add **2 eggs** slightly beaten, **1 teaspoonful salt, 1 tablespoonful sugar, 1 cup milk** and **1 teaspoonful butter.** Stir all together. Bake in a greased pan. Set in a pan of hot water, in a moderate oven. When it begins to thicken around the edges, stir, so the butter will be well mixed into the pudding. Bake until a silver knife inserted comes out clean.

Cucumber, a seed pod vegetable that is used mostly for pickles, also is used fresh for salad.

CUCUMBERS AND ONIONS

Peel **1 cucumber** and slice. Clean **1 onion** and slice. Sprinkle with **salt** and **pepper.** Add **vinegar** to season. Use water if vinegar is too strong to dilute. Mix together and serve.

Egg plant is a vegetable not so widely used as other vegetables. It may be prepared by first peeling it or it may be baked with peeling left on. Watch recipes for directions.

BAKED EGGPLANT

Butter a large baking dish or casserole and fill with **layers of peeled eggplant,** crisp bacon, hard cooked eggs, green pepper, cut fine, tomatoes, onion and crushed cracker crumbs. Use the proportions of **1 quart eggplant, 1 cup cracker crumbs, 1 pint tomatoes, 1 onion, 1 large green pepper, 4 hard cooked eggs** and **¼ pound bacon.** Make a layer of eggplant, then add some of each of the other ingredients. When filled, pour over remaining **tomato juice** and bacon fat. Add **milk** if needed for moisture. Bake until well done and quite dry.

BROILED EGGPLANT

Put **¼ cup butter** in broiler pan and heat until it is well melted and entirely covers the pan. Dip pieces of **unpeeled eggplant** in **beaten egg,** then roll in **cornflakes** that have been crushed fine. Lay on broiler pan. Dot each slice with **butter.** Broil under moderate flame until golden brown.

ESCALLOPED EGGPLANT

To **1 pint** of **peeled eggplant** use **crackers, butter** and **milk** with **salt** and **pepper** for seasoning. The bottom of a baking dish is covered with cracker crumbs (be sure that dish is buttered), then scatter eggplant over generously, also a few spoons or dots of butter. Add salt and pepper. Continue layers of crumbs and eggplant until all is used, allowing the crumbs to be the last layer. Cover with milk. Let stand 15 minutes. Add enough milk to nearly cover and bake in moderate oven until nicely browned. Of course, fresh eggplant that has been cooked can be used the same way.

EGGPLANT AND LAMB

Cut **1½ pound of lamb stew** into small pieces and brown in frying pan in a little **butter.** Cut **1 large eggplant** into small pieces (do not peel) about 2-inch cubes. Season with **salt** and **pepper.** Add to lamb with **1 cup tomatoes** and let simmer until done or put in baking dish and bake in moderately hot oven until both lamb and eggplant are done.

EGGPLANT RAGOUT

Boil **1 egg plant,** then peel and chop fine, add **2 medium onions,** chopped fine, **2 green peppers,** chopped fine, **1 cup nut meats** (English walnuts), chopped fine, **1 cup bread crumbs, 2 cups tomatoes** and **½ cup butter.** When well mixed put in baking dish that has been greased, and bake ½ to 1 hour in moderate oven. Serve as a meat substitute.

Dandelions are nature's own supply of greens. They can be had for the gathering. They are best when very young. They may be saved for future use by canning.

DANDELION GREENS

Cook **dandelion** or **other greens** in boiling water until tender. Lift out with fork. Mix with the following dressing: Beat **2 eggs slightly** and mix with **¾ cup sugar** and **½ teaspoonful salt.** Beat all together well. Add **⅜ cup vinegar,** cut **1/3 pound sliced bacon** in inch pieces and fry out slowly in skillet. Leave crisp bacon in grease and remove from fire, add vinegar mixture, stirring it in very quickly so dressing will be smooth. Return to fire and cook, stirring constantly, for a few minutes till dressing is smooth and thickened. This is enough for a very large dish of greens. This dressing is especially good on spinach.

DANDELIONS WITH TOMATO SAUCE

Cook **dandelion greens** in boiling water for about 5 minutes or until tender. Drain and squeeze all water out. Take **1 lb. hamburg** and make into little balls the size of marbles. Melt **2** or **3 tablespoonfuls lard** in frying pan and fry **2 kernels of garlic** until brown, then put in meat balls and fry until they are nicely browned. Next add **1 can tomato puree** and **1 cup water, salt,** and **pepper,** and cook about 10 minutes until thick. Pour this sauce over the drained dandelions and cook all about 2 minutes, then serve.

Endive and escarole are two greens which are not widely used. They are very good in salads and may be cooked the same as spinach or dandelion.

MOCK MUSHROOMS

Pick as many **dandelion blossoms** as you wish, without stems. Soak in salt water 3 or 4 hours or over night. Drain, roll blossoms in cracker crumbs, dip them in **beaten eggs** with **salt** and **pepper** added. Roll in crumbs again, fry in **hot butter** until well browned. Serve at once.

ENDIVE SALAD

Clean **1 lb. endive.** Break the longer leaves into shorter pieces. Put in a large bowl. When ready to serve sprinkle with **salt** and **pepper.** Add **1 tablespoonful vinegar** and **2½ tablespoonfuls olive** or **salad oil.** Toss together with two forks and serve. Excellent. Serve with French Dressing.

ENDIVE SOUP

Make a big pot full of **chicken** or beef **broth.** Clean **3 lbs. endive.** Put in large kettle with just the water that clings to it. When cooked down put into the broth. Do not use water drained from endive. Make tiny meat balls the size of marbles and add to the soup.

ENDIVE SOUP (Meat Balls)

Mix **1 lb. lean pork** (ground), **1 egg, ¼ cup dry bread crumbs, 2 tablespoonfuls grated Parmesan cheese, ¼ small onion,** cut in pieces and **salt** and **pepper** to taste. Mix together with hands, working until smooth. Shape in balls the size of marbles. Fry in small amount of **lard** until brown, then put meat balls into soup. After endive and meat marbles are in soup, cook all together for ½ hour. This makes enough soup for a large family of 8 or 10.

ESCAROLE

Take **2 lbs. of escarole,** wash 3 or 4 times. Put it in a 3-qt. sauce pan with just the water that clings to the leaves. Cover and let cook down, over a very slow fire. When cooked, drain off the liquid. Into another sauce pan, (the 2-qt. size will do,) put **3 tablespoonfuls olive oil** or **bacon drippings,** and **1 clove of finely chopped garlic.** Brown garlic slowly, then add cooked escarole. Add salt and pepper to taste. Cook altogether for another 15 minutes. This will serve 4 or 6.

Kale belongs to the cabbage family and may be cooked as such.

CASSEROLE OF KALE

Parboil **1 large head of kale** in salt water until leaves separate. Divide and place in buttered casserole alternately with **2 hard cooked eggs, 2 potatoes,** boiled and sliced or **1 cupful cooked rice, ½ pound ground meat, 1 tablespoonful grated onion, 1½ cups thin cream sauce** and **salt** and **pepper** to taste. Bake in a moderate oven 45 minutes. Serves 4 to 6.

STUFFED KALE HEAD

Parboil **1 large head of kale** in salt water until leaves separate. Stuff center with mixture made up of **½ pound ground meat, ¼ cup rice, 1 egg, ½ tablespoonful chopped onion, salt** and **pepper** to taste. Tie the head. Put in a deep casserole and pour over a sauce made as follows: brown **2 tablespoonfuls shortening** and **2 tablespoonfuls flour,** add **¼ clove garlic** or **½ teaspoonful chopped onion.** Add **2 cupfuls water.** Let simmer a few minutes. Then bake until kale is tender, about 1 hour in a moderate oven.

GREEN BEANS WITH BACON, POTATOES AND CORN

Have ready a large kettle with a tight cover. Clean and string **3 pounds of green beans.** Place in bottom of kettle. Bury a **1 pound piece** of **bacon** among the beans. Cover with water. Cook for about 2 hours or until both are tender. Place **12 new potatoes,** scraped, on top of beans and bacon. Cook 30 minutes longer, then place **12 roasting ears** on top of all. Cover and let corn steam until milk does not come out when a kernel is pierced. Serve corn on a platter, and bacon surrounded with potatoes on another. Beans may be served in tureen as usual. Serves 12.

BUTTERED GREEN BEANS

Wash, clean, and **string beans** if necessary. These beans may be left whole, broken into small pieces or run through a bean cutter which slices them diagonally. Their method of preparation is only a matter of choice with the cook. Drop into boiling salted water and cook 15 to 20 minutes or longer if desired. Remove from fire, drain (save liquid to add to soups), season with **melted butter** and more **salt** if necessary.

GREEN OR STRING BEANS WITH CHEESE

Cook **1 pound of string beans** either **green** or **yellow** or use **1** can of either of them. Drain. Put in mixing bowl, sprinkle with 4 ozs. of **grated cheese** and mix with **1 cup of medium white sauce.** Put in casserole and bake in moderate oven ½ hour. Proportions **for white sauce are 1 cup milk, 2 tablespoonfuls flour, 2 tablespoonfuls butter** and **½ teaspoonful** each of **salt** and **pepper.**

BAKED KIDNEY BEANS

Soak 3 **cupfuls red kidney beans** in water overnight. Next morning parboil them with **4 large onions.** Put into bean pot or baking dish and stir in **2 cups of canned tomatoes, 1 tablespoonful salt, 1 tablespoonful sugar** and **1/3 teaspoonful pepper.** Bury **½ lb. of salt pork** in the beans. Add just enough water to barely cover. Bake in slow oven until beans are done, then bring the pork to the top so it will brown. This recipe serves 8.

CHILI CON CARNE

Fry **2 pounds hamburg steak** in **butter** until it is a rich brown. Remove from frying pan to kettle and add **1 can kidney beans** (or **1 cup dry kidney beans** soaked overnight), **1 quart can tomatoes, 4 tablespoonfuls vinegar, 1 green pepper** chopped, **1 large onion chopped, 1 clove garlic minced fine, 1 tablespoonful sugar, ½ cup water or stock, ½ teaspoonful chili powder** and **salt** to taste. Simmer slowly for 1 hour.

When beans are dried they are classed as legumes and are a good meat substitute. **That is, the legume has a large amount of the food stuff called protein, which is in meat.**

Recipes for dried navy beans may be used for marrowfats and kidney beans.

Wash dried beans thoroughly before soaking. Then cook in water in which they were soaked.

BAKED BEANS

Cover **2 cups navy beans** with cold soft water or cold boiled hard water. Soak overnight. Drain, add cold water and **½ teaspoonful soda** to cover. Let simmer until skins are easily pierced, then drain. Additional water may be added. Place beans in casserole, cut **½ lb. salt pork** in ½ inch strips and bury thoroughly in beans. Mix **4 tablespoonfuls molasses (New Orleans), 2 teaspoonfuls salt, ¾ teaspoonful mustard** and **1 cup boiling water,** pour over beans in casserole. Water should be about half way up. If not, add more. Cover and bake slowly for 6 hours. Remove cover the last hour to brown. Brown sugar may be substituted for molasses.

Lentils are a small flat seed which are cooked only after being dried.

LENTIL ROAST

Soak **1 cup dried lentils** overnight. In the morning drain, add **2 qts. cold water, half an onion** and a **stalk of celery.** Cook until soft and rub through a sieve. Combine with **1 cup bread crumbs, ½ cup** or more **chopped walnuts, 2 beaten eggs, salt** and **pepper.** Form into a loaf and bake until brown, basting frequently.

SPROUTING SOYBEANS

Put in a bowl or some other container **soybeans** of the black variety. Add a **little chlorinated lime** to prevent mold, add a **little water** and set in dark. The beans soften and within five days send out white, yellow tipped shoots ready for eating.

LIMA BEANS

Cook **dried lima beans** slowly in plenty of water until thoroughly done. Drain off any remaining liquid. Season with plenty of **butter, salt** and a **little cream.** Do not stir until mushy.

CASSEROLE OF LIMA BEANS WITH PORK

Soak **1 pound dried lima beans** overnight. In the morning drain thoroughly, then add enough fresh water to cover well. Add **salt** to taste, and cook until almost tender. Into a greased baking dish put a layer of beans, then a layer of **ground pork,** a **tablespoonful brown sugar** and **⅛ teaspoonful dry mustard.** Continue until the beans and **1½ pounds of pork** have been used. Put **juice of beans** over all and bake in a slow oven about 2 hours.

LIMA BEANS EN CASSEROLE

Soak **1 pound dry lima beans** over night. Drain in morning, add fresh water to cover. Add salt and cook until tender. Peel **1 large onion** and cut almost through. Place in center of casserole. Add **1 tablespoonful dry mustard** to beans and pour into casserole containing onion. Fill half full of **milk** instead of bean juice. (Beans should be cooked so that they have very little juice on them when ready for the casserole.) Cover casserole with **slices** of **bacon** and bake in moderate oven until brown. It takes about ½ hour.

FRESH LIMA BEANS

Shell **beans.** Wash, drop into boiling salted water and cook quickly for 15 to 20 minutes, less if they are very tender. Drain, if there is any water left, although it is best to have just enough so that when beans are done nearly all water has evaporated. Season with **butter, salt, pepper** and **heavy cream** to give them moisture.

MOCK SAUSAGE

Soak 1 **cup lima beans** over night. Drain. Cook in boiling salted water until tender, then force through a sieve. Add **3 eggs, teaspoonful sage, 2 tablespoonfuls butter** and **2/3 cup bread crumbs.** Shape into sausages 3 inches long and 1 inch thick. Roll in **egg,** then in **bread crumbs.** Saute until brown. Serve with tomato sauce.

LIMA BEANS AND MUSHROOMS

Put 1½ **tablespoonfuls buttter** in sauce pan. Add **2 cups cooked Lima beans** and **2 cups fresh mushrooms.** Simmer for a few minutes, then add ½ **cup cream** or **evaporated milk.** Season with **salt** and **pepper.** Simmer until hot through, then serve on toasted biscuits or bread. If fresh mushrooms are used, one may parboil them 5 minutes before using.

The mushroom is a fungus growth which is very delicious in flavor. There is very little food value.

MUSHROOMS AND ASPARAGUS

Slice crosswise and very fine **1 lb. mushrooms.** Cut **asparagus** into small pieces until there are **2 cups.** Put both in same skillet and barely cover with water. Stew over slow fire 8 to 10 minutes with **2 tablespoonfuls butter** until done and tender. Serve over steak.

BROILED MUSHROOMS

Wash **mushrooms** and remove stems. Place the caps gill side down under flame of broiler for 2 or 3 minutes. Turn, sprinkle with **salt** and **pepper** and place a piece of **butter** in each cap. Broil under flame for few minutes longer. Lift carefully from broiler so that juices are not lost. Serve on buttered toast.

MUSHROOMS AND CAULIFLOWER

Wash **½ lb. mushrooms** in salt water. Cut **1 cauliflower** in pieces same size as mushrooms. Prepare cauliflower by cooking in salted water. When tender, add mushrooms and cook together until both are done. Drain, set aside. Prepare **cheese sauce** (see sauces). Mix mushrooms, cauliflower and cheese sauce together, place in casserole and brown in oven. Serve hot.

MUSHROOM VEAL LOAF

Wipe **1 cup of fresh mushrooms** and saute in fat for 5 minutes. Mix **2½ pounds of veal** and **½ pound of ham** that has been ground fine. Add **1 teaspoonful salt, ¼ teaspoonful white pepper, 4 tablespoonfuls catsup, 4 tablespoonfuls horse radish, 1 cup cracker crumbs, 1 green pepper** chopped fine and **1 onion** chopped fine. Beat **1 egg.** Cut mushrooms in small pieces and mix with other ingredients. When well mixed, place in well-oiled pan in the bottom of which 4 slices of bacon have been arranged. Save 2 slices for on top. Bake in a hot oven 1¼ hours, basting frequently. When serving this loaf, turn out on a hot platter and serve with a gravy made as follows: to **2 tablespoonfuls of liquid** left in pan add **1 cup sour cream, 1 tablespoonful butter** and **1 tablespoonful flour** mixed to a smooth paste with **2 tablespoonfuls water.** Add **salt, pepper,** and **paprika** to taste. Cook for 3 minutes.

STUFFED MUSHROOMS

Brush **12 large mushrooms.** Remove stems and chop finely. Peel caps if needed. (The commercial mushrooms do not need peeling.) Melt **3 tablespoonfuls butter.** Add **½ tablespoonful** finely chopped **onion** and **½ teaspoonful** finely chopped **parsley.** Cook 10 minutes. Add **1½ tablespoonfuls flour, cream** to moisten and **salt** and **pepper.** Cool and fill caps rounding well on top. Cover with **buttered cracker crumbs** and bake 15 minutes in hot oven (425° F.)

MUSHROOMS AND SWEETBREADS

Parboil, blanch and dice a **large pair of sweetbreads.** Chop **parsley,** chop **1 cup mushrooms,** and add to sweetbreads. Make **2 cups white sauce,** season well. Add **1 onion,** chopped fine, **cayenne pepper,** and **juice of 1 lemon.** Add sweetbread mixture to hot sauce. Let cook slowly 5 minutes. Have patty shells hot and fill them just before serving or one may use hot toast. Garnish with chopped olives and a dash of paprika. Nice for bridge luncheons.

Okra is a vegetable used extensively in the south. It has a slimy appearance which the northerner does not care for. Foods called gumbo usually contain okra.

OKRA

Wash **okra** thoroughly. Cut off stem ends and lay on top of boiling **green beans,** or **cabbage,** when they are nearly done. Okra can be boiled in clear water also. Lift out when tender and dot with **butter, pepper** and **salt.** Serve immediately.

BUTTERED OKRA

Cut stems off tender part of **okra pods** and cook whole in boiling salted water until tender. Drain and return to sauce pan with **plenty of butter,** a **taste** of **vinegar, salt** and **pepper** to season. Simmer slowly until they are thoroughly seasoned.

FRIED OKRA

Wash and cut stem end from **okra,** then cut in ½ inch pieces across pod. Sprinkle with **salt** and let stand few minutes. Roll in mixture of **one part flour** and **two parts cornmeal.** Fry in hot fat until lightly browned and tender. Especially good with green beans and sliced tomatoes.

OKRA, RICE AND TOMATOES

Wash **1 cup rice** and cook in boiling salted water until tender. Drain, add **2 tablespoonfuls butter, salt, pepper** and **paprika** to taste. Cut **1 quart okra** in slices and cook in small quantity of boiling water. When ready add ½ **can tomatoes** and rice. Serve hot.

SOUTHERN GUMBO

Wash **okra,** cut in small pieces. Have **2 tablespoonfuls bacon grease** or shortening in skillet. When hot, add **2 or 3 sliced onions.** Let cook a few minutes. Then add to this a **few sweet peppers,** cut in small pieces. Add okra and either a **can of tomatoes** or **4 or 5 fresh ones.** Cook about 30 minutes. Add **salt** and **pepper** and serve. This recipe is good also when hamburger steak is added and cooked with the above.

The onion is a bulb vegetable. There are several in this family; garlic, leeks, shallots and chives are all related. The bulbs are the edible portion of all, except chives. There the hollow leaves are used.

To peel onions so as not to have them get into your eyes either hold under water or hold bottom of onian up when peeling; the aromatic oils are not released so quickly when onion is held in that position.

To remove the odor of onions from hands, rub on freshly mixed mustard, then rinse in cold water.

BAKED STUFFED ONIONS

Parboil in salted water ¾ of an hour, **8 large onions**—Spanish preferred—which have been skinned. Drain and let cool. Fry **½ lb. ground veal, ½ lb. sausage,** and **4 slices bacon** until done. Scoop out centers of onions and stuff with the cooked meats chopped fine and seasoned with **salt** and **pepper.** Top with **bread crumbs.** Place in greased baking dish and bake in oven until crumbs are brown on top.

CREAMED ONIONS

Prepare **small whole onions** or slice larger ones, by removing at least 2 outside layers of the onion. This does away with the one layer that is so often tough. Cook in salted water until tender, allowing the water to cook away. Season with **salt** and **pepper, butter** and **cream.** Make a thickening of **flour** and **water** and add to onions while boiling in the cream if one desires them of a heavier consistency. Allowing the cream to evaporate will give the same results without the pasty taste which may result if the flour is not well cooked.

FRIED ONIONS

Slice **1 lb. white onions** and let stand in **milk** for 45 minutes. Remove from milk, drain, dip in **flour.** Fry either in skillet or in deep fat. **Salt** and **pepper.** Save milk to season some other preparation.

GLAZED ONIONS

Use **small uniform onions,** parboiling just a trifle so as to hold shape. Place in flat pan and cover with **sugar** and **butter.** Place in oven to bake until glazed.

Parsnips are a root vegetable having a very strong flavor. Parboiling will reduce this taste if one prefers it milder.

FRIED PARSNIPS

Pare **large parsnips,** cut lengthwise about ¼ inch thick, remove woody center. Boil until tender in water to which **1 teaspoonful of salt** and **1 tablespoonful sugar** has been added. Drain, dip in **egg,** then in **bread crumbs** and fry in **hot fat** (half butter and half lard) until brown.

PARSNIP FRITTERS

Boil 3 **large parsnips** until tender, then mash or put through a ricer, picking out any woody bits. Beat **1 egg** to a froth. Stir in mashed parsnips and beat well. Add **1 teaspoonful** salt and **1 tablespoonful butter,** then ½ **cup milk** and enough **flour** to make the batter firm. Make into balls and drop into **hot fat,** frying quickly. Remove from fat and place on absorbent paper to dry. *Editor's Note*: This is an English recipe and does not use baking powder but we think 1 teaspoonful of baking powder would improve the texture.

PARSNIP PUFFS

Mix **1 cup cold mashed boiled parsnips** with **2 tablespoonfuls grated cheese.** Add **1 egg,** well beaten, **1 teaspoonful sugar,** ½ **cup flour, pinch cayenne** and ½ **teaspoonful salt.** When well mixed roll out on floured board and cut in strips 1 inch wide and 3 inches long. Fry till brown in deep **hot fat.**

Peas are a most delicious vegetable, both green and dried. They are among the best sellers for canned vegetables.

BUTTERED NEW PEAS

Shell **peas**, wash, drop into boiling salted water and cook rapidly for 10 to 15 minutes, according to the age of peas. Drain. Season with **salt, pepper** and **butter.** Cream may be added, as a change in preparation.

Irish potatoes are perhaps the most widely used vegetable on the American market. For this reason we have collected many recipes so that there can be a change in their method of preparation.

New potatoes may be cooked with jackets on.

If potatoes for baking are placed in hot water for a few minutes before being put in oven they will bake quicker.

Rub the skins of potatoes with a little butter before baking to keep them soft.

Potatoes may be roasted in same pan with meat roast. Add them about 1 hour before roast is done, turning once to brown on all sides.

Potatoes for frying and mashing will cook faster if sliced before cooking.

BAKED POTATOES

Scrub thoroughly nice **medium sized potatoes.** Rub skins with **lard, substitute** or **butter.** Bake in a very hot oven about **1 hour.** When done, pierce with a fork, to allow steam to escape. Cut on top with a sharp knife both ways to form a cross, press with thumb and forefinger of each hand, making the opening bulge. Drop a **tablespoonful** of **butter** in this space with **salt** and **pepper.** Garnish over the top with **paprika.** The potato is eaten direct from the shell.

BAKED POTATO CAKES

Add **1 egg yolk, 2 tablespoonfuls flour, 2 teaspoonfuls of baking powder** to **2 cups of mashed potatoes.** Beat until smooth. Drop by spoonfuls into dish of **bread crumbs.** Roll around until well covered with crumbs. Put into greased baking pan. Press down and cover each cake with **grated cheese.** Bake in very hot oven until brown.

BAKED POTATOES WITH CHEESE

Cut **6 large baked potatoes** in half, lengthwise, and scoop out centers. Mash thoroughly. Add **2 cups grated cheese to 1/3 cup hot milk** and beat until smooth. Mix with potatoes. Add **2 teaspoonfuls salt** and **½ teaspoonful paprika** and whip until light and creamy. Refill potato shells, return to hot oven (450° F.) and bake until brown on top.

BAKED POTATOES WITH ONIONS AND CHEESE

Place in shallow pan a layer of **potatoes** and then a layer of **onions,** sliced thin. Sprinkle with **salt** and a little **pepper.** Dot with **butter** and **cheese.** Repeat the layers until pan is full, putting butter and cheese on top. Pour **water** or **milk** over contents until it is half way up sides of pan. Brown top in broiler few minutes, then cover and bake at 375° F. until done. This dish served with salad make a delicious Lenten meal.

POTATO BALLS (No. 1.)

Mix **1 cup mashed potatoes, 1 well beaten egg, 1½ cups flour, 2 teaspoonfuls baking powder, salt** to taste and enough **milk** to make a soft dough. Drop by spoonfuls in deep, **very hot fat** and fry until brown. Serve with syrup.

POTATO BALLS (No. 2.)

Wash and pare **potatoes,** then cut out balls with French cutter. If you do not have regular tool for so doing, use a round measuring spoon. A teaspoon will work but does not make such perfect balls. Save carefully all waste materials. Cook balls in salted water until done but not mushy. Drain. Add a generous amount of **butter** and **chopped parsley.** Reheat slowly until potatoes take on the flavor of parsley. Serve around meat used at this particular meal.

POTATO CAKES

Mash **five cold potatoes.** Add **1 egg,** beaten, **salt** and **pepper, 2 tablespoonfuls milk, 1 tablespoonful flour.** Mix well. Form into cakes and brown in fat.

POTATOES WITH CHEESE

Put layer of **cold boiled potatoes** that are cut in cubes or sliced, into a buttered baking dish. Sprinkle with **salt** and **pepper.** Cover with layer of **white sauce** then **layer of cheese** (Parmesan). Repeat this until the pan is full. Cover with **buttered crumbs** and bake until brown.

CREAMED POTATOES

Boil **6 large potatoes** with their jackets on. Cook until they can be just pierced with a fork. Let cool and remove the skins. Dice or slice. There should be 5 cups of potatoes. Put **3 tablespoonfuls butter** in bottom of a double boiler, add a layer of potatoes, a dash of **salt** and **pepper** and a sprinkling of flour. Continue to do this until potatoes are used. Pour over this **thin cream** or **top milk.** It should come to within 1 inch of the top of potatoes. Put on lid and set in the bottom part of boiler. Let cook one hour.

POTATOES AND EGGS

Alternate layers of **hard cooked eggs** with **cold potatoes** and **white sauce.** Bake for 20 minutes or until browned on top.

ESCALLOPED POTATOES

Wash, pare and slice thin, **Irish potatoes.** Place in a greased casserole or baking dish. Use a layer of potatoes and seasonings **(salt, pepper** and **butter).** Repeat until dish is full. Pour **milk** over all until dish is 2/3 full. Bake in moderate oven until potatoes are done and top has golden brown color. Cover potatoes while baking, but remove cover for browning.

ESCALLOPED POTATOES WITH CHEESE

Pare **6 or 7 potatoes** and slice very thin. Make a layer of potatoes, **strips of pimientos** and **grated cheese** (using **¼ lb.** for the whole recipe). Repeat these layers until potatoes are all used. Season each layer with **salt** and **pepper.** Cover all with **1 cup thin white sauce.** Cover all with **buttered bread crumbs.** Bake in moderate oven from 1 to 1½ hours. Too long or too slow baking will cause potatoes to turn black. Too fast cooking will make them watery.

GERMAN FRIED POTATOES

Boil **potatoes** in jackets and let stand until cold. Pare and slice. Heat 2 **large tablespoonfuls of clarified bacon fat** or kettle rendered lard in iron skillet until very hot. Add potatoes, **salt** and **pepper** to taste and fry for 5 minutes. Then turn and fry until brown on bottom and keep turning until nice and brown all through. About 5 minutes before serving add a **tablespoonful butter** and melt through. Serve very hot.

GERMAN RAW FRIED POTATOES

Pare **5 medium sized potatoes,** rinse, then dry with cloth. Slice thin (but not as thin as for potato chips). Put **2 tablespoonfuls lard** in skillet. When hot put in potatoes. Sprinkle with **salt** and **pepper.** Place lid on skillet. Keep potatoes on a hot flame as they should cook quickly. Without removing the lid shake the skillet a few times for the first few minutes they are cooking so the potatoes will not stick. When the potatoes are hot through, the ones in the bottom will be brown. Lift these over with a pancake turner so that others may become brown, too. Do not mash them or stir too often (about three times should be enough). It takes from 15 to 25 minutes to have them all nicely browned.

GERMAN POTATO SALAD

Cut 12 slices of bacon or **salt pork** into small cubes and fry very crisp. Let stand in hot skillet with all the drippings while slicing **6 medium sized potatoes** that have been boiled. Place potatoes in layers in a dish with a **few slices** of **onion** and sprinkle tiny meat cubes and a dash of **salt.** Pour drippings over it. Mix thoroughly. Heat ½ **cup vinegar** and pour over the mixture. Let stand in warming oven or on back of stove until well warmed.

HASHED BROWNED POTATOES

Fry out ¼ **lb. salt pork,** cut in small cubes. Remove the scraps. There should be about **1/3 cup fat.** Add **2 cups cold boiled potatoes** finely chopped. Season and mix potatoes thoroughly with fat. Cook 3 minutes, stirring constantly. Let stand to brown underneath. Fold as an omelet and turn on hot platter.

LYONNAISE POTATOES

Fry **1 onion** in fat and add **cold, chopped, cooked potatoes.** Allow to cook until nice and brown. Add **chopped parsley** before serving.

POTATO LAYERS

Cut **3 onions** and fry to a light brown. Grind any kind of **left-over meat** that is already cooked. Boil **10 potatoes** with skins on, then remove skins and slice. Butter baking dish and cover bottom with sliced potatoes. Add **salt** and **pepper.** Next slice **1 hard cooked egg** over this, then put a layer of meat, then a layer of onion and so on until all is used. Put **cracker crumbs** over top and pour on **milk** or **cream** with little lumps of **butter.** Bake 1½ hours.

MASHED POTATOES

Cook in salted water enough **potatoes** for your family. Drain. Mash with a potato masher or run through a ricer. Season with **salt, pepper, butter** and **hot milk,** adding a little at a time until they have acquired the taste desired. Beat thoroughly with an electric beater or a good wooden spoon.

NEW POTATOES AND PEAS

Parboil **new potatoes** with jackets on. When about half done, drain and remove skins. Add more hot water and salt, finish cooking. Cook **new peas** on top of stove without cover, by dropping new peas into boiling salted water. The amount of potatoes, peas and **white sauce** vary with the number served. When potatoes are done, drain and add with peas to white sauce. Serve while hot.

DAINTY POTATO PATTIES

Add **2 tablespoonfuls butter, ½ teaspoonful salt** and **3 egg yolks** to **2 cups** of **hot riced potatoes.** Beat. Using a pastry bag and tube shape into baskets, pyramids, crowns or roses. Brush over with beaten **egg** diluted with **1 teapoonful water.** Bake until golden brown in hot oven (425° F.)

This recipe is delicious served with fish.

One could use leftover mashed potatoes in the above recipe.

PARSLEY POTATOES

Cook **small new potatoes** with jackets on. When done, remove skins. Pour **melted butter** over top and sprinkle with **salt, pepper** and **chopped parsley.** Reheat in oven until ready to serve.

POTATO PUFFS

To **1 cup freshly mashed potatoes** add **¼ teaspoonful salt,** a dash of **white pepper** and **2 well beaten eggs.** Sift together **½ cup pastry flour** and **1 teaspoonful baking powder,** add to first mixture. Drop by teaspoonfuls into **hot, deep fat,** fry to golden brown. Drain and serve hot. Makes about 16 puffs.

PITTSBURGH POTATOES

Dice enough **potatoes** to fill **a quart measure.** Cut **1 onion** in small pieces and boil together about 5 minutes. Add **1 red** and **1 green pepper,** diced. Be careful not to over cook as the potatoes should be kept firm. Drain off surplus water and place mixture in baking dish. Make **1 cup white sauce** and add **1½ cups grated cheese.** Season with **salt** and **pepper** (a little **butter** if desired). Pour this over potatoes and bake until brown. This recipe could be divided for a small family.

POTATO ROSETTES

To **2 cups mashed potatoes** add **1 teaspoonful salt, pinch pepper, 1 egg** and **1/3 cup milk.** Beat **well.** Shape on pie plate or baking pan with pastry tube. Bake in 400° F. oven for 20 minutes.

POTATO SOUFFLE

Heat **2 cups mashed potatoes** in sauce pan. Add beaten **yolks** of **2 eggs, 3 tablespoonfuls cream** and **salt** and **pepper** as needed. Beat until well mixed. Carefully add **2 beaten egg whites.** Pile lightly in a greased baking dish. Bake until brown.

STUFFED POTATOES

Bake 6 medium sized potatoes, then cut lengthwise. Scrape out the inside with a spoon or fork and mash. Season with **½ teaspoonful salt, 2 tablespoonfuls butter, pepper** and **4 tablespoonfuls hot milk.** Add 2 beaten **egg whites,** reserving part of egg whites for top of potatoes. Fill skins with mixture and brush top with **egg** white. Return to oven, bake until brown. **Grated cheese** may be sprinkled over top if desired.

Peppers are a seed pod and are used as a vegetable or as seasonings.

After using a part of a can of pimentos cover with cooking oil or salt, if salt, wash before using. These will keep for some time with either method.

STUFFED PEPPERS

Boil 6 or 8 **sweet green peppers** 15 minutes in salt water. Grind **2 red peppers** and **3 onions.** Mix with **1 pound hamburg** or **smoked meat** or **leftover meat,** cook a few minutes. Add **bread crumbs** to make it firm enough for stuffing. Stuff green peppers. Cover with **1 small can tomatoes.** Bake in hot oven for ½ hour. Watch that they do not burn. If too brown before meat is done turn down fire.

Pumpkin is a large winter vegetable grown chiefly for pies. We advocate canned pumpkin unless your family is large enough to utilize a whole pumpkin. Left over pumpkin may be canned. Pumpkin is easily cooked, if baked in the shell. Cut in two, remove seeds and bake until soft.

ANGEL FOOD DUMPLINGS AND SAUERKRAUT

Cook **1 quart sauerkraut** with either **pork** or **beef** for **1 hour.** Mix **2 cups flour, 3 teaspoonfuls baking powder** and **¼ teaspoonful salt.** Add **1 egg** slightly beaten to 1 cup milk, then mix with the dry ingredients. Drop by spoonfuls into sauerkraut. Cover tightly, cooking slowly for 25 minutes.

SAUERKRAUT AND BRISKET OF BEEF

Place **2½ or 3 pounds of brisket of beef** in a baking dish and surround it with **1 large can** or **1 quart of sauerkraut.** Add just enough water to saturate the kraut well. Add 2 or 3 **medium sized onions** and sprinkle with **paprika** to suit the taste. Place in oven, and bake slowly until meat is done—about 2 hours. This dish may be boiled instead of baked, if desired. If boiled, it may be treated the same as spareribs and sauerkraut.

SAUERKRAUT AND HAMBURG

Place **1½ lbs. sauerkraut, 1 can tomato soup,** and **1 pint water** in kettle. Make small balls of **1 lb. hamburg** and **¼ cup uncooked rice,** drop into the sauerkraut mixture. Add **salt, pepper** and **paprika,** cook 1½ hours, adding water as needed.

Spinach, a leafy vegetable, high in iron content, and highly recommended for the daily diet.

SPINACH WITH BACON

Wash **1½ pounds of fresh spinach** well and place in a kettle, cover and cook until nearly done. In the meantime cut **3 slices of bacon** into small pieces and fry to a golden brown. Make a dressing by beating **2 eggs, 3 tablespoonfuls sugar, 4 tablespoonfuls vinegar, pinch salt** and **½ cup milk** together. Add to bacon and fat, let come to a boil. Pour over drained spinach. Serve hot.

BUTTERED SPINACH AND EGGS

Cook **fresh spinach** in its own water, there is enough water left on the leaves from washing to cook it thoroughly. If needed, a small amount of water may be added. Season with **salt** and **pepper.** Add a generous supply of **butter** and heat 1 minute more until butter cooks through the leaves. Serve with **hard cooked eggs** sliced over the top. Canned spinach may be used satisfactorily.

SPINACH RING (No. 1.)

Mix thoroughly 4 **cups cooked spinach,** chopped fine, **2 tablespoonfuls melted butter, 1 teaspoonful salt** and **2 eggs,** slightly beaten. Put in ring mold and bake in moderate oven 30 minutes. Turn onto platter. Fill center with **creamed mushrooms** and garnish with **deviled eggs.** Serves eight.

SPINACH RING (No. 2.)

Drain **1 No. 2½ can spinach** and chop slightly. Melt **2 tablespoonfuls butter** in sauce pan, add **2 tablespoonfuls flour** and blend thoroughly. Add **½ cup milk** and cook until thick, stirring constantly. Separate **3 eggs,** add beaten **yolks** to white sauce, add spinach, **1 tablespoonful chopped onion, 2 teaspoonfuls salt** and cook 2 minutes longer. Beat egg **whites** until stiff and fold into spinach mixture. Pour into well greased 8-inch ring mold. Set in pan of hot water so that water comes up ½ inch on side of mold. Bake in moderate oven for 30 minutes or until mixture sets. Turn out on warmed platter, fill center with **buttered peas** and around the outside of the ring. Arrange **diced** or **sliced beet** alternately with slices of **hard boiled eggs.** This serves 6 to 8. A little **horseradish** added to the beets gives them a piquant flavor.

Sweet potatoes are the roots of a plant which belongs to the morning glory family.

Sweet potatoes should be pared with a stainless steel knife and covered with salt water to keep edges from turning black.

CANDIED SWEET POTATOES

Boil quartered **sweet potato** until almost done, then drain. Heat heavy iron skillet and place in it **2 tablespoonfuls of butter** and **2 tablespoonfuls brown sugar.** Melt. When just starting to brown put in sweet potatoes. Turn fire low and cook until brown. Keep turning potatoes until golden brown on all sides. This is easy to do but care must be taken that the fire is not too hot as they burn easily.

CANDIED SWEET POTATOES WITH MAPLE SYRUP

Boil as many **sweet potatoes** as needed. Drain when nearly done. Slice either crosswise or lengthwise and place in shallow pan. **Mix 1 cup maple syrup, ½ teaspoonful salt, ¼ teaspoonful pepper** and **3 tablespoonfuls butter** together. Pour over sweet potatoes and bake ½ hour.

ORANGE CANDIED SWEET POTATOES

Combine **1 cup orange juice, ½ teaspoonful grated orange rind, 1 cup water, ½ cup sugar, 3 tablespoonfuls light corn syrup, ½ teaspoonful salt,** and **¼ cup melted butter.** Pour over **6 to 8 peeled, uncooked sweet potatoes** in baking dish. Bake covered in moderate oven until tender for 30 to 40 minutes. Baste occasionally. Remove lid last 10 minutes to brown, or put under broiler. Sweet potatoes thus cooked may be mashed and piled into orange shells, topped with marshmallows and browned, making individual servings.

STUFFED SWEET POTATOES

Bake **6 medium sized sweet potatoes.** Scoop out shells. Mash potatoes well, adding **3 tablespoonfuls butter, 1 teaspoonful salt, juice** of **1 orange, 1 cup shredded pineapple, ¼ cup chopped English walnuts** and **12 marshmallows,** cut up. Refill shell with mixture. Replace potatoes in hot oven until heated thoroughly.

FRYING SWEET POTATOES

Put **lard** in frying pan. Slice potatoes into the hot fat. Pour **½ cup sugar** and a **little water** over the potatoes. Cover and fry until soft. Turn very carefully so as not to make them mushy.

Squash is a vegetable of many varieties. They can nearly all be cooked over the same ideas as used in these recipes. It is a vegetable that needs a great deal of fat for flavor.

Cymlings are small, white, summer squashes and are usually cooked with skin and seeds, in boiling salted water. The water is evaporated and the squash seasoned with salt, pepper and plenty of butter.

BAKED SQUASH

Open **1 end of the squash** and remove all the seeds. Place the squash, open end downward, in a pie pan with a little water added. Bake for 2 hours or until tender. Remove the squash from the shell and season to taste with **plenty of butter,** some **salt** and **pepper** and **a little cream.** The squash may be baked the day before needed. Place cold squash in double boiler and heat thoroughly. Add seasonings.

CYMLINGS

The cymling is a **flat, round squash** with scallops around the edge. When young, skins, seeds and all interior are cooked. Just wash and remove stem. Cut into many small pieces. Cook until tender in **salted water,** cook until dry, draining if necessary, then reheating until dry. Season with **salt, pepper** and plenty of **butter.**

STUFFED SQUASH

Select either a round or long **summer squash.** Divide in halves. Remove seeds but save and add to meat. Pare if outside is tough. If tender, paring is not necessary. Fry in small amount of **butter, 1 pound ground meat,** beef preferred, **½ cup uncooked rice, 1 chopped onion** and **salt** and **pepper** to taste, until all are golden **cup water** and cover with **1 cup tomatoes.** Bake in moderately hot brown. Stuff squash with mixture. Place in baking pan, add **1** cup water and cover with 1 cup tomatoes, bake in moderately hot oven until done.

SQUAW DISH

Fry **½ cup diced bacon** slowly. Add **1 chopped green pepper** and **½ sliced onion,** continue frying until brown. Add to **1 can of corn** or **2 cups** of **fresh corn, 1 cup bread** soaked in **2 cups milk.** Lastly, add **2 eggs** that have been well beaten. Bake in moderate oven until set.

Swiss chard a leafy vegetable of the variety grown only for the leaves and stalks. Served mostly as a green.

SWISS CHARD

Remove **leaves** from **stalks** and cook separately. Serve leaves with **cooked salad dressing** and stalks with **butter, salt** and **pepper.**

SWISS CHARD

Remove leaves from stems of **Swiss Chard** to be used as greens. Cook in very little water and season either with **bacon, ham** or **sour cream.** Cook stems until medium tender in salted water, drain thoroughly. Then dip each stem and roll in **flour,** then fry brown in medium hot fat in which **one or two cloves of garlic** have been browned.

The tomato is seed pod of a plant formerly used entirely for garden decoration, as the fruit at that time was thought poisonous.

Tomato skins may be loosened by scraping them with back of knife before peeling. They may also be dipped in hot water for a few minutes, then in cold and peeled easily. If held on a fork over a flame until skins burst it will also help to peel them.

CREAMED TOMATOES

Melt **4 tablespoonfuls butter** or **margarine** in a sauce pan, blend in **4 tablespoonfuls flour** and cook until it starts to change color. Then add **3 cups of canned tomatoes** (or cut up fresh ones) and continue to cook and stir until all is smooth and flour cooked. Season with **salt** and **pepper** to taste. A little **sugar** may be added if one desires their tomatoes sweet.

TOMATOES, CORN AND CHEESE

Use either **fresh** or **canned corn** and **tomatoes.** Put a layer of **corn** in a buttered baking dish, then a layer of **tomatoes,** a layer of **grated cheese** and repeat until casserole is nearly full. Sprinkle **cracker crumbs** over top and dot with **margarine** and bake ½ hour at 375° F.

ESCALLOPED TOMATOES

Reserve **3 tablespoonfuls bread crumbs** from **2 cups of crumbs** and spread the rest on a pan. Brown in oven, do not burn them. Mix **2 cups tomatoes, browned crumbs, 1 teaspoonful salt** and a **dash of pepper** with **1 tablespoonful butter** or **margarine** and put in a shallow baking dish. Spread the unbrowned crumbs on top and dot with remainder of butter or margarine. Bake in moderate oven (350° F.) ½ hour.

TOMATO PUDDING

Toast enough **bread squares** on all sides to make **1 cup.** To **one 10 ounce can of tomato puree** add ¼ **cup boiling water, 1 scant cup of brown sugar** and ¼ **teaspoonful salt.** Boil 5 minutes. Place bread squares in casserole, pour over them ½ **cup melted butter or margarine** add hot tomato mixture and bake in covered casserole 30 minutes in a moderate oven (375° F.)

Turnips are a strong flavored root vegetable, but if grown properly, may have a very sweet agreeable taste.

BUTTERED TURNIPS

Pare **small turnips,** leave whole. Cook in salted water until tender. Season with salt, **pepper** and plenty of **butter.** These may be hollowed out and have buttered peas served in them. It makes a pretty and attractive way of serving peas.

RUTABAGA

Dice in ½ **inch cubes one yellow turnip** and cook until tender in small amount of salted water. Fry out several pieces of **fresh or salted side pork,** diced fine. When crisp remove and add to mashed turnips with a small amount of **fat** for **seasoning** plus a little **salt** and **pepper.** Add ½ **teaspoonful sugar** for added flavor.

SCALLOPED TURNIPS

Boil in salted water until tender **2 or 3 diced turnips.** Make a white sauce of **3 tablespoonfuls flour, 3 tablespoonfuls butter, 1 cup milk** and **½ cup liquid** in which turnips were cooked. Add **1 teaspoonful salt.** Add turnips to white sauce. Put into baking dish. Cover with **buttered crumbs.** Bake in moderate oven (350° F.) 15 minutes. **2 tablespoonfuls pimiento** may be added before baking if desired.

STUFFED TURNIPS

Cook **6 medium sized turnips** in boiling salted water until almost tender. Hollow out centers. Chop and add **½ cup bread crumbs** mixed with **1/3 cup grated cheese, salt, pepper,** and **paprika.** Fill turnips. Bake in moderate oven until brown.

Wine

BLACKBERRY WINE

Wash and mash well 1 **gallon blackberries.** Let them stand for 24 hours. Strain once or twice through cheese cloth, wringing as you strain. To each gallon of juice add **3 pounds of white sugar** and let stand in glass containers for 6 weeks in a cool dark place. When all fermentation is over, bottle and seal well.

DANDELION WINE

Pick **2 quarts of dandelion blossoms** — no green, pour over these, **1 gallon boiling water.** Let stand 2 days in a warm place, stirring occasionally. Strain and add **juice of 4 oranges, 3 lemons, 4 pounds granulated sugar** and **½ yeast cake.** Stir until sugar is dissolved. Put in a three gallon crock and place in cellar for about 6 weeks. Stir daily but keep crock covered. When 6 weeks' time is up, strain and bottle.

AMOUNTS REQUIRED TO SERVE 50 PERSONS

Coffee	2 pounds ground coffee, 2½ gallons water
Coffee cream	3 pints
Biscuits or rolls	2 to a person
Bread	2 to 5 loaves according to size
Butter	2½ pounds
Canned Corn	3 No. 10 Cans
Canned Green Beans	4 No. 10 Cans
Canned Peas	3 No. 10 Cans
Chicken Salad	9 quarts
Cole Slaw	10 pounds Cabbage
Cranberries	5 pounds cranberries, 5 pounds sugar
Creamed Chicken	20 pounds Chicken
Creamed Potatoes	1 peck potatoes
Escalloped Oysters	6 quarts oysters
Fruit Salad	8 quarts
Glazed Sweet Potatoes	20 pounds
Ham, boned and baked	10 pounds
Ice Cream, bulk	2 gallons
Ice Cream, brick	6 to 8 servings per quart
Layer Cake	4 large cakes
Lettuce	5 large heads
Macaroni and Cheese	4 pounds macaroni, 2 pounds cheese
Mashed Potatoes	1/3 bushel potatoes
Oyster Stew	8 quarts milk, 6 quarts oysters
Pie	6 servings to one 9-inch pie
Pork and Beans	5 pounds beans, 3 pounds salt pork
Roast Beef	25 pounds
Roast Chicken	40 pounds
Roast Fresh Ham	20 pounds
Roast Lamb	25 pounds
Sheet Cake	1 sheet 12 by 18 inches
Shortcake	8 quarts berries
Soup	3 gallons
White Sauce for Vegetables, Chicken or Macaroni	4 quarts

Index